MW00657324

THE CHICANO MOVEMENT

The largest social movement by people of Mexican descent in the U.S. to date, the Chicano Movement of the 1960s and 70s linked civil rights activism with a new, assertive ethnic identity: Chicano Power! Beginning with the farm workers' struggle led by César Chávez and Dolores Huerta, the Movement expanded to urban areas throughout the Southwest, Midwest, and Pacific Northwest, as a generation of self-proclaimed Chicanos fought to empower their communities. Recently, a new generation of historians has produced an explosion of interesting work on the Movement.

The Chicano Movement: Perspectives from the Twenty-First Century collects the various strands of this research into one readable collection, exploring the contours of the Movement while disputing the idea of it being one monolithic group. Bringing the story up through the 1980s, *The Chicano Movement* introduces students to the impact of the Movement, and enables them to expand their understanding of what it means to be an activist, a Chicano, and an American.

Mario T. García is Professor of Chicano Studies and History at the University of California, Santa Barbara.

NEW DIRECTIONS IN AMERICAN HISTORY

THE CHICANO MOVEMENT

Perspectives from the Twenty-First Century

Edited by
Mario T. García

Routledge
Taylor & Francis Group

NEW YORK AND LONDON

First published 2014
by Routledge
711 Third Avenue, New York, NY 10017

and by Routledge
2 Park Square, Milton Park, Abingdon, Oxon OX14 4RN

Routledge is an imprint of the Taylor & Francis Group, an informa business

© 2014 Taylor & Francis

Library of Congress Cataloging in Publication Data
    The Chicano movement : perspectives from the twenty-first century/edited by Mario T. Garcia.
    pages cm.—(New directions in American history)
    1. Chicano movement. 2. Mexican Americans—Politics and government—20th century. 3. Mexican Americans—Civil rights—History—20th century. 4. Mexican Americans—Social conditions—20th century. 5. Mexican Americans—Ethnic identity. 6. United States—Ethnic relations—History—20th century. 7. United States—Social conditions—20th century. 8. California—Ethnic relations—History—20th century. 9. California—Politics and government—20th century. I. Garcia, Mario T., editor.
    E184.M5C446 2014
    973'.046872—dc23
    2013038681

ISBN: 978-0-415-83308-0 (hbk)
ISBN: 978-0-415-83309-7 (pbk)
ISBN: 978-0-203-48913-0 (ebk)

Typeset in Bembo and Stone Sans
by Florence Production Ltd, Stoodleigh, Devon, UK

Printed and bound in the United States of America by
Edwards Brothers Malloy

For Sal Castro—a teacher

CONTENTS

ACKNOWLEDGMENTS

I want to first thank all of the contributors to this volume for their support and patience in the project. I also wish to thank all who participated in my February 2012 conference on the emerging historiography of the Chicano Movement that laid the foundation for this book. They are pioneers in Chicano Movement Studies. My gratitude also goes to the many sponsors of the conference held at UC Santa Barbara.

I want to thank Kimberly Guinta who initially expressed enthusiasm for this volume and whose enthusiasm and support never wavered. Thanks also to the staff at Routledge who worked with me over the different phases of the book.

I am especially grateful to Amber Workman, my research assistant, whose work was invaluable in helping to edit the manuscript and to format it for final submission.

FOREWORD: THE CHICANO MOVEMENT

Does Anyone Care about What Happened 45 Years Ago?

Jorge Mariscal

In a recent issue of the influential publication *Puro Pedo* magazine, readers were asked to respond to a survey that would determine their generational affiliation across the last four and a half decades. Question 1: "The book that changed my life is: a) *Yo soy Joaquin*, b) *This Bridge Called my Back*, c) *Always Running*, or d) *micro blogas*—'I don't read books.'" Question 2: "You're feeling nostalgic. You throw on the following *rola*: a) [CD] 'Viva Tirado' by El Chicano, b) the *La Bamba* soundtrack, c) a Latino house compilation, or d) 'Abrázame' by Los Rakas. Question 3: "You are organizing a high school conference for local youth. Your ideal keynote speaker would be: a) César Chávez, b) Jaime Escalante, c) Subcomandante Marcos, d) Jorge Ramos."

I begin with a comic tone because the questions I want to pose are quite serious. Our nervous laughter captures the discomfort we feel when we discuss the weight of generational difference and the potential distorting effect it has upon how our research is received, how effective our pedagogy is in the classroom, and how well we are able to mentor students and campus activists.

As we enter the second decade of the new century, one of the most obvious ironies is that at the same moment that public universities are turning their eyes away from local Spanish-speaking communities, the political class is expressing renewed interest in the so-called Hispanic electorate. In the wake of the 2012 election and President Obama's capturing of 73 percent of the Latino vote, the Republican Party launched a public campaign to "fix its Hispanic problem." Many Latinos found this move laughable and indeed the pandering of some figures such as John McCain was pathetic. But progressive Latinos snicker at their own peril. As the Latino community continues to grow, the internal divisions within the Latino voting bloc will become increasingly apparent. The fact that George W. Bush received 44 percent of the Latino vote in 2004 is a glaring reminder that conservative positions on the economy and numerous social issues can attract large parts of the Latino electorate. Hybrid political figures such as Ted Cruz in Texas and Marco Rubio in Florida deploy generic and decontextualized Hispanic personae in order to promote far-right policies, and even the Democrats, who during Obama's first term oversaw more deportations than in George W. Bush's two terms, are not beyond pandering to nativist concerns.

In a parallel move to the opportunistic concern for "Hispanics" within the general spectrum of political rhetoric, public university administrators pay cautious lip-service to "changing demographics" while rarely mentioning the term Latino. In states such as California and Texas, the rapid growth in the Latino college-age population has sounded alarms about a "wake-up call" and a "tipping-point," yet at the same time Chicano Studies programs at many colleges struggle to attract a fraction of the majors they enjoyed even 20 years ago. These declining majors, within the context of the slow-motion corporatization of public colleges and universities, will surely serve as a reason for the corporate downsizers to shrink Chicano Studies budgets and faculties. In the new "entrepreneurial" culture of privatized public universities, one's research agenda depends on pleasing donors and there are few donors, individual or corporate, eager to fund a discipline whose founding principles ranged from a critique of traditional liberalism and a demand for inclusion to a radical rejection of patriarchy and white supremacy, and the capitalist formations that sustained them.

On the cultural level, we must be realistic about the momentous shift that has taken place in Spanish-speaking communities over the last generation. Many of the children of immigrants who arrived in the 1990s and after report that the terms "Chicano" or "Chicana" do not resonate for them. Even those youth whose parents are closer to the Mexican American experience and know something about Chicano history eschew many of the core contributions of the Movement period, especially the "militant ethos" described by Ignacio García.[1]

Instead, twenty-first-century realities—hyper-individualism, debilitating student debt, lack of recognizable leadership, a depoliticized culture—drive these young people towards less threatening neo-assimilationist Hispanic identities and pragmatic courses of study that appear more viable for future employment opportunities and financial stability.

Given this new context, research on the Chicano Movement period is in many ways more crucial than ever. New studies by young scholars will shed light on the complexities of that earlier moment and, more important, may reveal strategies for political organizing in the twenty-first century. The studies presented in this volume edited by Mario T. García are the essential groundwork for both reassembling the past and mapping the future. But the question of how the past might best be conveyed to today's youth and whether or not it can even be received in a radically different context is the nagging issue with which we must all grapple. Beyond those who lived through it and those who study it, does anyone care about the Chicano Movement?

We are now 50 years away from the founding of the United Farm Workers (UFW) and the Alianza Federal de Mercedes, 45 years from the Crusade for Justice and the Blowouts, and 42 years from the Chicano Moratorium. For our students today, the *Movimiento* is as distant as World War I and the Hoover administration were to those of us who were college age in the late 1960s. Given the merciless march of history, how can we reinvest a past moment with meaning for the present?

My preliminary questions are the following: Does the Chicano Movement of the Civil Rights/Vietnam War era have anything to teach young Latinas and Latinos today? If so, in what specific ways can the experience of the Movement be translated for collective activism in 2014 and beyond? Given the enormous transformation of U.S. society and culture over the last 45 years, can we communicate at all across the generational divide? In short, what does the Chicano Movement mean to our students in a radically new context?

According to one historian of modernity, the impulse that drove late twentieth-century struggles for equal rights and economic justice derived from an Enlightenment belief in human emancipation. Broadly speaking, the goals were to achieve "the reduction or elimination of exploitation, inequality or oppression" and to address the "divisive distribution of power and resources."[2] "Emancipatory politics" was a politics of collective life chances that took place within the general framework of modern liberalism. I will have more to say about this later. For now, let me suggest that despite more radical agendas on the edges of the Chicano Movement, emancipatory politics were at the core of the vast majority of Movement organizations.

43 years ago at the University of California, Santa Barbara, activists declared: "We will move against those forces which have denied us freedom of expression and human dignity."[3] The phrase captures the emancipatory objective of every sector of what we call the Chicano Movement—from the farm workers to the youth in the cities, from the *revoltosos* in northern New Mexico to the women who demanded equality and respect in every organization. Listening to the pounding waves of anti-colonialist struggles around the world, the Chicana and Chicano rejected hierarchical domination in the United States and in effect helped to destroy an anti-Mexican Jim Crow regime imposed almost 50 years before *Plessy v. Ferguson*. They contributed to the realization of liberalism's promise of equal opportunity even as they critiqued liberalism's fundamental flaws.

Fast-forward to 2014 and we see troubling conditions for Spanish-speaking communities that remind us of the pre-Movement period. Rather than elaborating upon the details of the new anti-Latino racism—the disproportionate impact of the housing crisis on Latinos, mass deportations, a still broken K-12 system, reduced access to higher education, the hyper-militarization of the border, and so on—I will simply say "Arizona" and assume that most readers understand that there are ominous clouds threatening the future for Latinos in the United States. My larger claim is that all of these twenty-first-century challenges are emerging on a post-emancipatory landscape. This is a landscape referred to by some as post-racial. Clearly we are not post-racial in any sense. I will argue, however, that the contemporary context is post-liberal and that this post-liberal condition is called (ironically) neoliberalism.

Neoliberalism, globalization, and the new technology together have produced in U.S. culture a fantasy "common sense" that the great battles against exploitation and injustice have been more or less won. For many people, including our students, the Obama presidency heightens this confusion. My hypothesis is that an emancipatory politics has been displaced by a politics of individual self-development; the frame is no longer life chances (for the collective or the community), but rather life choices for each individual. This is not to say that the emancipatory model has disappeared; it is just that it has been moved off center stage.

Under assault from the pervasive culture of twenty-first-century capital, specifically financial speculation, niche-marketing, digitalized consumerism, and social media individuation, the master narratives of emancipatory political agendas have been displaced by an emphasis on short-term desire—imagine the fleeting timeline on Facebook where issues appear suddenly and then scroll out of sight in a matter of seconds. As Bernard Stiegler puts it, the political space and time of the public sphere is assaulted by capital's "liquidation of social relations" and "liquidation of solidarities."[4] The formation of collective projects and long-term investments in the future is made more difficult, and the elaboration of continuities across generations becomes less likely.

In *Brown-Eyed Children of the Sun*, I argued that a tension existed in the Movement between various forms of ethnic nationalism and a more expansive internationalism.[5] In the most productive resolution of that tension, attention and commitment to local struggles were combined with an analysis and understanding of international struggles. An emancipatory politics began at home and was linked to structurally analogous movements abroad—anti-colonialism, Third World solidarity, etc. These connections across space were complemented by connections across time to earlier historical actors and cultures that inspired Movement ideologies: Zapata and las Adelitas; Maya and Nahua resistance to invasion and occupation; the foundational myth of Aztlán itself; and an imagined bronze continent without national boundaries.

Under the new regime of the post-emancipatory politics of life choices, international solidarity is displaced by a kind of deracinated global cosmopolitan-ism; in worst-case scenarios local histories and struggles are muted or erased entirely. Individuals now may "do activism" by "liking" or linking his or her "status" to issues thousands of miles away while never engaging directly with the human actors engaged in those struggles. More important, local struggles may be ignored—leap-frogged over by the power of social media and the globalized diffusion of the activist impulse. In elite university settings, Latina students may be less inclined to engage with local communities of color and more inclined to express solidarity with movements in Cairo or Santiago de Chile. This erasure of the local has been exacerbated for over 20 years by a sustained critique of a revisionist caricature of "cultural nationalism." This ideology, assuming that it ever was a coherent system of thought during the Movement period, is now presented in elite academic circles as a wholly negative and exclusionary impulse.

In this new world of cosmopolitan long-distance "activism" (referred to by some as "clicktivism"), to what extent can earlier social movements, especially those founded on working-class values, with ethnic nationalism as their organizing principle, and born in conditions dramatically different from our own, how can such movements speak to contemporary youth? Two of the questions I hear most often in my undergraduate course on the Chicano Movement are "Why were they so angry?" and "What did they want?" (here I would remind you that I teach at the heavily corporatized and elitist UC San Diego, a science and engineering campus whose culture discourages any kind of grounded political analysis. My comments are tainted by that reality. I have no doubt that Chicano Studies take different forms at different kinds of institutions). Many of my students are eager to hear about what happened "back in the day"—some of them are impressed by the fact that young Latinas and Latinos of their age forced through significant reforms at every level of U.S. society. And yet because they live in a post-emancipatory universe, my students struggle to connect to that earlier moment and struggle even more to make sense of its lessons for their own generation.

Let me return then to the basic framework I have outlined. If the dominant mode of youth politics today is premised upon individual life choices rather than collective mobilization, we will need to understand the historical changes that have produced this situation. For those of you who are thinking, but what about the Occupy movement?, let me suggest that the Occupy movement is less a radical critique of American liberalism than it is a call for a return to New Deal-style policies that, like the New Deal itself, suffered from a weak anti-racist component. Given that the term "occupation" has a negative connotation for most ethnic Mexicans in the United States, Chicano activists from the Vietnam War era surely would find it difficult to identify with the Occupy brand; in fact, the participation of youth of color in the Occupy movement, even at its peak, was minimal.

Because the conference that produced this volume took place where the Plan de Santa Bárbara came into being in 1969 and because most of us are teachers, I will focus specifically on the transformation of the educational sector. The authors of the Plan put the problem succinctly:

> Chicanos must come to grips with the reality of the university in modern society. The university is a powerful modern institution because it generates and distributes knowledge which is power . . . The role of knowledge in producing powerful social change, indeed revolution, cannot be under-estimated. But it is equally important to recognize that research will not

only provide Chicanos with *action oriented analysis of conditions*, it will also aid significantly in politically educating the Chicano community.[6]

Allow me to restate one of my introductory questions: What is the relationship between the university, as it existed for the authors of the Plan, and the university we know today? Long gone are the days of the California Master Plan. In its place, a semi-privatized University of California system in which most campuses receive less than 10 percent of their budget from state taxpayer money—projections for the next 20 years show flat admission targets for California residents and ever-increasing targets for out of state, especially foreign students. As the numbers of Black and Brown students decrease, or even if they remain at current levels, and as the numbers of Chicana and Black faculty remain artificially low, the potential for the production and distribution of knowledge focused on domestic minority communities is weak. Although Movement activists on the campuses faced tremendous obstacles, the cost of a UC education was nominal; today, most students graduating with a BA face years of indebtedness. In short, the "university" experienced by Movement activists was markedly different from the "university" we know today. Moreover, as I have already argued, an earlier politics of collective liberation has been displaced by a politics of individual life choices.

The long road from liberal to neoliberal higher education was not direct and therefore not easily identifiable for many people within university contexts. The economic bubbles of the 1990s tended to disguise the inexorability of the neoliberal project, and during this long period university "ethnic studies" programs seemed to be flourishing. Humanists and social scientists were especially blind to the changes taking place, since their professional cultures did not depend on external funding as did those of their science and engineering colleagues. But by the end of the first decade of the new century and the Great Recession produced by neoliberal economic policies, it was clear to everyone that the relative comfort of the state-funded university had been snatched away and most likely would never return. The proponents of structural adjustment or "austerity" projects, already completed in the manufacturing and other sectors, had finally set their sights on public higher education.

Two areas that would suffer the most under the new regime were 1) the stimulation of a radical critique of the status quo—what the liberal UC president Clark Kerr called the "critical evaluation of society"—and 2) the inclusion of historically under-represented minority groups among the ranks of students, staff, and faculty. Since the days of the Cold War public university, these two areas had been linked by residual ideologies that promoted the idea that it was necessary to pass on traditional knowledge to younger generations and, from the late 1960s on, that there was a moral imperative to dismantle the exclusionary practices inherent in New Deal/Great Society liberalism in the United States, especially around categories of "race," gender, and economic status. As the first stages of neoliberalism took shape in the late 1970s (in those early days called Reaganism), the social movements that had forced open the curriculum, and to a lesser extent faculties and student bodies, receded. Elite universities defaulted back to their "best practices." Gender, sexuality, and "race" now could be studied at various locations on campus, but faculty prejudices against research areas that were considered to be inherently "biased" and less "serious"—Black studies, gender studies, Chicano studies, etc.—produced barriers that blocked individual faculty advancement and programmatic funding. For traditional faculty, those disciplines with origins in the mass mobilizations of the late 1960s and 1970s were an inconvenience and not to be taken seriously, especially when they diverged from embedded social science methodologies that produced racialized and gendered outcomes or when they stimulated critiques of liberal institutional practices that were inherently elitist.

What would this mean for the production of knowledge linked to social change? From its inception, Chicano Studies was an interdisciplinary project that the liberal university viewed with suspicion. It had been allowed on campus only because of pressure from the Chicano Movement mobilizations, and only tolerated due to continued advocacy from students and local communities. As the transformation of state-funded public colleges proceeded throughout the 1980s, how could the goals outlined by Movement activists be realized? If the neoliberal university was now simply one part of the economic regime, as opposed to a public investment within a broader liberal democratic vision, why should anyone care if the local cultures and histories of racialized, working class communities were taught only sporadically and if only token numbers of students from those communities had access to advanced studies?

UC Santa Barbara scholar Christopher Newfield has argued persuasively that from the mid-1980s through the Clinton years both liberal and conservative intellectuals crafted a careful retreat from "minority matters." By the early 1980s, most grassroots organizations in Black and Brown communities born during the Vietnam War period had been defused; conservative ideologies now turned their attention to the colleges and universities. As Newfield points out: "The culture wars were creating the conditions in which liberals would help conservatives in denouncing the instruments of meaningful equal opportunity, that is, the kind that would have reduced racial disparity of *outcomes*."[7]

What was becoming clear was that only a small subset of students—the already privileged—would have access to the best schools; the consequences for working-class students of all colors would be dire. Sociologist Sheila Slaughter summarizes the trend this way:

> The increased significance of revenue considerations that comes with academic capitalism leads to a greater concentration of institutional energies and monies on students already privileged and served by higher education, with a lesser focus on those student populations that historically have been undeserved.[8]

But there was even more change on the way. By the turn of the century, the structural transformation imposed by global capital and the new technologies had accelerated the demise of liberal notions of the commons and the public good. The enthusiasm among elites for globalization was dampened only slightly by the pushback from local communities that viewed the new global order as an existential threat—the Zapatistas are probably the most relevant example here and it should be noted that they generated a renewed activist impulse among some sectors of Latino and Latina youth in the United States that continues even today, despite the awkward spectacle of American college students "performing" a decontextualized *zapatismo* on elite campuses in the global north.

In the domain of higher education, it is important to distinguish between two distinct albeit related terms—globalization and internationalization. If globalization is the economic, political, and societal forces pushing twenty-first-century higher education toward greater global involvement, internationalization is composed of the specific policies and practices of higher education institutions that respond to globalization by coping with its effects and reaping its benefits. As two scholars of education explain:

> Globalization may be unalterable, but internationalization involves many choices. Globalization tends to concentrate wealth, knowledge and power in those already possessing these elements. International academic mobility similarly favors well-developed education systems and institutions, thereby compounding existing inequalities.[9]

The "many choices" made by higher education institutions to enact internationalization are reflected in a wide variety of policies and curricular reforms:

- The creation and expansion of academic programs and departments that focus on international dimensions. Such courses may feature issues of racial and gender formations in countries abroad as well as quantitative studies of populations outside the United States.
- New or expanded majors focusing on areas outside the United States such as International Studies, Global Justice, International Business, and others. The attraction for students is obvious since the "international" brand strikes them as more transferable to a career than "Chicano" or even "Latino" studies. This is especially true for first- and second-generation students from immigrant families for whom the term "Chicano" holds particular and not always positive meanings.
- Expanded trends in hiring international faculty (those born and educated outside the United States). At my university, colleagues from abroad are often presented as examples of the administration's commitment to "diversity." Thus, eight new "Hispanic" faculty hires usually means two U.S. Latinos, six Latin Americans, and one Spaniard.

- The expansion of recruitment of international students who study in U.S. institutions as either short-range visiting students or degree-seeking students. Such students pay higher fees than local students.
- The creation of new and/or expanded administrative positions and structures (with commensurate resources) to increase internationalization in Academic Affairs and/or Student Affairs.
- Expanded public relations materials and campaigns touting the institution's "global" reputation and connections.

By the end of the last decade, it was not difficult to find "Research 1" campuses where international faculty outnumbered U.S. minority faculty by four or five to one. Those who called attention to this disparity, while not quite being accused of xenophobia, were labeled "nationalists" or "protectionists," although the point was simply that universities were not recruiting U.S. minority faculty with the same single-minded focus that they placed on foreign faculty. A 2007 joint study by Princeton University and the University of Pennsylvania found that many institutions now privilege international Black (i.e., African) and "Hispanic" (i.e., Spanish or Latin American) students and faculty over domestic African Americans and Latinos because the former tend to be wealthier, carry less "cultural baggage," and therefore are perceived to be "easier to get along with."[10]

In one literature department, liberal white faculty decided to do their Chicano colleagues "a favor" by hiring a Mexican writer as a visiting professor. What the well-meaning faculty did not understand was that this particular Mexican author had written extensively about Chicano/as as "wannabe Mexicans" with no real culture of their own except a bastardized "Taco Bell" and "McBurrito" culture. Mexican Americans were, he said, like the Tijuana donkey that had been painted to resemble a zebra—a hybrid spectacle with no real identity. With little understanding of (or interest in) the economic inequalities faced by the majority of Spanish-speaking people in the United States, renascent anti-Mexican racism, or reduced access to higher education for working-class students, the attitudes of these professors and their Mexican guest writer reproduced fossilized cultural assumptions and allowed privileged students to perpetuate racializing stereotypes and biases.

In effect, the problem had less to do with ethnic identities within the Mexican and Mexican American/Chicano population than with divisions based on class privilege. A "border bourgeoisie" composed of young Mexican professionals that live and work in both the U.S. and Mexico share a common culture with their white middle-class U.S. counterparts, an aestheticized culture founded in large part on middle-class privilege and the othering of or at least a distancing from working-class communities on both sides of the border. As a variation on the long-standing problematic of *pochismo*, that is, the notion in Mexican culture that Mexican Americans are "whitewashed" creatures without any linguistic or cultural identity, the new phenomenon is rooted in the tension that exists between the working class and their wealthier compatriots in both countries who have benefitted from the neoliberal dispensation.

Now let me be clear. I am not arguing that we ought to oppose the presence of international faculty and students. I am suggesting that one of the goals of the Chicano Movement—the insertion of Mexican Americans into every level of university life—has been achieved only partially, and that these partial victories are in danger of being rolled back. In other words, inclusion must mean not only international students, faculty, and curricula, but U.S. minority students, faculty, and curricula as well and, more than ever, U.S. Latinos especially, given the demographic projections for California and the nation as a whole.

Why are elite universities pursuing internationalization so vigorously? The reasons sharpen the contrast between what the public university was in 1969 and what it is today. With state revenues shrinking, the primary reason is the financial motive. As one commentator notes:

> The contemporary emphasis on free trade stimulates international academic mobility. Current thinking sees international higher education as a commodity to be freely traded and sees higher education as a private good, not a public responsibility . . . Earning money is a key motive for all internationalization projects.[11]

Internationalization flows concurrently with the trend toward the increased privatization of public higher education that has been studied now for some 15 years. Since the economic crisis of 2008, critiques of privatization have increased and student movements to combat it have surfaced and then receded sporadically over the last several years.

Let me move toward a conclusion now with a short meditation on the status of Chican@, Latin@, and Ethnic studies at research universities. What happens to the teaching of "race," gender, and class once they are separated from the potential for praxis? If these categories are theorized only in seminar rooms and critique remains frozen at the intellectual level, the potential for creating tactical interventions designed to challenge the neoliberal university will be minimal. The neoliberal regime even more than its liberal predecessor can easily tolerate courses on the history of oppressions, decolonization, and the like as long as that critique stays inside the classroom or at elite conference venues. It can easily accommodate faculty who claim to be "interrogating" corporatized academic practices when those same faculty advance their career by pursuing hyper-professionalization and self-promotion and preach those values to their graduate students and junior colleagues.

Whereas the liberal university could congratulate itself for "embracing" Chicano curricular offerings (usually after protracted efforts to reject them or underfund them), the neoliberal university simply imposes a "pay as you go" regime in which those programs unable to raise external funding begin to disappear. There are very few foundations, corporations, and wealthy donors eager to fund academic programs that challenge the status quo by engaging too deeply in Clark Kerr's "critical evaluation of society" much less a full-blown transformation of the university as Movement activists had demanded. As Arlene Dávila showed in *Latinos, Inc.*, the Latino community has been reduced to just one more market segment.[12] In order to survive, will the Chicano studies programs of the future be forced to include a Pan Bimbo Endowed Chair, a Jarritos Lecture Series, or a Carlos Slim Research Fellowship? And once they do, will the rubric "Chicano Studies" even be relevant? Will the identifying labels "Chicana" and "Chicano" themselves be replaced once and for all by the deracinated and depoliticized term "Hispanic"?

Today, the warning issued almost 50 years ago by another University of California employee, Herbert Marcuse, rings especially true:

> For if 'education' is more and other than training, learning, preparing for the [already] existing society, it means not only enabling man to know and understand the facts which make up reality but also to know and understand the factors that establish the facts so that he can change their inhuman reality.[13]

Or as the authors of the Plan de Santa Bárbara put it: "For this reason, Chicano students must give priority to structural change activity which aims to affect the conditions that oppress Chicano people."[14]

This means that the teaching of Chicana/Chicano studies at neoliberal educational institutions in the twenty-first century will be an incomplete project that is complicit with neoliberal market values whenever it is not accompanied by reform movements led by student, staff, non-academic organizations, and faculty coalitions. Being "radical" at the level of personal relations is not being "radical" at the level of institutional change. At elite research campuses, for example, theorizing "race" (even in juxtaposition to other categories) is easily co-opted and therefore rarely produces a challenge to institutional racial and gender inequities. The shift from radical critique to "diversity training," "individual caring," and "understanding oppression" coincides with neoliberalism's exaltation of "individual freedom," dehistoricized identities, and "humanitarian military intervention." At the undergraduate level, students from historically excluded groups are forced to contend with structural obstacles that make their academic success more unlikely while the stratified institutional culture remains intact.

Research on the Chicano Movement, no matter how critical the method-ologies employed, will be received by students in a totally new context that is inextricably linked to novel forms of identity formation, the new social tech-nologies, and above all the hegemonic force of privatization and its accomplices—short-term speculation, generic diversity, "paper or armchair revolutionism," and their ultimate enabler—class-based elitism—known throughout the UC system as "excellence." It will be a multi-generational struggle to roll back these enemies of a democratic system of higher education. That struggle is only just beginning.

Please allow me to conclude, then, with an informal summation of what I see as the social and historical reality that confronts us as teachers and students. It is in the form of a message I sent to my friend Roberto Rodríguez at the University of Arizona after the forced removal of Chicano-themed books from Mexican American studies high school classrooms in Tucson:

> Estimado Roberto: From our privileged location here at a University of California campus, we are witnessing a related transformation that is different in its details, more subtle, and less aggressively racist. We have no Hornes or Huppenthals. But we do have invisible technocrats slowly destroying the public university and converting it into a corporate bastion where students from California are displaced by foreign students (who pay more), where students are "taught" in classes of 900 people, and where faculty are forced to become "entrepreneurs." The campus administration at San Diego recently published its top three priority areas for the future—all of them had to do with creating products for the market; the word "education" was not mentioned once. The academic areas that emphasize history and critical thinking are either shrinking or becoming parodies. The push for on-line education is strong—no need to interact with real students. We simply sell them on-line courses and use underpaid TAs to grade the work. Administrators brag that UCSD is no longer a California university; it's a global university.

So what is to be done? As the cost of higher education goes up, Raza and African American students will slowly be denied access as will a majority of working-class youth; the few that make it in will have to take on serious debt to finish their degree. The future? Education for the already privileged and for a few tokens. Education as preparation for the stratified job market. Education as the site of market-driven research. Education to train elites from around the world. No more critique of the status quo. No more engagement with local populations. No more critical pedagogy in the classroom.

Education for the market does not permit education that empowers the working class. I've always thought the radical conservatives in Arizona hated Mexican American Studies more for its pedagogy than for its curriculum. "Ethnic Studies" at elitist universities is simply an inverted version of the dominant elitist, professionalized, and jargon-infused pedagogy that the institution promotes. In that sense, it poses no threat to the status quo. The attack on Mexican American Studies, therefore, has almost nothing to do with the political situation of a Department of Ethnic Studies at a UC campus. So again, this fight has less to do with the content of ethnic studies courses than with what the *Movimiento* demanded over 40 years ago—a university that serves the community and a pedagogy that empowers our youth. In many ways, the struggle that lies ahead is more difficult than the one faced by Movement activists. ¡Que siga la Causa!

Notes

1 Ignacio García, *Chicanismo: The Forging of a Militant Ethos Among Mexican Americans* (Tucson: University of Arizona Press, 1997).
2 Anthony Giddens, *Modernity and Self-Identity: Self and Society in the Late Modern Age* (Palo Alto, CA: Stanford University Press, 1991).
3 Chicano Coordinating Council on Higher Education, *Plan de Santa Bárbara: A Chicano Plan for Higher Education* (Oakland, CA: La Causa, 1969), 9.
4 Bernard Stiegler, *For a New Critique of Political Economy* (Cambridge, UK: Polity, 2010).
5 Jorge Mariscal, *Brown-Eyed Children of the Sun: Lessons from the Chicano Movement 1965–1975* (Albuquerque: University of New Mexico Press, 2005).
6 Chicano Coordinating Council on Higher Education, *Plan de Santa Bárbara*, 78.
7 Christopher Newfield, *Unmaking the Public University: The Forty-Year Assault on the Middle Class* (Cambridge, MA: Harvard University Press, 2008), 110.
8 Sheila Slaughter and Larry Leslie, *Academic Capitalism: Politics, Policies, and the Entrepreneurial University* (Baltimore: Johns Hopkins University Press, 1999), 76.
9 Philip Altbach and J. Knight, "The internationalization of higher education: Motivations and realities," *Journal of Studies in International Education*, vol. 11, 2007: 291.
10 James Donaldson, "Outsourcing Affirmative Action: Colleges Look Overseas for Racial Diversity," ABC News on-line (March 8, 2007): http://abcnews.go.com/US/story?id=2931345&page=1 (accessed February 2, 2013).
11 Altbach and Knight, "The internationalization of higher education," 291–292.
12 Arlene Dávila, *Latinos, Inc.: The Marketing and Making of a People* (Berkeley: University of California Press, 2001).
13 See Marcuse's 1968 Postscript in Herbert Marcuse, *A Critique of Pure Tolerance* (New York: Beacon Press, 1968).
14 Chicano Coordinating Council on Higher Education, *Plan de Santa Bárbara*, 79.

INTRODUCTION

The Chicano Movement and Chicano Historiography

Mario T. García

I would like to introduce this volume on the emerging historiography of the Chicano Movement from a twenty-first-century perspective, by addressing nine key questions about the Chicano Movement.

What was the Chicano Movement?

The Chicano Movement was the largest and most widespread civil rights and empowerment movement by Mexican-descent people in the United States. The key years of the movement are between 1965 and 1975 although the new historiography, as noted in this volume, is pushing the movement further into the late 1970s and 1980s. Nevertheless, that 10-year period between 1965 and 1975 had without question the most intense years of the movement. Why begin in 1965? That year marked the beginning of the famous grape strike in California's Central Valley (San Joaquin Valley) led by César Chávez, Dolores Huerta, and the farm workers to establish a union for farm workers that would not only bring them much-deserved wage and benefit increases, but a sense of dignity for their labor and for themselves. The courage of the predominantly Mexican-origin farm workers along with the national attention they acquired, in turn, influenced many Chicano youth throughout California and the Southwest, where the majority of Mexican Americans lived, to become politically involved and laid the foundation for the emergence of the Chicano Generation—a new political generation—that spearheaded what came to be known as the Chicano Movement, especially in the urban areas. The year 1975 is a more arbitrary marker but it is the year when the U.S.'s longest and most controversial war to that time—the Vietnam War— came to an end with the failure of the American intervention in that country and a humiliating loss. The war had generated a great deal of the historic social protests of the so-called "Sixties" that actually spilled over into the early 1970s. The end of the war led to an elimination of one of the key sources of protest politics in the massive anti-war movement, and the beginning of the decline of such protests including those of the Chicano Movement. Although the movement would continue in one form or another and certainly its spirit of Chicano empowerment also continued, still much of the militant dynamics of the movement clearly began to dissipate in the post-Vietnam era.

The Chicano Movement was characterized at one level by the continuation of a longer civil rights movement, led initially by what I call the Mexican American Generation of the 1930s through the 1950s that initiated the first major civil rights movement by Mexican Americans in the United States.[1] The Mexican American Generation was composed of either second-generation children of the mass number of Mexican immigrants who entered the U.S. in the early twentieth century or the smaller number of descendants, such as in south Texas, of those Mexican Americans who were already residing in the Southwest and California at the time of the U.S.–Mexico War that led to the American conquest of El Norte, or the northern part of Mexico, in that conflict. It was this generation, beginning in the 1930s when U.S.-born Mexican Americans were becoming the majority population among Mexican-descent people in the U.S., that forged this first civil rights struggle. This movement was expressive of U.S.-born Mexicans who knew more about what their rights were and how through racism, discrimination, and segregation they had been denied those rights. As a result they organized new associations among themselves to represent their civic and political interests. Such organization before and after World War II included the League of United Latin American Citizens (LULAC), the Mexican American Movement, the Spanish-Speaking Congress, the American G.I. Forum, the Community Service Organization (CSO), the Asociación Nacional México-Americana (ANMA), and the Mexican American Political Association (MAPA).[2]

Through these organizations and others, new Mexican American leaders organized efforts to desegregate the notorious so-called Mexican schools throughout the Southwest, including California, as well as the desegregation of public facilities such as restaurants, hotels, parks, swimming pools, beaches, movie theatres, etc.[3] They also fought for better jobs and living wages for Mexican-origin workers. They confronted jury discrimination especially in Texas. Politically, especially after the war, they promoted greater voting by Mexican Americans as well as encouraging Mexican Americans to run for public offices such as for school boards and city councils.[4] This civil rights movement, while diverse, limited, and scattered, nevertheless achieved significant breakthroughs and achievements. These included major legal cases to confront school segregation such as: in the Mendez Case in Orange County, California in 1946; the confrontation on jury segregation in the Hernández Case that went all the way to the U.S. Supreme Court; opening better jobs for Mexican Americans by the encouragement to join the new militant CIO (Congress of Industrial

Organizations) unions; and greater effective political representation by the election of more Mexican Americans to public offices highlighted by the election of Edward Roybal to the Los Angeles city council in 1949, and the election of Raymond Telles as mayor of El Paso in 1957.[5]

While the Mexican American Generation civil rights movement led to important reforms, it did not by any means eliminate a deeply seated racialized class system in the Southwest that relegated most Mexican-origin people to pools of cheap and exploitable labor. As a result, much discrimination and segregation remained into the 1960s.[6] It was the new Chicano Generation that took up the torch of combating such a second-class system even though it did not know much about or appreciate the earlier efforts by the Mexican American Generation. Nevertheless, in their own and more militant and radicalized way the Chicano Generation had no choice but to further this civil rights legacy with respect to educational, economic, political, and cultural race and class discrimination.

But the Chicano Generation went further than civil rights and also focused on its own version of the anti-colonial and Third World theme of self-determination. It called not for integration as had the Mexican American Generation, with integration meaning breaking down obstacles to equal opportunities with other Americans, but instead it called for the Chicano community to be able to control its own resources and determine its own future. It called for community control of its schools, its economy, its politics, and its culture. This was a Chicano version of self-determination. How exactly to accomplish this was never very clear but what was important was the concept of "Chicano Power" meaning self-empowerment. Hence, the Chicano civil rights movement differed from that of the Mexican American Generation in that civil rights in the Chicano Movement's case was not intended to achieve integration per se with other Americans—although this in fact was achieved in part—but through these struggles to achieve community empowerment. This was the Chicano Movement.

What is the Relationship of the Chicano Movement to Chicano History?

First of all, Chicano history as a field of study and as part of Chicano Studies is a Chicano Movement creation. The Chicano Generation understood that as part of its self-empowerment, it had to have a sense of its history—a history that had been denied it in the schools. Mexicans were not supposed to have a history in the U.S., yet the Chicano Generation instinctively recognized that it had a history or counter-history that it needed to discover. This meant exploring its indigenous and *mestizo* (Indian and Spanish, and even African and Asian) past: its roots in Mexican history including Mexico's war with the U.S.; the Mexican Revolution of 1910; and the history of Mexican immigrants to the U.S. But this was a history it only knew through family and community lore and not systematically studied by historians. This search for a relevant and useable past led to the development of the field of Chicano history as part of the movement's efforts to establish Chicano Studies programs at universities and colleges.[7]

As Chicano history developed and led to the first broad-based study of the history of Mexicans in the U.S. by professionally trained historians, most of Chicano background, it became possible to recognize that the Chicano Movement did not exist in a historical vacuum. Whether it was aware of it or not, it was the recipient of a historical legacy. Part of that legacy was that the first generation of Mexican Americans began its experience within the U.S. as a conquered people, or what I call the Conquered Generation in Chicano history. This was the result of the U.S.–Mexico War (1846–48) that, as noted, led to the U.S. annexation of close to half of Mexico's territory that became the American Southwest. Those Mexicans who found themselves living on the northern side of the new border were incorporated for the most part as U.S. citizens. However, they were not treated as first-class citizens but as second-class ones. Their conquest led to the dispossession of their farm and ranch lands and, through the introduction of American racism and a capitalist class system, to their subjugation as a cheap labor source. Some Mexican Americans rebelled against this treatment and rose up in revolt, only to be repressed. This was part of the Chicano Movement's legacy.[8]

That legacy also included the beginning of mass immigration from Mexico in the early twentieth century, as over a million Mexican immigrants entered from 1900 to 1930. This represented what I call the Immigrant Generation in Chicano history.[9] Uprooted in their land by economic modernization influenced by the infusion of American capital to channel Mexican commercial agriculture and mining development to American imperialistic and industrial desires and needs, thousands of peasants, small farmers, and others were displaced, and eventually moved north and crossed the border in search of jobs and better economic opportunities. But their movement also coincided with many of those same American economic interests such as the railroads, mining corporations, and agri-business which had invested in Mexico and now also invested in the Southwest in search of new and exploitable resources. Such exploitation, however, necessitated new sources of cheap labor and hence the attraction of Mexican immigrants.

Once across the border, Mexican immigrants became racialized and were considered members of an inferior race—Mexicans or "dirty Mexicans." This inferiority status, in turn, led to the justification for their exploitation and lack of development through "Mexican jobs," "Mexican wages," and their U.S.-born children being subjected to "Mexican schools." This is part of the legacy of the Chicano Movement including those immigrants who in their way attempted to defend themselves against their discrimination and segregation by a process of community-building, including asserting their pride in their Mexican culture and heritage. This legacy further included those who entered the U.S. as former revolutionaries in Mexico's major civil war, the Mexican Revolution of 1910. The Chicano Generation would rediscover this revolutionary heritage.[10]

Finally, as previously observed, the Chicano Generation as part of its historical legacy was directly and indirectly influenced by the civil rights struggles of the Mexican American Generation. Although the Chicano Movement would reject what it unfairly labeled the accommodationist politics of the previous political generation, still it benefitted from that generation's civil rights struggles that created somewhat more educational, economic, and political advantages for their children—the Chicano Generation.

As part of its historical legacy, the Chicano Generation inherited its very name. The term "Chicano" was first introduced by early Mexican immigrants as part of the Immigrant Generation. However, the term was appropriated by U.S.-born Mexican Americans in the hardcore *barrios* or communities of the Southwest such as south El Paso and East Los Angeles by the World War II period. The so-called pachucos and zootsuitors of the era in particular used the term Chicano as part of their countercultural identity formation.[11] Later youth urban groups including the rising gang movements of the 1950s further utilized the term as an expression of an identity that rejected both mainstream U.S. and Mexican American cultures. It represented a term of rebellion of rebels with or perhaps without a cause. The Chicano Generation, seeing itself also as countercultural and rebellious against the forces of integration, assimilation, and Americanization, re-appropriated the term Chicano as part of this generation's effort of self-empowerment; in this case, the right and power to name themselves—Chicanos.

All of this previous history and legacy, and more, provides a historical contextualization for understanding the rise of the Chicano Movement and its particular politics.

What is the Relationship of the Chicano Movement to U.S. History?

The Chicano Movement is U.S. history. It is part of the history of the Sixties and, in particular, of the protest movements of the period that included the Black civil rights movement led by Dr. Martin Luther King, Jr., the Black Power movement, the anti-war movement against the Vietnam War, the feminist movement, and the countercultural movement, among other manifestations of protest led by a new generation of young Americans. Having said this, it is unfortunate that in the writings on the history of this major period of American political upheaval, the history of the Chicano Movement has not been well integrated. Outside of mention of César Chávez and the farm workers movement, most histories of this era omit or give short shrift to the role of Chicanos in making part of this history. For example, much has been written about the anti-war movement but without taking into consideration that Chicanos organized the largest anti-war effort by any "minority" in the country highlighted by the massive Chicano Anti-War Moratorium on August 29, 1970 in East Los Angeles when 20,000 or more mostly Chicanos demonstrated against the war. They protested that Chicanos, like Blacks, were being disproportionally drafted into the military and sent to Vietnam in addition to the war expenses cutting back on social programs that aided Chicanos. The fact is that, at all levels, Chicanos contributed to the history of this period whether it had to do with: the issues of civil rights; the farm workers movement; the land grant movement in New Mexico led by Reies López Tijerina; the student movement; the search for political alternatives such as the effort to build an independent Chicano political party—La Raza Unida Party; countercultural movements through the expression of Chicano art and literature known as the Chicano Renaissance; and, of course, the anti-war movement. In all of these manifestations and more especially localized ones that this volume brings attention to, the Chicano Movement represented a significant part of mid-twentieth-century American history and it needs to be acknowledged especially now when Chicanos/Latinos represent, with over 55 million people and some 16 percent of the total U.S. population, the largest minority in the country. This volume is one effort to do so.

What were the Causes of the Chicano Movement?

The causes of the Chicano Movement were both internal and external.

Internally, the Chicano Movement led by the Chicano Generation was reacting first to the continuation of many years of racism, discrimination, segregation, and poverty facing Mexican Americans in the United States. While the earlier Mexican American Generation had made some inroads in combating such conditions, it was not able to eradicate all of them and hence, into the 1960s, Mexican Americans continued to face significant disparities with other American ethnic groups including African Americans in education, jobs, wages, housing, medical services, political representation, and ethnic/cultural respect. Hence, the Chicano Movement in its own and more militant way took on these social problems since it affected the activists of the movement and their communities.

Second, the Chicano Generation was consciously and unconsciously reacting to and benefitting from a legacy of Mexican American struggles for civil rights and dignity. Chicanos in the 1960s and 1970s may not have known much about the earlier history of Mexican Americans but perhaps in their families they had parents who had participated in earlier protests such as against the lack of educational opportunities for their children. Protest and civil rights struggles were not new in the Chicano communities and, to a degree, the new Chicano Generation responded to this either by acknowledging this legacy or by believing in a critical way that these earlier movements represented failed ones and so it was up to the Chicano Movement to supersede them.

A third internal cause concerns what is called "rising expectations." That is, many of the Chicano Generation activists, despite the long-standing conditions of racism and lack of educational and economic opportunities in the Mexican American communities, were in fact experiencing some level of mobility. As a result of the earlier civil rights efforts by the Mexican American Generation, younger Chicanos were completing high school and, more than ever before, were beginning by the early and mid-1960s to attend college. Many benefitted from their fathers as military veterans themselves going to college, utilizing the G.I. Bill of Rights to fund their education. As a result, some of the World War II or Korean War veterans became teachers, lawyers, doctors, or skilled technicians. In turn, they as role models encouraged or insisted that their children went to college. The result was that the Mexican American community into the 1960s was displaying a juxtaposition of poverty and progress. That progress, for some, generated among the Chicano Generation a sense of rising expectations whereby they being the recipients of some progress and mobility recognized that more progress and mobility was still needed and so in the Chicano Movement began to demand it. Many social movements, as was the case in the student movements of the time including the Chicano student movement, were and are led by people who in fact are experiencing mobility, but that only whets their appetites for more mobility not only for themselves but for those in their communities left behind. This was the politics of rising expectations that affected the Chicano Movement.

Finally, the Chicano Generation was motivated by family socialization. By this I mean that it appears that many, perhaps most, movement activists may have been socialized by their parents to stand up for their rights and not allow others to demean them or insult them because they were of Mexican origin. This socialization included being proud of one's Mexican heritage and culture. This type of family socialization may have laid the basis for activists who became inspired to combat racism and discrimination in their own way.

While these internal causes may help explain the origins of the Chicano Movement, at the same time there are external causes as well that influenced the Chicano Generation. This included what was happening in the world around them, such as the other civil rights and protest movements of this period. Chicanos did not live in a bubble. They were, for example, part of the TV generation. They witnessed the civil rights demonstrations of Blacks; they were inspired by Dr. King's "I Have a Dream" speech in 1963; they learned of the Free Speech Movement in Berkeley in 1964; they recognized the beginning of what would become unprecedented anti-war marches; and they learned of how many affluent young whites were turning away from a middle-class culture that they believed to be hypocritical and shallow and by contrast looked toward countercultural expressions such as in the hippie movement and the drug culture. Chicanos saw a domestic world in crisis and in turmoil and the establishment being challenged by a more questioning and skeptical youth generation displaying an ambivalence if not open opposition to the traditional avenues of social change via the two-party electoral system, the courts, etc. Instead, new protest movements, both black and white, increasingly used not only more radical critiques of the American racialized capitalist system, but also militant strategies of social change such as direct action in the streets via marches, mass demonstrations, sit-ins, picketing, and even, in some cases, the use of violence. The Chicano Movement, in turn, became radical and militant because it came of age in a radical and militant protest time. In this sense, the movement was in step with its historical context.

But it was not only domestic upheavals that influenced the Chicano Movement from an external perspective, it was what was happening in many parts of the world as well. Chicanos were especially influenced by the so-called Third World movements of liberation in Asia, Africa, and Latin America. These anti-colonial and anti-Western movements for national liberation and self-awareness touched a historical nerve among Chicanos as they began to learn that they shared some similarities with these Third World struggles. Chicanos asserted that they had begun their experiences in the U.S. as a conquered and colonized people in the nineteenth century and that they had lived in an internal form of colonialism into the twentieth century. Just as Third World people were discovering their pre-colonial and native cultures, so too were Chicanos beginning to rediscover their Mexican cultural and historical roots. Like Third World people, Chicanos were also recognizing the right to name themselves—Chicanos! Of all these Third World movements, there is no question that the Chicano Movement especially reacted to the Cuban Revolution of 1959 led by Fidel Castro and Che Guevara. This was a nationalist revolution against Yankee imperialism and neo-colonialism in the Spanish language and with Latin American roots that particularly appealed to Chicanos. Hence, the Chicano Movement, for example, re-appropriated the iconic image of Che Guevara in the movement's iconography. So much was the image of Che used that probably some Chicanos believed that Che was Chicano. But what this expressed was that the Chicano Movement identified with Third World movements for liberation and saw itself as part of this movement, utilizing the very terms of these struggles such as self-determination and liberation in addition to applying the internal colonial analogy to a historical explanation of Chicano history.

The Chicano Movement did not occur in a vacuum. It was very much a part of its internal history and its external reality. Both came together to influence the movement and its particular character.

What were the Goals of the Chicano Movement?

As noted, the Chicano Movement combined a civil rights agenda with an effort to achieve self-determination for the Chicano communities through self-empowerment. It rejected integration and pluralism and certainly assimilation, and instead embraced community empowerment. But the theme of community empowerment was loosely constructed and shows that the larger goals of the Chicano Movement were ambivalent. What did self-determination mean? What did community empowerment mean? The answers or responses were ambivalent. The movement saw itself as being "revolutionary," but what did this mean? The movement regarded Chicanos as being an internally colonized people, but what did this mean with respect to what needed to be done? Was the movement revolutionary? Was the movement irredentist in that it aimed at regaining the Southwest, or Aztlán, as Chicanos began to refer to the region, to rejoin the conquered homeland back to mother Mexico? Or was the movement, despite the radical and militant rhetoric, basically a liberal reform movement? There were no simple or clear answers to such questions. The movement, like most of the other social protest movements of the Sixties, knew better what it didn't like than what would replace it. At the same time, while the existential goals of the movement were ambivalent, what was clearer was that the movement aimed to first empower the new Chicano Generation by achieving a re-education and re-awareness by Chicanos of their ancestral and parental Mexican historical and cultural roots and that it would be on the basis of this new cultural nationalism that the movement would then organize to take up the challenge to the historic racism and economic exploitation of Chicanos. "¡Ya Basta!" was the cry of the movement—we have had enough!

Did the Chicano Movement have a Particular Ideology?

The Chicano Movement's ideology was referred to as Chicanismo. It was not a set document or plan but an evolution of ideas, themes, and an ethos or spirit. It was centered on cultural or ethnic nationalism or what some refer to as the politics of identity. Cultural nationalism meant the bonding of an ethnic group, Chicanos, based on a common cultural heritage. The politics of identity suggested that the core or essential identity of Chicanos was their ethnicity. Chicanismo further suggested a type of monolithic Chicano experience and avoided the actual heterogeneity of Mexican Americans; however, in the heat of the political moment, it was felt essential to propose a common unity in order to build a political and social movement. Such a movement could not be organized on a fragmented identity.[12]

Chicanismo filled certain key needs for the movement. It confronted the identity question. Were Chicanos Americans, Mexican Americans, or what? Chicanismo said "you're Chicano, be proud of it and move on." Were Chicanos white or a people of color? Chicanismo said "you're of indigenous and mestizo [Spanish and Indian] background and hence a people of color." Why were Chicanos lagging behind other Americans? Chicanismo said, "because you are a colonized people."

The key themes of Chicanismo included that of Chicanos being an indigenous people. As such, they represented the descendants of the Aztecs and lived in the ancestral homeland of the Aztecs—Aztlán—which Chicanos conveniently argued was the Southwest where the majority of Chicanos lived. Aztlán was the Chicanos' historical homeland—their origin myth. But Aztlán also constituted a Lost Homeland in that in the U.S.–Mexico War the U.S. had captured and colonized Aztlán. This gave rise to the internal colonial model. At the same time, the Chicano

Generation symbolized La Raza Nueva or born-again Chicanos who had become conscious and proud of their Chicano heritage. Chicanismo also embraced the sanctity of La Familia, or the family, but expanded support for the nuclear family as the bedrock of Chicanismo to include an expansive concept of La Familia to embrace the entire Chicano community. Other key themes of Chicanismo included: Carnalismo, or a sense of brotherhood; barrio culture, or the proposal that the "authentic" culture of Chicanos was to be found in the hard-core barrios such as East Los Angeles; revolutionary heritage, or the idea that Chicanos possessed a revolutionary tradition going back to the Mexican Revolution of 1910 with rebels such as Emiliano Zapata and Pancho Villa; and finally the theme of self-determination, or Chicano Power.

Chicanismo, or cultural nationalism, was over time not as essentialist or monolithic as at first thought.[13] It accommodated or was challenged by other ideologies such as Marxism, a Third World consciousness or internationalism, and by feminism. In the end, Chicanismo was not dogmatically cultural nationalist.

What were the Major Manifestations of the Chicano Movement?

The major manifestations of the Chicano Movement or those that are best known about—although, as this volume suggests, there were many more localized manifestations that more recent scholars are documenting—include the following:

The farm workers' insurgency led by César Chávez and Dolores Huerta represents a major and seminal manifestation. This historic struggle that led to the initial success of the farm workers' union, the UFW (United Farm Workers), in securing contracts from California growers was, as noted, a major stimulus to the development of the Chicano Generation as a political generation and the Chicano Movement. The farm workers' story is not a precursor of the movement but an essential and leading part of it.[14] While the connection between labor and the Chicano Movement has been largely confined to the farm workers' struggle, the chapters by Lorena Márquez and Max Krochmal expand this connection to include labor movements in Sacramento and San Antonio that were linked to the Chicano Movement.

The land grant movement in northern New Mexico led by Reies López Tijerina marked another initial manifestation. Tijerina's militant movement upholding the land rights of rural Mexican Americans further caught the imagination of young Chicanos in the cities who saw Tijerina and his movement as "revolutionary," providing an additional inspiration for the Chicano Movement.[15]

The Chicano student movement both in the colleges and in the high schools was a clear expression of the Chicano Generation, as noted by Gustavo Licón and Marisol Moreno in their chapters. Chicano college students through their campus organizations such as MEChA (*Movimiento Estudiantil Chicano de Aztlán*) were a key component of the movement both on the campuses (recruitment of more Chicano students and the establishment of Chicano Studies), as well as in the community, such as support for the farm workers and other manifestations of the movement. High school students in their own right pushed for improvement in their schools and added the right to a good education as part of the movement's civil rights agenda. The Chicano high school movement was highlighted by the historic 1968 so-called Blowouts or walkouts by thousands of Chicano students protesting inferior education in the East L.A. public schools.[16]

The Chicano anti-war movement over the U.S. role in the Vietnam War was without question one of the most important manifestations of the Chicano Movement. Chicanos began to recognize that the war was a Chicano issue because, for one, Chicanos were being disproportionally drafted (since they were not encouraged to stay in school or go to college) but also being disproportionally sent to the war front, bearing heavy casualties. Moreover, the war was diverting much-needed resources and funds from domestic programs that could help the Chicano community. The Chicano anti-war movement staged the largest demonstration of the movement when some 20,000, mostly Chicanos, protested the war in East L.A.[17]

Disenchanted with the traditional two-party system that Chicanos believed had done nothing over the years for Chicanos, the movement promoted the organization of the independent political party, La Raza Unida Party (RUP), to more effectively represent the interests of Chicanos and assist in the political empowerment of the communities. Spearheaded by José Ángel Gutiérrez in Texas, the RUP experienced initial electoral success in small rural communities of south Texas where Mexican Americans formed the majority of residents. This involved election to city councils, boards of education, and country commissions. In the larger southwestern cities, the RUP faced more difficulties, as José Moreno observes in his chapter, since Chicanos represented minorities in such urban areas. While no doubt in some of these cases the RUP hoped for victories, at the same time it used the electoral process to put forth the agenda of the Chicano Movement and to politicize the people. In 1972, the RUP held its first and only national convention in El Paso, Texas. However, due to key rivalries between Gutiérrez and Rodolfo "Corky" Gonzales of Denver over the RUP leadership, the RUP began to decline thereafter.[18]

Immigration, especially protection of the undocumented immigrants, most of them Mexican, likewise became an issue taken up by some movement activists, as noted by Jimmy Patiño in his chapter on San Diego. With the termination of the Bracero labor contract program between Mexico and the U.S. in 1964, some employers such as in agribusiness encouraged and hired an increasing number of undocumented Mexican workers that were likewise used as strikebreakers against the efforts to unionize farm workers by César Chávez in California. Urban services and other industries necessitating cheap labor also recruited the undocumented. Moreover, in response to this immigration increase, the California state legislature and the U.S. Congress considered punitive measures to stem this flow.

In addition, the federal government began to detain and deport thousands of such immigrants. In reaction, movement activists in California led by Bert Corona, a long-time Mexican American organizer and a crossover figure between the Mexican American Generation and the Chicano Generation, organized to protect the undocumented and to oppose anti-immigration laws. As such, the movement included immigration issues as part of its agenda.[19]

The Chicana feminist movement represented still another major manifestation of the movement. Women played important roles in the movement but often confronted sexism and gender discrimination. Some women therefore evolved from being just cultural nationalists to also expressing feminist views calling for the elimination of any discriminatory treatment of women in the movement. They became both cultural nationalists and feminists. Chicana feminists organized their own conferences and organizations, as well as publications. Rosie Bermúdez's chapter, for example, highlights one prominent Chicana feminist, Alicia Escalante, who led the East L.A. Welfare Rights Organization.[20]

Finally, the Chicano Movement inspired a major artistic and literary revival of artists, poets, and writers who used their artistic talents in support of the movement. This came to be referred to as the Chicano Renaissance. Such artists were inspired by the movement and, in turn, became movement artists. They rejected a traditional view that art and politics should not mix. They believed that all art was political and hence they were just being open about their politics.[21]

These manifestations constituted some of the major struggles of the Chicano Movement but there were many more localized ones that the new Chicano historiography on the movement is beginning to reveal. Examples of such more localized studies include the chapters by Lorena Márquez concerning the movement in Sacramento, Oliver Rosales on the movement in Bakersfield, and Luis Moreno's study of the movement in Oxnard, California.

What is the Legacy of the Movement?

The legacy of the Chicano Movement appears on several fronts.

Above all, the movement made Chicanos and, by extension, other Latinos into national political actors for the first time. This was the origins of the major political influence that Latinos now wield in contemporary American politics as witnessed by the key and decisive role that Latinos played in the re-election of President Barack Obama in the 2012 election. The Chicano Movement succeeded in bringing Chicanos/Latinos to national public and media attention. This attention and influence has only increased over the last four decades and more especially with the impressive growth of the Latino population.

The movement also accomplished major reforms. Even though the movement saw itself as being revolutionary and not reformist, the fact is that in the end it achieved reforms rather than revolution. The American racialized capitalist system remained, but the movement forced it to acquiesce to allow Chicanos more opportunities within the system. These included more access to colleges and universities including graduate programs. Within this academic system, Chicano and Latino Studies programs, departments, and research centers were formed for the very first time. A entire new generation of Chicano/Latino scholars/intellectuals came out of the movement. Professor Jorge Mariscal and myself represent that generation in this volume. Some of the authors in this text represent the latest wave of Chicano historians, for example, but scholars who are building on the shoulders of those who came before. In addition, the movement forced the system to provide more opportunities in business careers, the law, the media, medicine, engineering, and other more skilled and technical positions. Furthermore, the movement created a whole generation of elected and appointed Chicano/Latino politicians and this has only further increased over time. In all, the movement helped to create a new and aspiring middle class, but one in many cases was still empowered by the ethos of the Chicano Movement and thus more demanding of the system.

The Chicano Movement further established and promoted a new and empowering ethnic consciousness that over time has politically energized the Chicano and Latino communities. The ongoing push against anti-immigration policies and for comprehensive immigration reform comes from a new generation of leaders who directly and indirectly have been influenced by the legacy of the movement. Chicano Power has become translated into Latino Power and there is no looking back. The movement demanded respect for Chicanos and Latinos in the U.S. and this demand has only been reinforced by newer generations.

Finally, I would argue that one of the legacies and perhaps the most important legacy of the Chicano Movement is that, without necessarily acknowledging it, the Chicano Movement advanced the struggle for social justice and democracy in the United States. The movement, along with many of the other social movements of that era, recognized that the American democratic agenda was still an unfulfilled one and that this effort could only be achieved by struggles from below—by the people. The movement assisted in that struggle to achieve full democracy but did not complete it. Hence, it is up to the new generations, as Jorge Mariscal notes in his Foreword, to take up that struggle especially at the grass-roots level, but inspired by the Chicano Movement as well as by the other movements of the Sixties. In that sense the Chicano Movement is not dead but is alive in the continuing legacy and spirit of oppositional politics.

How have Historians Dealt with the Movement and What is the Contribution of this Volume?

Historians in Chicano history have examined the Chicano Movement but not as extensively as other periods of either the nineteenth century or twentieth century especially. Part of the reason may have to do with that Chicano historiography, as a particular area of study, coincided with the Chicano Movement and, while inspired by the movement, was much too close to it for a historical perspective. Since that period some studies have been done that are either overviews of the movement such as that by Carlos Muñoz or have a focus on particular aspects or locations of the movement such as Ernesto Chávez's study of the movement in Los Angeles, Lorena Oropeza's major examination of the Chicano anti-war movement or Jorge Mariscal's nuanced view of Chicano cultural nationalism.[22] While these represent pioneering and groundbreaking studies they are still limited in terms of coverage of the movement and more complete examinations of the movement have been sparse until now. The chapters in this volume showcase some of the exciting and emerging historiography of the movement but they represent only a portion of much larger studies by these historians. When published in book form each of these complete histories will constitute the first concerted and major wave of what can now be called Chicano Movement Studies. The three sections of this text note the focus of the studies in the areas of community struggles, the student movement, and the geographic diversity of movement studies. While the area of community struggles still has some focus on Los Angeles as a major location of the movement, other contributions expand to include areas less studied or not previously studied, such as Oxnard, Sacramento, and Bakersfield. As noted, university students played a major role in the movement, and the two chapters in that section advance our knowledge of this aspect of the movement. Gustavo Licón provides an intriguing insight into the politics of the evolving history of the MEChA student movement in California not only during the movement years, but also in the post-movement ones and reveals the tensions between cultural nationalism and Marxism in that evolution. In one of the first important studies of the Chicano student movement at the community colleges, Marisol Moreno provides an analysis of such a movement at East Los Angeles College. Finally, historians Max Krochmal, Nora Salas, and Norma Cárdenas expand our knowledge of the movement beyond the Southwest to include the states of Texas, Michigan, and Oregon.

Conclusion

The origin of this publication is a conference that I organized at UC Santa Barbara in February of 2012 on "Chicano Power! The Emerging Historiography of the Chicano Movement."[23] I wanted to call attention to the increased interest especially by younger historians in the Chicano Movement. As I identified some of these scholars, I invited them to participate in the conference. The 2-day event, in my opinion, was very successful in exposing this new and significant historiography on a major period in Chicano history. In addition to papers on a variety of forthcoming books or dissertations on the Chicano Movement, one special panel was composed of the authors of recent books on the movement. These included: David Montejano's astute study of the Brown Berets in San Antonio; Maylei Blackwell's pioneering history of Chicana feminism during the movement; Brian Behnken's path-breaking comparative history of Chicano and African American civil rights struggles in Texas including during the period of the Chicano Movement; Lee Bebout's stimulating intellectual history of the movement; and my own testimonio/oral history of Sal Castro and the 1968 Blowouts in Los Angeles.[24] I am planning on additional such conferences as I discover more historians who are focusing on the movement. I was fortunate that Routledge was excited to publish some of the conference papers along with others that I solicited, and the result is this book. My hope is that this text with its exciting studies of the Chicano Movement will, at one level, inspire additional young scholars to work on still other facets of the movement, and, second, inspire students who read this volume to take up the torch of the Chicano Movement to fulfill the dream of a complete American democracy. This would be the ultimate legacy of the Chicano Movement and of the struggle for Chicano Power.

Let me add a note about terminology. During the period of the Chicano Movement, the movement just used the term *Chicano*. This is how I and some other authors in this volume refer to the movement. However, other authors choose to use the more contemporary term Chicana/o to indicate that both men and women were involved in the movement. It should be said that, in Spanish, the term *Chicano* includes both genders.

Notes

1   On the Mexican American Generation, see Mario T. García, *Mexican Americans: Leadership, Ideology & Identity, 1930–1960* (Berkeley and Los Angeles: University of California Press, 1989) and Richard A. García, *Rise of the Mexican American Middle Class: San Antonio, 1929–1941* (College Station: Texas A&M Press, 1991).

2   Cynthia E. Orozco, *No Mexicans, Women or Dogs Allowed: The Rise of the Mexican American Civil Rights Movement* (Austin: University of Texas Press, 2009); Benjamin Márquez, *LULAC: The Evolution of a Mexican American Political Organization* (Austin: University of Texas Press, 1993); Carl Allsup, *The American G.I. Forum: Origins and Evolution* (Austin: University of Texas Press, 1982).

3   On the Mexican Schools, see Gilbert G. Gonzales, *Chicano Education in the Era of Segregation* (Philadelphia: Balch Institute Press, 1990) and Guadalupe San Miguel, *"Let All of Them Take Heed": Mexican Americans and the Campaign for Educational Equality in Texas, 1910–1981* (Austin: University of Texas Press, 1987).

4   See Ignacio M. García, *Hector P. García: In Relentless Pursuit of Justice* (Houston, TX: Arte Publico Press, 2002); Ignacio M. García, *White But Not Equal: Mexican Americans, Jury Discrimination, and the Supreme Court* (Tucson: University of Arizona Press, 2009); Michael A. Olivas, Ed., *Colored Men and Hombres Aquí: Hernández v. Texas and the Emergence of Mexican American Lawyering* (Houston, TX: Arte Publico Press, 2006); Emilio Zamora, *Claiming Rights and Righting Wrongs in Texas: Mexican Workers and Job Politics During World War II* (College Station: Texas A&M Press, 2009); Carlos Blanton, forthcoming biography of George I. Sánchez from Yale University Press; Michael A. Olivas, Ed., *In Defense of My People: Alonso S. Perales and the Development of Mexican-American Public Intellectuals* (Houston, TX: Arte Publico Press, 2012).

5   On the Mendez Case, see Philippa Strum, *Mendez v. Westminster: School Desegration and Mexican-American Rights* (Lawrence: University Press of Kansas, 2010).

6   On the process of racialization, see Michael Omi and Howard Winant, *Racial Formation in the United States: From the 1960s to the 1980s* (New York: Routledge, 1986).

7   See Rodolfo F. Acuña, *The Making of Chicana/o Studies: In the Trenches of Academe* (New Brunswick, NJ: Rutgers University Press, 2011) and Michael Soldatenko, *Chicano Studies: The Genesis of a Discipline* (Tucson: University of Arizona Press, 2009).

8   See Rodolfo F. Acuña, *Occupied America: The Chicano's Struggle Toward Liberation* (San Francisco: Canfield Press, 1972); Mario Barrera, *Race and Class in the Southwest: A Theory of Racial Inequality* (Notre Dame: University of Notre Dame Press, 1972); Robert Blauner, *Racial Oppression in America* (New York: Harper & Row, 1972).

9   Mario T. García, *Desert Immigrants: The Mexicans of El Paso, 1880–1920* (New Haven, CT: Yale University Press, 1979). See also, Alberto Camarillo, *Chicanos in a Changing Society: From Mexican Pueblos to American Barrios in Santa Barbara and Southern California* (Cambridge, MA: Harvard University Press, 1979); Ricardo Romo, *East Los Angeles: History of a Barrio* (Austin: University of Texas Press, 1983); Vicki L. Ruiz, *Cannery Women/Cannery Lives: Mexican Women, Unionization, and the California Food Processing Industry, 1930–1950* (Albuquerque: University of New Mexico Press, 1987); George J. Sánchez, *Becoming Mexican American: Ethnicity, Culture, and Identity in Chicano Los Angeles, 1900–1945* (New York: Oxford University Press, 1993); Zaragoza Vargas, *Proletarians of the North: A History of Mexican Industrial Workers in Detroit and the Midwest, 1917–1933* (Berkeley and Los Angeles: University of California Press, 1993); Douglas Monroy, *Rebirth: Mexican Los Angeles from the Great Migration to the Great Depression* (Berkeley and Los Angeles: University of California Press, 1999); Matt García, *A World of Its Own: Race, Labor, and Citrus in the Making of Greater Los Angeles, 1900–1947* (Chapel Hill: University of North Carolina Press, 2001); Gabriela Arredondo, *Mexican Chicago: Race, Identity, and Nation, 1916–1939* (Urbana: University of Illinois Press, 2008).

10   George J. Sánchez, *Becoming Mexican American: Ethnicity, Culture, and Identity in Chicano Los Angeles, 1900–1945* (New York: Oxford University Press, 1993).

11   See Luis Alvarez, *The Power of the Zoot: Youth Culture and Resistance during World War II* (Berkeley and Los Angeles: University of California Press, 2008); Mauricio Mazón, *The Zoot-Suit Riots: The Psychology of Symbolic Annihilation* (Austin: University of Texas Press, 1984); Eduardo Obregón Pagán, *Murder at the Sleepy Lagoon: Zoot Suits, Race, and Riot in Wartime L.A.* (Chapel Hill: University of North Carolina Press, 2003); Catherine S. Ramírez, *The Woman in the Zoot Suit: Gender, Nationalism, and the Cultural Politics of Memory* (Durham, NC and London: Duke University Press, 2009).

12   See Ignacio M. García, *Chicanismo: The Forging of a Militant Ethos Among Mexican Americans* (Tucson: University of Arizona Press, 1997).

13   See Jorge Mariscal, *Brown-Eyed Children of the Sun: Lessons from the Chicano Movement, 1965–1975* (Albuquerque: University of New Mexico Press, 2005).

14   The literature on the farm workers is extensive but selected texts include Richard Griswold del Castillo and Richard A. García, *César Chávez: A Triumph of Spirit* (Norman: University of Oklahoma Press, 1995); Jacques Levy, *César Chávez: Autobiography of La Causa* (New York: W.W. Norton, 1975); Miriam Powell, *The Union of Their Dreams: Power, Hope, and Struggle in César Chávez's Farm Worker Movement* (New York: Bloomsbury Press, 2009); Frank Bardacke, *Trampling Out the Vintage: César Chávez and the Two Souls of the United Farm Workers* (London and New York: Verso Press, 2011); Matt García, *From the Jaws of Victory: The Triumph and Tragedy of César Chávez and the Farm Worker Movement* (Berkeley and Los Angeles: University of California Press, 2012); Mario T. Garcia, *A Dolores Huerta Reader* (Albuquerque: University of New Mexico Press, 2008).

15   On Tijerina, see Rudy V. Busto, *King Tiger: The Religious Vision of Reies López Tijerina* (Albuquerque: University of New Mexico Press, 2005); José Ángel Gutiérrez, Ed.,

Reies López Tijerina, *They Called Me "King Tiger": My Struggle for the Land and Our Rights* (Houston, TX: Arte Publico Press, 2000); Richard M. Gardner, *Grito! Reies López Tijerina and the New Mexico Land Grant War of 1967* (New York: Bobbs-Merrill, 1970).

16 Mario T. García and Sal Castro, *Blowout! Sal Castro and the Chicano Struggle for Educational Justice* (Chapel Hill: University of North Carolina Press, 2011); Carlos Muñoz, Jr., *Youth, Identity, Power: The Chicano Movement* (London: Verso Press, 1989); Armando Navarro, *Mexican American Youth Organization: Avant-Garde of the Chicano Movement in Texas* (Austin: University of Texas Press, 1995).

17 Lorena Oropeza, *¡Raza Si! Guerra No! Chicano Protest and Patriotism during the Vietnam War Era* (Berkeley and Los Angeles: University of California Press, 2005); Jorge Mariscal, *Aztlán and Viet Nam: Chicano and Chicana Experiences of the War* (Berkeley and Los Angeles: University of California Press, 1999). For an excellent and moving fictional account of the impact of the Vietnam War on Mexican American families, see Stella Pope Duarte, *Let Their Spirits Dance* (New York: Harper Perennial, 2002).

18 Ignacio M. García, *United We Win: The Rise and Fall of La Raza Unida Party* (Tucson: Mexican American Studies & Research Center, University of Arizona, 1989); Armando Navarro, *The Cristal Experiment: A Chicano Struggle for Community Control* (Madison: University of Wisconsin Press, 1998); Armando Navarro, *La Raza Unida Party: A Chicano Challenge to the U.S. Two-Party Dictatorship* (Philadelphia: Temple University Press, 2000); Marc Rodríguez, *The Tejano Diaspora: Mexican Americanism & Ethnic Politics in Texas and Wisconsin* (Chapel Hill: University of North Carolina Press, 2011).

19 See Mario T. García, *Memories of Chicano History: The Life and Narrative of Bert Corona* (Berkeley and Los Angeles: University of California Press, 1994); David G. Gutiérrez, *Walls and Mirrors: Mexican Americans, Mexican Immigrants, and the Politics of Ethnicity* (Berkeley and Los Angeles: University of California Press, 1995).

20 Alma A. García, Ed., *Chicana Feminist Thought: The Basic Historical Writings* (New York: Routledge, 1997); Maylei Blackwell, *¡Chicana Power! Contested Histories of Feminism in the Chicano Movement* (Austin: University of Texas Press, 2011).

21 See, for example, Richard Griswold del Castillo, Teresa McKenna and Yvonne Yarbro-Bejarano, Eds., *Chicano Art: Resistance and Affirmation, 1965–1985* (Los Angeles: Wright Art Gallery, UCLA, 1991).

22 Ernesto Chávez, *¡Mi Raza Primero! Nationalism, Identity, and Insurgency in the Chicano Movement in Los Angeles, 1966–1978* (Berkeley and Los Angeles: University of California Press, 2002); Lorena Oropeza, *¡Raza Si! Guerra No!*; George Mariscal, *Brown-Eyed Children of the Sun*; Carlos Muñoz, *Youth, Identity, Power*.

23 In addition to the scholars mentioned in the Introduction, other participants included Lauren Araiza, Gordon Mantler, Jerry García, Karla Alonso, Virginia Espino, and Marisela Chávez. The keynote speakers were Jorge Mariscal and the late Sal Castro.

24 David Montejano, *Quixote's Soldiers: A Local History of the Chicano Movement, 1965–1981* (Austin: University of Texas Press, 2010); Maylei Blackwell, *¡Chicana Power! Contested Histories of Feminism in the Chicano Movement* (Austin: University of Texas Press, 2011); Brian D. Behnken, *Fighting Their Own Battles: Mexican Americans, African Americans, and the Struggle for Civil Rights in Texas* (Chapel Hill: University of North Carolina Press, 2011); Lee Bebout, *Mythohistorical Interventions: The Chicano Movement and Its Legacies* (Minneapolis: University of Minnesota Press, 2011); and Mario T. Garcia and Sal Castro, *Blowout! Sal Castro and the Chicano Struggle for Educational Justice* (Chapel Hill, University of North Carolina Press, 2011).

PART ONE

Community Struggles

1

"ALL I WANT IS THAT HE BE PUNISHED"

Border Patrol Violence, Women's Voices, and Chicano Activism in Early 1970s San Diego[1]

Jimmy Patiño

In the midst of increasing incidences of brutality at the hands of immigration authorities, Martha Elena Parra López, a Tijuana resident, was raped by Border Patrol agent Kenneth Cocke on May 31, 1972.[2] A few days later, Martha Elena responded by detailing the event to San Ysidro activist Alberto García who, with area Chicano activists, created an uproar about the injustice. San Diego Chicano activists, already incensed by a series of harassment and brutality incidents undertaken by U.S. Customs and Border Patrol officers against Mexicans and Mexican Americans, called for immediate action from authorities for this atrocious act against who they described as a "young attractive Mexican National" and "mother of two children."[3] For them, this brutality was part of a larger attack on "La Raza"/"our people," as they called for a broader investigation of the local effects of deportation-oriented immigration policies.[4] For Martha Elena, telling her story to Chicano activists and to the public was an act of defiance, as she later stated, "All I want is that he (Agent Cocke) be punished."[5]

The rape occurred after Martha Elena was apprehended with two companions, María Sandoval and Teresa Castellanos, while visiting their friend Vera León's Chula Vista residence in south San Diego County. Martha Elena was a resident of nearby Tijuana and married to a professional basketball player there. She was likely from "central Mexico" as one report noted that her 11-year-old son was living with relatives there. She had moved to Tijuana with her spouse 6 years preceding the incident.[6] Another report noted that she was a mother of two, suggesting that another child resided with her and her spouse.[7] She stated that while living in Tijuana she had only crossed the U.S.-Mexico border on two occasions, both times for brief visits. She had been in Chula Vista, only about 15 miles from Tijuana and the border, for a week when she was apprehended.[8]

Revealing the level of crisis growing among law enforcement agents concerning "illegal immigration" the Border Patrol was tipped off by Chula Vista police who contacted INS officials after discovering that Martha Elena, María, and Teresa were undocumented.[9] Agent Cocke apprehended the three women at about 6:30 in the evening and transported them to the San Ysidro Border Patrol office.[10]

Demonstrating Cocke's emboldened attitude within his daily work at the Border Patrol, he began sexually harassing Martha Elena at the San Ysidro station where she and her two companions were further interrogated and processed.[11] Affirming Agent Cocke's questioning about her marital status, Martha Elena reported that he then used obscenities as he remarked that she "must have many admirers" because she was "good looking."[12] Cocke then documented routine information including Martha Elena's height and weight and the number of children she had. He then checked her face and arms for any evidence of needle marks from drug use. Martha Elena was then "made to sign a paper" that she apparently did not understand nor was informed of what it was, although Cocke then gave her a copy of it.[13] The form most likely gave consent for a voluntary departure, an expulsion status where migrants admit to entering the country without documentation and are then immediately sent back to their home countries, particularly utilized to remove Mexican migrants.[14] Martha Elena was then detained in another room while both of her companions, María and Teresa, were also processed.[15]

Soon after, Cocke drove the three women to a major crossway, the San Ysidro border entrance, where the officer instructed only María and Teresa to follow the flow of pedestrians into Mexico. Revealing the women's insistence on staying together, María and Teresa reportedly responded to Cocke, "All three of us will leave or all three of us will stay."[16] The officer became visibly upset with the women's refusal to follow his orders and drove along the international border into an obscure area about 15 to 20 minutes away from the San Ysidro border entrance. Martha Elena recalled, "I became very frightened when he insisted on dropping us off in the dark, out by the airport."[17] The airport under reference was Brown Field airport, about a mile north of the border in the Otay Mesa community. A barbed-wire fence, in bad repair and easily crossed, separated this part of the San Diego area from Mexico's La Libertad district of Tijuana at this time in the early 1970s.[18]

Once in this much darker, remote border site, Cocke again instructed María and Teresa to cross the border through the meager border fence. They again refused. Martha Elena recounted "I wanted to also to go with them but he grabbed me by the arm and threw me in the front seat."[19] Cocke then threatened the women, asserting that María and Teresa "better get going" or he would "do something" to them or to Martha Elena. As Martha Elena stated, "In other words he threatened us."[20] As María and Teresa had consistently refused Cocke's instructions to separate them, they made what must have been a painstaking decision to leave the scene (and Martha Elena) rather than test an armed law enforcement agent's threat of violence. Indeed, Martha Elena recalled the intimidating character of the officer, "He was a large, blond man. I was afraid of him from the start. He had a uniform and authority."[21]

Interlacing official inspection procedures with sexual harassment, Cocke stood in front of Martha Elena, who was trapped in the front seat, and asked her to remove her clothing. She refused, after which he insisted. Agent Cocke then took out a flashlight and instructed, "Take your brassiere off, I want to see if they are real and also take your panties off so that I can see if you have concealed money or documents."[22] Martha Elena then claimed, "After a long struggle with this officer until my strength was out, he stripped me completely and violated me, he made a statement and said 'I hope you do not have any disease,' he then told me to get dressed and to get out of the patrol car and go to my country."[23]

The next day she contacted Vera León, whose home she had been visiting in Chula Vista when she was apprehended, to inform her about what had happened. Vera contacted San Ysidro activist and notary Alberto García who, a few days later on June 7, listened to Martha Elena's report of the incident and notarized an affidavit.[24] She also visited a San Diego area hospital where she was treated for bleeding due to the sexual assault, an injury she also reported in the affidavit.[25]

While Martha Elena Parra López was not a frequent border crosser, and the actions of Agent Cocke were seemingly isolated and extreme, her voice is instructive in revealing how the increasing number of Mexican migrants entering the United States in the early 1970s were subject to arbitrary acts of harassment and violence through the official questioning and search procedures mandated by U.S. immigration policy.[26] U.S. border agents consistently subjected migrants and other border crossers to procedural inspections that aimed to identify drug-users, drug-smugglers, economic burdens, illegal aliens, and others that were perceived as potential hazards to the well-being of U.S. society. In 1966, Border Patrol apprehensions peaked back up to more than 100,000—a level they had not reached since 1954. By 1970 the rate was at half a million, on its way to reaching just under one million by 1977.[27] Through reports of official Border Patrol procedures emerged cases of abuse, including physical assault, unwarranted strip searches, and as in the case of Martha Elena Parra López, sexual harassment and rape.

Martha Elena's testimony is of particular significance because not only was the migrant stream from Mexico growing to unprecedented levels, but it was also becoming increasingly female as employers recruited Mexican women to work in *maquiladoras* (assembly plants) proliferating on the Mexican side of the border and domestic labor demands in the U.S. increased. When coupled with dozens if not hundreds of complaints by Mexican-immigrant, Mexican American, and other border crossing women from 1970 to 1972 concerning humiliating experiences of being strip searched, Martha Elena's voice helps unmask the ways that male dominance and gender inequality were part of the systematic acts of racial and class subjugation unfolding at the border.[28] These women's voices revealed that invasive and humiliating violations of their self-possession were occurring within the everyday procedures of border patrolling alongside physical beatings, verbal intimidation and racial profiling.

The association between "illegal aliens" and the historic racialized image of "Mexicans" led to racial profiling in which Mexican Americans were also subject to many of these intimidating and invasive experiences at the San Diego border region in the early 1970s. Historically many Mexican American civil rights organizations had sought to differentiate themselves from undocumented migrants up to the 1970s. Yet groups in San Diego such as a local chapter of the statewide Mexican American Political Association (MAPA), the Center for Autonomous Social Action (CASA), and the Chicano Movement third party front *La Raza Unida*, alongside homegrown organizations such as the United California Mexican American Association and the coalitional Ad Hoc Committee on Chicano Rights, reacted by asserting that the collective abuses experienced by Mexican immigrants and Mexican Americans at the hands of border agents were systematic attacks against "our people," suggesting an evolving cross-border notion of Chicano or Chicano/Mexicano identity. Martha Elena's act of holding accountable Agent Cocke, alongside the many border women who came forward with complaints that border officials had unduly strip-searched them, revealed the participation of Mexican immigrant and Mexican American women within this immigrant rights contingent of the Chicano Movement, which was officially led by mostly Mexican American men. Women border crossers participated in these campaigns by telling stories that influenced, contested and informed Chicano activist calls for social justice within immigration politics. The refusal of these women and other victims of border official violence to remain silent created a context in which an important number of Chicano Movement and Mexican American civil rights organizations began to pay closer attention to the immigration issue, advocate undocumented migrants and Mexican American victims of Border Patrol harassment, and critique what they saw as adverse effects of border patrolling on what they began to define as their mixed-legal status, transnational ethnic community.

Demographic Shifts and the (Re) Emerging Immigration Debate

Rising incidents of Border Patrol violence and engagement by Chicano Movement activists in immigrant rights in the early 1970s were indicative of an unprecedented demographic revolution of the ethnic Mexican population in the U.S. The total Mexican immigrant population in the U.S. grew from 454,000 in 1950, hit 760,000 in 1970, and by 1980 would reach about 2.2 million.[29] The number of Mexican-origin people in the U.S. grew almost ten-fold between 1960 and 1980 from 1.7 million to 8.7 million, in large part due to this migration.[30] This rise followed a brief hiatus of migration from Mexico in the mid-1960s after the Bracero Program, a binational guest worker agreement, was abolished in 1964.[31] The mid-1960s also witnessed an improving economy in Mexico called the "Mexican Miracle" that was credited in large part to U.S. investments. By 1967 this rapid development in Mexico had created a widening gap between rich and poor as job creation failed to keep up with the needs of an increasing population.[32] In this way, the late 1960s/early 1970s surge in Mexican immigration to the U.S. demonstrated sociologist Saskia Sassen's contention that migration is exacerbated, rather than curbed, by the general policy of an emergent globalized economic system.[33] In the hierarchical arrangement of globalization developing in the early 1970s, first world nations such as the United States invested in developing nations such as Mexico to "promote export-oriented growth" as part of creating a global market and breaking down barriers to trade.[34] This is significant in understanding the roots of the new, intensified migration of Mexicans to the United States in that these shifts were not only brought about by the poverty and unemployment within Mexico, but had more to do with U.S. investment activities and pressures from global market institutions such as the International Monetary Fund. These outside influences contextualized decisions made by the Mexican state toward intensifying the globalization of capitalist relations. These political economic shifts manifested in the U.S.-Mexico region via agricultural commercialization and the Border Industrialization Program, which uprooted rural farmers and created migration to urban centers in Mexico, new industries in the north Mexico border region, and low-wage jobs in the U.S.

Indeed these same global economic shifts affected U.S. society as manufacturing jobs were increasingly sent to developing nations in this period leading to the expansion of a service economy.[35] In addition to the nearly 100-year-old practice of recruiting migrant laborers to work for agribusiness in the U.S., the expanding service economy in the 1970s alongside other industries such as construction and domestic work increasingly relied on migrant labor, which was often undocumented.[36] Furthermore, the Immigration Act of 1965 created an administrative situation in which undocumented immigration dramatically increased, leading to intensifying contact and conflict with the Border Patrol. By placing annual quotas on immigration from the Western Hemisphere for the first time, with a 40,000 quota on any one nation, while about 200,000 migrant laborers from Mexico were projected to be needed in the U.S. labor market alongside another 35,000 Mexicans with applications for regular permanent residency, the number of "illegals" would inevitably exceed the scant new quota.[37] Employers in industries reliant on migrant labor would continue to recruit migrants regardless of their legal status. Indeed, many employers preferred undocumented workers as was demonstrated during the Bracero Program in which employers actively sought to avoid the requirements to pay guest workers better wages and provide livable work conditions by opting to hire undocumented workers.[38] While the end of the Bracero Program was in large part due to the work of Mexican American activists battling against the exploitative nature of the program's inability to abide by its human rights components, its end marked the emergence of a dramatic increase of undocumented migration as employers continued and expanded the informal decades-old processes of migrant labor recruitment.[39]

The increase in migration from Mexico in the 1960s and 70s was also characterized by intensifying participation of women. The Bracero Program actively recruited Mexican men and, following its abolition, Mexican migrant women's participation and network creation ensued and expanded.[40] With the rise of the *maquiladora* industry at this time, scholars have noted that employers of these assembly plants in the border region targeted Mexican women as a cheap, exploitable labor force both in Mexico and the United States.[41] In Mexico this shifted gender relations and migration patterns as industrial work was not provided at the same levels for under-employed and unemployed men.[42] This process, intended to develop Mexico, socialized many Mexican women to rely on industrial work while *maquiladora* jobs failed to provide needed stability, inducing migration to other industrial jobs often along the border and the United States in industries such as microelectronics and apparel manufacturing.[43] U.S. industries intensified the recruitment of jobs historically circumscribed for Mexican migrant women in the U.S. including domestic work as maids, elderly care, house and office cleaning, childcare, and healthcare. Sociologist Yen Le Espiritu explains the preference for female migrants, particularly Latina and Asian workers, by U.S. manufacturing employers as being due to "the patriarchal and racist assumptions that women can afford to work for less, do not mind dead-end jobs, and are more suited physiologically to certain kinds of detailed and routine work."[44] The result of these developments was that Mexican women formed a larger share of the rising number of Mexicans migrating to the U.S. in the 1970s and onward, arriving not only as dependents of male workers, but as workers themselves.

The rising number of Mexican immigrants was met in the U.S with the discourse of the "illegal alien." While based in a history of anti-Mexican sentiment rooted in the Mexican–American War of 1848 and the racial nativism of the repatriation drives of the 1930s and 1950s, debates over the rising numbers of "illegals," the new anti-immigrant discourse of the early 1970s, again depicted migrants as a drain on U.S. society in a moment of recession. Indeed, a series of hearings led by Representative Peter Rodino (D-New Jersey) in 1971 produced a five-volume Congressional document on the dangers and negative effects of undocumented migration on U.S. citizens, particularly in employment and wages. Concerns were also mounting regarding the suggested migrant tendency toward crime and the association between Mexico and illicit drugs.[45]

With this discourse proliferating within public debate, Mexican immigrants, usually imagined as male unskilled workers, were characterized as occupying jobs in place of U.S. citizens, bringing their families to consume public services, and engaging in criminal activities. Mexican women were characterized as not only invaders, but reproducers of the invading population. Analyzing national magazines since 1965, anthropologist Leo Chávez identifies three themes relating to fears of Mexican women's reproduction: 1) high fertility and population growth, 2) reconquest, and 3) overuse of medical and other social services.[46]

Local and national elites depicted the entrance of "illegals" as a crisis, reinforcing the logic of militarized law enforcement efforts. Geographer Joseph Nevins argues "beginning in the late 1960s, there was growing public perception of the international boundary with Mexico as dangerously out of control, as a porous line of defense against unprecedented numbers of potentially threatening unauthorized migrants entering the United States from Mexico."[47] Indeed, concern about immigration among politicians and the media was increasingly articulated in military language depicting the need to stop an invading force. As a 1972 *Los Angeles Times* article exclaimed, "Holding the line against the tide of illegal entrants are 350 U.S. Customs, Immigration and Border Patrol officers."[48] While at times considering the immigrant side of the issue, the media often depicted federal border officials as weary combatants protecting the country against "illegal entrants."

Border Patrol Violence and the Chicano Movement in San Diego

The increased concern about "illegal entrants" alongside increasing numbers of border crossings from Mexico in the early 1970s made San Diego a primary site where routine acts of violence, harassment, and brutality against Mexican immigrants and Mexican Americans occurred through official border enforcement efforts of U.S. Customs and the Border Patrol.[49] For this reason, Chicano Movement activists in the borderlands were among the first to engage the immigration crisis in a new era. The Chicano Movement was a series of mobilizations beginning in the late 1960s based on an ethnic nationalism that sought to unite Mexican Americans as a people through celebration of cultural difference, recognition of a history of racial oppression, and a strategy of forging community self-determination as a way of organizing for basic civil and human rights.[50] While the Chicano Movement put forth a vehement rejection of white supremacy and Mexican-American assimilation strategies through an assertion of pride in Mexican heritage, it was ironically silent on the issue of Mexican immigration in its early years in the late 1960s.[51] The exception was the 1968 founding of CASA, *el Centro de Acción Social Autónoma*, in Los Angeles by veteran trade unionists Soledad "Chole" Alatorre and Bert Corona, the latter of which was a leader in the statewide MAPA organization. CASA sought to provide services to undocumented immigrants and worked to politicize them into Chicano Movement activism. Indeed, Corona and Alatorre were key influences on San Diego Chicano leader Herman Baca's thinking on the immigration issue in their interactions in

MAPA. According to Baca, a rift developed within the Chicano Movement in the early 1970s along the lines of those who advocated for undocumented migrants versus those that wanted to concentrate on Mexican-American (U.S. citizen) issues separate from immigration issues. Baca would help organize a CASA in south San Diego County later in 1972. Baca recalled, ". . . there was a lot of misunderstanding, really a sense of irrelevancy that the issue (immigration) didn't have nothing to do with us."[52]

The emergence of Chicano political efforts that expressly included Mexican migrants must be contextualized within the complex history of relations between Mexican Americans and Mexican immigrants. The creation of deportation-oriented immigration policies in the 1920s with the bureaucratization of the category "illegal alien" alongside the creation of the U.S. Border Patrol shaped this volatile relationship by fragmenting the Mexican-origin community along the lines of legal status. In a context of mass deportation of "illegal aliens" during the Depression era, Mexican American civil rights organizations articulated differing approaches to Mexican immigrant populations. While some sought to incorporate Mexican immigrants into the fold of the ethnic community, particularly Mexican American leaders within the trade union movement, as fellow workers, there were others, best exemplified by the League of United Latin American Citizens (LULAC), who sought to differentiate themselves from Mexican immigrants and supported restrictive immigration policies as a way of authenticating Mexican Americans' official citizenship.[53] Therefore Chicano Movement efforts that formulated solidarity and inclusion of migrants, albeit in varied and sometimes limited ways, emerged within this historical context of political fragmentation among Mexican American activists on the immigration question that was by no means resolved by the 1970s. Indeed, the rising numbers of migrants in the 1970s exacerbated this debate within Mexican American activist circles, and its intensification was experienced especially in San Diego where Border Patrol harassment was also on the increase.[54]

State policies added further fuel to the flames of concern over "illegals" in San Diego and wider California. For example, the California State legislature passed the Dixon Arnett Bill in November of 1971 seeking to fine employers who hired undocumented immigrants. Herman Baca, Carlos "Charlie" Vásquez, and other San Diego Chicano activists in local MAPA and La Raza Unida chapters participated in a statewide effort for the next several months against the bill's implementation in March of 1972. Baca argued that the law would "create an adverse effect on a specific ethnic group—Mexican-Americans—who make up the largest portion of the state's alien population."[55] This statement represented well this Chicano activist contingent's emerging position that hysteria over "illegal aliens" led to discrimination against Mexican Americans.

The Parra López incident of May 1972, therefore, occurred as an important contingent of local Chicano Movement organizations were already confronting the ways that immigration policing was affecting ethnic Mexican communities.

In addition to the San Diego area chapters of MAPA and La Raza Unida, as early as 1970 the newly created Office of Mexican American Affairs in San Diego County directed by former Urban League organizer Victor Villalpando, and Alberto García's United California Mexican American Association came to address immigration issues in response to numerous complaints from ethnic Mexicans of all citizenship statuses who were discriminated against by employers, detained, deported, racially profiled, and made the victims of Border Patrol and law enforcement violence.[56] In 1970, noting how many of his friends had recounted Border Patrol harassment, local newspaper columnist Joe Viesca reported this July 24, 1970 encounter:

> The official asked what I had done in Tijuana. Since I believe this was an insulting question, I merely told him it was a personal matter. This was sufficient for him to send me to the second inspection point . . . (where) an official took me by the arm and twisted it toward the spine and if I would have resisted in the least he would have broken my arm. When I commenced to tell him that as an American citizen I was fully aware of my rights he said: "No B____ (sic), S.O.B. Mexican has any rights here." He took me, making a showing of unnecessary violence, to the office where he ordered me to put all my personal belongings on the counter. He began to check all my personal documents and looked for "contraband" in the cards and papers that were in my wallet. When I tried to smoke he slapped my face.[57]

Viesca's account reveals that Mexican Americans, despite a claim to official U.S. citizenship, could be subject to harassment and violence by border agents. Indeed, as a generic "Mexican" Viesca was informed he had no rights and, like Parra López, was subject to violence within the official procedures of the Border Patrol, being slapped and strong-armed as they searched through his belongings.

Also in 1970, a young Anglo-American woman and an African-American woman underwent an invasive strip search when crossing the border together with two Mexican-American men who were pat-searched. The Anglo woman's mother reported that a matron inspector had checked her daughter's vagina and rectum with a flashlight. They were never put under arrest nor told why they were being searched. Her mother explained,

> My daughter told me it was a very humiliating experience. I asked her why she thought she had been searched, and she told me she had long hair, was wearing blue jeans and was with a black girl and two Mexican-American men and she thought she represented the counter culture to the customs officials.[58]

Another woman retail worker from National City who described her ethnicity as French and American Indian recalled how she was stopped twice in one week and one time strip-searched. On both stops she was accompanied by two African Americans and one Anglo-American acquaintance.[59] A registered nurse from Chula Vista, whose ethnicity was not revealed, recalled a similar experience when she was strip-searched on May 28, 1971 when crossing the border. As a nurse, she testified that the search, in addition to being humiliating, was unsanitary. Revealing again the blurred line between harassment and official border authority procedures, another young woman reported that a male customs officer had twisted her arm and put his hand in her brassiere in a supposed search for narcotics.[60] In some cases, male crossers were also strip-searched, as well as being beaten and abused. For example, a San Diego shipyard welder told of being strip-searched, internally examined and slapped.[61] These cases reveal that the Customs agents' and Border Patrol's concerns about concealing contraband often took the form of strip-searching women on suspicion that their bodies might be harboring contraband. These cases seem to reveal that race was a primary factor in deciding which female border crossers might be harboring such contraband as this practice was extended to white women in situations where they were accompanied by people of color.

These reports of harassment at the border came to the fore after Joe Viesca published his account in 1970 and especially when the account of Antonio Cuevas was reported in February of 1972. Cuevas was a Mexican American who claimed he was beaten twice when attempting to cross back into the U.S. after visiting friends in Tijuana in December of 1971. He was beaten while in the presence of an Immigration Department supervisor and beaten again when he remarked that he would report the Border Patrol agent, Agent Ecerkt, who beat him.[62] According to a letter from Vic Villalpando, director of the Mexican American Affairs Office of San Diego County, to Baca and other Chicano activists, the documentation of the Cuevas case represented an opportunity to record and publicize the wider harassment by the Border Patrol of Mexican immigrants and Mexican Americans. Villalpando asserted, "Heretofore, I have been appraised (verbally) of mal-treatment cases against Chicanos crossing the Border by Immigration and Customs officials, but I was never able to attain written statements that could be used in a court of law."[63] Villalpando's concern for "Chicanos" crossing the border undoubtedly included Mexican Americans and Mexican immigrants as he referenced cases of brutality experienced by both groups. For Villalpando, the Cuevas case was also important because, unlike the numerous other cases of Border Patrol brutality, it was recorded and covered by the media and its exposure could work to reveal numerous other incidents embedded within ethnic Mexican life in the borderlands. San Ysidro activist Albert García, leader of the United California Mexican American Association, asserted that after the *National City Star-News* ran a story on Cuevas' beating, he received more than 60 additional complaints charging U.S. customs and immigration officers with brutality.[64] Villalpando asserted, "We know, either personally or vicariously, that incidents of brutality by Border officials against our people are frequent and almost common-place."[65]

Indeed, activists began referring to Chicanos and Mexican nationals as "our people" and members of "La Raza," even including undocumented migrants within their reference to the "Chicano community." In February of 1972 Villalpando called for a "Border Project" that would document the harassments and brutalities that border communities often experienced in their everyday lives. With the notary Albert García of the United California Mexican American Association he requested that Herman Baca's MAPA chapter and other Chicano Movement organizations assist in this project. Here Villalpando publicized a kind of border sentiment held by both Mexican migrants and U.S.-born Chicanos ("our people"): a shared experience of racialization at the hands of border officials.

Many of the individuals who came forward to record what they perceived as harassment and abuse by border officials were women complaining about strip searches. As Chicano activists sought to document mounting cases of border violence against Mexicans and Mexican Americans, one source reported that by 1972 several hundred women had come forward to complain about being strip-searched by Customs agents.[66] These women, many if not most of Mexican origin, utilized the Chicano activist call to record the legal violence of border policing to reclaim their bodies and refuse the normalized practice of strip searches utilized by border agents. Indeed, their stories challenged the racial and gendered assumptions that underpinned the perception that the bodies of Mexican-origin women were probable harboring places of contraband. For instance, Roberta Baca (no relation to Herman Baca) filed suit against the San Diego Immigration and Naturalization Service (INS) District Supervisor Vernon Han after being strip-searched without explanation in January of 1972.[67] Roberta Baca's complaint was exemplary of a series of other complaints when she asserted that inspectors unjustifiably strip-searched and interrogated her upon her return to the United States from Mexico. She stated that for no apparent reason she, her children, and a friend, Isabel Loranzana, were asked to go into INS offices at the San Ysidro border crossing on January 15, 1972. After being asked to empty their purses, inspectors confiscated Baca's identification card as well as Loranzana's boyfriend's which she happened to be carrying. Roberta and Isabel were denied explanation of why they were being detained as they were made to wait in the office. They were told that they could not make any phone calls because they were not under arrest. Furthermore, because they were not under arrest, they were told they had "no rights." A female inspector then took Roberta into a separate room where she was told to be quiet and stand in the corner. The officer asked Roberta if she had anything concealed on her body to which she replied that she did not. Roberta then claimed,

> She had me bend over and through all this she kept asking me repeatedly
> if I had anything concealed on my body. She made me stand with my feet
> about two feet apart and put my hands on my knees with my back toward
> her. She then had me bend way over and place my hands on my buttocks

and spread my buttocks apart. She proceeded to check the inside of my vagina with a flashlight, to see if I had anything concealed.[68]

After being instructed to put her clothes back on, the inspector asked if Roberta was on welfare, if her husband was the father of her children, and if she had ever been arrested. Isabel was then taken to the room where she was pat-searched and asked the same questions.[69] Revealing no probable cause other than the women's ethnicity and gender, the inspector's interrogation following the strip search reveals the perspective by the INS that Mexican women in particular were threats to the well-being of the nation. As potential welfare recipients, concealers of illegal substances, and reproducers of an unwanted population, these women, who appeared to have legal status in the U.S., were assumed to be a threat. This account further reveals the role that gender and race played in the interface between immigration policy, practice and popular stereotypes of Mexican immigrants. As anthropologist Leo Chávez observes in his analysis of post-1965 media coverage:

> Rather than an invading army, or even the stereotypical male migrant worker, the images (of Mexican immigrant women) suggested a more insidious invasion, one that included the capacity of the invaders to reproduce themselves. The women being carried into U.S. territory carry with them the seeds of future generations. The images signaled not simply a concern over undocumented workers, but a concern with immigrants who stay and reproduce families and, by extension, communities in the United States. These images, and their accompanying articles, alluded to issues of population growth, use of prenatal care, children's health services, education, and other social services.[70]

Furthermore, the accounts of Roberta Baca and other border crossing women reveal Mexican-origin women as perceived threats to the idealized nuclear family as they were suspected of having children out of wedlock and/or from a number of different fathers. As Chávez notes, popular discourse post-1965 has dichotomized between Mexican-origin women's fertility as "irrational, illogical, chaotic and therefore threatening" in contrast to Anglo women's fertility as "autonomous, responsible . . . of sound mind, as in a legal subject."[71]

Based on these complaints of border official harassment, particularly by Mexican and Mexican American women, Villalpando and Albert García demanded a congressional hearing on the prevalence of strip-searching and abuse at the border. Chicano activists perceived the proposed hearing as an opportunity for the Chicano community, including Mexican immigrants, to testify against the systematic practices of Customs and the Border Patrol. Herman Baca and the MAPA-National City chapter urged state officials to investigate "a problem that has been prevalent in this area for too long . . . the continual violation of Chicano's and Mexican Nationals' civil and God-given rights by the U.S.

Immigration Department and the U.S. Customs Bureau." Baca accused the two departments of being,

> more representative of the KGB and the Gestapo than organizations that are supposedly representative of a constitutional government . . . we are tired of this type of attitude and treatment and whole heartedly support the investigation being called for by Mr. Albert García and Mr. Vic Villalpando.[72]

Responding to Chicano activist appeals was Mexican American Congressman Edward Roybal who, as chair of the Congressional Treasury Committee which held U.S. Customs within its jurisdiction, agreed to hold a hearing on border issues in San Diego on April 28, 1972. Countering the INS' depiction of Mexican women as welfare-hungry, decadent child bearers, activists argued that Border Patrol, Customs, and local law enforcement agents physically brutalized Mexican men and violated women's bodies attacking what might be perceived as "*La Familia de la Raza*" a popular Chicano Movement conception of a united ethno-racial community organized as a family.[73] Indeed, the gendered dimensions of Chicano Movement activism were evident in the preparation for the hearings, where García categorized border brutalities in two areas, "women being searched illegally," and "men beaten or abused."[74] In García's testimony he demonstrated the anti-family policies of the Border Patrol, for example, by recalling how a busload of Mexican children, aged 8–10, returning from a visit to the San Diego zoo were stopped and apparently strip-searched at the border crossing. Chicano activists and border community members sought to counter the depiction of Mexican men and women as threats to the notion of the U.S. family by revealing the anti-family practices of the Border Patrol who strip-searched and harassed women and children and physically abused men.

Ethnic Mexican victims of border brutality displayed their grievances to members of the House Appropriations Committee investigating the Treasury Department. Noting the role of women in the hearing, Roybal would report that out of the 1,800 women stripped and searched at the border in 1971, only 285 were found to be carrying any contraband. Of those carrying contraband very few actually concealed it in their body cavities.[75] Like Parra López, these women struggled for the possession of their own bodies by protesting and making public the ways in which searches at the border subjugated them to humiliation and loss of dignity.

The accomplishment of the April 1972 hearing marked an important development within Chicano Movement politics. The systematic Border Patrol violence on ethnic Mexicans across citizenship statuses led many San Diego Chicano activists to develop a cross-border notion of "Chicano" identity, inclusive of undocumented migrants, as a basis for the struggle. Grappling with legal violence at the border, activists constructed the parameters of a transnational Chicano community by speaking of a shared experience of brutality by both Mexican Americans and Mexican immigrants at the hands of border agents. A coalition of Chicano activists was part of the hundred or so participants in a demonstration outside the Federal Courthouse in downtown San Diego against the various brutalities experienced at the border. The *El Mexicano* newspaper observed,

> To the shout of "Chicano Power," and "Raza sí, Migra no" (Our people, yes, the Border Patrol, no!), a group of Americans of Mexican ancestry, walked in a great oval outside of the Federal Court, with placards and slogans that repudiated the attitude of customs and immigration agents.[76]

According to *El Mexicano* more than a hundred Chicano activists led by Herman Baca sought to call attention to the federal hearing inside the courthouse and the repeated brutalities of the Border Patrol and Customs agents.[77] As these "Raza sí, Migra no" activists asserted, "The issue of immigration brutality, both psychological and physical, is one that affects all Chicanos and Mexicanos throughout the *frontera* of the Southwest."[78] Through Chicano Movement mobilization as a united "Raza," activists created space through which abused ethnic Mexicans of all citizenship statuses could voice their resistance. Yet mobilization as a united community was limited in its ability to articulate the complex ways that legal status and gender differences within the Mexican-origin community shaped social relations at the border in the early 1970s. As the mostly male, U.S.-born Chicano response to the Parra López case reveals, there were also significant limits to the gendered construction of "Raza." Furthermore, most of the women and men who spoke out in the hearings were U.S. citizens, mostly Mexican American, suggesting challenges to grappling with the unique and subjugated experiences of the undocumented.

Chicano Activists Respond to the Rape

The rape of Martha Elena Parra López further reveals that the particular violations of women's bodily possession was a key experience of subjugation for Mexican and Mexican American female border crossers in the early 1970s. Scholarship on more recent periods in the 80s and 90s suggests that rape is an experience that may be more prevalent to undocumented women, suggesting a key differential experience with the social effects of border policing based on legal status. As historian Eithne Luibhéid asserts in her study of cases in which Border Patrol agents raped undocumented women in the 1990s, "The fact that raped undocumented women have virtually no mechanisms for protest means that rape is also a site for the inscription of documented versus undocumented as salient."[79] In other words, the divide between the protections offered by documented and undocumented status are made evident, if not normalized, by the border officials' rape of undocumented women. This scholarship on more recent incidents of rape of migrant women therefore reveals the systematic and routine nature of sexual violence at the border within the social context of militarization of the border that began in the 1960s and 70s.[80]

Citing Beverly Allen's study of rape as a weapon of imperialist war and Tim Dunn's assertion that U.S. immigration policy has militarized into a practice of low-intensity warfare, Sylvanna M. Falcón argues:

> The level of militarization produces warlike characteristics that make rape and other human rights violations an inevitable consequence of border militarization efforts ... Warlike conditions at the border reinforce a climate that sustains the rape and systematic degradation of women. Agent impunity and the absence of accountability contribute to a border climate in which rape occurs with little consequence.[81]

Like the other forms of legal violence reported by border crossers and Chicano activists, Agent Kenneth Cocke's rape of Martha Elena occurred within the militarized procedures of border policing. Agent Cocke's remark following the rape, "now go back to your country," reveals the act as part and parcel of the deportation process, or at least enabled by it, as Martha Elena was literally expelled into Mexico. Cocke's comment that "I hope you do not have any disease" might reflect the larger anti-immigrant narrative that characterizes un-authorized Mexican immigration, particularly female migration, as a threat presence invading the cultural and racial "health" of the U.S. society. These hierarchical discourses on race and nation further legitimized a labor system of superexploitation as "illegal" status maintained and reinforced the subjugation of a racialized labor force that was, and continues to be, a permanent feature of the United States economy. Furthermore, the redeployment of violence targeting women of color was indication of the ways that the authorities responded to the increasing incidence of female border crossing within the economic shifts that deliberately recruited migrant women labor beginning in the late 1960s.

The intersections of nation, race, gender and sex within border policing are important in relation to how research has explored these intersections within Chicano Movement activism. Chicano Movement research has revealed that while activism asserted counterhegemonic politics that challenged racism and discrimination, many organizations tended to reproduce structures of patriarchy practiced within and outside of the ethnic Mexican community. As mentioned, the dominant concepts of ethno-racial unity and the nuclear family were important intellectual bases of articulating the politics of the Chicano Movement. Historian Ramón Gutiérrez notes that the assertion of Chicano masculinity was central to movement rhetoric, within concepts such as *La Familia de la Raza* (collective practices of community extended from the notion of family) and strong male symbolism depicted from Aztec and Mexican history.[82] This counter-assertion of masculinity responded to a history of social emasculation and cultural negation implemented by the imposition of a white supremacist U.S. society. Gutiérrez asserts, "Young Chicano men, a largely powerless group, invested themselves with images of power—a symbolic inversion commonly found in the fantasies of powerless men worldwide, a gendered vision that rarely extends to women."[83] These precedents often normalized almost exclusive male leadership in many cases, centralized male subjectivity within dominant articulations of "Chicano" identity and reproduced notions of Chicano men as the rightful protectors and proprietors of the Chicana body.

The archives reveal that these patriarchal assumptions were a key part of how Chicano activists struggled for justice on behalf of Martha Elena Parra López. At the same time, Parra López and other border women entered the realm of Chicano politics to contest its limited framework that valued women only in the domestic realm. Coverage of the rape in the San Diego County *La Raza Unida Newsletter* describes her on two separate occasions as "attractive" and a "mother." By highlighting Martha Elena's sexual appeal, the description "attractive" implies that her sexuality was taken by the Border Patrol agent from its proper place under the protection of Mexican men. Indeed, in reporting on Martha Elena's affidavit, the article reiterates her affirmative answer to Cocke that revealed her marital status. While this is seemingly objective in its reporting of what Martha Elena stated in the affidavit, matched with the article's description of her as "attractive" and a "mother of two" the event is framed within the confines of the domestic sphere. The article suggests that Martha Elena's "attractive" sexuality was displaced from the appropriate domain of her (Mexican) husband and her duties as nurturer to her children. More broadly speaking, this reflects the gender constructions which are often part of the Chicano Movement discourse and activism. As Alicia Schmidt Camacho asserts:

> The discourse of El Movimiento hailed women as the symbolic mothers of citizens and bearers of culture. Through their domestic labors, women would defend and redeem la raza. The coercive force of the nationalist trope of *race as family* did not exclude women from political activity but, rather, delimited their participation so as to foreclose the capacity of Chicanas to voice their interests with any autonomy.[84]

Placing Martha Elena's sexuality and role as "mother" within *la familia de la Raza* was a key way in which Mexican immigrants were imagined as "Chicanos" and part of the same "Raza" as Mexican Americans. Furthermore, it reveals how developing notions of a transnational community were articulated through the patriarchal notion of the nuclear family, mobilizing to assert a Chicano/Mexicano masculinity in competition with hypermasculine state violence. Chicano activists advocated for Parra López and other victims of *migra* repression in part by acting as defenders against the disruption of ethnic Mexican families who protected Mexican women from being taken away from their roles as wives and mothers by the invading Border Patrol. This type of description worked as a strategy in bolstering Chicano activists' claims against the brutality of border enforcement policy on their community by highlighting the Border Patrol's role in disrupting family life, in this case violating a woman's role as a wife and mother.[85] At the same time, while these transnational Chicano Movement proponents criticized the hegemonic practice of immigration policy and border enforcement, they did not consider how the notion of the nuclear family itself upheld hierarchies within and outside of their community.[86]

In addition, by ignoring the patriarchal dimensions of the rape and publicizing it as only another attack on La Raza, Chicano activists failed to conceive of the ways in which the Chicana/Mexicana experience at the border could not be deduced to racial oppression without considering its intersection with sexist practices both within and outside of the Mexican and Mexican American community. Instead, Chicano Movement activists painted the event as another case of the Border Patrol embodying the white political structure's attack on their transnational ethno-racial community. After San Diego County District Attorney Edwin Miller failed to bring Cocke up on charges, arrest him or even question him, Herman Baca of the Mexican American Political Association (MAPA) criticized him for dragging his feet, arguing that, "if the suspect would have been a Chicano, he would have been in jail long ago."[87] Baca also exclaimed, "This travesty of justice only serves to symbolize the immorality, brutality, and all the injustices that are committed against *Mexicans* and *Chicanos* (my emphasis) daily along the international border by the racist Immigration Department."[88] In a later critique of officials in handling the case, other Chicano activists in MAPA, commenting in the *La Raza Unida San Diego County Newsletter,* used it as evidence of a systemic "double standard . . . one for whites and the other for non-whites."[89] By modifying the rape into the domestic sphere via race as family then eliding the gender and sexual categories of power at play within this act by defining it as solely an attack on their ethno-racial community, Chicano activists deployed traditional gender roles of male breadwinner/protector and female domestic caretaker to forge Chicano/Mexicano notions of transnational community.[90]

Nevertheless, Chicano activists never wavered on Martha Elena's assertion that she was raped by Agent Cocke even as officials suggested that the sex was consensual. Indeed, officials seemed reluctant to even handle the case. San Diego County District Attorney Ed Miller refused to, calling it a federal matter and citing a lack of evidence to convict the accused of rape.[91] Appealing then to the District Attorney of the State of California, Evelle J. Younger, Chicano activists were appalled to hear him defend Miller's decision and argue that a rape did not occur. Younger explained, "While the evidence does reveal that an act of sexual intercourse did occur . . . the evidence also reveals that the Border Patrol officer did not use such threats of force" that would fall within the description of rape under the California Penal Code.[92] In other words the San Diego County and

California State District Attorneys agreed with the alleged perpetrator Kenneth Cocke's assessment that the sex was consensual. Later in 1974, the newly appointed INS commissioner, General Leonard Chapman, responded to continued pressure from Chicano activists to address the rape case by re-asserting Cocke's contention that he gained consent from Parra López. The INS did proceed with misconduct and removal action against Cocke under which he resigned in October of 1972. No criminal charges were pursued. Congressman Roybal criticized officials for failing to act, but also considered Cocke's assertion that he gained consent from Martha Elena. Roybal asserted, "He (Cocke) must be guilty of something, even if the girl consented."[93]

Chicano activists were appalled because there seemed to be ample evidence that could bring the Cocke case to a grand jury. Aside from Martha Elena's statement that she was indeed abducted and raped, her companions whom Cocke forced to leave the situation, María Sandoval and Teresa Castellanos, were witnesses to the events. Furthermore, a medical examiner at University Hospital in San Diego verified that there were physical indications of bruising, vaginal bleeding and use of force.[94] The failure of the San Diego District Attorney, California Attorney General, and the INS to proceed with criminal prosecution led Chicano activists to conclude and dramatize the role that race might have played. García revealed the frustration experienced by activists in this case when he deduced that "I understand this rape case was stopped in Washington so that no further publicity would be issued."[95] Indeed, with the failure to even put forth a trial on these offensive allegations, Chicano activists learned that state actors were not to be relied upon.

Martha Elena and other border women entered the realm of Chicano politics to contest its limited framework that valued women only in the domestic realm. Furthermore, women in all likelihood utilized domestic identities such as "mother" or "wife" as a way of asserting their rights. Yet Martha Elena's insistence on sharing her terrifying experience with the public reveals the agency, although fragmented within the archival sources, of an undocumented migrant woman that suggests an alternative political subjectivity beyond the domestic realm. Indeed, the fact that her friends refused to leave her side demonstrated an oppositional solidarity among Mexicanas all too aware of the consequences of being left alone with a *migra* officer.[96] This Mexicana oppositional sentiment revealed a conscious-ness of and resistance to not only systematized national/racial exclusion and exploitation of physical labor, but also routine exploitation of their bodies, being sexually objectified and violently violated in a way that disciplines Mexican immigrant women in particular. Martha Elena also worked with her friend Vera León to document her story with activist Alberto García, revealing cross-border women's networks of support and solidarity across differences in legal status. Furthermore, that Martha Elena shared her story with León reveals her refusal to accept sexual violence at the hands of a U.S. state official as routine, and a struggle for the possession of her own body and dignity despite her undocumented status. This Chicana/Mexicana solidarity shows an awareness of and resistance to forms of sexual exploitation not only at the border, but within work sites, community life, and relationships. Indeed, the experiences that Martha Elena and her *compañeras* struggled through reveal a class experience shaped by legal status, gender, race, and national affiliation.[97] Therefore, Parra López's refusal to remain silent might reveal a nuanced transnational Mexicana politics beyond the domestic realm of wife and mother and the limited rhetoric articulated by Chicano activists. Instead, it asserts a de-essentialized and variegated political subjectivity as simultaneously a migrant, a member of a community of border women, and a participant in a transnational network of survival. This political subjectivity often worked outside of the confines of the nation-state, the male gaze within the ethnic Mexican community and U.S. society, and the diversifying forms of exploitation endemic to the evolution of global capitalism.

Conclusion

While an emergent transnational Chicano Movement provided space for Mexican and Mexican-American women to voice their struggles, the gender conceptions deployed within the notion of *familia de la Raza* proved to limit the evolution of Chicano immigrant rights activism. This might reveal a gap between the Chicana feminist movement that was ongoing within Chicano Movement activism in other spaces/places and the "Raza Sí, Migra No" activism developing, in part, in the San Diego border region.[98] This was significant at a crucial moment when activists within the Chicano Movement in San Diego were beginning to split over moderate and radical critiques of the immigration crisis. While a liberal/moderate strategy sought traditional mechanisms of redress to serve as a corrective to glitches in the otherwise democratic practices of U.S. society, a transnational Chicano/Mexicano politics emerged to criticize immigration policy as a systematic practice that served the globalizing interests of capital. Indeed, as radical activists within Chicano Movement organizations in San Diego, including the Centro de Accion Social Autónoma (CASA), local chapters of La Raza Unida Party, and the emerging Committee on Chicano Rights in San Diego, sought to illuminate the systematic class exploitation embedded within immigration policy, the voices of Mexican and Mexican-American female border crossers have offered the opportunity to further unveil the use of differential forms of subjugation by capital within incipient global economic shifts through not only race and legal status, but also gender and sexuality.

The stories by migrant women in particular depict a more nuanced analysis beyond an all-out Border Patrol attack on a monolithic La Raza. For instance, while it appears that women were more likely to report instances of strip-search, it is apparent that male border crossers were also subject to this procedure. This occurrence might suggest that border women were less likely to shame themselves into silence over such a humiliation as dominant notions of masculinity might influence male victims. Many migrant women insisted on holding individual Border Patrol agents accountable and even the practice of border patrolling more broadly in this regard. Furthermore while Martha Elena's report was the only account of such an incident in the early 1970s, the power conferred to Border Patrol agents and the vulnerable positions of undocumented migrant women in particular uncovers the various forms of legal violence against ethnic Mexican women and men within the border patrolling process. As sociologist Sylvanna M. Falcón asserts in her study of sexual violence perpetrated by Border Patrolmen in the 1980s, the power conferred to agents in a context with little or no supervision enables incidents of sexual violence, harassment, and intimidation.[99]

In this way border women revealed the ways that racialized targeting of migrants was gendered in the particular fears concerning Mexican immigrant women's bodies that justified strip searches and the dangerous position in which these assumptions could put undocumented women such as Martha Elena Parra López. These gender-specific assumptions within the racial logic of border patrolling subjected many female border crossers to invasive official procedures and power differentials that could be used to commit non-official abuses such as sexual violence. Thus, Mexican-immigrant and Mexican-American women in the border region influenced and bolstered Chicano activism's critique of making public the systematic marginalization of "La Raza" and confronting institutions that reproduced these inequalities while articulating how this repression was experienced *differently* in relation to gender and legal status especially. By including this array of voices emerging from Mexican-immigrant and Mexican-American border communities, scholars can reveal an important set of contested modes of resistance to the U.S. state's intensifying implementation of a border patrolling logic that attempted to manage and control the mass movement of working-class communities from Mexico and the United States.

By considering the experience of racialized migrant women, the critique of deportation-oriented immigration policies as exploitative could be further augmented by illuminating the systematic nature of sexual violence at the border. As cultural critic Lisa Lowe articulates, global restructuring of the capitalist mode of production toward transnational circuits of exchange, including international migration, and access to global markets, has created what she refers to as a "new social formation." In this new social formation, capital thrives not from homogenizing "but through differentiation of specific resources and markets that permit the exploitation of gendered and racialized labor" many of which have come to "specifically target female labor markets where women are disciplined by state-instituted traditional patriarchy" as well as "racialized immigration laws."[100] Therefore, a nuanced understanding of the relationship between gender and racial systems of exploitation within immigration policy could illuminate the ways in which "capital profits from mixing and combining different modes of production" at the U.S.-Mexico border. By attempting to illuminate these "complex structures of a new social formation" through Martha Elena's eyes, social justice might be gauged from the marginalized positions at the intersection of race, gender, sexuality, and legal status. With regard to resistance to the very logic of border patrolling, as Chicano activists initiated in early 1970s San Diego, the archival fragments of Martha Elena's experience call forth the "interventions and modes of opposition specific to those" exploitative structures at the U.S.-Mexico borderlands and beyond.[101]

Notes

1 I wish to thank Ramón Gutiérrez, the Twin Cities Chican@ Studies Writing Group, especially Lorena Muñoz, Cindy García and Yolanda Padilla; and Mario García and all the participants of the Conference on the Emerging Historiography of the Chicano Movement in February of 2012 for solidarity and dialog regarding the writing of this essay.

2 Affidavit of Martha Elena Parra López, June 7, 1972, Box 6, Folder 1, Herman Baca Papers, Mandeville Special Collections Library, University of California, San Diego, (Henceforth referred to as "Baca Papers").

3 "Border Patrolman Accused of Rape," *La Raza Unida Party San Diego County Newsletter*, July 2, 1972, Box 14, Folder 8, Baca Papers.

4 A note on ethno-racial terminology: I use the term "ethnic Mexican" and "Mexican-origin" interchangeably to refer to people of Mexican heritage regardless of their nationality (American or Mexican) or legal status in the United States (citizen, resident, undocumented, etc.). I use the term "Mexican American" to refer to born or naturalized citizens of the United States that are of Mexican heritage. I use the term "Chicano" in reference to individuals who identify with the "Chicano Movement," who use the term as a self-referent, and in reference to how these individuals are using the term to describe their community. I use the term "Mexicano" or "Mexican immigrant" to refer to Mexicans from Mexico who are in the U.S. I use Chicana and Mexicana in reference to women in the same framing as above. I choose not to employ the "a/o" or "@" as in Mexicana/o or Chican@ for clarity. Similarly I use "Chicano" in the phrase "Chicano Movement" to emphasize that it was mostly men leading the movement's organizational efforts, at least in this case. Ethno-racial identity and terminology is always a contentious and ongoing process and therefore cannot be utilized without some degree of ambiguity. I utilize primarily the theoretical work on identity of Stuart Hall as exhibited, for example, in Stuart Hall, "Old and New Identities, Old and New Ethnicities" in Anthony D. King, Ed., *Culture, Globalization, and The World System* (Binghamton: SUNY Department of Art and Art History, 1991) and the concept of "racial formation" as developed by Michael Omi and Howard Winant, *Racial Formation in the United States: From the 1960s to the 1990s* (New York: Routledge Press, 1994).

5 Dial Torgerson and Frank Del Olmo, "Tension Grows in Battle of 'Chain Link Curtain,'" *Los Angeles Times*, July 30, 1972, B3.

6 Torgerson and Del Olmo, 1972.

7 "Border Patrolman Accused of Rape," July 2, 1972.

8 Torgerson and Del Olmo, 1972.

9 On this historic link between local police and federal border patrolling see, "Hands-Off' Policy On Aliens Aired: Only Immigration Authorities May Hold Suspects, Lawmen Told," *San Diego Union* April 26, 1973, Box 22, Folder 3, Baca Papers.

10 Affidavit of Martha Elena Parra López, June 7, 1972, Baca Papers.

11 According to sociologist Paula A. Bar, scholarly definitions of sexual harassment describe conduct that is "unwelcomed or unsolicited, is sexual in nature, and is deliberate or

repeated," including verbal comments, gestures and physical contact. Legal scholar Catharine MacKinnon's definition highlights how sexual harassment occurs "in the context of a relationship of unequal power." Paula A. Bar, "Perceptions of Sexual Harassment," *Sociological Inquiry*, 63, No. 4 (1993): 461; Catharine MacKinnon, *Sexual Harassment of Working Women: A Case of Sex Discrimination* (New Haven, CT: Yale University Press, 1979), 27. For a useful review of more recent scholarship on sexual harassment see Christopher Uggen and Amy Blackstone, "Sexual Harassment as a Gendered Expression of Power," *American Sociological Review*, 69, No. 1 (February 2004): 65–68.

12 Affidavit of Martha Elena Parra López, June 7, 1972, Baca Papers.

13 Ibid.

14 In order to make alien removal more efficient, the U.S. Immigration Service initiated voluntary departures in 1927 to avoid hearings and detention. This process was expanded at different moments since and continues to be a key part of expulsions at the U.S.-Mexico border. See Mae M. Ngai, *Impossible Subjects: Illegal Aliens and the Making of Modern America* (Princeton, NJ: Princeton University Press, 2004), 60; Kelley Lytle Hernández, *Migra! A History of the U.S. Border Patrol* (Berkeley: University of California Press, 2010), 76, 80; and Transactional Access Records Clearinghouse, "Controlling the Borders," (Syracuse, NY: University of Syracuse, 2006), accessed February 28, 2013, http://trac.syr.edu/immigration/reports/141/

15 Affidavit of Martha Elena Parra López, June 7, 1972, Baca Papers.

16 Affidavit of Martha Elena Parra López, June 7, 1972, Baca Papers.; "Border Patrolman Accused of Rape," July 2, 1972.

17 Torgerson and Del Olmo, 1972.

18 Ibid.

19 Affidavit of Martha Elena Parra López, June 7, 1972, Baca Papers.

20 Ibid.

21 Torgerson and Del Olmo, 1972.

22 Affidavit of Martha Elena Parra López, June 7, 1972, Baca Papers. Sylvanna M. Falcón asserts that the power conferred to Border Patrol agents in a context with little or no supervision enables incidents of sexual violence, harassment, and intimidation. Sylvanna M. Falcón, "Rape as a Weapon of War: Militarized Rape at the U.S.-Mexico Border," *Social Justice*, 28, No. 2 (2001).

23 Affidavit of Martha Elena Parra López, June 7, 1972, Baca Papers.

24 Ibid.

25 "Border Patrolman Accused of Rape," July 2, 1972; Affidavit of Martha Elena Parra López, June 7, 1972, Baca Papers.

26 Harassment and violence are defined within Ian Haney López's notion of "legal violence." Haney López asserts, "The massive police presence, the constant police brutality, the hostile judges, and the crowded jails convinced Chicanos they were brown. 'Law' for Chicanos . . . means the police and the courts, and legal violence refers principally to the physical force these institutions wield. Law carried out on the street—as opposed to law on the books . . ." In a similar way U.S. Customs and Border Patrol officers, and other mechanisms of immigration law, consistently enacted violence on Mexicans and Mexican Americans in the border region both psychological and physical. Ian Haney López, *Racism on Trial: The Chicano Fight for Justice* (Cambridge, MA: Belknap Press at Harvard University, 2003), 9.

27 Pew Hispanic Center, "Mexican Immigrants in the United States, 2008," (Washington, DC, 2008). Pew Hispanic Center, 2008 and David G. Gutiérrez, "*Sin Fronteras?* Chicanos, Mexican Americans, and the Emergence of the Contemporary Immigration Debate," *Journal of American Ethnic History*, 10, No. 4 (Summer 1991): 5–37.

28 The director of the immigrant service organization CASA Justicia, Carlos "Charlie" Vásquez claims that about 300 women came forth in early 1972 with complaints of

being strip-searched. Interview with Carlos Vásquez, Tape 1, September 7, 2006, Herman Baca Oral History Collection, Baca Papers.

29 Pew Hispanic Center, 2008.

30 According to the U.S. Census Bureau the Mexican-origin population in 1960 was approximated at 1.7 million, 4.5 million in 1970, and 8.7 million in 1980. The Census reported that the Mexican-origin population was at 28.3 million in 2006.

31 Gutiérrez, "*Sin Fronteras?*" 1991.

32 See David G. Gutiérrez, "Ethnic Mexicans in the Late Twentieth Century: Globalization, Labor Migration, and the Demographic Revolution," in David G. Gutiérrez, Ed., *A Columbia History of Latinos in the U.S. Since 1960* (New York: Columbia University Press, 2004); Saskia Sassen, "America's Immigration 'Problem,'" *World Policy Journal*, 6, No. 4 (Fall, 1989): 811–832.

33 Saskia Sassen, "Globalization and Immigration," in David G. Gutiérrez, Ed., *Between Two Worlds* (Wilmington: Scholarly Resources, Inc., 1998).

34 Ibid.

35 Sassen, "America's Immigration 'Problem,'" 1989.

36 Gutiérrez, "Ethnic Mexicans in the Late Twentieth Century," 2004 and Sassen, "Globalization and Immigration," 1998.

37 Rudy Acuña, *Anything But Mexican: Chicanos in Contemporary Los Angeles* (New York: Verso Press, 1994), 114. Also see Mae Ngai, *Impossible Subjects: Illegal Aliens and the Making of Modern America* (Princeton, NJ: Princeton University Press, 2004), 261. In 1976 the U.S. Congress imposed a 20,000 person quota on immigration from Mexico, exacerbating the shift from legal to illegal migration. Furthermore, this 1976 act closed loopholes that allowed the children of undocumented migrants born in the U.S. to legalize their status.

38 See David G. Gutiérrez, *Walls and Mirrors: Mexican Americans, Mexican Immigrants and the Politics of Ethnicity* (Berkley: University of California Press, 1995) Chapter 5.

39 Ibid.

40 Pierette Hondagneu-Sotelo, *Gendered Transitions* (Berkeley: University of California Press, 1994).

41 Norma Iglesias Prieto, *Beautiful Flowers of the Maquiladora: Life Histories of Women Workers in Tijuana* (Austin: University of Texas Press, 1997); Alicia Schmidt Camacho, *Migrant Imaginaries: Latino Cultural Politics in the U.S.-Mexico Borderlands* (New York: New York University Press, 2008).

42 Patricia R. Pessar, "Engendering Migration Studies: The Case of New Immigrants in the United States," *American Behavioral Scientist*, 42 (1999); Sassen, "Globalization and Immigration," 1998; Camacho, *Migrant Imaginaries*, 2008.

43 Pessar, 1999, 580.

44 Yen Le Espiritu, *Asian American Women and Men* (Thousand Oaks, CA: Sage Press, 1997).

45 Joseph Nevins asserts, "the end of the 1960s/early 1970s saw the emergence of a conservative-led war—with the Nixon administration at the helm—on crime and illicit drug use, one that often pointed the finger at Mexico for being a source of the illicit commodities." Joseph Nevins, *Operation Gatekeeper and Beyond: The War on "Illegals" and the Remaking of the U.S.-Mexico Boundary* (New York: Routledge, 2002), 78.

46 Leo R. Chávez, "A Glass Half-Empty: Latina Reproduction and Public Discourse," *Human Organization*, 63, No.2 (Summer 2004).

47 Joseph Nevins, *Operation Gatekeeper and Beyond: The War on "Illegals" and the Remaking of the U.S.-Mexico Boundary* (New York: Routledge Press, 2nd edition, 2010), 77–78.

48 Torgerson and Del Olmo, 1972.

49 See Joseph Nevins, *Operation Gatekeeper and Beyond*, 2010, for notions of San Diego as an actual borderland geographic space in which territorial boundaries are divided, crossed and policed. On this notion of border and borderlands as specific geographic

sites I use Roberto Alvarez, "The Mexican-U.S. Border: The Making of an Anthropology of Borderlands," and Josiah McC. Heyman and Howard Campbell, "Recent Research on the U.S.-Mexico Border," (Review Essay), *Latin American Research Review*, 39, No. 3 (2004): 205–220. Conceiving of the ways in which territorial borders shape social relations beyond the actual border I utilized the work of Alvarez, 2004 and Eithne Luibhéid, *Entry Denied: Controlling Sexuality at the Border* (Minneapolis: University of Minnesota Press, 2002).

50 For recent writing on the Chicano Movement see, Maylei Blackwell, *Chicana Power! Contested Histories of Feminism the Chicano Movement* (Austin: University of Texas Press, 2011); Ernesto Chávez, *Mi Raza Primero! Nationalism, Identity, and Insurgency in the Chicano Movement in Los Angeles, 1966–1978* (Berkeley: University of California Press, 2002); George Mariscal, *Brown-Eyed Children of the Sun: Lessons from the Chicano Movement, 1965–1975* (Albuquerque: University of New Mexico Press, 2006); Ian Haney López, *Racism on Trial: The Chicano Fight for Social Justice* (Cambridge, MA: Belknap Press of Harvard University Press, 2003), and Lorena Oropeza, *Raza Si! Guerra No!: Chicano Protest and Patriotism in the Viet Nam War Era* (Berkeley: University of California Press, 2005). A classic book on the Chicano Movement remains Carlos Muñoz, *Youth, Identity, Power: The Chicano Movement* (New York: Verso Books, 1989, revised edition, 2007).

51 For the evolution of Chicano thinking on the issue of Mexican immigration and the significance of Mexican immigrants to the "Chicano Movement," see Esteban Flores, "Post-Bracero Undocumented Mexican Immigration and Political Recomposition," (Ph.D. diss., University of Texas, Austin, 1982); Gutiérrez, "*Sin Fronteras?*", 1991, 5–37; and Camacho, *Migrant Imaginaries*, 2008, 152–193.

52 Herman Baca Papers/Herman Baca Oral History Collection, Tape 13, Session 11, September 13, 2006. On this rift see also veteran activist Bert Corona's analysis in Mario García, *Memories of Chicano History*; and Gutierrez, *Walls and Mirrors*, 1995, 179–205.

53 Gutierrez, *Walls and Mirrors*, 1995.

54 Geographer Joseph Nevins argues that the increased anti-immigrant discourse that began in the late 1960s emerged from lawmakers in Washington, D.C. Soon, however, San Diego elites took an active part in constructing a "crisis" concerning "illegal aliens" entering the U.S. and draining its resources.

55 Nancy Ray, "Chicano Picket Chacon's Offices: Assemblyman's Vote Favoring Ban on Jobs for Illegal Aliens Assailed," *San Diego Union*, February 11, 1972.

56 Herman Baca Papers, September 13, 2006.

57 José T. Viesca, translation of the column Aqui Estamos! *National City Star-News*, July 30, 1970, Baca Papers, Box 17, Folder 8.

58 Jean Crowder, "Congressmen hear minorities," *National City Star-News*, April 30, 1972.

59 Ibid.

60 Ibid.

61 Ibid.

62 Vic Villalpando to Herman Baca, et al., February 15, 1972, Box 6, Folder 3, Baca Papers; and Crowder, 1972.

63 Villalpando to Baca, 1972

64 "60 persons claim brutality by U.S. Border officials," *National City Star-News*, February 17, 1972.

65 Villalpando to Baca, 1972.

66 Interview with Carlos Vásquez, Tape 1, September 7, 2006, Herman Baca Oral History Collection, Baca Papers.

67 Roberta Baca v. Vernon Hann, 1972–73, Box 3, Folder 16, Baca Papers.

68 "Statement taken from Mrs. Roberta Baca on January 20, 1972 at 1:00 P.M.," Box 3, Folder 16, Baca Papers.

69 Ibid.
70 Chávez, "A Glass Half-Empty," 2004.
71 Ibid., 175.
72 Herman Baca to Congressman Lionel Van Deerlin, March 20, 1972, Box 13, Folder 7, Baca Papers.
73 Ibid.
74 "Immigration and Customs Hearing," Flyer, Box 3, Folder 16, Baca Papers.
75 Rep. Edward Roybal, "Some Strange Customs at the Border," *Los Angeles Times*, June 19, 1972.
76 Enrique Sánchez Díaz, "Las Revisiones en la Frontera un Atentado Contra la Dignidad," *El Mexicano*, Sábado 29 de Abril de 1972. See Box 17, Folder 8, Baca Papers.
77 Ibid.
78 "Picket Picket Picket" Flyer, April 1972, Box 3, Folder 16, Baca Papers.
79 Luibhéid, 2002, 130.
80 I build off the work of Falcón, 2001; and Luibhéid, 2002. The more recent incidents of rape at the border, as explored by Falcon and Luibhéid, reveal the more systematic documentation of these occurrences as organizations such as Human Rights Watch, Amnesty International, government entities such as the Office for the Inspector General, American Friends Service Committee, media outlets, as well as grassroots community organizations have recorded these incidents since the 1980s, unlike the 1970s and earlier.
81 Falcón, 2001.
82 Ramón Gutiérrez, "Community, Patriarchy and Individualism: The Politics of Chicano History," *The American Quarterly*, 45, No.1 (March 1993): 44–72. I also refer to the work of Alicia Schmidt Camacho, *Migrant Imaginaries: Latino Cultural Politics in the U.S.-Mexico Borderlands* (New York: New York University Press, 2008), 165–178; Richard T. Rodríguez, *Next of Kin: The Family in Chicano/a Cultural Politics* (Durham: Duke University Press, 2009); and Blackwell, *Chicana Power*, 2011 in conceptualizing family, gender and patriarchy within the Chicano Movement.
83 Gutiérrez, "Community, Patriarchy and Individualism:," 1993, 45–46.
84 Camacho, *Migrant Imaginaries,* 2008, 169.
85 "Border Patrolman Accused of Rape," July 2, 1972.
86 I am influenced by the Chicana feminist writings in response to sexism in the Chicana/o Movement that explored the complexities of ethnic nationalism's tendency to mobilize as a people against racism without addressing patriarchy and other social hierarchies internal to the Latina/o community. See Alma García, *Chicana Feminist Thought: The Basic Historical Writings* (New York: Routledge, 1997).
87 "Border Patrolman Accused of Rape," July 2, 1972.
88 Ibid.
89 Ibid.
90 Conceiving of gender as a major modality through which a racialized community was imagined on transnational grounds is related to the notion articulated by Stuart Hall that "race is the modality through which class is lived." See Stuart Hall, "Race, Articulation and Societies Structured in Dominance," in *Sociological Theories: Race and Colonialism* (Paris: UNESCO, 1980).
91 Albert García to Congressman Lionel Van Deerlin, November 24, 1972, Box 20, Folder 19, Baca Papers. On Miller's alliance with MAPA for his election see Herman Baca Oral History Collection, Tape 2, Baca Papers.
92 Evelle J. Younger to Albert García, Ad Hoc Committee on Border Brutalities; and Robert R. López, San Diego Human Relations Agency, May 4, 1973, Box 20, Folder 19, Baca Papers.
93 "Delay irks Roybal in rape prosecution," *Los Angeles Times*, August 27, 1972.

94 "Border Patrolman Accused of Rape," July 2, 1972; Affidavit of Martha Elena Parra López, June 7, 1972, Baca Papers.
95 Albert García to Senator Allan Cranston, April 4, 1974, Box 17, Folder 8, Baca Papers.
96 "*Migra*" is a colloquial term used among Mexicans, Mexican Americans and other Latinos as a derogatory reference to the Border Patrol or other border officials. Embedded within this term is the collective understanding that border officials are anti-Mexican and anti-Latino.
97 "*Compañera*" translates to "companion" or "comrade," referencing a close friend that one struggles alongside.
98 On the Chicana feminist movement developing simultaneously but seemingly out of dialog with the transnational Chicano activism discussed here, see García, *Chicana Feminist Thought, 1997*; and Blackwell, *Chicana Power!, 2011*.
99 Falcón, "Rape as a Weapon of War," 2001.
100 Lisa Lowe, Immigrant Acts: On Asian American Cultural Politics (Durham, NC: Duke University Press, 1996), 161.
101 Ibid.

2

REINSCRIBING THE VOICES OF *LA GENTE* IN THE NARRATIVE OF THE CHICANO MOVEMENT[1]

Lorena V. Márquez

This chapter investigates the overarching effects of the Chicano Movement on *la gente* (everyday people) by focusing on cannery workers—specifically at the Libby, McNeill & Libby plant—and their struggle for labor rights in Sacramento, California. As will be made clear, some of the ideals of the Chicano Movement had permeated many aspects of Chicano life and work. As a case in point, when ethnic Mexican cannery workers in Sacramento organized the Cannery Workers Committee (CWC) in 1969—at the height of the Chicano Movement—they single-handedly transformed local labor practices and did so by positioning themselves in the larger rubric of civil rights.[2] Their organizing tactics and rhetoric, articulated in both print media and meetings, demonstrate how the Chicano Movement moved beyond what some have argued were largely symbolic cultural issues centering on personal and collective identity to bread-and-butter economic issues central to all segments of the Chicano community.

This paper situates labor organizing in the framework of Sacramento Chicano community politics, but also in the context of the larger Chicano Movement. It argues that the Chicano Movement was far-reaching and influenced unionization efforts by uniting workers and providing them with the rhetoric to articulate race and gender oppression in the workplace. In the early 1960s and ending in the late 1970s a political consciousness of being *mexicano* in the United States gave rise to what historian Ignacio M. García, has called the "militant ethos"—a "body of ideas, strategies, tactics, and rationalizations that community uses to respond to external challenges."[3] This ethos sought to synthesize the problems of the ethnic Mexican community by addressing years of discrimination, violence, and neglect from the American mainstream.[4] The role of specific groups of workers in the Chicano Movement remains largely understudied, yet in the 1960s it is clear that ordinary Chicanos became increasingly impatient with low-wage labor and especially with the lack of opportunities for advancement.[5] Likewise, Mexicans in Sacramento understood and had firsthand experience with racism and sexism and nowhere was this more prominent than on the cannery floor. Although Mexican cannery workers endured multiple forms of race and gender discrimination and had voiced their grievances since the 1930s, and in some cases before, their pleas and complaints often went unattended.

By examining the workplace, we can begin to fully comprehend the transformative and regenerative actions on the ground or what social historians call "everyday people." This idea is not altogether new; during the 1960s British scholar E. P. Thompson (and others) urged us to study "history from the bottom up"—a counter-academic culture aimed to challenge the "top down" approach.[6] The Thompson school of thought encouraged a new breed of scholars—known as social historians—to study the complex and multifaceted histories of marginalized communities and groups such as women, the working class, and people of color.[7] This work adds to this body of literature and posits that we must continue to study *la gente* in order to gain a better and more comprehensive understanding of how social movements function and how they are received/perceived by all segments of society—including the working poor.

Indeed, the founding of the CWC demonstrated what was possible when ethnic Mexicans came together to demand race and gender equality during an epic political moment. They were able to change worker conditions by claiming that the canneries had long held both people of color and women in subordinate positions. Furthermore, the CWC utilized programs created during the 1960s such as the Equal Employment Opportunity Commission, the California State Fair Employment Practices Commission, the Sacramento City-County Human Relations Commission, and the Federal Employment Opportunity Commission to halt racist and sexist practices at local canneries. The establishment of these commissions came about in the aftermath of the signing of the 1964 Civil Rights Act—a landmark piece of legislation that made it illegal to discriminate in the workplace or public facilities.[8] Because the government agencies were in place to finally deal with race and gender discrimination claims, the CWC was able to take advantage of these programs and make formal complaints to the authorities. In turn, the involvement of these agencies added outside pressure to cannery employers who found themselves having to answer not only to their own employees, but also to state and federal officials.

At the center of this story is Rubén Reyes. Originally a transplant from Arizona, he came to Sacramento in 1949 to work in its expanding canning industry. He eventually settled, married, and had seven children in the capitol city and led perhaps one of the most aggressive campaigns against racial and gender discrimination; he did this through the establishment of the CWC, where he served as its president.[9] Reyes was profoundly influenced by the racial social order in Phoenix and grew to resent whites who upheld a system of inequality and subjugation. By the mid-twentieth century segregation was rampant in the American Southwest, white supremacy was upheld in legal, public, and social spaces. Reyes explained this harsh reality, "I grew up in a place where they wouldn't serve me food, they wouldn't allow me in any restaurants, we couldn't swim in your swimming pools."[10] Racial segregation caused hostility and distrust between Mexicans and Anglos in Phoenix and these social divisions lasted well into the twentieth century. Reyes reflected, "The memories and the experiences that I had had in Arizona were very strong and I was very angry with the system. And I was very, very anti-white. I think I still am."[11] Reyes experienced social trauma from what he viewed as an abuse of power by whites. He explained that from the time he had reason, he was able to discern that whites had a clear socio-economic advantage over Mexicans. In turn, he held a deep level of resentment against the status quo. Although this article focuses on Reyes's leadership, by contextualizing his life and work, it also attempts to shine light on the contributions and courage of fellow co-workers who dared to make their grievances known and voices heard—risking their employment and, indeed, their very livelihoods.

Historiography

By the late 1960s the Chicano Movement had moved beyond the realm of youth activists and "militant" organizations and into the homes, work, and life of *la gente*. Yet, workers' connections and contributions to the *movimiento* have been largely overlooked by scholars who tend to focus on more overt forms of resistance.[12] This oversight has had a profound impact on the way we comprehend the overarching effects of the Chicano Movement. To date, few studies look at the role of *la gente* and the workplace. Ever since the first regional canneries were established in the nineteenth century, cannery workers have tended to represent the Southwest's increasingly polyglot working class. For more than a century, cannery workers have tended to be a mix of immigrant and native-born "minority" workers, underpaid, not proficient in English, and deeply gender-stratified. For these reasons their needs often mirrored those articulated by members of the larger Chicano community and it is their demands as a marginalized workforce that resonated with the larger goals of the Chicano Movement. The Chicano Movement was mostly led by working-class youth who demanded access to a quality education, a fair opportunity for upward mobility, and representation in positions of power.[13] In many ways, then, their needs and desires did not differ from those espoused by the cannery workers.

The term "Chicano Movement," used in this study, is in the masculine form because in its time it was known as the "Chican*o* Movement" and because through most of its existence the Movement ignored or shamed Chicanas into taking secondary leadership or obscure positions.[14] Throughout the 1970s, the initial generation of self-proclaimed Chicana feminists viewed the struggle against sexism within the Chicano Movement and the struggle against racism in the larger society as central ideological components of their feminist thought. Chicana feminists began to challenge *machismo* in the movement and the portrait of the so-called "ideal Chicana" drawn by Chicano cultural nationalists who glorified the traditional gender roles for Chicanas.[15] Outward examples of their subordination in the Movement became ever more glaring since women were denied leadership roles. Instead, as was also true within civil rights groups such as the Student Non-Violent Coordinating Committee and the anti-war group Students for a Democratic Society, women in the Chicano Movement were "relegated to cleaning up, making coffee, executing the orders men gave," and otherwise "servicing their needs."[16] If women did manage to assume leadership positions, as some did, they were often ridiculed and charged with being "unfeminine, sexually perverse, promiscuous, and all too often, taunted as lesbians."[17]

The contributions of Chicanas have been largely overlooked because of the often narrow classifications of leadership and activism. Chicana scholars have made great inroads in expanding the confines of what was understood as "political activism," arguing that it must be studied in its many forms and shapes—for it is often fluid and subtle.[18] In other words, not every person contributes to a movement or social cause equally or similarly. For instance, participation can come in waves—at times one can be more involved, while at others—depending on family and work obligations—becoming even inactive. Additionally, one does not necessarily have to serve in a front and center leadership position to classify as a "leader," but can work behind the scenes, spearhead committees, fundraise, or simply serve as a general member. While this type of work is equally important, it often goes unnoticed. Unfortunately, this was particularly true of women during the Chicano Movement who were often not given the opportunity to organize in "leadership" roles by their male counterparts, yet managed to give of their time, energy, and attention to the cause with little recognition or acknowledgement of their efforts.[19]

Although recent scholarship has developed a more complex and encompassing portrait of the Chicano Movement, for the most part, it still generally tends to dismiss or fails to make the connection to *la gente* or what David Montejano calls people "from below."[20] Indeed, Chicano Movement studies tend to focus on individuals such as Oscar "Zeta" Acosta, José Angel Gutiérrez, organizations such as the Brown Berets, United Farm Workers union, Mexican American Youth Association, or major events such as the Chicano Moratorium or the East LA Blowouts.[21] The works of Chicana scholars (Lorena Oropeza, Vicki L. Ruiz, Dionne Espinoza, and Maylei Blackwell) have begun to challenge the once male-centered paradigm by giving voice and place to Chicana activists in the *movimiento*. This chapter, in a small way then, hopes to move beyond "traditional" Chicano Movement historiography and examine the critical ways in which *la gente* connected with Chicano Movement ideologies.

History of Canneries in Sacramento

For most of the twentieth century, Sacramento served as a significant site for canneries because of its prime location at the intersection of the rich agricultural hinterlands of both of California's central and northern valleys. Hence, the longevity and success of canneries in Sacramento is due to its prime location, surrounded by lucrative agricultural fields that yield an abundance of crops to sustain profits. Sacramento historian Steve M. Avella traces their important development to the opening of the Panama Canal in 1914, which facilitated trade operations. Consequently, there was a sharp increase in demand for canned goods that generated the building of new canneries in California. The larger Sacramento Valley benefited greatly from this demand. For example, Hunt Brothers launched canning operations in nearby Davis and Marysville. Libby, McNeill & Libby's Sacramento facility had grown to become one of the largest canneries in the Golden State.[22] Without question, California's canning industry boomed with the onset of World War I. Indeed, the U.S. troops and their allies were estimated as requiring some 200 million cans of fruit and vegetables.[23]

California cannery workers have historically lacked union representation due to their short-term employment and because they have been largely regarded as passive. Historian Elizabeth Reis explains that cannery workers have held an ambiguous worker position because they "straddled a line between factory workers and agricultural laborers."[24] Like farm workers they were seasonal but at the same time, they resembled factory workers; their work was tedious and repetitive, located in urban areas, and non-migratory. Furthermore, the largely female workforce was mistakenly regarded as docile and unlikely to launch formal complaints. To further complicate matters, the fact that there was a high worker turnover, and many were immigrants who lacked English language fluency, made it all the more challenging to organize workers. For these reasons, labor unions showed little interest in representing cannery workers. Indeed, cannery workers have been largely misunderstood and underestimated by both employers and unions. For instance, when the mostly female, Italian immigrant cannery workers staged a boycott for higher wages and safer worker conditions in San Francisco in 1917, their efforts caught many by surprise. They were labeled as militant and anti-American.[25] Chicanos were simply the most recent example of workers organizing against cannery worker abuse.

The expansion in the packing and canning industry also allowed for the emergence and development of a vibrant working-class culture. Indeed, canneries represented one of the most diverse workplaces in Sacramento because its employees were largely composed of immigrant women, many of whom sought to augment their impoverished family incomes. Avella notes that "the net result of the increasingly diverse workforce was a slow but steady increase in Sacramento's population."[26] The arrival of the Reyes family to Sacramento was part of this growth and demonstrates the strong pull of job opportunities in

Sacramento canneries. Undeniably, the continuous accessibility of workers to fill labor-intensive posts added to the region's cannery industry success. In the beginning, Sacramento's canning workforce comprised mostly immigrants from various European countries including Germany, Italy, Spain, and Yugoslavia. This was also the case in the San Francisco Bay area where a mostly Italian workforce labored in the canneries.[27]

The cannery business, however, was not always booming and, like so many industries, was severely weakened by the Great Depression. In Sacramento, the first industry to be affected by the economic crisis was the seasonal canning industry. Indeed, as early as September 1930, 153 employees of the California Cooperative Producers Canning Company—a Sacramento company—were laid off without pay when demand plunged for canned goods. Families were financially too stretched to purchase this once-desired commodity. To make matters worse, in early December 1932 a dreadful freeze hit valley citrus crops and destroyed at least half of the citrus trees, particularly oranges. Cannery officials, now under heated public pressure, promised to keep operations going.[28] All the while, there was an increased social and political backlash against Mexican immigrant workers who became the scapegoats for the nation's economic problems.

In an effort to appease and calm the social anxiety and the perceived threat of immigrants, local, state, and federal officials pressured an estimated 350,000 to 500,000 Mexican nationals—and an unknown but surely sizable number of their U.S.-born children—into leaving the U.S. in a massive repatriation.[29] These efforts began in early 1931 and were most starkly felt in Los Angeles where by the year's end nearly one third of its Mexican population had been repatriated. Similar efforts took place in Sacramento and although it is not clear how many local Mexicans were repatriated, accessibility to train rides undoubtedly facilitated the removal of "undesired" Mexican nationals.[30] In Sacramento as well, the canning industry pledged to employ only "local residents"—meaning they would refrain from hiring Mexican immigrants.[31]

World War II presented new challenges, but also opportunities for local canneries and their workers. For instance, the war effort placed a heavy demand on canned goods to feed and supply U.S. troops at home and abroad, as well as the increased needs of civilians on the home front. In response to the overwhelming demand, packing houses and canneries were awarded thousands of federal U.S. contracts and California's agribusiness, in particular, benefited greatly.[32] According to historian Vicki L. Ruiz, from 1939 to 1950 California led canned fruit and vegetable production in the nation and "in 1946 the state's share in the U.S. fruit pack was approximately 50 percent."[33] By 1947 the canned fruit and vegetable industry had made tremendous economic headway and was the largest manufacturing employer in California.[34]

Now facing completely different economic circumstances than just a decade earlier, the canning industry could not fill enough posts to meet production demand. California's canning industry again began to successfully expand while, at the same time, the defense industry was also booming. Both industries began competing for the same pool of workers—there were simply not enough workers to fill the posts needed. Canning companies, however, found themselves at a disadvantage as they could not meet the higher wages offered in the defense industry. Thus, by the early 1940s, "cannery operatives, who were usually at the bottom end of the socio-economic scale," had become what Ruiz calls "labor aristocrats," if only in a situational sense.[35] This was the case in Sacramento where the predominantly European immigrant workforce began to leave the canning industry for employment opportunities in the defense industry in the San Francisco Bay Area, southern California, and elsewhere in the West.[36]

The impact of both experienced workers leaving to work for better paying jobs in defense industries and the recruitment of able-bodied men to enlist in the military created a severe labor shortage. It was at this crucial moment that the shift from a predominantly white cannery workforce to one of Mexican origin took place in Sacramento. This change was augmented by the 1942 labor agreement between the U.S. and Mexico, known as the Bracero Program. The agreement had a far-reaching impact, dramatically altering work conditions in Californian agricultural businesses. Immediately after its signing, thousands of *braceros* began harvesting California crops and also canning fruit and vegetables. *Braceros* not only endured severe worker conditions, but were largely viewed as cheap, indispensable, and scab labor. Worse yet, at a moment's notice they could be fired, replaced, or let go without pay for hours worked.[37]

The transition from a European immigrant workforce to a predominantly ethnic Mexican one gave rise to a stark example of a racially stratified workforce in the Sacramento Valley. The concentration of ethnic Mexicans in low-status occupations in many ways helped to reinforce and perpetuate negative stereotypes about Mexicans' native abilities. Unfortunately, over time whites began to associate ethnic Mexicans with only the hardest, dirtiest, most dangerous, and least-paid kind of labor. Historian David G. Gutiérrez explains that "this status became institutionalized in some ways by the emergence of an ethnic division of labor characterized by a dual wage structure, in which Mexican workers were consistently paid less than 'white' workers performing the same work."[38] Hence, by the 1940s this unfair pay structure was systematically practiced in the Southwest, and Sacramento was no exception. Ruiz found similar conditions in her study on cannery work in southern California. She notes, "It should be pointed out that many Mexican and Filipino farm workers did not experience any upward mobility as the result of World War II."[39] Indeed, ethnic Mexican and Filipinos continued to labor in the fields alongside the newly arrived *braceros*. Thus, unlike their European immigrant co-workers they continued to be relegated to low-pay, low-skill employment.

Sacramento canneries benefited greatly from the Bracero Program which not only augmented its workforce but also helped to depress wages and exacerbate unfair labor practices.[40] At first, *braceros* were not able to make fair labor practice demands because they were under contract. Both the U.S. and Mexican governments were supposed to protect them under the bi-national program, however, the agreement failed to put into place an administrative structure to address the outpouring of labor complaints. Thus, Rubén Reyes was not surprised by the way cannery employers responded to the Mexican national workforce. He explained:

> The mentality of the white man is that "hey all of a sudden we don't have white people in the canneries anymore. All of the Mexicans are taking over. It's time for a change, a radical change." So it just shows you what white people think of other people, you know, and basically what they see the Brown people as in this country. . . . That they didn't feel that we as Mexicans, or Chicanos, were worth as much as the whites that were working there before.[41]

Clearly for Reyes, whites "basically" disregarded people of color and this was no exception. To make matters worse, in practice *braceros* routinely earned less than what their contracts promised. This was justified because they made more than they would have received for the same work in Mexico. Matt García in his work on citrus workers in the San Gabriel and Pomona Valleys in eastern Los Angeles county notes that "by 1958, the hourly wage for Mexican American workers rose slightly to between 80 cents and $1, depending on the season, but employers often paid braceros between 10 and 15 cents less than their local co-workers."[42] Furthermore, in her work on the Mexican immigration policies, Kitty Calavita found that by the early 1950s the Bracero Program, in partnership with the Immigration and Naturalization Service administration, were closely allied with growers to maintain a steady legal workforce and to control illegal crossings.[43]

The Rise of the Cannery Workers Committee (CWC)

By the 1960s, Chicanos had become increasingly impatient with low-wage labor and especially with the lack of opportunities for advancement. Although Mexican cannery workers had voiced their grievances since the 1930s, and in some cases before, in most cases, their pleas and complaints went largely unattended. However, it is important to note that in many regions in the nation this rhetoric was found among Chicano labor organizers *before* the Movement. For instance, in the 1930s and 1940s, Emma Tenayuca, labor activist and Communist Party member, organized and regarded all Mexicans north of the border as one people and endorsed a form of political unity between Mexican Americans and Mexican nationals based on a combination of cultural and class affinities and goals. She reasoned that they were bound together as a predominant working-class people, shared a "common history, culture, and oppressed condition" on the North American continent.[44] Earlier worker organizing efforts helped inform and shape labor activism during the Chicano Movement; the 1960s represented an instance of historical activist continuity and not necessarily a new phenomenon.

In 1971, CWC, under plaintiff Rubén Reyes, sued Libby, McNeill & Libby, and Cannery Workers Union Local 857 on the grounds of racial discrimination. Reyes courageously charged that Libby and the union had not only discriminated against him, but also that these practices were widespread against ethnic Mexicans and women. Reyes sued and on May 8, 1971 the court found that Libby, McNeill & Libby had deprived ethnic Mexicans of promotions to higher paying positions and failed to adequately promote such opportunities by not making material available in Spanish. Furthermore, it ruled that the Cannery Workers Union Local 857 had discriminated against Reyes and ethnic Mexicans by failing to: carry out grievance procedures in an expeditious manner; resolve complaints; and provide by-laws and other pertinent documents in Spanish considering that 40 percent of their members were Mexican immigrants and had limited command of the English language.[45] For the first time in memory, Reyes's victory against his long-time employer and union altered workplace conditions for marginalized cannery workers and held union representatives accountable to the *gente* they supposedly represented. Although the lawsuit was brought by an individual, the legal action actually represented a collective effort. Indeed *Reyes v. Libby* brought charges forward on behalf of all ethnic Mexicans noting that "Libby, McNeil [sic] & Libby had discriminated against Mr. Reyes and other Mexican Americans."[46]

The formation of the CWC was, in short, a response to decades of neglect at the hands of cannery employers and their unions. Rudolph "Rudy" Ávila, CWC former member and worker at Libby's, recently explained:

> The reason we formed the committee was because there was no upward movement for the Mexicans working there [Libby, McNeill & Libby]. All the lower paying jobs were held by Mexicans and [there was] not a chance to be promoted to higher paying jobs—even though a lot of the Mexicans had more seniority than the whites. The whites were the ones getting referred for the higher positions. Their excuse was that we were not qualified.[47]

Clearly, Ávila and his fellow cannery workers were well aware that the company had long maintained a racist institution where it was commonly practiced to overlook ethnic Mexicans for promotions. Through the CWC, ethnic Mexicans were able to come together as workers and have a platform on which to air their grievances and foster community. Indeed, there was a true interest and need to create an alternative to the company union. The CWC carried the slogan of justice and a promise of true worker representation. When it formed in 1969, Reyes urged his co-workers, "WE HAVE TO MAKE OUR MOVEMENT NOW AND WE CANNOT REST FOR ONE SECOND."[48]

Word of the lawsuit's success spread quickly, and, consequently, within a year, CWC chapters expanded to canneries throughout Northern California, eventually making it one of the most powerful unions in the region including Woodland, Fairfield, San Jose, Merced, Salinas, Yuba City, and Marysville.[49] CWC not only operated as a union and advocate for cannery workers, it also was instrumental in setting up a series of investigations that led to legal penalties against employers who discriminated on the basis of race and gender. For instance, the Equal Employment Opportunity Commission (EEOC) launched an investigation on behalf of five CWC members against three canneries and two unions on January 27, 1971.

CWC members saw themselves as part of the larger Chicano Movement and employed the rhetoric of civil rights to mobilize fellow cannery workers to join their cause. This was best illustrated in the CWC newsletter publication, which was first published in 1976. *The Cannery Worker*, where iconography and symbols of the United Farm Workers (UFW) eagle, the power fist, and images of Emiliano Zapata and Ernesto "Che" Guevara appeared frequently. The newspaper was widely circulated in canneries in Northern California and the first year's publication was free to all cannery workers, although a 6-dollar donation was encouraged. *The Cannery Worker* was a bilingual newspaper, taking into account its large Spanish-language readership.[50] The first managing editor Rudolph "Rudy" Ávila explained that the function of the newspaper was to educate the workers "telling them the stories about other canneries in Northern California. Also, advising them of their rights and all that."[51] Reyes, himself, identified as Chicano and grounded his philosophy in ideals espoused by the Chicano Movement. By identifying as Chicano openly and espousing the ideals of the Chicano Movement to CWC members through *The Cannery Worker*, Reyes helped link the Chicano Movement to cannery workers. For Reyes and those involved in the newsletter, at the very least, the plight of the worker was intimately linked to the goals of the Chicano Movement.

For CWC members, the call for justice, equity, access, and fairness not only represented the goals of the Chicano Movement, but the very objectives of cannery workers. Ávila recently explained this connection in an interview when asked if he thought the plight of workers was linked to the Chicano Movement: "Yes, we tried to improve our conditions, our working conditions, because we helped the economy right here [Sacramento]. Our jobs helped the economy in the U.S." In a real sense, then, for Ávila the role of the worker was intimately linked to the U.S. economy, and by organizing better working conditions they were challenging racism head on. Likewise, as chairperson of the CWC, Reyes often employed civil rights rhetoric in his speeches such as "*unanse al movimiento y hay que demandar nuestros derechos*" ("join the movement and let's demand our rights").[52] Furthermore, he linked the Chicano worker struggle with those of other racially oppressed groups in the U.S. such as Chinese Americans and, more particularly, African Americans. In this sense, he made claims of shared experience and struggle. Reyes and the CWC also viewed the Mexican cannery worker cause in alignment with the goals of the Civil Rights Movement. The CWC made claims that as workers, residents, and taxpayers of the state they merited and earned equal access and opportunities.[53]

As discussed above, Reyes's upbringing in racially segregated Arizona made him increasingly impatient with the progress in civil rights, especially when it came to Mexicans in the U.S. Reyes began working at Libby, McNeill & Libby in 1949, shortly after the Teamsters union takeover of Sacramento canneries. Although he arrived after the tumultuous Teamster victory he noted, "It didn't take me long to find out that we didn't have a union when I came to work there."[54] For Reyes, then, although the Teamsters Union was supposed to represent the best interest of the workers, the opposite was true. The Teamsters were clearly aligned with the companies, and their loyalties and commitment were to protect the profit and gains of employers. Already by the 1950s the workforce at Libby's was about 35 percent Mexican and the Teamsters Union was doing little to address their needs. Essentially, Reyes explained, the canneries did as they wanted and had a tradeoff with the Teamsters to control the retirement and pension plan funds.

Cannery workers often complained of harassment by supervisors who regularly abused their power. Reyes also made note of this abuse at Libby,

> When I formed a [Cannery Workers] Committee in 1969, they were still grabbing people by the back of the neck. You know, and running them "HEY!", just like a little school kid. "Hey, you get over there!" and grabbing them by the arm, physically handling people.[55]

The combination of both verbal and physical harassment added stress to a job that was not only physically demanding but also failed to pay its workers adequately. Cannery workers were under constant pressure to work faster and harder and the tactics used to keep them in "their place" were humiliating, degrading, and outright abusive.

Gender Discrimination on the Cannery Workshop Floor

To make matters worse, Mexican women were often relegated to low-pay, low-skill posts, while their Anglo co-workers often received promotions or supervisory positions.[56] Vicki Ruiz explains this phenomenon noting that "[a]n ethnic division of labor existed side by side with a division of labor by gender."[57] In Sacramento, Mexican women often endured more rigorous and stringent work and were also the first to be reprimanded for not meeting factory production quotas. Reyes acknowledged, "Women have it worse. They put most of the women on the belt—the toughest job in the cannery."[58] It appears that Reyes was keenly aware of the "triple oppression" under which Chicana cannery workers labored. In this sense Reyes challenged Chicano nationalist-sexist impulses. Dominant views on the inferiority of the Chicana body, and consequently on their limitations, contributed to a situation in which Chicana and Mexicana cannery workers were usually the last to be considered for promotions. This rationalization, which was commonplace at the time, is best explained by sociologist Denise A. Segura who notes that "women are viewed at a very deep level by employers as mothers (or future mothers), [thus] they encounter discrimination in job entry and advancement."[59] All these factors made for a degrading workplace for *mexicanas* and helped justify the positioning of women in low-pay jobs.

Work conditions for Chicanas at Sacramento canneries were not only deplorable but also posed health hazards. Mexicanas generally worked the belts, considered to be the harshest and most demanding position. Reyes described the intolerable working conditions women workers were exposed to:

> When you work the belt, it is awfully hard work to stand in one place, the steam, the heat, or the cold, and this belt moving in front of your eyes for eight hours. Women used to faint up there. Plus the handling of the product itself was such that women [were at] the nurses' office every day before each shift was full of women, they couldn't tend to all of them because they would come in and get bandaged up. What was happening was that they were handling the product coming in off the fields full of insecticides. They developed sores, what have you. Rashes. They thought [from the] peach fuzz, or the acid from the tomatoes. This is the explanations [sic] the canneries gave. It took us years to find out what was really going on.[60]

Reyes was referring to the harmful side effects of pesticides later discovered. In the 1980s, the UFW led a taskforce to investigate the effects of pesticides on farm workers. Startling U.S. government reports found that in the 1980s farmers used approximately 2.6 million tons of chemical pesticides per year and that at least 300,000 people suffered serious illness due to its use. Not only were farm workers exposed to this poison, but also their children who lived and played near agricultural fields. In fact, the mere act of sharing the same living headquarters exposed children to unusually high rates of pesticides. The most devastating effects were the large numbers of cancer clusters, with unusually high rates of disease, especially among the young, which divided small communities in the San Joaquin Valley, just south of Sacramento, and again pitted the local power establishment against farm worker advocates.[61] Although there is no known medical report of pesticide effects on cannery workers in Sacramento at this time, clearly they were not immune to such chemicals.

Chicanas were not only exposed to hazardous pesticides, but were also paid less than their male counterparts. For instance, they were not given the opportunity to work in the warehouse, run machinery, or drive trucks or forklifts, which were not only considered "easier" jobs, but were much better paid. At best, Reyes noted, there were a handful of "cute white women," in his words, who worked in these positions and "the foremen would be patting them on the behind."[62] The blatant sexual harassment often went unchallenged and women found little refuge in reporting this abuse to union officials or cannery administrators.

Chicanas on the cannery shop floor were also often victims of racialized sexual harassment. Sumi K. Cho explains that racialized sexual harassment denotes a particular set of injuries resulting from the unique complex of power relations facing women of color in the workplace. She notes that race and gender combine to alter conceptions of both the "primary injury" (the offending conduct legally recognized as sexual harassment) and the "secondary injury" (the actions of employers and institutions that ally with harasser).[63] She argues further that this dual form of exploitation derives from a much longer and more complicated tradition of "colonial and military domination that is interwoven with more contemporary forms of sexual domination to provide the 'ultimate western male fantasy.'"[64]

Additionally, while men in the packing and canning industry were usually afforded the opportunity to work all year round, the overwhelming majority of women were often limited to seasonal positions forcing them to be unemployed for the better part of the year.[65] This was commonplace in canneries statewide.[66] To add insult to injury, when women went on maternity leave, they lost all rights to their pensions even after working 10 to 15 years for a cannery. Reyes believed this to be one of the biggest "rip offs" to take place by cannery management. Canneries were able to get away with this because they cited it as "a break in service," under the bargaining agreement, which allowed for pension plans to be wiped out. Reyes protested:

> So consequently, you have thousands, and I'm talking about thousands of women in the cannery who worked for years, who periodically had a break in service and ended up relinquishing their pensions to the Teamsters, only because they weren't informed of their rights or educated in the break in service clause.[67]

Reyes, concerned about this discrepancy, informed long-time cannery worker advocate lawyer Tony Ganston, who then referred him to the Senior Citizens Law Center located in San Francisco.[68] Women were also paid an estimated three slots lower than the lowest paid position held by men, according to Reyes.

Because of his insight and knowledge on cannery rights, Reyes was hired by the Senior Citizens Law Center to interview hundreds of mostly white women about their pension plan. The women who retired in the 1970s were of German, Yugoslavian, Russian, and Spanish descent and had worked in canneries before the predominately Mexican workforce had replaced them. Reyes reported that some of these women had worked in the canneries for 40 years and were only receiving $30 a month. The Senior Citizens Law Center sued on behalf of these cannery workers. Reyes cited one of the major problems as getting the retirees to understand their rights. Information was distributed by mail, but after receiving little feedback from the retired cannery workers the Senior Citizens Law Center held meetings to try and inform workers of their pension benefits, which ended up being a "monumental task" according to Reyes.[69]

Racial Discrimination on the Cannery Workshop Floor

Reyes was keenly aware of how triple oppression, the compounding of race, class and gender oppression, affected women workers long before they retired.[70] He believed that the "hierarchy in the canneries was both racist and sexist." He noted that this was most apparent in the division of the seven employment brackets, where Chicanas/os seldom made it into the top three positions. In Sacramento, only two top positions were filled by Chicanos, and none by Chicanas, regardless of the fact that this ethnic group had long made up the majority of workers in California canneries.[71] Sociologist Tomás Almaguer in his work on the origins of white supremacy in California notes that "differences among racialized populations in class, gender, and ethnicity functioned as intervening markers that had important consequences in each group's collective history."[72] Clearly for Mexicanas who labored in canneries their work was not only viewed as obsolete because of its "menial" nature, but was also regarded as insignificant. This was despite the fact that, by the mid-1970s, 60,000 workers were employed at 74 canneries in California, at peak season, 58 percent were women, of which 62 percent were minorities. Most of the workers on the "regular" list were male, while virtually all persons on the seasonal list were female.[73]

The abuses Reyes witnessed at Libby, McNeill & Libby reminded him of the racial and economic injustices he had experienced in Arizona, and this motivated him to action. Reyes became involved in workers' rights when the Libby management asked him to interpret for newly arrived Mexican immigrants, who did not speak English, during work related disputes. He explained:

> What happened, the way that they would beat the Mexicans and deny them the opportunities, was that they would tongue lash them. And most Mexicans, not being able to deal with the language, this was basically the biggest weapon that the canneries had against the Mexicans.[74]

Being exposed first-hand to verbal abuse toward Mexican immigrants opened his eyes to the overt racism in the canneries. Although he himself had experienced work-related exploitation, participating as a go-between politicized him even further. It was at this critical moment that Reyes began to speak up against such maltreatment. According to Reyes, *mexicanos* were routinely screamed at in front of their peers on the shop floor. Intimidated by such tactics, embarrassed by the public humiliation, and afraid of losing their jobs, most Mexican immigrants when confronted with this situation would simply put their heads down and walk away.

Reyes viewed this abuse as methodical and sustained through a system of racism over centuries in the United States. From his standpoint, Libby, McNeill & Libby operated under this structure and would continue to do so if left unchallenged. He explained how blacks and Mexicans had taken the brunt of racial injustice:

> Basically, the attitude of the white guy, that he was in charge, since, you know, very few Mexican foremen, if any, very few Mexican mechanics, very few minorities, and blacks were the last to be hired and first to be fired. And at the tail end of all the machines where all the hard stacking is done, it was always a black guy. When the season started, there was always this saying, "Hey, we're getting, starting like number 9, get us a couple of niggers or buckers." So at the tail end of the machines were the black guys doing the stacking, doing the dirtiest work.[75]

Reyes believed that racism was commonplace and regularly practiced against both Mexicans and blacks. Clearly, blacks and Mexicans were subject to racist practices according to the specific racial stereotypes held by their employers. Black workers were assigned the most physically demanding jobs, while Mexicans were not allowed into supervisory positions—keeping both ethnic groups in subordinate positions.

Reyes's view on race and racism was consistent with civil rights beliefs at the time. Michael Omi and Howard Winant in their work on racial formation in the United States explain that the later 1960s signaled a "sharp break" from the early Civil Rights Movement, which subscribed to the belief that integration would be the vehicle through which to overcome racial prejudice. However, the failed promises of *Brown v. Board of Education* made it clear that racial inequality and injustice had much deeper roots. Indeed, racial discrimination had been in existence from the country's founding and had become entrenched in U.S. society; it was ingrained in structural and legal policies that had for too long relegated and maintained persons of color in an almost permanent second-class status. Omi and Winant argue that "it was this combination of relationships—discrimination, and institutional inequality—which defined the concept of racism at the end of the 1960s."[76] This was the understanding of racism with which Reyes worked.

Because of his advocacy and activism on behalf of workers, Reyes earned the reputation of being a "troublemaker" among members of the Libby, McNeill & Libby management team. Soon after protesting about demeaning practices, he was separated from the Mexican immigrant workers and given jobs that did not require him to be on the "line." Consequently, Reyes was moved out of his position in the warehouse and became "weigh master" whose duties included grading, shipping, receiving, and weighing the product. He noted that this was a difficult job because it required extensive math skills, but he gradually learned and mastered the position, ultimately working in that capacity for 10 years. When Libby, McNeill & Libby dismissed the two workers who assisted him, he filed arbitration for a strenuous workload and won. The ruling in his favor was based largely on the fact that the cannery had violated its own worker contract. To compensate for the short-handedness, Libby, McNeill & Libby gave Reyes a 10 cent an hour raise.

Target a Worker: Rally a Community

The CWC perhaps met its greatest challenge when Rubén Reyes received a suspension in 1971 and was eventually dismissed from his employer of 20 years for refusing to take down a poster of Mexican Revolutionary icon Emiliano Zapata from his office wall.[77] Reyes would only concede to removing the Zapata poster if Libby, McNeill & Libby would strip off restroom graffiti of "nigger" and "spic." Reyes suggested, "Paint it over man. Paint is cheap."[78] Since Libby did not meet Reyes's request, Reyes did not remove the Zapata poster from his office and was consequently suspended for failing to comply with company rules and orders. Libby held that others felt threatened by the revolutionary figure and therefore they were merely acting on worker complaints. On the other hand, Reyes questioned the cannery's true intentions when nothing had ever been done to address the numerous complaints of racial slurs written on bathroom walls, a communal space where workers were constantly exposed to racist propaganda.

Reyes sought the representation of Nathaniel Colley, attorney at law and NAACP (National Association for the Advancement of Colored People) West Coast legal counsel, to fight his case against Libby, McNeill & Libby. Colley reported on the case, "Mr. Reyes is not a slave. I have advised him that he was perfectly within his rights to hang the poster. What he did was no different than if I had hung a poster of George Washington crossing the Delaware."[79] Reyes's suspension lasted four and a half months and was lifted only after union arbitration found that he was within his civil rights to hang the poster. At the time, Reyes had to provide for his seven children and wife yet was only compensated for 2 months of lost earned wages.[80] While Reyes awaited deliberation on his complaint, he was forced to apply for public assistance to help feed his family. Reyes's suspension did not alter his activism and leadership role in the CWC. On the contrary, this only confirmed his belief that canneries would use their power to dismantle and squash any dissent from workers who fought against worker injustice.

After the union arbitration board found in his favor, his supervisors at Libby, McNeill & Libby continued to target Reyes. Libby made new charges against him, alleging that he failed to report to work on September 30, 1972 without prior notification. When Reyes showed up to work as scheduled on Monday, October 2, 1972, he was immediately instructed to go the personnel office where he met with David Childs, Libby's manager. Childs requested that Reyes sign a suspension notice for missing work without permission, but Reyes tore up the notice while still in the office. He refuted the charges, maintaining that he had taken proper protocol by asking for the day off well in advance. Childs set an unlimited suspension against Reyes pending an investigation by the Cannery Workers Warehousemen Union, Local 857, which represented Libby's employees. Reyes believed that his suspension was a reprisal for his role in CWC over the years and more specifically a recent dispute with the company and union wherein the cannery workers had requested higher pay and a 40-hour work week, instead of the usual 48-hour work week that included Saturdays with no overtime compensation. Libby, McNeill & Libby had denied their demands.[81]

The Chicano community activists of Sacramento came to Reyes's defense. For example, Tony Vásquez, executive director of the Urban Coalition, publicly stated that:

> Rubén's suspension only reinforces the belief of the minority working man that he is really without opportunities. It is no wonder that minorities have struck out in such frustrated anger these recent years. The system does not work for them and what else can they do? Libby's arbitrary action may well backfire on them [the company and union] because they may have succeeded in really making Rubén a martyr and solidifying his position as a rallying point for all the minority cannery workers.[82]

For Vásquez, then, the civil unrest of the late 1960s materialized because those who were oppressed continued to get doors slammed on them until they could no longer control their frustration. Cannery workers were part of this movement; at Libby the persecution of Reyes became a "rallying point" for their cause.

The CWC gained momentum by not only accessing different community and government agencies, but through press coverage. Most notably, *The Sacramento Bee* and *The Sacramento Union*, the two major newspapers in Sacramento, extensively covered stories on the CWC's efforts to address racial discrimination at local canneries. Thus, media coverage became an essential recruitment tool for the CWC because it helped increase local membership and, most importantly, assisted in spreading word of the union's success to cannery workers in nearby cities. Not only was the CWC able to grow in membership, but at last they were able to get the attention of federal agencies. By February 1972, CWC had effectively organized a broad-based charge of discrimination against minorities and women at all 76 canneries in Northern California through the assistance of Commissioner William H. Brown III of the U.S. Equal Employment Opportunity Commission. The charge was also made against labor unions and canners' employer associations that deliberately allowed discrimination practices to continue.[83]

The Outcome

The persistence of the CWC eventually paid off when on March 7, 1972 the California Fair Employment Practice Commission released a report titled: "Nine

Canneries in Sacramento, Yolo, and Solano Counties." The nine canneries included American Home Foods, Basic Vegetable Products, Inc., Campbell Soup Company, Contadina, Del Monte Plants No. 11 and No. 238, Hunt-Wesson Foods, Libby, McNeill & Libby, and Sacramento Foods. The report found that not only were Chicano cannery workers systematically discriminated against by their employers but they were widely discriminated against by the policies and practices of their own unions where they represented 40 percent of the membership but yet were only 10 percent of the union structure. The report went on to note that the union further discouraged Chicano involvement in the union by holding elections in the off-season, when the Chicano membership was at its lowest percentage. Moreover, the union had denied repeated requests to publish minutes, reports and other union notices in Spanish for its constituents.[84]

Never before had cannery workers in Northern California assembled in such an organized fashion to challenge status-quo racial and gender discrimination. The CWC steering committee was made up of: Rubén Reyes, president of the Sacramento chapter; Rudy García and Pete Naranjo from San Jose; Agapito Aguirre from Vacaville; and Adrián Mondajano, Peter Zeygolis, and Anna Zavella of King City. Together they brought charges against the canneries alleging that minority employees were not proportionately represented in higher skilled jobs, that they were given separate pay rates for the same types of work, and that they were harassed because of race and national origin. They also charged that the cannery unions were violating collective bargaining agreements, failing to represent minority employees' complaints of discrimination, and were discouraging minorities from taking part in union activities, especially in their quest for union officers.[85] Finally, CWC forcefully brought more general awareness to issues of sex and race bias in Northern California at cannery plants. However, the victories of the CWC were short-lived as the canneries were slow to respond to these demands or complaints even after the court had ruled in their favor.

Reyes and CWC continued to make known that it was not only the canneries themselves that had discriminated against Chicanas/os, but the Teamster union's operatives as well. Indeed, at a State Fair Employment Practices Commission hearing in San Francisco, cannery workers from Sacramento, King City, Gilroy, Vacaville, Woodland, and San Jose testified about the ill-treatment of Mexican workers and other minorities by both companies and unions.[86] In the eyes of Chicana/o cannery workers, unions and companies alike were using their power to keep worker rights at bay. Findings of state and county labor organizations supported the workers' view. Agencies including the California State Fair Employment Practices Commission, Sacramento City-County Human Relations Commission, and the Federal Employment Opportunity Commission found institutional discrimination in the state food processing industry. The City-County Commission ruled that although minorities made up 40 percent of the area's cannery workforce, they held only 2 percent of the better-paying jobs. The Federal Commission also found that seventy-six canneries in Northern

California discriminated against women and minorities in hiring, wages, and promotions. Metropolitan Sacramento Urban Coalition chairman, Alden W. Brosseau, noted that, despite these findings, the aforementioned agencies were not successful in resolving these problems. Brosseau stated, "As the legitimate aspirations of the minority workers continue to be frustrated, we conclude that justice can only be achieved in the courts."[87]

It was not until 1973 when Congress amended the 1964 Civil Rights Act, allowing the EEOC to sue and act on legal grounds against discrimination in the workplace. Previously, the Commission was empowered only to investigate complaints of discrimination.[88] However, this lawsuit would take another 3 years to litigate. On May 6, 1976 Judge William H. Orrick of the U.S. District Court in San Francisco ordered in a consent decree that women and minorities be given a promotion priority over white males when they bid for higher-bracket jobs. Canneries kept a seniority promotion list of year-round "regulars" who had accumulated 1,400 hours of work a year, and "seasonals" who worked less than that. As a rule, each year seasonal workers went to the bottom of the list even if they had been hired long before the regulars, because seniority did not begin until a worker became a regular. The decree also found that "females and minorities have been denied opportunities to obtain high bracket and regular positions with the industry." It set a guideline that all women and minorities who had bid for better jobs since July 2, 1965, the date of the Civil Rights Act, could move up in seniority according to their original date of hire, not the date they were made "regular."[89]

As might have been anticipated, representatives of the canneries first opposed the decree. Patricia L. Palafox, director of the Affirmative Action Trust Fund, noted that "They [canneries] only decided they wanted it after they decided it would be better than fighting it in court." Frustrated by the unwillingness and constant resistance of canneries to adhere to the decree, Palafox placed her 2-week resignation notice on July 27, 1976. When questioned as to why she had made such a severe decision, she simply replied, "Let Rubén Reyes's comments speak for themselves."[90] Reyes acknowledged that Palafox had been placed in a difficult position because she was not getting compliance from the canneries and Teamsters concerning the broad spectrum of civil rights, and that she "was forced to quit." Reyes commented, "The canneries are keeping the decree a secret. They don't want the workers to know the decree allows for a $5 million compensation trust fund, and that they can get some of that money if they have a justified grievance."[91] According to the decree, the money was to be paid by the canneries and distributed by a panel of Teamsters and cannery representatives. At last, after nearly a decade, the CWC received some form of validation by gaining compensation for the cannery workers they had so vigilantly tried to defend.

Despite the numerous victories, the Cannery Workers Committee disbanded for reasons that remain unclear. Perhaps it was due to leadership exhaustion and the failure to replenish it with new energy. Nevertheless, in the late 1970s

Sacramento's CWC began to fade and by the early 1980s seemed to have disappeared without much of a trace. Reyes believed that the CWC came to an end because it was infiltrated. He stated that the

> Government came in after their investigation and they came up with what they called a Consent Decree. They rammed it through the Federal Courts in San Francisco. We were double-crossed by some of the attorneys that we had hired to represent us. At one point, we were trying to kick them out.[92]

Reyes believed that the long list of government agencies that were supposed to aid cannery workers, such as the Employment Opportunity Commission, Human Relations Commission, and the Fair Employment Practices Commission, had conspired with company lawyers to settle with a Consent Decree that cheated workers of their rights. Based on what is admittedly an incomplete record, Reyes seemed to have been disappointed with himself—as if he had somehow let his fellow co-workers and organizers down.

Reyes's involvement in cannery unionization ultimately "destroyed" his family life and left him in economic ruin. He noted, "I never made any money in organizing. I did it because I wanted to do it. But I paid a price. The price was that I lost my job in 1972. They kicked me out."[93] Years later, in an interview with Rosana Madrid in 1983 at his home, he broke down at one point and sobbed when he sadly pointed to his surroundings, "If I took you through this house you would understand half of my story. This house is just falling apart."[94] To make matters worse, his wife left him in 1973 because he was overly committed to organizing and spent very little time at home. Eventually the pressure was too much to bear for his family. He explained, "We never got together again, you know. It was something that changed our whole lives. She never could understand why I was in it."[95] Moreover, Reyes commented, "The end result of my work is that I have been blacklisted," he could not secure employment.[96] For Reyes the ultimate downfall of his life was symbolized by the ruins of his home. At one point the housing authority intervened because he had a gaping hole in his roof for 15 months. Unfortunately, he did not have the financial means to fix the roofing problem. Like many activists, Reyes's life story reflects the high costs paid by many civil rights leaders. In essence, Reyes's story and that of the Cannery Workers Committee merits a place in Chicano Movement history because it represents the voices of *la gente*. Their struggle for equality and justice provides an important teaching point for all of us about what it means to believe that change is possible and that it's worth fighting for.

Looking at the emergence of the CWC in Sacramento, the struggles of Rubén Reyes and the cannery workers at Libby, we can see how worker struggles were a key, yet to-date, understudied chapter in the Chicano Movement. While historians have successfully noted the organizing of the UFW as a watershed in our past, the struggle of other laborers against discrimination and harassment remain markedly understudied. The life and activism of Rubén Reyes whose struggle "rallied" workers at Libby, demonstrates that there is much to be learned from these struggles. Reyes, while a worker and activist in the 1960s and 1970s, was able to speak out against structural racism, to articulate the rights of women facing gender discrimination and what today we call "triple oppression." Organizations such as the CWC, utilizing the language of the Chicano Movement were both a product of and constitutive of the rights struggles of the era. Like so many, Reyes paid a high price for his activism, yet the legacy of his activism and of the CWC continued long after the CWC faded into memory.

Notes

1   With much gratitude to David G. Gutiérrez and Linda Heidenreich for offering their insight and revisions to this article. I would also like to thank the two anonymous reviewers and Mario T. García for their helpful comments. Lastly, I thank my other dissertation committee members for their review and suggestions to the earlier chapter version in my dissertation, "Sacramento en El Movimiento: Chicano Politics in the Civil Rights Era" (2010): Miroslava Chávez-García, Nayan Shah, Vicky L. Ruiz, and Jorge Huerta.

2   I use the term "Mexican" or "ethnic Mexican" to refer to the combined population of the people of Mexican descent and heritage in the United States regardless of their actual nationality and/or citizenship status. The term "ethnic Mexican" was coined by historian David G. Gutiérrez to address the complexity of "legality" in Latino communities in the U.S. I employ the term "Latino" as an umbrella term for descendents and nationals of Mexico, Central America, South America, and the Caribbean who reside in the U.S. regardless of nationality and/or citizenship status. Since the 1980s, large numbers of political refugees from Central and South America have settled in California and other states in the U.S. Thus, the term "Latino" played a more significant role during the 1990s than in previous decades when Mexicans were culturally dominant in California and the U.S. Southwest. Since the Chicano Movement of the late 1960s, many Chicano and Latino activists (including myself) have viewed the term "Hispanic" as derogatory. They argue that the term strips them of their indigenous and African ancestry. In the cases where the term appears, (usually in reference to government documents or reports) it will be in quotation marks. The term "Chicano" is often used when referring to persons of Mexican ancestry raised and/or born in the United States. However, the term also carries political meaning— those who self-identify as "Chicano" often adhere or subscribe to a philosophical set of political convictions that grew out of the social activism of the Civil Rights era. They believe in the formation of a self-determined "imaginary" nation that aims to improve the conditions of its people in the U.S. For purposes of this paper, I will use the terms Chicano and Mexican interchangeably and will employ it when dealing with students and/or persons who exercise political action against what they perceive to be racial, social, and economic injustices. Furthermore, given that this study is situated in the midst of the Chicano Movement, and many of the persons involved identified as Chicano, the term "Chicano" is perhaps more applicable.

3   Ignacio M. García, *Chicanismo: The Forging of a Militant Ethos among Mexican Americans* (Tucson: University of Arizona Press, 1997): 4.

4   Ibid.

5   This is ironic given the strong histories of Chicano labor available for earlier time periods. For example, Vicki Ruiz, *Cannery Women, Cannery Lives: Mexican Women, Unionization, and the California Food Processing Industry, 1930–1950* (Albuquerque: University of New Mexico Press, 1987); Juan Gómez Quiñones, *The First Steps: Chicano Labor Conflict and Organizing, 1900–1920* (Los Angeles: Aztlán Publication, 1973) and *Development of the Mexican Working Class North of the Rio Bravo Work and Culture among Laborers and Artisans, 1600–1900* (Los Angeles: Chicano Studies Research Center Publications, University of California, Los Angeles, 1982); Mario T. García, *Mexican Americans: Leadership, Ideology, and Identity, 1930–1960* (New Haven, CT: Yale University Press, 1989).

6   E. P. Thompson, *The Making of the English Working Class* (London: Victor Gollanez, 1963).

7   Some of these scholars are mentioned in note 5.

8   Clayborne Carson, David J. Garrow, Gerald Gill, Vincent Harding, and Darlene Clark Hine, Eds., *The Eyes on the Prize Civil Rights Reader: Documents, Speeches and Firsthand Accounts from the Black Freedom Struggle* (New York: Penguin Books, 1991): 594.

9   Robert Dávila, "Rubén Reyes Obituary," *The Sacramento Bee*, 15 September 2007.

10 Rubén Reyes, interview by Rosana Madrid, 5 December 1983. Transcribed by Lee Ann McMeans. "Sacramento Ethnic Community Survey-Chicano Oral Histories," Sacramento Archives and Museum Collection Center (Sacramento, CA): 10.

11 Reyes, interview by Rosana Madrid, 5 December 1983, 2.

12 For a more in-depth study on both subvert and overt forms of resistance and the ways the underclass resist oppression refer to: James C. Scott, *Everyday Forms of Peasant Resistance* (New Haven, CT: Yale University Press, 1984).

13 Carlos Múñoz, *Youth Identity and Power: The Chicano Movement* (New York: Verso, 1989): 15.

14 For works on Chicanas in the Movement see: Beatriz M. Pesquera and Denise A. Segura, "With Quill and Torch: A Chicana Perspective on the American Women's Movement and Feminists Theories," in David R. Maciel and Isidro D. Ortiz, *Chicanas/Chicanos at the Crossroad: Social, Economic, and Political Change* (Tucson: University of Arizona Press, 1996); Alma M. García, Ed., *Chicana Feminist Thought: The Basic Historical Writings* (New York: Routledge, 1997); Francisca Flores, "Comisión Femenil Mexicana," *Regeneración* Vol. 2 (1971); Roberta Fernández, "*Abriendo caminos* in the Borderland: Chicana Writers Respond to the Ideology of Literary Nationalism," *Frontiers* Vol. 14/2 (1994); Ramón Gutiérrez, "Community, Patriarchy and Individualism: The Politics of Chicano History and the Dream of Equality," *American Quarterly* Vol. 45 (March 1993); Lorena Oropeza and Dionne Espinoza, *Enriqueta and the Chicano Movement: Writings from El Grito del Norte* (Houston, TX: Arte Público Press, 2006); María E. Montoya, "Class, Gender, and Culture as Challenges to Chicano Identity," in Refugio I. Rochín and Dennis N. Valdés, Eds., *Voices of a New Chicana/o History* (East Lansing: Michigan State University Press, 2000): 188–189; Yolanda Broyles-González, *El Teatro Campesino: Theatre in the Chicano Movement* (Austin: University of Texas, 1994): Maylei Blackwell, "Contested Histories: Las Hijas de Cuauhtémoc, Chicana Feminisms, and Print Culture in the Chicano Movement, 1968–1973," in *Chicana Feminisms: A Critical Reader* by Gabriela F. Arrendodo, Aída Hurtado, Norma Klahn, Olga Nájera-Ramírez, and Patricia Zavella, Eds. (Durham, NC: Duke University, 2003); Maylei Blackwell, *Chicana Power!: Contested Histories of Feminism in the Chicano Movement* (Austin: University of Texas, 2011).

15 Quoted in Alma M. García, Ed., *Chicana Feminist Thought: The Basic Historical Writings* (New York: Routledge, 1997): 5. Taken from Francisca Flores, "Comisión Femenil Mexicana," *Regeneración* 2 (1971): 6.

16 Ramón Gutiérrez, "Chicano History: Paradigm Shifts and Shifting Boundaries," in Refugio I. Rochín and Dennis N. Valdés, Eds., *Voices of a New Chicana/o History* (East Lansing: Michigan State University, 2000): 100.

17 Ibid.

18 Cynthia Orozco, *No Mexicans or Dogs Allowed* (Austin: University of Texas, 2009), 196–97.

19 Maylei Blackwell, *¡Chicana Power!: Contested Histories of Feminism during the Chicano Movement* (Austin: University of Texas, 2011): 50.

20 David Montejano, *Quixote's Soldiers: A Local History of the Chicano Movement, 1966–1981* (University of Texas Press, 2010): 7.

21 Lorena Oropeza, *¡Raza Si! Guerra No!: Chicano Protest and Patriotism during the Viet Nam War Era* (Berkeley: University of California Press, 2005): 80. For additional works on the Chicano Civil Rights Movement see: Armando Navarro, "El Partido de La Raza Unida in Crystal City: A Peaceful Revolution," (Ph.D. diss., University of California, Riverside, 1974); Ignacio García, *Chicanismo: The Forging of a Militant Ethos Among Chicanos* (Tucson: University of Arizona Press, 1997); Armando Navarro, *The Cristal Experiment: A Chicano Struggle for Community Control* (Madison: University of Wisconsin Press, 1999); Carlos Múñoz, Jr., *Youth, Identity and Power: The Chicano Movement* (New York: Verso, 1989); and Ernesto Vigil, *The Crusade for Justice: Chicano Militancy and the Government's War on Dissent* (Madison: University of Wisconsin Press, 1999); Yolanda Alaniz and Megan Cornish, *Viva La Raza: A History of Chicano Identity and Resistance* (Seattle, WA: Red Letter Press, 2008).

For additional works on the Chicano student movement refer to: Gerald Paul Rosen, "The Development of the Chicano Movement in Los Angeles, from 1967 to 1969," *Aztlán* Vol. 4 (Spring 1973), 155–184; Juan Gómez-Quiñones, *Mexican Students Por La Raza: The Chicano Student Movement in Southern California 1967–1977* (Santa Barbara, CA: Editorial La Cause, 1978); Armando Navarro, *Mexican American Youth Organization: Avant Garde of the Chicano Movement in Texas* (Austin: University of Texas Press, 1995); Carlos Múñoz, "The Politics of Protest and Chicano Liberation: A Case Study of Repression and Cooptation," *Aztlán* Vol. 5 (Spring and Fall 1974), 119–143; Carlos Múñoz and Mario Barrera, "La Raza Unida Party and the Chicanos Student Movement in California," *Social Science Journal* Vol. 19 (April 1982), 101–120; Mario Barrera, *Beyond Aztlán: Ethnic Autonomy in Comparative Perspective* (New York: 1988); Mario T. García and Sal Castro, *Blowout: Sal Castro and the Chicano Struggle for Educational Justice* (Chapel Hill: University of North Carolina Press, 2011).

22 Steve M. Avella, *Sacramento: Indomitable City* (Charleston, SC: Arcadia Publishing, 2003): 59–60.

23 Elizabeth Reis, "Cannery Row: The AFL, the IWW, and Bay Area Italian Cannery Workers," *California History* Vol. 64, No. 3 (Summer 1985), 176.

24 Reis, "Cannery Row," 179.

25 Ibid., 179–83. For more works on Cannery Workers see: Carol Lyn McKibben, *Beyond Cannery Row: Sicilian Women, Immigration, and Community in Monterey, CA, 1915–1999* (Urbana: University of Illinois Press, 2006); Elizabeth Reis, "Cannery Row: The AFL, the IWW and Bay Area Cannery Workers," *California History* Vol. 64, No. 3 (1985), 174–191; William V. Flores, "Mujeres en Huelga: Cultural Citizenship and Gender Empowerment in a Cannery Strike," *Humboldt Journal of Social Relations* Vol. 22, No. 1 (1996): 57–81; Victor B. Nelson-Cisneros, "UCAPAWA and Chicanos in California: The Farm Worker Period, 1937–1940," *Aztlán* Vol. 7, No. 3 (1976), 453–477; Dan McCurry, *Cannery Captives: Women Workers in the Produce Processing Industry* (New York: Arno Press, 1975); Vicki L. Ruiz, "Una Mujer Sin Fronteras," *Pacific Historical Review* Vol. 73, No. 1 (February 2004), 1–20; Rene Pérez Rosenbaum, "Unionization of Tomato Field Workers in Northwest Ohio, 1967–1969," *Labor History* Vol. 35, No. 3 (Summer 1994), 329–44.

26 Avella, *Sacramento: Indomitable City*, 59–60.

27 Elizabeth Reis, "Cannery Row.: The AFL, the IWW, and Bay Area Italian Cannery Workers," *California History* Vol. 64, No. 3 (Summer 1985), 174–91.

28   Avella, *Sacramento: Indomitable City*, 97.
29   David G. Gutiérrez, Ed., *Between Two Worlds: Mexican Immigrants in the United States* (Wilmington, DE: Scholarly Resources Inc., 1996), xiii-xiv. Also see: Francisco E. Balderrama and Raymond Rodríguez, *Decade of Betrayal: Mexican Repatriation in the 1930s* (Albuquerque: University of New Mexico Press, 1995).
30   Avella, *Sacramento and the Catholic Church*, 219.
31   Ibid., 97.
32   Vicki L. Ruiz, *Cannery Women, Cannery Lives: Mexican Women, Unionization, and the California Food Processing Industry, 1930–1950* (Albuquerque: University of New Mexico Press, 1987): 80.
33   Ibid., 23.
34   Patricia Zavella, *Women's Work and Chicano Families: Cannery Workers of the Santa Clara Valley* (Ithaca, NY: Cornell University Press, 1987): 51.
35   Ruiz, *Cannery Women, Cannery Lives*, 80.
36   Rubén Reyes, Interview by Rosana Madrid, 5 December 1983. Transcribed by Lee Ann McMeans. "Sacramento Ethnic Community Survey-Chicano Oral Histories," Sacramento Archives and Museum Collection Center (Sacramento, CA): 45.
37   Ruiz, *Cannery Women, Cannery Lives*, 56.
38   Gutiérrez, *Walls and Mirrors*, 25.
39   Ruiz, *Cannery Women, Cannery Lives*, 56.
40   Avella, *Sacramento: Indomitable City*, 109.
41   Reyes, interview by Rosana Madrid, 5 December 1983, 25.
42   García, *A World of Its Own*, 175.
43   Kitty Calavita, *Inside the State: The Bracero Program, Immigration, and the I.N.S.* (New York: Routledge, 1992): 110–111. Also see: Devra Weber, *Dark Sweat, White Gold: California Farm Workers, Cotton and the New Deal* (Berkeley: University of California Press, 1994).
44   Mario T. García, *Mexican Americans: Leadership, Ideology, and Identity, 1930–1960* (New Haven, CT: Yale University Press, 1989): 154. For additional information on Emma Tenayuca see: Gabriela González, "Carolina Munguía and Emma Tenayuca: The Politics of Benevolence and Radical Reform" *Frontiers* Vol. 24 (2003): 200–229; Zaragoza Vargas, *Labor Rights are Civil Rights: Mexican American Workers in Twentieth-Century America* (Princeton, NJ: Princeton University Press, 2007).
45   Rubén Reyes vs. Libby, McNeill & Libby and Cannery Workers Union Local 857, Case No. 70–29, May 18, 1971, "Findings, Conclusions, and Recommendations."
46   Rubén Reyes vs. Libby, McNeill & Libby and Cannery Workers Union Local 857, Case No. 70–29, May 18, 1971, "Findings, Conclusions, and Recommendations."
47   Rudolph Ávila, interview by author, 2 February 2013, Sacramento, California, audio recording.
48   Rubén Reyes, appears in caps and quoted in 1969, "CWC Celebrated Anniversary: A Synopsis of The Cannery Committee," *The Cannery Worker* Vol. 1, No. 4 (February 1977), 1.
49   Ávila, interview, 2 February 2013.
50   "Special March Edition," *The Cannery Worker* Vol. 1, No. 4 (February 1977), 1.
51   Ávila, interview, 2 February 2013.
52   Rubén Reyes, CWC Meeting recording 1974, Bob Barber Collection, Walter Reuther Library.
53   For studies on Chicana/o labor studies see: Carey McWilliams, *Factories in the Field: The Story of Migratory Farm Labor in California* (Berkeley: University of California Press, 1935); Matt García, *A World of Its Own: Race, Labor and Citrus in the Making of Greater Los Angeles, 1900–1970* (Chapel Hill: The University of North Carolina Press, 2001); Patricia Zavella, *Women's Work and Chicano Families: Cannery Workers of the Santa Clara Valley* (Ithaca, NY: Cornell University Press, 1987); Zaragosa Vargas, *Proletarians of*

the North: A History of Mexican Industrial Workers in Detroit and the Midwest, 1917–1933 (Berkeley: University of California Press, 1993); Erasmo Gamboa, *Mexican Labor and World War II: Braceros in the Pacific Northwest, 1942–1947* (Seattle: University of Washington Press, 1990); José M. Alamillo, *Making Lemonade out of Lemons: Mexican American Labor and Leisure in a California Town 1880–1960* (Urbana: University of Illinois Press, 2006); Pierrette Hondagneu-Sotelo, *Doméstica: Immigrant Workers Cleaning and Caring in the Shadows of Affluence* (Berkeley: University of California, 2001); Vicki L. Ruiz, Ed., *Las Obreras: Chicana Politics of Work and Family* (Los Angeles: Chicano Studies Resource Center Publications, 2000); and Vicki L. Ruiz, *Cannery Women, Cannery Lives: Mexican Women, Unionization, and the California Food Processing Industry, 1930–1950* (Albuquerque: University of New Mexico Press, 1987).

54 Reyes, interview by Rosana Madrid, 5 December 1983, 28.
55 Ibid.
56 Ibid.
57 Ruiz, *Cannery Women, Cannery Lives*, 29.
58 Quoted in, "Reyes Speaks on California Canning Situation," *The State Hornet*, 14 September 1976.
59 Denise A. Segura, "Ambivalence or Continuity?: Motherhood and Employment among Chicanas and Mexican Immigrant Workers," in Vicki L. Ruiz, Ed., *Las Obreras: Chicana Politics of Work and Family* (Los Angeles: UCLA Studies Research Center Publications, 2000): 185.
60 Reyes, interview by Rosana Madrid, 5 December 1983, 40.
61 Susan Ferriss and Ricardo Sandoval, *The Fight in the Fields: Cesar Chavez and the Farmworkers Movement* (New York: Harcourt Brace & Company, 1997): 234.
62 Reyes, interview by Rosana Madrid, 5 December 1983, 40.
63 Sumi K. Cho, "Converging Stereotypes in Racialized Sexual Harassment: Where the Model Minority Meets Suzie Wong," in Adrien Katherine Wing, Ed., *Critical Race Feminism: A Reader* (New York: New York University Press, 2003): 350.
64 Ibid., 351.
65 Reyes, interview by Rosana Madrid, 5 December 1983, 40.
66 Ruiz, *Cannery Women, Cannery Lives*, 72.
67 Reyes, interview by Rosana Madrid, 5 December 1983, 43.
68 The National Senior Citizens Law Center was founded in 1972. It advocates before the courts, Congress, and federal agencies to promote the independence and well-being of low income elderly Americas, especially women, people of color, and other disadvantaged Americans.
69 Reyes, interview by Rosana Madrid, 5 December 1983, 43.
70 For information on the concept of triple oppression see: Beatriz M. Pesquera and Denise A. Segura, "There is No Going Back: Chicanas and Feminism," in Norma Alarcón, Rafaela Castro, Emma Pérez, Beatriz Pesquera, Adaljiza Sosa Riddell, and Patricia Zavella, Eds., *Chicana Critical Issues* (Berkeley, CA: Third Women Press, 1993).
71 "Reyes Speaks on California Canning Situation," *The State Hornet*, 14 September 1976.
72 Tomás Almaguer, *Racial Fault Lines: The Historical Origins of White Supremacy in California* (Berkeley, CA: University of California Press, 1994): 209.
73 "Promotion Decree: Another Issue Stirs in Strike," *The Sacramento Bee*, 27 July 1976.
74 Reyes, interview by Rosana Madrid, 5 December 1983, 29.
75 Ibid., 5 December 1983, 28–29.
76 Michael Omi and Howard Winant, *Racial Formation in the United States: From the 1960s to the 1990s*, second edition (New York: Routledge, 1994): 69.
77 For information on Emiliano Zapata see: Samuel Burk, *Emiliano Zapata!: Revolution and Betrayal in Mexico* (Albuquerque: University of New Mexico Press).
78 Quoted in "For Cannery Workers, Hearings but No Relief," *The Hornet* (Sacramento State University student newspaper), 6 March 1973.

79   Quoted in "Foreman Plan suit as Libby Extends Suspension over Zapata Poster in Office," *The Sacramento Bee*, 10 March 1971.
80   "For Cannery Workers, Hearings but No Relief," *The Hornet* (Sacramento State University student newspaper), 6 March 1973.
81   "Workers will ask Kleinsdienst Aid" *The Sacramento Bee*, 8 October 1972.
82   Quoted in "Zapata Picture in Office, Cannery Foreman: Poster Coast Job," *The Sacramento Bee*, 5 May 1971.
83   "US Claims 76 North State Canneries Discrimination," *The Sacramento Bee*, 24 February 1972.
84   Linda Neal, Consultant, "The Cannery Union and Discrimination," May 1972 (SAMCC, Rubén Reyes Collection, Sacramento, California).
85   "Chicano Workers Map Bias Battle," *San Jose Mercury*, 11 March 1972.
86   "Cannery, Union Probe Goes to Attorney General," *The Sacramento Bee*, 6 June 1972.
87   Quoted in, "Kleindienst Asked to Act on Cannery 'Bias," *The Sacramento Bee*, 28 September 72.
88   "EEOC sues to Enforce Civil Rights Act," *The Sacramento Bee*, 6 April 1973.
89   "Promotion Decree: Another Issue Stirs in Strike," *The Sacramento Bee*, 27 July 1976.
90   Quoted in, "Promotion Decree: Another Issue Stirs in Strike," *The Sacramento Bee*, 27 July 1976.
91   Ibid.
92   Reyes, interview by Rosana Madrid, 5 December 1983, 21.
93   Ibid.
94   Ibid.
95   Ibid.
96   Ibid.

3

"HOO-RAY GONZALES!"[1]

Civil Rights Protest and Chicano Politics in Bakersfield, 1968–1974

Oliver A. Rosales

> The 30th Assembly District is a typically gerrymandered legislative district. With most of east Bakersfield and cities like Arvin, Lamont, Delano, Shafter, Wasco, McFarland, the population is both heavily Latino and Democratic. Kern County is 47.1 percent Latino, a plurality in the county. Clearly, the 30th District needs dramatic voter registration drives, citizenship efforts and political education in the broadest sense. The candidates should have a sense of missionary zeal, which would lead them to hit the streets in efforts to get people, especially Latinos, to become registered voters so that they can determine their own political destinies.[2]
>
> Raymond Gonzales, *La Voz de Kern*, 2010

> All those people who've been snickering at us shall take another look. . . . It's now fashionable to talk about the encroachment of government on people's lives: we in Kern County have been saying it and voting it all along. I think we'll get stronger as the resentment against government rise[s]. . . . Kern County will become typical of representative government and politics. There is nothing peculiar or backward about Kern County or its politics. We're the future.[3]
>
> William (Bill) Thomas, 1978

Mexican Americans, African Americans, and their white liberal allies mobilized politically throughout the civil rights struggles of the late 1960s and early 1970s in Bakersfield and Kern County, California. Urban African Americans and Mexican Americans voiced their political and social concerns and agitated against the local antistatist conservative body politic—embodied in the Bakersfield city council's majority vote. Both Mexican Americans and African Americans continued a post-World War II tradition of grassroots political engagement in Kern County that eventually reaped political rewards in 1972.

The "politics of the fields" during the tumultuous 1970s were marked by support for, or condemnation of, the United Farm Workers (UFW). The Delano grape boycott (1965–1970) and opposition to police brutality engendered a unifying effect on the political thinking of African Americans and Mexican Americans in Bakersfield. The farm worker movement tangentially generated protest against police brutality and support for federally subsidized rural health care as well.[4] Each social cause mobilized the political left and right in Bakersfield in the late 1960s and early 1970s. The political left, composed of urban Chicana/os, African Americans, and white liberals marshaled the first grassroots Chicano political victory in Kern County in 1972, with the election of Raymond Gonzales to the California state assembly. Gonzales' brief tenure in the California assembly (1972–1974) reveals tremendous insight into the changing nature of politics, civil rights, and racial coalition-building in Kern County during the Chicano movement era. His relationship with the UFW contributed to both his maiden election victory and his re-election defeat in 1974 to local Republican Bill Thomas. Gonzales' defeat also marked a regional eclipse of grassroots racial coalition-building and political activism on the liberal left.

The Politics of the Field: Civil Rights during the Delano Grape Strike

From 1965–1970 the UFW waged an epic farm labor strike including the secondary boycott against Delano area grape growers. The farm labor struggle, while national and international in scope, had an intense and vilifying local aspect in Kern County. Despite expansive research documenting the history of the Delano grape strike, the localized aspect of the farm labor struggle remains largely unaddressed.[5] In 1968 the Bakersfield city council took action to officially oppose the grape strike. Urban civil rights groups mobilized in response to back the UFW. Support for the UFW intersected increasingly with civil rights reforms in venues outside the farm labor movement.

On September 16, 1968, the third anniversary of the announcement of the Delano grape strike, the Bakersfield city council passed by a 5 to 2 vote margin Resolution No. 87–68. Officially entitled "A Resolution of the City Council of the City of Bakersfield Regarding Labor-Management Disputes Outside of the Jurisdiction of Member Municipalities of the National League of Cities," the resolution positioned the city council in clear opposition to the UFW grape boycott. The resolution called for political pressure on the National League of Cities to prevent elected, as well as non-elected, municipal officials from entering "into labor-management disputes which involve areas outside their jurisdiction, so that economic and irrevocable injury to another municipality is prevented."[6] Bakersfield city council members demanded that other U.S. municipalities should forego politicizing Kern County's 3-year farm labor dispute and, in effect, limit the financial losses to Kern County growers. César Chávez acknowledged local government resistance to the boycott before the Congressional Education and Labor Committee in October 1969.

> We have experienced things that we never dreamed we would be confronted with when we began the strike. These small communities are so well knit and the grower influence is so predominant that when we struck in Delano, we not only had the growers against us, but we had the other public bodies like the city council[s], the board of supervisors, the high school and elementary school districts, passing resolutions and propaganda against the strike and against the union. . . . [T]he community wanted to destroy us as soon as possible . . .[7]

Chávez testified. As historian Devra Weber notes, valley towns in Central California had been transformed economically by agrarian capitalism since the 1920s. The valley towns that Chávez organized through the grape strike and boycott were marked historically by a social milieu of migrant workers and growers who embraced a style of "quasi-welfare capitalism" designed to control agriculture workers.[8]

Throughout 1968 the Delano grape boycott underwent significant tactical changes. In spring that year, César Chávez engaged in a hunger strike to call attention to the importance of maintaining non-violence in the farm labor struggle. Violence on both sides of the dispute had become ugly. Chávez was summoned to the Kern County courthouse in downtown Bakersfield that year to answer questions about the escalation of violence in the fields. UFW organizers Marshal Ganz and Leroy Chatfield seized the court appearance as an opportunity to take over the public space, turning the area outside the courthouse into a peaceful mass demonstration supportive of the Delano grape boycott.[9] The goal was to convert the Kern County courthouse "into a cathedral," Ganz later recalled.[10] The UFW also sent representatives across the United States and abroad to key consumer markets to advocate support for a secondary boycott against California grapes— including a young Jessica Govea, whose parents were active in founding the Bakersfield Community Service Organization (CSO).[11]

Even though Delano was outside the municipal jurisdiction of Bakersfield, the city council felt compelled to issue an anti-union resolution. Conservatives reasoned that the permanent unionization of farm workers, a likely outcome if the grape boycott succeeded, spelled financial ruin for Kern County agribusiness. African Americans mobilized against the city council's resolution in support of the farm workers, demonstrating racial solidarity with Mexican Americans. This racial alliance was part of a longer tradition of mutual support regarding labor and civil rights activism between the region's two most predominant racial minority groups.[12] External municipal support for the Delano grape strike continued as a contentious issue in local politics through 1969. Tensions heightened when African American Los Angeles city councilman and mayoral candidate Tom Bradley publicly endorsed the Delano grape boycott at a UFW convention in East Los Angeles. The Bakersfield city council passed a resolution condemning Bradley's endorsement and affirmed that

> this Council does not inten[d] to tell Councilman Bradley how to take care of a special situation in Watts. . . . It is important for this Council and the Board of Supervisors and all the people to stand together in opposition to outside influence bent upon courses of action that could be disastrous to all.[13]

Upset at the city council's perceived attack on a rising African American leader, the Bakersfield NAACP (National Association for the Advancement of Colored People) argued that local African Americans supported the grape boycott because in addition to being an issue concerning minority groups, it was "also a moral issue."[14] Local NAACP officials argued that the city council had unfairly and in open bias sided with growers and that their anti-boycott resolution "had an ulterior racial motive. . . . If Mr. Bradley had not been a black man, the resolution would not have been offered."[15] Such support from African Americans advanced racial solidarity with Mexican Americans in the struggle for labor and civil rights. By supporting the UFW, African American activists followed the mandate from the regional and national NAACP leadership, such as West Coast regional director Leonard Carter. The latter had been at the forefront of the NAACP-WC's efforts to encourage the national NAACP body to support the UFW. At the 58th annual NAACP convention in Boston in July 1967, the NAACP offered its first official resolution in support of the UFW.[16] Local NAACP support reflected a larger regional support from African Americans for the UFW, including the Black Panthers of the San Francisco Bay area.[17]

"Hoo-ray Gonzales!": Civil Rights Protest and Grassroots Chicano Politics

Within a context of rural and urban multiracial civil rights reform—marked by continued support for the UFW, protests against police brutality, the expansion of the rural welfare state, and continued antistatist opposition to civil rights— Mexican Americans, African Americans, and their white liberal allies mobilized politically behind local liberal Chicano civil rights leader and educator Ray Gonzales for political office. Gonzales' political approach was complex, ahead of its time, and symbolized the efforts of the liberal left in Kern County in the early 1970s.[18] He was the first Latino assemblyman elected in a majority white conservative city and county. At the time only 8 percent registered Latino voters occupied his district—meaning that Gonzales was elected by a majority white vote.[19]

Gonzales built his public career as an educator and civil rights leader. Having begun his teaching career at Bakersfield College, he completed a doctorate at the

University of Southern California in Latin American Studies and joined the founding faculty at California State College, Bakersfield. Later he served as a founding faculty member of the Chicano Studies program at California State University, Long Beach. In addition to his educational career, he was an integral part of the civic unity movement and helped broker the McGraw Hill media concessions in late 1971—a landmark in the history of Chicano media reform.[20] His 1972 campaign agenda for state assembly included the following political platform: 1) make the tax structure fair, 2) meet changing needs in education, 3) reach full employment, 4) insure the survival of the family farm, 5) obtain the same benefits for farm employees that industrial workers enjoy, 6) stop the pollution of the natural environment, and 7) fill the so-called "generation gap" with trust and reason.[21]

A staunch Democrat, Gonzales' campaign flier declared that "many people believe there is very little difference between the two major [political] parties." As a corrective, Gonzales suggested,

> there is a great deal of difference between the party of Franklin Roosevelt, Harry Truman, and John Kennedy on the one hand and that of Herbert Hoover, Dwight Eisenhower, and Richard Nixon on the other. The . . . fundamental difference is that the Democratic Party feels that it is the duty of government to protect the interest[s] of individual citizens, while the Republican Party feels that it must protect the interests of big business.[22]

Gonzales' criticism of Republicans helped him gain grassroots support for the Democratic Party in an age of growing political cynicism and third party politics, especially among Chicanos—the latter evidenced by the rise of *La Raza Unida* Party.[23] Gonzales stressed to Kern County voters that loyalty to the Democratic Party and its principles benefitted all citizens, including Chicanos.

Despite Gonzales' Democratic partisanship, his candidacy seemed a long shot in conservative Bakersfield. "The State Democratic Party and leadership of the Assembly did not support me when I ran," Gonzales recalled. "They could not see a liberal Chicano Democrat winning against a three-term Republican incumbent."[24] Despite the state party leadership's unenthusiastic response, Gonzales, highly educated, articulate, and a devoted community activist, made political inroads into a historically white conservative district. Historically, the region had a reputation for an independent voting record, writes historian James Gregory.[25] Recalling his early assembly campaign, Gonzales recalled that California senator "Alan Cranston spoke for me. He rarely supported anybody in the [Democratic] primary but he supported me because of a friend we had in common, Fleming Atha. I was a long-shot for the state assembly but he supported me."[26] Atha was active as a member of the California Democratic Council (CDC) and helped organize that group's 1966 annual meeting in Bakersfield.[27] Atha and

Gonzales were also colleagues for several years in the Kern Council for Civic Unity (KCCU). After Gonzales' victory, he established working relationships with California Democratic heavyweights such as U.S. Senators Alan Cranston and John Tunney, as well as labor leader Jack Henning (the latter executive secretary-treasurer of the AFL-CIO)—all of which unsettled Kern County's Republican establishment.

Grassroots mobilization provided a base for Gonzales' assembly election. Bakersfield College Chicano student activist and Viet Nam War veteran Duane Goff helped lead registration of new voters. "I think we registered about 1,100 new Democratic voters," Goff recalled. "I had just finished the semester . . . and wasn't receiving my G.I. Bill during the summer. Ray called me up and asked me to work for his campaign, so I said 'sure.'"[28] Steve Barber, a resident from Taft—a majority white town with a long racist history just southwest of Bakersfield[29]—was put in charge of Gonzales' political campaign. "My campaign office was on the street corner of Kentucky and Baker in East Bakersfield. Steve walked into the office one [summer] day. He was unemployed and recently graduated from college. [He] had read an article about me being active in the ACLU [American Civil Liberties Union], and he had been active in the ACLU, [so] he started volunteering on the campaign. He was one major reason I won. He became my campaign manager and worked for one year for no pay," Gonzales remembered.[30] Once Gonzales was elected, Barber served as his full-time field representative in the assembly district. Barber's tireless efforts and political savvy added clarity to Gonzales' shoestring campaign budget, including the $85 per month rented office space in old town (East) Bakersfield.

Gonzales' assembly campaign hyped partisan differences between Democrats and Republicans, particularly over the issue of campaign financing. White liberals, African Americans, and Chicano Democrats opposed the alliance of big business with the Republican Party.[31] Running a multiracial campaign in the civic unity tradition, Gonzales appealed to Mexican American voters by launching his campaign in the Lamont-Arvin area (a Latino enclave), where over 600 people attended a rally commemorating his bid for the 28th Assembly District seat.[32] Gonzales expressed multiracial appeal to reporters who covered his campaign. "If I'm a crusader, I'm a crusader for human needs. Many are Chicano needs, many are black needs, and many are women's needs—but almost always they are Anglo needs as well," he told reporters.[33] Gonzales' public campaign financing was grassroots in character. Rather than relying on large financial donors to fill his election coffers, as many area Republicans had done before him, Gonzales solicited grassroots contributions.

Such support from below propelled Gonzales in the primary election, helping him oust Democratic city councilman Bob Whittemore in June 1972 by a margin of just 87 votes. The primary race was close, but Gonzales' organizing activities in eastern Kern County (the high-desert area) turned the voting tide in both the primary and later general election. After defeating Whittemore, Republican incumbent Kent Stacey targeted his Democratic opponent. Gonzales faced a potentially insurmountable conservative opponent in Stacey, bankrolled by the Republican establishment. Republicans cast Gonzales as a liberal-radical and political outsider. Gonzales acknowledged his liberalism on civil rights, but denied allegations that he was a far-left liberal. "I'm not that liberal. . . . I guess because I once studied for the priesthood that I'm kind of a Puritan but I'm considered a liberal because of my involvement with civil rights," he told reporters.[34] Such a moderate tone was an effective political statement in a community as religiously cultured as Kern County, yet indicated Gonzales' missionary zeal concerning issues of social justice.[35]

Gonzales' connection to the Chicano youth vote was vital to his election. Young Chicanos brought energy to his campaign regardless of his political inexperience and lack of large financial supporters. At Bakersfield College the annual student-led *Semana de La Raza* festival created a sense of community among young Chicanos, both within the academic setting and larger community. As part of the 1972 celebrations, guest speakers included Dr. Octavio Romano, professor at UC Berkeley and editor of *El Quinto Sol* publications, Margaret Govea, CSO activist and mother of UFW organizer Jessica Govea, and assembly candidate Dr. Ray Gonzales. Gonzales' participation denoted the scope of the Chicano youth movement's interests in union rights, higher education, political empowerment and reform—all under the banner of Chicano civil rights. Beyond the ethnic pride associated with the possibility of electing Kern County's first Latino legislator, the meeting of Chicano youth activists with the electoral process demonstrated a central goal of the Chicano power movement. Accepting an invitation to speak at the *Cinco de Mayo* festival connected Gonzales with his former campus, yet also gained him support from the youth vote.[36] Gonzales' mobilized youth vote campaign even utilized the energies of those not yet old enough to cast a ballot, through door-to-door campaigning. Further gaining support from young Chicanos, Gonzales, a former Marine, spoke out against the Bakersfield city council's use of their public platform to express support for President Richard Nixon's escalation of the war in Viet Nam in 1972. His position was thus in line with the larger sentiments of the Chicano youth power movement, specifically opposition to the Viet Nam War.[37]

The *Bakersfield Californian* endorsed Gonzales for office 1 week before the general election, a key factor in his victory over the Republican incumbent. The editorial endorsement described Stacey as lacking an impressive legislative record. Gonzales was characterized, on the other hand, as an ethnic minority who overcame numerous obstacles to gain his position as a college professor, demonstrating that he was more than qualified for public office. Prior to Stacey's defeat, however, the Republican machine in Bakersfield attempted to smear Gonzales' campaign as a puppet of California's Democratic Party. Fleming Atha, a long-time Anglo Democrat from Bakersfield and treasurer of the Gonzales Committee for the 28th assembly district, challenged a statement made by Republican Bakersfield city councilman Richard Stiern. The councilman suggested publicly that the Gonzales Committee had received $100,000 from the Democratic state assembly caucus committee. Atha countered the charge as grossly inflated, noting that the committee to elect Ray Gonzales received only $500 from the state caucus as aid to register voters. Atha further charged that "big money" corporate interests bankrolled Richard Stiern's "right wing" candidates, not Gonzales.

Atha's criticism of the collusion between monied interests and the political right proved a rallying point for Gonzales as a freshman politician in the California assembly. Once in office Gonzales embraced open transparency and proffered a strong critique of the influence of money in politics.[38] Such outspoken criticism of Sacramento's political culture did not win Gonzales new friends among business interests and legislators, but his position highlighted the role that grassroots organization held in his election. A principled politician, Gonzales was not beholden to special interests, but to the people. Once in office, he adopted a reputation as a political maverick, controlled neither by agribusiness nor the UFW—the latter position unique for a Chicano Democrat in California in the early 1970s.[39] In brief, both UFW and agribusiness loyalties shaped political alliances in California politics after 1965 in complex ways.[40]

Gonzales' rise as a Chicano Democrat raised both ire and hope by unseating an incumbent Republican. The fact that he came from the Central Valley—the land of agribusiness and the UFW—signaled a larger ascendancy of Chicano political power, or so it seemed to many political observers at the time. Gonzales "arrived here [in Sacramento] with more advanced notice than most of the others [15 new assemblymen] and got a lukewarm reception from many of his new colleagues,"[41] the *San Francisco Chronicle* reported. Gonzales would become either the state assembly's new "golden boy" or political pariah. Once in office, Gonzales was a principled opponent of gifts from lobbyists, a political culture practice that, in his mind, showed a character-shortcoming among numerous Sacramento politicians. In addition to opposing lobbyist contributions, Gonzales spoke out against the use of profanity on the assembly floor and made his opposition to these practices known in Sacramento and his home district. These unpopular positions made political waves for the neophyte Chicano assemblyman from Bakersfield. According to one journalist, Gonzales "shocked the legislative establishment" by sending $600 back to a lobbyist with a "No thank you" note attached,[42] showing reporters and his legislative colleagues the freshman legislator's political gravitas on the issue of influence peddling among state capitol lobbyists.

Revising the California state tax code was one of Gonzales' first efforts to follow through on his campaign promises once in office. Gonzales challenged specifically tax loops that benefitted growers and large landholders.[43] Reforming the tax code appealed to urban and rural Chicanos, especially those swayed by political rhetoric critical of agriculture elites who benefitted from public policies at the expense of the poor. Criticism of the Williamson Act commanded Gonzales' attention. This legislation, (known as the California Land Conservation Act) authored by Kern County Democratic assemblyman John Williamson in 1965, gave tax breaks to large landowners who declared to keep land as open space in an effort to prevent suburban sprawl. Williamson Act supporters and industry sympathizers argued that growers and large landowners needed large tax breaks in order to keep agrarian (non-urban land) productive and financially competitive. The Williamson Act rationalized that "farmland under contract [would] . . . be assessed on the basis of its actual income rather than on the market value." Kern County landowners signed up in droves, commanding 1.4 million acres out of a statewide allocation of 11 million acres. The state was obliged under this legislation to backfill counties for the loss of tax revenues, but did not acknowledge its financial commitment to counties until the early 1970s.[44] Gonzales criticized the Williamson Act on the basis that the law lowered potential tax revenues for Kern County. Of all California counties at the time, Kern County had the most land benefitting from lower taxes under this legislation.

To the chagrin of the Kern County board of supervisors, Gonzales claimed before "the Assembly Select Committee on Open Space Lands that the law annually cost the county $10 million in lost revenue."[45] Gonzales opposed the Williamson Act as part of his campaign mandate to create a more fair and balanced tax code that improved public expenditure such as education. Gonzales argued that "in Los Angeles County where 'urban sprawl' is a fact and measures should be taken to deter this force, the Williamson Act has not been implemented at all. In Kern County where there is little fear of 'urban sprawl,' the law has been enacted to the fullest, if not abused."[46] Corporate greed under the Williamson Act limited available financial resources for public education, Gonzales pressed. The largest recipients of tax breaks under the Williamson Act included "Tenneco West, Tejon Ranch Company, [and] Buena Vista Ranch," all large-scale companies that collectively illustrated to Gonzales that the Williamson Act in its present form was "a sham and a fraud."[47] Such political posturing appealed to liberal Democrats, particularly the notion that agribusiness benefitted disproportionately under a corporate welfare state. The latter political trend explained, in part, the shift of the valley's population away from its New Deal Democrat origins to a Republican majority. Civil rights era politics and activism fomented a rightward shift in Kern County politics, particularly concerning defense of agricultural subsidies.

African Americans and Mexican Americans found unity on other fronts during Gonzales' assembly tenure. In February 1974, tempers flared over the naming of the Holloway-Gonzales Library in Bakersfield's impoverished southeast corridor. The controversy represented an opportunity for civic agreement between Chicanos and African Americans, evidenced by the selection of names (Raymond Gonzales and Ruth Love Holloway) for the new southeast Bakersfield public library. Fifth district supervisor John Mitchell opposed naming the library after Gonzales and Holloway, despite wide support for naming the library in honor of the two prominent racial minority educators.[48] Mitchell especially raised minority ire by asserting publicly at a board meeting, "Who are Holloway and

---

Gonzales?" Many argued the supervisor's commentary to be disrespectful. Dr. Ruth Love Holloway was a native southeast Bakersfield resident and at the time the U.S. Director of the "Right to Read" program, in addition to being a former Oakland School District superintendent. Dr. Raymond Gonzales was also an area resident, incumbent state assemblyman for the district, and the only member of the California assembly with a doctorate. Gonzales had also recently been appointed as chairman of the Assembly Education Committee by Speaker Leo McCarthy, the first freshman ever appointed to the position.[49] "It is comforting to know that I have such high quality representation to my [local] government," read one *Bakersfield Californian* editorial letter sarcastically following Mitchell's comments.[50] The controversy over the naming of the Holloway-Gonzales Library was especially partisan since Gonzales was up for re-election that year, and local Republicans were committed toward ousting the Chicano incumbent.[51]

Gonzales and the Divisive Politics of Farm Labor Legislation

Maintaining a political base that reflected a united constituency proved more difficult for Gonzales during his re-election campaign, particularly as African American and Mexican American racial solidarity encountered new challenges. In addition, antistatist racial conservatives seized political opportunities opened by the fracturing of racial coalitions to compound Gonzales' 1974 re-election campaign. No more clearly was this political precariousness demonstrated than in the controversy within the California assembly's Chicano political caucus regarding farm worker legislation backed by the UFW in 1974. The southern California Chicano caucus was not as electorally impacted in their home districts as Gonzales was by support for UFW-backed legislation. Furthermore, the civic unity that characterized Gonzales' 1972 campaign, with solid alliances between Chicanos, African Americans, and white liberals, was not replicated to the same degree in 1974. Part of this political fracturing within the Democratic base was due to controversy over Gonzales' position on farm labor legislation, as well as the racial politics put forth successfully by Republicans in 1974.

The emergence of five Chicano California assemblymen in 1972 marked an ascendancy of growing Chicano political power in Sacramento. Chicano voters mobilized in 1972 to defeat Proposition 22 (Prop 22). That campaign helped contribute to the election of Ray Gonzales, Joseph Montoya, and Richard Alatorre to the California assembly—increasing the percentage of Mexican Americans in the assembly by 150 percent.[52] The grower-sponsored Prop 22 called for banning secondary boycotts by labor unions, a direct attack on the UFW and its use of the secondary boycott, given the union's exclusion from the National Labor Relations Act. Labor scholar and activist Randy Shaw notes that "Proposition 22 . . . include[ed] the standard provisions forbidding boycotts and strikes and add[ed] . . . extreme provisions . . . barring farm worker unions from bargaining on work rules."[53] Gonzales opposed the proposition on the grounds that he would champion equal rights for farm workers that paralleled labor rights enjoyed by industrial workers.[54] The working relationship of the UFW to the Chicano political caucus was paramount to the future of Chicano politics in Los Angeles and southern California. In his speeches, assemblyman Richard Alatorre, who championed UFW-sponsored farm labor legislation in the assembly, frequently invoked *la causa* as critical when reviewing the progress Mexican Americans had made as a racial group since World War II.[55] Yet, other caucus members were free from the hostility Gonzales faced as a Kern County legislative representative. Gonzales' Central Valley constituency was more racially divided between white, Latino, and African American than in the districts of his Chicano caucus colleagues. The UFW levied pressure on the Chicano caucus to support UFW-sponsored legislation—a more politically feasible position for Los Angeles and southern California caucus members given their greater proportion of Latino voters and the distance from ground-zero of *la huelga*. For Gonzales, the proximity of this geopolitical reality would deal him a political deathblow.

Prior to his confrontation with the UFW over farm labor legislation, Gonzales had articulated publicly the historical significance of farm workers to California agriculture. In a 1973 *Sacramento Bee* editorial, Gonzales opined

> one segment in the history of California agriculture that traditionally has been overlooked has been the farm labor force. It is this failure of recognition which has led to many of the agricultural disputes that have plagued the industry in the past.[56]

Such recognition of farm workers from both an academic and political perspective was significant, especially as Gonzales clamored for a farm labor bill in Sacramento that same year. His argument before the voting public and his legislative colleagues rested upon the idea that farm workers had built the legacy of California's agricultural success for over a century. Gonzales reasoned that this alone should have prompted the legislature to broker a reasonable bill to end the conflict in the fields. In 1973, rather than renewing a majority of UFW contracts, growers instead signed "sweetheart contracts" with the Teamsters union, creating fierce competition between the UFW and Teamsters over the future unionization of farm workers and contempt for support of UFW boycotts.

Gonzales' tensions with organized labor were visible soon after taking office when he experienced discord from some segments of Kern County's labor movement. In January 1973, only weeks after being in office, Mel Rubin, president of the Kern, Inyo, and Mono Counties Central Labor Council (CLC-AFL-CIO), pressed Gonzales to fulfill his campaign promises to the labor movement. Rubin specifically wanted Gonzales to appoint two labor members (of the five Gonzales could appoint) to the state Democratic Central Committee. Gonzales informed Rubin that he wanted to appoint a black, a Latino/a, a woman, and a youth representative in light of Rubin's request that he select two names from a list given by Rubin himself. Gonzales preferred instead to select from a list of names submitted to him from the general Kern County labor council. Rubin interpreted this move as the Chicano politician working to fragment organized labor.[57] "Mel was just trying to let me know who was boss," Gonzales later mused.[58]

The potential to pass farm labor legislation, however, influenced Gonzales' political positioning as both an assembly candidate and upon assuming office. For Chicanos running for state assembly, the UFW held major influence in determining political rhetoric, a liberty Gonzales was not afforded given the conservative nature of Kern County politics. If Gonzales was to have a future as a Democratic legislator in Kern County, he needed to have the support of the UFW, but appear not entirely beholden to the demands of the predominantly Mexican-American labor union. In a letter to Gonzales in August 1972 during the assembly campaign season, Los Angeles assembly candidate and future Chicano caucus member Art Torres informed Gonzales that he supported the UFW and the AFL-CIO position that opposed federal regulation of farm workers parallel to "the National Labor Relations Act [NLRA], as amended by Taft-Hartley."[59] If farm workers were brought under the NLRA, the secondary boycott, the UFW's principal weapon against growers, would have become illegal under labor law. Torres visited candidate Gonzales' headquarters in Bakersfield to discuss potential farm labor legislation. At the meeting, Gonzales stressed the nature of Kern County politics to the Los Angeles candidate. Following their meeting, Gonzales would write to Torres, "You realize of course that running a political campaign in con-servative Kern County is difficult to begin with for any candidate, and more so for a liberal minority candidate."[60] While Torres ultimately viewed support for UFW-sponsored legislation as a litmus test for Chicano candidates, albeit with little political fallout for himself, Gonzales was skeptical of unbridled support for a farm labor bill that did not address the issue of the secondary boycott in order to appeal to a major segment of his Kern County constituents.

Among Gonzales' other key constituents, however, was César Chávez. Weeks after Gonzales' 1972 election victory, the assemblyman contacted César Chávez to discuss his relationship with the UFW. Explaining his reasoning for comments made regarding the ongoing UFW lettuce boycott, Gonzales wrote,

> I had to make a choice as to either being a leader in the boycott drive or an effective legislator in Sacramento. I do not feel that the two things are compatible here in Kern County. I am sure you know that the boycott will not be won in our area; it will be won out-of-county perhaps even out-of-state. To the residents of this county this is an emotional issue. I prefer to deal in realities.[61]

Such brash statements from Gonzales won him no favors at UFW headquarters. UFW officials drafted a response. "Consider the precepts which formed a major part of your campaign," a UFW staffer wrote to the assemblyman. The UFW then encouraged Gonzales to bring a lettuce boycott resolution before the California legislature.[62] Gonzales declined.

Despite early grumblings with the UFW that he would be an independent Democrat in the assembly, Gonzales tried to submit legislation in 1973 to solve the farm labor problem that existed in his district. In drafting legislation, Gonzales walked a fine line between supporting farm workers and trying to appear an impartial public servant supportive of labor rights. Gonzales declared to his supporters:

> Our most immediate priority is to put an end to the violence in the fields. [O]nly when men and women meet together as brothers and sisters with a commitment to solving mutual problems through rational deliberations and just compromises can true progress be made.[63]

Local journalists in Bakersfield kept pressure on Gonzales to push a farm labor bill representative of all his constituents in Bakersfield and Kern County. "Possibly the single most important vote in the eyes of Kern County residents couldn't be cast this year because the legislature . . . failed again to bring the issue of farm labor legislation to the floor of either house," wrote Bakersfield journalist Mary K. Shell.[64] With political pressure at home to solve the farm labor crisis, Gonzales wrote to Chávez in July 1973 proposing a temporary solution while legislation pended deliberation in the assembly. "Much has been said by many about the necessity and propriety of holding elections as the only reasonable means to settle the current conflict. Yet no one has stepped forward to initiate any action toward this end. . . . I am willing to establish a panel of persons . . . for the purpose of holding elections to determine which union a particular grower's employees sought to represent them. . . . This proposal would be a one-time only measure [sic]."[65] Gonzales' proposal, however, gained no traction with the UFW. The union focused on mobilizing other members of the Chicano political caucus and the California assembly toward support of a farm labor bill fully couched in terms set by the union. Gonzales recalled telling Chávez "no union can do that [the secondary boycott]. I told César you don't need the law to do that, just do it. They didn't care about me. César had one issue and the union was it."[66] The lack of support for Gonzales' reelection campaign from the UFW hindered the incumbent Democrat's grassroots support that had helped elect him in 1972. Gonzales' position on the farm labor bill resembled, moreover, especially to young Chicano and Chicana voters, calls from the Kern County Farm Bureau to bring farm workers under the National Labor Relations Act (NLRA)—its key provision, of course, outlawing the secondary boycott—the UFW's principal weapon to fight growers.[67]

Conflict continued to emerge between Richard Alatorre, César Chávez, and Ray Gonzales over the crafting of farm labor legislation in 1974. The conflict centered around Alatorre's sponsorship of assembly bill 3370 (AB 3370). Gonzales proposed amendments to Alatorre's bill that, in his estimation, would have made the measure more palpable to Kern County voters. Gonzales recalled,

> I knew the bill [AB 3370] was not going anywhere, but as a show of my commitment to the cause of the workers, I wanted to vote for it. But I had a problem with it, which was the use of the secondary boycott. That is why I offered my amendment. I figured if I could get my amendment in, I would vote for the bill, even if it cost me.[68]

As written, AB 3370 set up a three-man commission to supervise elections and also allowed secondary boycotts, recognitional strikes, and challenges to existing contracts—all provisions that UFW staffers knew opponents would find uncompromising and too far reaching.[69] The main point of debate between Gonzales and the Chicano political caucus surfaced over the prohibition of secondary boycotts by a union that had lost a certification election.[70] The latter was a concern for the UFW since the Teamsters' union was competing with UFW organizers in the field—often using violent tactics to intimidate workers to not support the UFW boycott and strike. Giving up the boycott to legislation, moreover, was not an option according to the UFW. Chávez was skeptical that potential farm labor legislation might ultimately ban the secondary boycott. The UFW leader in fact only supported farm labor legislation as a compromise to the United Auto Workers and that union's $1.7 million donation to the UFW.[71] In 1974, for example, the UFW had embraced the larger tenets of the American labor movement's anti-immigrant position through its "Campaign against Illegals," the latter César Chávez argued as "more important than the strike, second only to the boycott."[72]

Although the UFW pushed AB 3370 hard in Sacramento, union organizers did not expect AB 3370 to ever become law. Their strategy ultimately aimed to pressure a state constitutional amendment in 1976 that was "far more preferable to a law that [potentially] could be eroded by future legislators."[73] Nevertheless, as AB 3370 became a major political campaign issue in 1974, legislators in Sacramento threatened "to water-down the measure on the Assembly floor."[74] Gonzales was chief among Democratic legislators who argued that AB 3370 should contain an amendment prohibiting secondary boycotts, identical to the secondary boycott provision contained under the NLRA—thus keeping his campaign promise to make farm workers' rights parallel to New Deal era protective legislation for industrial workers. To Chávez and UFW attorneys, note UFW chroniclers Susan Ferris and Ricardo Sandoval, any potential farm labor bill had to

> preserve the farmworkers' right to secondary boycotts. Setting up picket lines in front of grocery store chains that sold boycotted products . . . was the union's only truly effective tool against growers who refused to negotiate contracts,[75]

thus positioning the union directly against the Chicano assembly candidate they had supported in 1972.

The UFW and Alatorre announced they would drop sponsorship of AB 3370 if Gonzales' amendment against the secondary boycott was included. Later in the legislative session, when AB 3370 was called for a vote, many Democrats who initially supported Gonzales' amendment changed position. Confounded by what was suddenly happening on the assembly floor, Gonzales recalled hearing from his Democratic colleague and San Francisco Bay area assemblyman Dan Boatwright, who sat directly in front of him, "Ray, Jack Henning called me and said that if I supported your amendment, he would cut off my labor money. What should I do, Ray?" In reply, Gonzales told him, "Dan, just save your ass!"[76] To Gonzales, the political posturing of Alatorre and other Democrats critical of amending AB 3370 showed that ultimately they were not interested in enacting "secret ballot" elections for farm workers, but rather maintaining their own political "clout" in California's agricultural fields and assembly districts, particularly since there was no expectation that AB 3370 would ever pass. "It [the farm labor bill] was all tied up with gubernatorial politics and union power," Gonzales later lamented. "No one was really concerned about the needs of farm workers," and in Gonzales' case, helping maintain the incumbent Chicano Democrat's chance for re-election.[77]

The *Bakersfield Californian* condemned César Chávez, the UFW, and the fate of AB 3370. The *Californian* portrayed Gonzales favorably, however, noting that he voted against AB 3370 given that his amendments were not included in the final draft voted on by the legislature. Legislators "succumbed to extremely heavy lobbying . . . [,] supporters of this bill were not the least bit interested in the farm worker,"[78] Gonzales told reporters. The assemblyman's political fortunes clearly hinged on his ability to rationalize to Kern County voters that he championed farm labor legislation that would solve sooner, rather than later, Kern County's agriculture labor crisis.

Despite his efforts to pass farm labor legislation respective of his diverse Kern County constituents, Gonzales' position on farm labor legislation became a valuable campaign issue for his 1974 Republican opponent, Bill Thomas. "Bill Thomas speaks *YOUR* kind of government!" read one Republican campaign advertisement.[79] Portraying Gonzales as a far-left supporter of labor and civil rights, the Republican challenger favored farm worker legislation friendly to growers, particularly legislation that would prevent a labor strike at harvest time. Thomas argued further that Gonzales had clearly failed to spearhead grower interests in the state assembly.[80] As the political mean season heated up in June 1974, two major issues defined the Republican campaign against Gonzales: 1) Gonzales' moral conscience vote against the death penalty in 1973 (Gonzales was an ardent Catholic and one-time seminarian), and 2) Gonzales' alleged silence on farm labor legislation, particularly the outlawing of secondary boycotts. At the time of his candidacy for state assembly, Thomas was a political science professor at Bakersfield

College and Gonzales' former colleague. Recalling the growing bitterness between
Thomas and himself over the Republican's political tactics, Gonzales lamented,

> Bill Thomas and I were friends. . . . Our wives exchanged maternity clothes.
> We played handball. We were hired in the same year [at Bakersfield College].
> He was a Republican but always considered himself a moderate. He . . .
> looked down on the Bakersfield/Kern County Republicans as yokels. He
> was smarter than they were. He supported me when I ran the first time
> [and] gave me a contribution under the table. We were neighbors [and]
> wanted to come up with a busing plan that would be acceptable, because
> federal law had come in and school districts were resisting. Bill Thomas
> came up with a busing plan and gave it to us, [the Kern Council for Civic
> Unity], but told us not to put his name on it. He did not want to be identified
> with it because he had become a member of the Republican Central
> Committee. Thomas was not a racist or a bigot but there were Republicans
> who were. I was getting ready to run for re-election and he was telling
> me you're in good shape and we can't get anyone to run against you, you're
> too strong. He was going to run against Walter Stiern in the state Senate.
> Ken Maddy and the Republican leadership in the assembly got in contact
> with him [and] told him if he ran against Stiern he was on his own. But
> if he ran against me, they would bankroll him. Steve Barber called me and
> told me Bill Thomas filed. I called Thomas and I asked him "what's going
> on?" He told me the story [and] then he said "I guess I never realized how
> ambitious I really [am]." He tells me we can run a classic campaign, two
> college professors, talk to the issues, and keep it high level. I told him "Bill,
> I'm the incumbent, a strong incumbent, you said so yourself. I know that
> in order for you to beat me, you have to come at me with a claw hammer,
> how can I look at you and say you're my friend and we're running for the
> same office. And if you're willing to do that how can I say this is my friend
> Bill?" I never talked to him again after that [sic].[81]

   Thomas soon abandoned his friendship with Gonzales in pursuit of a more
polarized discursive political campaign against the incumbent Democrat. "The
time to begin the dialogue is now. . . . Gonzales has been conspicuously quiet as
to where he stands on farm labor issues vital to the people of Kern County,"
Thomas remarked publicly.[82] Gonzales responded quickly to Thomas' challenge.
The incumbent Democrat encouraged a debate to occur later in the election
cycle as he was busy in Sacramento maintaining his voting record. Gonzales'
commitment to legislative purpose, however, left open the public forum to Thomas
and local Republicans to control the political dialogue against his incumbency.
Gonzales' multiracial base moreover had splintered by late 1973 over farm labor
legislation. Competition over federally subsidized rural health care dollars between
African Americans and Mexican Americans, in addition to Gonzales' controversial

conscience vote against the death penalty, further undermined his re-election campaign. Thomas took political advantage of both Gonzales' coalition fracturing and the space it opened to appeal to Kern County's "law and order" voters surrounding the county's overwhelming support for the death penalty. "Thomas' campaign was very racial. He ran pictures of me with [César] Chávez and his ads would say 'elect one of us,'"[83] Gonzales later recalled of his Republican opponent's strategy. Thomas' challenge to his former friend and colleague would be remembered as "a move that established Thomas' reputation for ruthlessness and arrogance," wrote *Bakersfield Californian* columnist Vic Pollard in 2005.[84]

Following defeat by his Republican challenger, on his last day as a California assemblyman, Gonzales wrote a letter to César Chávez. His letter reflected an assessment on the future of farm labor legislation in the California legislature, as well as the future of the UFW in Kern County:

> The majority of Chicano farm laborers are not impressed with your operation. . . . They are either tired of the struggle or disillusioned with the entire movement. . . . They are enraged by the violent and insulting tactics employed by some of your supporters. . . . There is a growing resentment toward the union and I feel it stems from the poor public relations policy carried out by your union officials. . . . In your effort to carry on your boycott at the national and international levels you have lost contact with your true constituency. . . . Only Jack Henning's pressure and money, and the fact that it was an election year got you the 41 labor votes from the Democrats [for AB 3370]. . . . Unless you begin to mend your fences with a majority of Mexican American farmworkers you will not be winning elections when and if a farm labor bill is passed. . . . I hope I have not offended you again with these candid remarks. I only make them because, contrary to the belief of some of your volunteers, I am concerned about the destiny of farm workers in this country. I worked in the Delano grape fields before most of them had ever heard of the place. . . . The growers . . . blinded by their own greed, bigotry, and disgust for your movement . . . will never trust a Chicano.[85]

Gonzales' words proved prophetic in light of the troubles the UFW later encountered winning elections in the field following passage of the Agricultural Labor Relations Act in 1975. Additionally, as recent UFW historians have documented, dramatic internal conflicts within the UFW's rank-and-file leadership in the late 1970s ultimately undermined the union's success at organizing farm workers.[86]

Conclusion

The election loss of Ray Gonzales to Bill Thomas for the California assembly in 1974 marked a turning point in the shifting fortunes of grassroots political action among multiracial liberal coalition groups in Bakersfield and Kern County. Multiracial alliances from below had propelled Gonzales from academia to the political arena in 1972. He drew upon the multiracial heritage of the civic unity movement[87] and, at the same time, from the growing political importance of young Chicanos and Chicanas during the heyday of the Chicano power movement. Holding together racial alliances, however, proved untenable for the Chicano Democrat in conservative Kern County. Moreover, the controversy surrounding UFW-sponsored farm labor legislation guaranteeing the preservation of the secondary boycott was equally divisive among Gonzales' core constituents. In the end, conservative political mobilization for the Bill Thomas campaign unseated the Chicano Democrat, eclipsing the political progress that grassroots multiracial coalitions had made in Kern County up until this point in California's Central Valley. For Thomas, 1974 marked the beginning of a remarkable career as a Bakersfield Republican legislator, leading eventually to his chairmanship of the House Ways and Means Committee until his retirement from Congress in 2007.

Following election defeat, Ray Gonzales worked in Governor Jerry Brown's administration and was appointed to the Public Employment Relations Board, adjudicating labor disputes between teachers, state employees, and management, followed by federal service in the diplomatic corps in Latin America.[88] He later taught political science at CSU Monterey Bay until retirement. He also would run unsuccessfully for Kern County supervisor against the former *Bakersfield Californian* reporter (who covered much of Gonzales' tenure as a state assembly-man) and Republican Mary K. Shell. Despite his political misfortunes, Gonzales maintained a steadfast commitment toward civil rights and political empowerment, particularly among Latinos. His work in the 1990 redistricting efforts in southeast Bakersfield proved to be a watershed in helping establish a Latino seat for Kern County's growing Latino population—at the supervisorial, as well as state assembly, senate, and U.S. Congressional levels.

Yet, the multiracial grassroots coalition-building that characterized his 1972 campaign has not been replicated in Kern County Latino politics. Corporations have played a more significant role in financing candidates, including the evolution of the UFW from a grassroots union into what journalist Miriam Pawel has described as an organization mastering the "art of cashing in on Latino political power [,] . . . parlaying the memory of César Chávez into millions of dollars in public and private donations."[89] Pawel's declension narrative of the UFW legacy is not alone. Numerous books have emerged highly critical of the UFW. This chapter reiterates, however, that in an age of historical narratives geared toward chronicling the 50-year anniversary of *la huelga*, it is vitally important to explore the political dynamics of historical grassroots civil rights organizing beyond the fields. Doing so more fully demonstrates the strategic historical limitations of farm worker organizing in championing the broad scope of civil rights reform and political empowerment in conservative Bakersfield and Kern County among the region's historic racial minority groups, specifically, Mexican Americans.

Notes

1   "Hoo-ray Gonzales" was the title of Ray Gonzales' 1972 campaign button for the California assembly.
2   Raymond Gonzales, "Will Parra-Florez Assembly Race Turn Into the Family Feud Part II," *La Voz de Kern*, 2010.
3   Maureen McCloud, "The Kern Brand of Politics—Conservative, Populist, Humorless," *California Journal*, July 9, 1978.
4   For an exploration of these issues beyond the scope of this chapter, see Oliver A. Rosales, "'Mississippi West': Race, Politics, and Civil Rights in California's Central Valley, 1947–1984" (Ph.D. diss., University of California, Santa Barbara, 2012).
5   On recent UFW historiography, see Miriam Pawel, *The Union of Their Dreams: Power, Hope, and Struggle in César Chávez's Farm Worker Movement* (New York: Bloomsbury, 2009); Randy Shaw, *Beyond the Fields: César Chávez, the UFW, and the Struggle for Social Justice in the 21st Century* (Berkeley: University of California Press, 2008); Frank Bardacke, *Trampling Out the Vintage: César Chávez and the Two Souls of the United Farm Workers* (London: Verso, 2011); Todd Holmes, "The Economic Roots of Reaganism: Corporate Conservatives, Political Economy, and the United Farm Workers Movement, 1965–1970," *Western Historical Quarterly* Vol. XLI, No. 1 (Spring 2010): 55–80; Matt García, *From the Jaws of Victory: The Triumph and Tragedy of César Chávez and the Farm Worker Movement* (Berkeley: University of California Press, 2012); and Lauren Araiza, *To March for Others: The Black Freedom Struggle and the United Farm Workers* (Philadelphia: University of Pennsylvania Press, 2013).
6   "Resolution 87–68," Resolutions of the Bakersfield City Council, September 16, 1968, www.bakersfieldcity.us/administration/citymanager/cityclerk/city_records.html, hereafter BCCM, accessed February 10, 2011.
7   "Statement of César Estrada Chávez, director, UFWC AFL-CIO," Transcript of Public Hearing, October 1, 1969 (available at farmworkermovement.org).
8   For an excellent overview of the historical development of valley towns in Central California concerning tensions between growers and labor, see Devra Weber, *Dark Sweat, White Gold* (Berkeley: University of California Press, 1994), 17–47.
9   Marshall Ganz interview by Leroy Chatfield, 2009, Oral History, Farmworker Movement Documentation Project, http://farmworkermovement.com/medias/oral-history, accessed February 18, 2014.
10 Ibid.
11 On Jessica Govea, see Gloria Alday, "Organizing a Movement: Jessica Govea—Chicana, Feminist & Labor Organizer" (Undergraduate Honors Thesis, Yale College, 2007). I thank CSO Project director Gretchen Laue for bringing this source to my attention.
12 On the role of Filipinos in the farm labor movement, see Philip Vera Cruz, *Philip Vera Cruz: A Personal History of Filipino Immigrants and the Farmworkers Movement* (Los Angeles: UCLA Labor Center, Institute of Industrial Relations & UCLA Asian American Studies Center, 1992).
13 Minutes of the Bakersfield City Council, April 28, 1969, BCCM, accessed July 18, 2010.
14 Ibid.
15 Ibid.
16 Lauren Ariaza, "For Freedom of Other Men: Civil Rights, Black Power, and the United Farm Workers, 1965–1973" (PhD diss., University of California, Berkeley, 2006), 59.
17 Ibid.
18 On contemporary politics in Kern County, see Steve Singiser, "Forget Mark Sanford: Here is a special election with real lessons for 2014," *Daily Kos Elections*,

http://cached.newslookup.com/cached.php?ref_id=93&siteid=2089&id=2154630&t
=1370221756, accessed June 18, 2013.
19   Statement by Raymond Gonzales, Californian Radio, September 13, 2011,
www.bakersfield.com/CalifornianRadio/x322743277/Californian-Radio-Sept-13-
2011, accessed June 18, 2013.
20   On the Chicano fair media movement, see Rosales, "Mississippi West," 121–190.
21   1972 Campaign Flyer, P1010543, Book 1, Ray Gonzales Collection, hereafter RGC
(in author's possession).
22   "Brochure on bio of Ray Gonzales," P1010546-47, Book 1, RGC.
23   See for example Armando Navarro, *La Raza Unida Party: A Chicano Challenge to the
US Two-Party Dictatorship* (Philadelphia: Temple University Press, 2000).
24   Raymond Gonzales, email correspondence to author, October 5, 2011.
25   See James Gregory, *The Southern Diaspora: How the Great Migrations of Black and White
Southerners Transformed America* (Chapel Hill: University of North Carolina Press, 2005),
286–290.
26   Ray Gonzales, interview by Oliver Rosales, 2009.
27   "The 14th annual convention of the California Democratic Council," Box 31, Folder
10, California Democratic Council Records, Southern California Library, Los Angeles,
California.
28   Duane Goff, interview by Oliver Rosales, March 2010.
29   On white supremacy and the Ku Klux Klan in Taft, see Edward Humes, *Mean Justice*
(New York: Simon & Shuster, 1999); Rick Wartzman, *Obscene In the Extreme: The
Burning and Banning of John Steinbeck's The Grapes of Wrath* (New York: Public Affairs,
2008); Alicia Rodríguez, "The Kern County Klan Local KKK members, including
Bakersfield's police chief, were outed 90 years ago," *Bakersfield Californian*, May 7,
2012.
30   Gonzales interview, 2009.
31   Ray Gonzales, political campaign flier, P1010546, Book 1, RGC.
32   "Ray Gonzales opens campaign," *La Voz*, August 10, 1972, P1010549, Book 1, RGC.
33   "Ray Gonzales reviews busy first year in state assembly," P1010785, Book 2, RGC.
34   "Ray Gonzales spends busy day stumping," P1010578, Book 1, RGC. Kern County
Democrats still echo Gonzales' conservatism as a Democrat, appropriating the term
"Valleycrat" to describe their brand of pragmatic politics. See "'First Look': Leticia
Perez emphasizes practical approach to issues," *Bakersfield Californian*, June 4, 2013,
www.bakersfieldcalifornian.com/local/x1047453917/First-Look-Leticia-Perez-
emphasizes-practical-approach-to-issues, accessed June 18, 2013.
35   Although there needs to be more work done on the historic religiosity of California's
Central Valley residents, for a useful introduction on the impact of southern migration
to the American West in terms of religiosity, see Gregory, *The Southern Diaspora*,
197–235.
36   "East Students to Join in Celebrating Cinco de Mayo," P1010516, Book 1, RGC.
37   "He feels council acted out of turn," P1010575, Book 1, RGC on Chicano opposition
to the war in Vietnam, see Lorena Oropeza, *¡Raza Si, Guerra No! Chicano Protest and
Patriotism in the Vietnam War Era* (Berkeley: University of California Press, 2005).
38   "Gonzales Campaign," P1010574, Book 1, RGC.
39   "Blowing the Whistle: Assemblyman Fights System," P1010573, Book 1, RGC.
40   See Holmes, "The Economic Roots of Reaganism: Corporate Conservatives, Political
Economy, and the United Farm Workers Movement, 1965–1970."
41   "More tolerant of its shortcomings: Gonzales mellows after year in Legislature,"
P1010774, Book 2, RGC.
42   "Foe of Cussing and Gratuities: A maverick legislator," *San Francisco Chronicle*, March
12, 1973, P1010607, Book 1, RGC.
43   "Gonzales Assails Williamson Act," P1010554, Book 1, RGC.

44 "Ag preserves: Need or sham?," P1010720, Book 2, RGC.
45 "Gonzales asked to clarify 'tax fraud,'" P1010517, Book 1, RGC.
46 "Dr. Gonzales scores open space act," P1010544, Book 1, RGC.
47 Mary K. Shell, "Nothing but a 'Sham and Fraud,'" *Bakersfield Californian*, April 1, 1973.
48 "Tempers flare over name for library," P1010533, Book 1, RGC.
49 Raymond Gonzales, email correspondence to author, October 5, 2011.
50 "Letter to the editor," P1010733, Book 2, RGC.
51 "Editorial: Let citizens decide," P1010735, Book 2, RGC.
52 Herman Sillas, "Mexican-Americans and the Political Mainstream," *Los Angeles Times*, November 22, 1972.
53 Shaw, *Beyond the Fields*, 151.
54 "Candidates booed, grilled," P1010569, Book 1, RGC.
55 Various documents from the Richard Alatorre collection demonstrate this tendency of Alatorre during speaking engagements. See for example Statements and Speeches 1973–74, Box 6, Folder 4, Richard Alatorre Collection, John F. Kennedy Memorial Library, California State University, Los Angeles.
56 "The California Farmworker: Forgotten man in history of agribusiness," *The Sacramento Bee*, April 22, 1973, P1010616, Book 1, RGC.
57 Raymond Gonzales, email correspondence to author, October 5, 2011.
58 Ibid.
59 Art Torres to Raymond Gonzales, August 16, 1973, Box 13, Folder 28, UFW Administration Files, United Farm Workers Organizing Committee, Archives of Urban and Labor Affairs, Wayne State University, hereafter ULA-WSU.
60 Raymond Gonzales to Art Torres, August 9, 1972, Box 13, Folder 28, UFW Administration Files, ULA-WSU.
61 Ray Gonzales to César Chávez, November 25, 1972, Box 13, Folder 28, UFW Administration Files, ULA-WSU.
62 César Chávez to Ray Gonzales, November 30, 1972, Box 13, Folder 28, UFW Administration Files, ULA-WSU.
63 "The Gonzales Report," P1010666, Book 1, RGC.
64 "How our very own legislators voted," P1010719, Book 2, RGC.
65 Ray Gonzales to César Chávez, July 27, 1973, Box 3, Folder 34, UFW Work Department, United Farm Workers Organizing Committee, Archives of Urban and Labor Affairs, Wayne State University.
66 Gonzales interview, 2009.
67 Ernest Gallo to William Ketchum, June 27, 1974; Fred L. Starrh to John Tunney, May 8, 1974, Unions, William Ketchum Papers, California State University, Bakersfield, Walter Stiern Library.
68 Ray Gonzales, email correspondence to author, October 20, 2011.
69 Jerry Gillam, "Assembly OKs Secret Farm Ballot Measure," *Los Angeles Times*, August 20, 1974.
70 Ibid.
71 See Pawel, *The Union of their Dreams*, 147.
72 Quoted in Bardacke, *Trampling Out the Vintage*, 488.
73 Pawel, *The Union of their Dreams*, 149.
74 Ibid., 148.
75 Susan Ferris and Ricardo Sandoval, *The Fight in the Fields: César Chávez and the Farmworkers Movement* (New York: Hancourt Brace, 1997), 197.
76 Gonzales interview, 2009.
77 Ibid.
78 "Editorial: The workers are ignored," P1010725, Book 2, RGC.
79 "[Ad] Compare the Issues [with Thomas]," P1010618, Book 1, RGC.

80   "Thomas raps Gonzales for farm labor bill role," P1010724, Book 2, RGC.
81   Gonzales interview, May 11, 2009.
82   "Candidate Thomas asks Gonzales to debate now," P1010814, Book 2, RGC.
83   Gonzales interview, 2009.
84   Vic Pollard, "Kern's Mercurial Mastermind: Bill Thomas (R-CA) will leave indelible mark," *Bakersfield Californian*, October 30, 2005.
85   Ray Gonzales to César Chávez, December 1, 1974, Box 45, Folder 28, UFW Office of President, ULA-WSU.
86   On the decline of the UFW see Burdacke, *Trampling Out the Vintage*; Pawel, *The Union of their Dreams*; Shaw, *Beyond the Fields*; and Garcia, *From the Jaws of Victory*.
87   On the civic unity movement in California, see Mark Brilliant, *The Color of America Has Changed: How Racial Diversity Shaped Civil Rights Reform in California, 1941–1978* (New York: Oxford University Press, 2010); and Shana Bernstein, *Bridges of Reform: Interracial Civil Rights Activism in Twentieth-Century Los Angeles* (New York: Oxford University Press, 2011).
88   Raymond Gonzales, email correspondence to author, October 5, 2011.
89   Pawel, *The Union of Their Dreams*, 329.

4

ALICIA ESCALANTE, THE CHICANA WELFARE RIGHTS ORGANIZATION, AND THE CHICANO MOVEMENT

Rosie C. Bermúdez

> I have experienced the life of a welfare recipient, I have seen what it can do to people. This has inspired me to do something about it. There came the day over 5 years ago that I was ready, that I was looking, that I was hurt enough to fight back! I grasped for something that would enable me to gain back everything that I had lost. They had tried to strip me, as a woman, as an individual, as a human being.[1]

In 1973, Alicia Escalante, a Chicana welfare mother from East Los Angeles, wrote these words in one of the first Chicana feminist journals,[2] on the founding of the East Los Angeles Welfare Rights Organization (ELAWRO).[3] Escalante and several single welfare mothers had founded the ELAWRO, a grassroots community organization, 6 years earlier in 1967. In the 1960s, many welfare recipients in the East Los Angeles area were single Chicana and Mexicana mothers.[4] One of the major objectives of the ELAWRO was to protect the rights of welfare recipients and to advocate for social and economic justice in the welfare system. Although the organization sought to advocate for all welfare recipients, such as the disabled, elderly, and those who were unable to find steady employment, its main focus was the single Chicana and Mexicana welfare mother. Chicana mothers made up the leadership and in large part the membership of the organization. These welfare recipients organized out of necessity, finding themselves propelled into activism by their personal and familial needs. These needs included everyday necessities, including enough money for food, clothes, rent, accessible healthcare, and meaningful employment. In addition to these needs they wanted to be treated with respect and dignity by the welfare administration. The conditions they faced from the welfare system included racist, discriminatory and culturally insensitive social workers, staff and administrators, a lack of local offices in the Chicana/o community, and degrading and oppressive policies and eligibility requirements. Additionally, welfare recipients constantly had endured the public stigma attached to being a welfare recipient in United States society.[5]

The ELAWRO emerged out of a period of history marked by social and political upheaval by what the U.S. Government termed its "minority" populations. The African American Civil Rights movement had been going strong for over a decade. Many hard-fought gains had been made with the passage of the 1964 Civil Rights Act, and the 1965 Voting Rights Act.[6] The Chicana/o movement, under full swing by the mid to late 1960s, included several regional struggles, among them the farm workers' struggle in California, the land grant struggle in New Mexico, the East Los Angeles high school Blowouts, Chicana/o student activism at the colleges and universities, the Chicano and Chicana anti-war movement, and the struggle for self-determination and against police brutality in several Chicano communities.[7] The welfare rights movement was also underway and had become a national movement bridging the poor in many locations.[8] The Vietnam War was raging and President Lyndon Johnson's War on Poverty was dwindling due to national resources being sucked dry by the war machine. During this period there was also global de-colonial struggles being waged by colonized peoples. The ELAWRO represented an emerging manifestation of the Chicana/o Movement, which has generally gone unrecognized and unhistoricized, even among Chicana/o Studies scholars.

At the heart of this chapter is a narrative recovering and interpreting the history of the East Los Angeles Welfare Rights Organization and its founding member Alicia Escalante. Escalante and the ELAWRO have been consistently cited as one of the earliest Chicana organizations that emerged during the Chicano Movement.[9] Escalante has also been briefly historicized as a leading Chicana activist, but both Escalante and the organization remain on the margins of the history of the Chicana/o Movement.[10] One importance of historicizing this organization and Escalante's role in it concerns the formulation of a distinct form of Chicana feminism articulated by poor women. Also important is providing an interpretation of Escalante as an integral and vital leader who was able to successfully navigate and negotiate between multiple organizations and activist collectives. The activities of Escalante and the ELAWRO reflect a very multifaceted commitment to several social movements. These social movements were the Chicano movement, the Chicana movement, the welfare rights movement, the women's movement, and the Poor People's movement. Escalante and the ELAWRO were active in the fight against racism, sexism, economic injustice, educational inequity, corruption within the Catholic Church, and the Vietnam War. These multiple fronts of activism speak to Escalante's and the larger organization's commitment to the Chicana and Chicano community, the poor, and the advancement of Chicana and Mexicana women.

Alicia Escalante's Early Activism and the Foundation of the ELAWRO

In 1966, social services in California were subject to immense cutbacks under the governorship of Republican Governor Ronald Reagan. Part of these cutbacks impacted the Medi-Cal program, which provided healthcare coverage to low-income families and welfare recipients. Escalante and her five children were among those welfare recipients who relied on Medi-Cal to cover their medical expenses. On a visit to Dr. Carlo, the Escalante family's physician, he informed Escalante that he would probably not be able to see her or her children any longer due to these budget cuts. Dr. Carlo also told Escalante about an upcoming demonstration scheduled to occur in downtown Los Angeles against these cutbacks. Escalante recalled the conversation:

> And so the demonstration was taking place a few days after seeing the doctor. That day after I had sent my kids off to school and packed their lunches I took the bus. Sure enough as soon as I got off the bus there was a large group of people physically disabled in wheelchairs and so forth going back and forth in front of the city hall.[11]

This was the beginning for Escalante, marking her entrance into activist politics. Following this first demonstration, she attended a strategy meeting for groups that were involved with organizing against the Medi-Cal cutbacks. Representatives from the South Central Los Angeles area and different disabled rights groups came to this meeting. Escalante stated that there had been no Mexican Americans or Chicanas/os at either the demonstration or at this organizing meeting. She remembered, however, that, "By the time I left that meeting, I was the chairwoman of East L.A."[12] Soon thereafter, she informed Dr. Carlo that she had gone to the demonstration and meeting and was now involved with organizing efforts against the Medi-Cal cutbacks. He was very happy about this and extended his help to Escalante to provide rent for office space and to pay for a phone line. Escalante was reluctant to take Dr. Carlo's help at first, but knew that she could use it.

The first thing that Escalante did was to organize a meeting in East Los Angeles at a local community center regarding the Medi-Cal cutbacks. Escalante remembers spending countless days and hours on publicity and informing the Mexican American and Chicana/o community. She created fliers, made several phone calls (her sister Irene also helped out), went door to door, and recruited people from Dr. Carlo's office, all in an effort to get the community organized around an issue that was going to directly affect them. "I remember walking to the center and thinking to myself, 'I wonder if anybody is going to be there,'" she said. "[Then] I walked in there [and] it was standing room only and I've never forgotten that, standing room only." Through the organizing efforts on the part of several groups, including Escalante and members of the East Los Angeles community, the Medi-Cal cuts were not initiated. This victory propelled Escalante to continue to organize on behalf of the Mexican American and Chicana/o community but this time in the area of welfare rights. Through her organizing against the Medi-Cal cuts Escalante learned of groups such as the National Welfare Rights Organization (NWRO). She also knew of two local African-American welfare rights activists in Los Angeles, Johnnie Tillmon and Catherine Jermany.[13] Escalante began attending local welfare rights meetings, explaining:

> I started first just observing, going to their meetings and observing to see what issues they were addressing because they influenced me and I wanted to see if it was the right thing to do to join them. I liked what I saw them doing, so I thought I would become a part of the National Welfare Rights Organization.[14]

Soon after, Escalante reasoned that, since she already had an office, support from the community, and a strong group that had been successful against the Medi-Cal cuts, she would petition for incorporation under the name East Los Angeles Welfare Rights Organization in 1967.[15]

Although the ELAWRO had its early beginnings with the NWRO, the ELAWRO quickly split with the national organization. Escalante asserted that during her participation with Los Angeles welfare rights activities she often was the only Mexican American or Chicana who was present. She also stated that "in many instances I don't think they were fully aware of the issues that we as a Spanish-speaking community [faced]."[16] Escalante explained that she attended one of the NWRO's conferences (she did not remember exactly where and when it took place), but what she did recall is that she attempted to pass a resolution that addressed the "Spanish-speaking community." She recounted the moment:

> my thinking was, okay, I think the first thing that I need to do is request a resolution for acceptance of certain issues that I felt were lacking. Though I listened a lot and observed a lot it was quite obvious that they were not very culturally aware of our needs and I drafted a resolution that basically addressed the issue of bilingual workers, translation of welfare forms into Spanish and that sort of thing and walked around them to see if there was support. The resolution didn't pass . . . I regrettably felt that the only thing to do was, just go on my own. I respected them for what they were doing and I respected the leadership, but I had to go on my own because the resolution meant what my goals were. All welfare forms were in English and they were not in layman's language, they were in legal mumbo jumbo. So that half of the people that came [to the ELAWRO office] were, "can you translate this for me" or something or the other. The other ones, it's the same thing; you walked into a welfare office and you didn't see a brown

face. Things that I felt were necessary to open up communication for the people. So I went out on my own, I got a lot of criticism from some of them but that's ok, it was the best thing I ever did.[17]

Escalante's choice to disassociate from the NWRO was a reflection of the need of Chicana welfare recipients to organize on their own behalf. She explained her reasoning in a speech delivered in 1974:

[t]he Chicano Movement also greatly influenced the ELAWRO in the late 60s. We chose to place more emphasis on the special needs and problems of the Raza communities. It was for this reason that a break was made from the national organization. Though basically the same goals were kept, the operation of Chicana Welfare Rights Organization has been more in keeping with our culture and tradition.[18]

Although the ELAWRO chose to split from the NWRO they still maintained ties and would later come together to organize around the Talmadge Amendment, which directly affected all welfare mothers regardless of race.

The ELAWRO Fighting for Justice on Multiple Fronts

The structure of the organization, from Escalante's perspective, functioned as a *familia*. Escalante and the membership largely consisted of single Chicana welfare mothers who ran the office, which they shared with the local police malpractice center.[19] The organization's main focus was to protect and inform welfare recipients of their rights as recipients and as human beings. One of the many issues that Escalante and the organization took on was the translation of welfare forms into Spanish. Additionally, the organization fought to establish new welfare offices within the Spanish-speaking community, and called on the Department of Social Services to hire bilingual and bicultural social workers. Escalante stated that there was no real communication between the welfare system and the people it was attempting to serve. In order for the ELAWRO to take on such issues, they familiarized themselves with the policies and regulations of the welfare system. The bureaucracy that existed within the system was structured on three levels: local, state, and federal. The ELAWRO found that there was a lack of communication between the levels of the bureaucracy and that this, in turn, hurt the recipients who were in great need of aid.[20] Escalante spoke about this situation, saying:

Whenever there were discrepancies at the local level, we documented them and brought it to the attention of the administrators. We would ask to meet with the director of welfare and if he tried to avoid meeting with us, we would go to the County Board of Supervisors. We would write politicians concerning issues like the Talmadge law, or pilot projects affecting large communities. We would undertake surveys and conduct research. And if we had to, we would take the county to court. We tried to pursue an issue until it was resolved.[21]

Due to the lack of communication between the Mexican American and Chicana/o community and the welfare system, and the maltreatment experienced by welfare recipients, the ELAWRO also wanted the recipients to be involved with the hiring process of new social workers and with policy-making that directly affected them. Escalante and ELAWRO members took on individual cases and assisted recipients with filing for fair hearings and were present during these hearings. The ELAWRO also organized demonstrations and protests in order to combat the injustices being perpetuated by the welfare system.

By 1968, the ELAWRO had become very well known in East Los Angeles, and also on a larger scale throughout California and across the United States. Escalante and the ELAWRO became so influential that they were invited by the Southern Christian Leadership Conference (SCLC) to participate in the Poor People's Campaign in Washington D.C. in the Spring of 1968.[22] Escalante received the call at the organization's office and was asked to organize a group of recipients and their families to attend. The SCLC provided for everything, a Greyhound bus for transportation, food, and a monitor, who was Jesse Jackson. Escalante's group was one among several groups who boarded buses headed to Washington D.C. from East Los Angeles. Upon their arrival, arrangements had already been made for them to stay at a schoolhouse by Corky Gonzales from the Denver-based Crusade for Justice.[23] Escalante had also brought her teenage daughter Lorraine along for their month-long stay in the nation's capitol.[24] While in Washington D.C. Escalante participated in a demonstration at the capitol building along with twenty-eight other welfare mothers against an anti-welfare bill (PL90–248), which resulted in their arrest.[25] Escalante and ELAWRO's presence at the Poor People's Campaign was significant as it represented the experiences of poverty from the perspective of the Chicana/o community. More importantly, as noted in this chapter, they represented the experiences of poor Chicana mothers on welfare in a multi-racial struggle against poverty. Following the Poor People's Campaign, Escalante returned home to East Los Angeles in the midst of a struggle being waged in the community's high schools.

In March 1968, the East Los Angeles high school "Blowouts" took place, with thousands of local high school students walking out of their classrooms in response to an inadequate education, racism in the schools, a 50 percent drop-out rate, and an unresponsive school board.[26] Sal Castro, a history and social studies teacher at Lincoln High School who had inspired and helped organize the student strike, was arrested, along with twelve others, in connection to the Blowouts and was dismissed from his teaching position. In response to his dismissal, organizing efforts culminated in several protests and an 8-day sit-in at the Board of Education in Los Angeles. Thirty-five members of the Chicano and Chicana community, including Alicia Escalante, participated in the sit-in.[27] In a special issue of *La Raza* magazine, Escalante asserted,

> I am a Chicana mother and was one of the 35 arrested at the Board of Education sit-in. . . . My two oldest children are involved with the movement of the Chicano . . . Castro's case was just one of our many victories to come. We in the Movement will at least be able to hold our heads up and say that we haven't submitted to the gringo or to the pressures of the system. We are brown and we are proud. I am at least raising my children to be proud of their heritage, to demand their rights, and as they become parents they too will pass this on until justice is done . . . For those of you mothers who think I may not be a good mother because I am militant, on the contrary, my children are very well taken care of in every respect. Viva la Raza![28]

The Blowouts hit close to home for Escalante as her children attended school on the east side of Los Angeles. Escalante's words are quite powerful and moving, as she situated herself as part of the "Movement" as a Chicana mother. This image of a Chicana mother as a Chicano Movement activist and leader is far from the image of the activists that are usually portrayed in the leading narratives of the Chicano Movement, which typically focus on the "great men" (e.g. César Chávez, Corky Gonzales, Reies López Tijerina, José Ángel Gutiérrez, and even Sal Castro).[29] Escalante and ELAWRO members were not just committed to the struggle for welfare rights, they were also committed to the struggle of the Chicano and Chicana people and the self-determination of the community.

Due to the exposure that Escalante and the ELAWRO received as a result of their activism, Escalante began to accept invitations to speak. Not only would these speaking engagements serve as a method to disseminate information about the Chicana struggle for welfare rights, it also improved the organization's financial well-being. Escalante traveled extensively throughout the United States to speak about Chicana welfare rights. She spoke in Denver, Chicago, and New York. Escalante also participated in speaking engagements locally. She was a part of a panel at one of the earliest Chicana activist gatherings at the University of California, Los Angeles (UCLA) in November 1969. The gathering was the Corazón de Aztlán Conference, also known as the "Chicana Symposium."[30] Escalante was one of several Chicana activists invited to speak, which also included Enriqueta Vásquez and Elizabeth "Betita" Martínez, editors of New Mexico's *El Grito Del Norte*, Gerry Gonzales of the Crusade for Justice, Dolores Huerta of the United Farm Workers, and female members from UMAS/MEChA de UCLA, which included Susan Racho. Escalante was clearly recognized as a prominent Chicana activist and Chicano Movement activist, as were the other Chicana women that were invited to speak that day.

In addition to speaking on a national and local level, Escalante also had the opportunity to travel the world in 1969. She was awarded a scholarship by the National Council of Churches to attend a "nutrition seminar on hunger." This seminar took twenty-seven women, many of them middle-class professionals, to several different countries, visiting places such as Paris, Rome, Lebanon, India, Thailand, the Philippines, Hong Kong, Taiwan, South Korea, and Tokyo. Escalante was the only Chicana; the "only grassroots person." She explained,

> I saw a lot of poverty, actual starvation, especially in India. I felt deeply and sincerely for these people, but I knew my work was here, with my own people. I came to the conclusion more than ever, that this is the richest country in the world, and for hunger of any kind to exist here is inexcusable![31]

This experience definitely contributed to Escalante's understanding of poverty, and what it meant to be a poor Chicana mother in one of the wealthiest nations in the world. Soon after her return Escalante participated in the Chicano and Chicana anti-war movement in Los Angeles. She, along with ELAWRO members, attended the first Chicano Moratorium in December 1969, where she declared, "I'd rather have my sons die for *La Raza* and *La Causa* than in Vietnam."[32] Escalante and members of the organization also attended the second Chicano Moratorium demonstration on February 28, 1970 known as the "March in the Rain." They also attended the famous August 29, 1970 Chicano Moratorium, the largest Chicana/o anti-war protest, which ended with police violence and the death of three people, including journalist Rubén Salazar.[33]

In December 1969, following the first Chicano Moratorium, Escalante was arrested in connection with her involvement with the *Católicos Por La Raza* (CPLR) Christmas Eve demonstration at St. Basil's Church on Wilshire in Los Angeles.[34] CPLR was a community-based organization that sought to end discrimination within the Catholic Church. The protest was organized as a result of several issues, which included the disconnection between the community and the Church. Another impetus for the demonstration was "the closing of a Catholic parochial school, Our Lady Queen of Angels High School, which had an 87 percent Mexican American enrollment, at the same time as the archdiocese had finished construction of a new 3-million-dollar church, St. Basil's, in the trendy Wilshire district."[35] Escalante recalled that she was asked to organize a group of recipients to attend the demonstration and that it was to be peaceful. Upon her group's arrival, which included families and elders she sensed that there was going to be violence. She had seen plain-clothes officers everywhere in addition to helicopters. A few moments later the demonstration erupted into violence. Escalante had her then 6-year-old son, Alex, with her and during the commotion she lost him in the crowd. She was very afraid that he would be hurt and as she attempted to find her son an officer was pushing her back. Escalante stated, "[a]ll I know is I picked up my hand [and] as soon as he was close enough to me, I hit him right where it hurts."[36] She was immediately handcuffed and hauled off to jail.[37] Several demonstrators were beaten which included men and women, young and old. An indictment made on behalf of the Los Angeles archdiocese led to additional arrests a few weeks later. Escalante was convicted of assaulting a police officer and was sentenced to 30 days in Sybil Brand women's prison and 1 year of probation.

Following her jail time, Escalante decided to leave Los Angeles in early 1970 for a while. Her decision to move away was influenced by the police repression that was occurring against Chicano Movement leaders following the arrests in connection with St. Basil's and advice she had received. Prior to Escalante's decision to leave, she had been involved in an ongoing dialogue with Crusade for Justice leader Corky Gonzales and his wife Gerry Gonzales about her possibly going to Denver. Both Corky and Gerry Gonzales wanted Escalante to help expand welfare rights organizing in Denver with women who had been active in the Crusade and who worked at the organization's Escuela Tlatelolco. So Escalante and her children headed for Denver, and stayed in the same colonia where Corky and Gerry Gonzales lived. During this period, the ELAWRO's influence expanded with the emergence of the National Chicana Welfare Rights Organization and *La Causa de los Pobres*. These two new organizations were developed in an effort to be inclusive of welfare rights organizational efforts in other locations, such as Denver. Escalante worked with women who were seeking to develop their own welfare rights organization and also taught Spanish at the Crusade's Escuela Tlatelolco. While she was away, her sister, Irene Villalobos, who was also a welfare rights activist in the city of El Sereno, and ELAWRO members stepped up and maintained the organization and their activities. After living in Denver for almost a year, Escalante and her family returned to Los Angeles as she had to attend court given the fact that the Los Angeles City District Attorney was attempting to give her more time for the St. Basil's demonstration.[38]

Escalante and the ELAWRO played a significant role in the Chicano Movement. Escalante was a Chicana community leader and the ELAWRO was a Chicana community organization. They focused on multiple issues that concerned them as members of the Chicano and Chicana community, as welfare recipients, and as mothers. Escalante explains, "it wasn't just welfare, [it was about] advocacy for any and all that were seeking justice."[39] She stated,

> one of the things that we always tried to do was if there were other issues, which there were, within the community we all supported each other and even though the goal of the organization was to address all the issues that had to deal with the single mom and with the welfare system we always got called when there were other issues facing the community.[40]

This statement is a reflection of the leadership role that Escalante and the organization itself played in the Chicano and Chicana community. Their participation in multiple struggles also speaks to the organization's commitment to several social movements. "We played a supportive role in any issue that dealt with other movements. Because that's the unity we always showed together."[41]

The Chicana Welfare Rights Organization v. The Talmadge Amendment, Forging a Chicana Feminist Identity and Politics

By 1970 the ELAWRO was also identified as the Chicana Welfare Rights Organization (CWRO).[42] Escalante articulates how she felt about identifying as a Chicana,

> [w]ell for me. I always saw myself as a Chicana . . . was born and raised a Chicana . . . that was the terminology that was used definitely in the 1960s and so I think my efforts sought to include every woman that saw themselves as Chicana.[43]

A very important issue that the CWRO tackled during their organizing efforts in the early 1970s was the Talmadge Amendment. The Talmadge Amendment was an amendment to the Social Security Act, which was initially passed in response to the Great Depression in the 1930s. It was introduced, debated, and passed in Congress in 1971. It went into effect in July of 1972. This amendment required able-bodied persons to register for work with the Human Resources Development program. The main group that it targeted was welfare recipients and their families, more specifically welfare mothers with dependent children. According to the CWRO and other welfare rights organizations, the aim of this amendment was to reduce the welfare rolls. The CWRO argued that the Talmadge Amendment would not help people get off welfare, but rather would keep them on it. The training that was established through this amendment was often inadequate and prepared workers for minimally paid jobs that did not require any skill, so in reality they were really just making them work for their checks. At times, the jobs that the welfare department was trying to place them in were non-existent. An article published in the *Eastside Sun* by Eddie Prado states that:

> The women's group has listed the following as the primary complaints against the law: Inadequate day services are provided by the law, the law does not give a woman a choice between staying at home to care for her children or working to be an eligible recipient, the law takes no steps towards meaningful job training. The bill was designed to eliminate the Aid to Families with Dependent Children program; the jobs provided for recipients amount to slave labor.[44]

The CWRO also argued that this amendment would just create another level of bureaucracy that recipients would have to deal with and that this would be financially ineffective and wasteful. It also asserted that, rather than spending millions of dollars on a new layer of bureaucracy, the government should put the money towards offering poor women adequate training, childcare, and assistance with education, in addition to other recommendations. As Escalante wrote in *Encuentro Femenil,*

> Forced labor is the means by which the welfare system helps to manipulate the labor market to the advantage of only the employers, the owners of industry, business and finance. . . . Forced work does not create jobs, nor does it enable people to become self supporting. On the contrary, it has the effect, the intentional effect, of driving wages down by increasing the competition of already scarce jobs. In short, the purpose of forced labor is to undercut the bargaining power of labor. And of course, it does not even begin to resolve the welfare mess or the problems of mass unemployment and poverty![45]

Although the CWRO had geared its focus towards assisting the Chicano community primarily, the organization also sought to cross racial and class barriers that existed in society. An article published in *La Raza* magazine on the Talmadge Amendment, for example, reads, "It is their hope (CWRO) to arouse concern of all women of all races and classes, to help fight for the abolishment of an amendment which does not provide meaningful employment or training for the poor."[46] The CWRO led a fierce campaign against the Talmadge Amendment. A part of their efforts included utilizing Chicana and Chicano Movement publications, and local print media, and forming coalitions with other organizations, political groups, and individuals.

Several articles concerning the Talmadge Amendment were produced in *Encuentro Femenil* and *Regeneración,* two of the earliest Chicana feminist publications to emerge out of the Chicana Movement. Within these two publications, Chicana activists Alicia Escalante and Francisca Flores opened up dialogue around the Talmadge Amendment.[47] Flores' article, "A Reaction to Discussions on the Talmadge Amendment," argued that the struggle against the Talmadge Amendment could become a platform to include others in the struggle for economic justice. She asserted,

> it is one thing to oppose Congressional and or administrative repudiation of social legislation and quite another to call on the community to oppose a piece of legislation such as the Talmadge amendment solely on the basis and interest of one group affected by it.[48]

Escalante replied in her article, "A Letter From the Chicana Welfare Rights Organization," that:

> [Flores] first get herself informed about what the East Los Angeles Chicano
> Welfare Rights is all about and what it is really doing before she starts forming
> or giving her opinions. Constructive criticism, yes: destructive no. We are
> not playing politics with each other.[49]

Although Flores and Escalante differed in opinion, they both were Chicana activists
who sought social and economic justice for *La Chicana*. This discussion illustrates
the diversity in opinion and ideology among Chicanas who were organizing
during the same time period. Participating in Chicana print culture proved to
be a very important method of communication between individual activists and
organizations. Maylei Blackwell articulates the importance that Chicana print
culture served during the Chicana Movement,

> The *Hijas de Cuauhtémoc* newspaper and *Encuentro Femenil* created a vital
> Chicana feminist print culture in which new political identities, discourses
> and strategies were constructed and debated. This vital print culture created
> a Chicana Feminist counterpublic that opened up spaces for Chicana
> dialogue across regions, social movement sectors, activist generations, and
> social differences. Moreover, it provided a space for women to contest the
> limiting masculinist politics embedded in the gendered project of Chicano
> nationalism that articulated the subject-citizen of Aztlán as male.[50]

Although the CWRO and the *Comisión Femenil Mexicana Nacional* (CFMN),
headed by Francisca Flores, were both focused on the needs of Chicanas, they
differed in their organizing methods and their origins. CFMN was considered to
be a Chicana organization that was headed by professional and educated women.
Its members focused on providing employment training, leadership skills, and
childcare services to Chicanas so that they could work outside the home. CFMN
received government funding to run their programs and centers such as the Chicana
Service Action Center and the Centro de Niños. The CWRO, on the other
hand, worked primarily with single welfare recipient mothers who were
unemployed or, if they worked, performed low-skill menial labor. The CWRO
began as a grassroots organization, and although it was incorporated under the
title ELAWRO it did not receive any type of substantial government funding,
but rather relied on the limited resources its members could muster.

The CWRO gained a large amount of momentum behind its campaign to
abolish the Talmadge Amendment. Its supporters included other women's
organizations, political groups and several politicians. Among them were:

> [the] National Women's Political Caucus, Calif. State Assemblyman Willie
> L. Brown, Jr., Calif. State Senator Mervyn M. Dymally, Calif. State
> Assemblyman John Vasconcellos, Calif. State Assemblyman Bob Moretti,
> Calif. State Senator Alfred H. Song, U.S. Congressman Calif. Edward

Roybal, 3rd World Women's Group, Chicana Political Caucus, National Council of Churches, [and the] National Welfare Rights Organization.[51]

Although they were able to build a strong campaign, the CWRO was unsuccessful at abolishing the Talmadge Amendment. Despite this unsuccessful struggle, the CWRO successfully built coalitions with individual politicians, with other women's organizations and political groups.

Escalante and the CWRO had been publishing articles and advertisements for the organization as early as 1967. *La Raza* newspaper and later *La Raza* magazine served as a vehicle for the organization to disseminate information about their organizing efforts and the issues that they were tackling. From 1967 through 1974 Escalante and the CWRO consistently contributed to *La Raza*. In addition to Escalante writing about welfare, several others also published articles on welfare and welfare rights. Some examples of these other articles are three pieces that were published in *La Raza* in 1968 that dealt with the stigma attached to being a welfare recipient, and the myth of the welfare recipient. The first of these articles was published in February titled, "Are Welfare Recipients Human?" which revealed "in a pretty strong way, how some very powerful people feel about welfare, and people on welfare." The article stated:

> Notice to all welfare clients: You're not tax payers, you don't support yourselves. You don't take good care of your kids; they are hungry, dirty, not clothed properly. You have boyfriends in your homes, and have illegitimate children. You are no good; you should be sterilized; your kids put in homes; you should be made to go to work; you should be ashamed of yourselves for living.[52]

The second article published on March 1, 1968, "Are Welfare Recipients Represented," reflects the experiences of Mexican Americans and Chicanos/as on welfare and the reality that they face.[53] The third article, "Welfare doesn't help people," pointed out that,

> The basic philosophy of welfare, as expressed in the regulations and laws of all welfare departments in this country, is NOT to provide a basic income or to (God Forbid!) help people OUT of poverty, but to give poor people just enough to keep their children from becoming beggars on the streets. To prevent them from becoming a visible embarrassment. To keep their stomachs just so full that they won't riot.[54]

The article also argues that politicians and the news media kept the general public ignorant about welfare and hateful of its recipients. All three articles, and many others like them, ended by calling people to fight back and become active in the cause for welfare rights. Others who wrote articles were Clemencia Martínez,

Sandra Ugarte, Mike García, The Los Angeles Social Workers Union–Local 535, and a social worker organization called SALUD (Social Action Latinos for Unity Development).[55] The fact that these articles were published in *La Raza* is significant given that many of them were republished in other Chicano Movement publications as a result of *La Raza* being a member of the Chicano Press Association.[56]

In addition to Chicana and Chicano Movement publications, Escalante also consistently published articles in the local newspapers such as the *Eastside Sun*. An article entitled "ELA Chicana Welfare Rights Report" provides an example of the maltreatment experienced by welfare mothers in East Los Angeles.

> 1. Mrs. Ramírez goes into the department with an emergency. Her four week old daughter is very ill. She is badly in need of a medical card. She waits an amount of six hours, and only to be told that she is to be given another appointment and told to come back. 2. Mrs. Esperanza Jaramillo goes into the department to apply for food stamps. She has gone eight times, and has not been helped! Each time she waits four to five hours. She is ill and has to leave her children alone each time. 3. A working mother, Armancleica Torres, has gone five times in one week, because of her income tax return. Each time jeopardizing her job, because she has to take time from work. 4. Esther Romero did not receive her check, has gone to the department four times, waits five hours each time, in order for her to get to the department she has to hitchhike.[57]

This quote illustrates many of the frustrations and bureaucratic hoops that all welfare recipients had to jump through in order to receive assistance. In 1973, when this article was published 21.5 percent of Hispanic families reported in the U.S. Bureau of Census were under the poverty level, and 57.4 percent of female-headed households were under the poverty level.[58]

The CWRO's struggle to defeat the Talmadge Amendment offers an example of its gendered critiques. The organization argued that the Talmadge Amendment targeted mothers with children over 6 years old specifically since they made up what the welfare system defined as "able bodied" workers. The CWRO argued:

> we are firm in our position that women should have the right to choose what their roles as mothers, housewives or whatever is to be; if women are going to be dictated to by the government as to what these roles are to be, then the government should be consistent and demand this of all women—not just the poor.[59]

The CWRO emphasized that women should have the right to choose whether they were going to join the workforce or to stay at home and care for their children. Another important critique put forward was the fact that women's labor in the home was not considered "work," which the CWRO argued it was. Anna Nieto Gómez provided a similar critique of the Equal Rights Amendment in her article titled, "madres por JUSTICIA." She explained that it:

> is an injustice when the Equal Rights Amendment which demands equal pay for equal work does not extend to the mother whose work is not considered a part of the labor force. Society forgets that she is responsible for the maintenance of the labor force.[60]

The CWRO believed in a united front of all women in the struggle for welfare rights. Unity was important to the CWRO as this was considered essential to creating change. Escalante articulated the need for unity among Chicanas in an article published in *Encuentro Femenil*. As she stated,

> The real welfare picture will eventually come out if we as Mujeres, Madres, Chicanas get together and communicate and help each other. The road of the welfare mother is a lonely one. And our Hermanas, no matter what walk of life they come from, will have to join us.[61]

Escalante and the CWRO expressed a Chicana feminist identity and politics through their organizing efforts against the Talmadge Amendment and for Chicana welfare rights. Although Escalante and the CWRO were involved with multiple struggles and social movements, at the heart of their activism was justice specifically for the single Chicana welfare mother. This emphasis placed on poor Chicana women's needs is expressive of a Chicana feminist identity and politics that has yet to be explored fully. Indeed, Escalante and the CWRO's feminist politics do not fit neatly into dominant articulations of feminism, thus the importance of this area of research. Like Maylei Blackwell, I argue that Escalante and the CWRO practiced a multiple insurgent feminism as Blackwell asserts,

> Many feminist practices of women of color, lesbians and working class women are not clearly registered in dominant frames because they involve political subjects who have multiple identities and who most often engage in multi-issue organizing or work on several political fronts, not all of which put gender at the center. Further many of these forms of feminist consciousness were produced by being in between movements and coalitions. These particular practices have produced new forms of analysis and new political identities that are often not registered in feminist epistemologies based on rigid typologies such as Liberal, Social, or Radical.[62]

When I asked Escalante if she and the CWRO practiced their own brand of feminism she responded,

[a]bsolutely, but not in the sense that the Anglo woman was looking at it. Because I have never lived in a white woman's world, in the sense that I knew my own identity, I always have. I know who I am as a person and to be liberated, to have equality, I always felt was a right of all human beings . . . [63]

The CWRO utilized several methods of organizing against an unjust welfare system. First and foremost, the CWRO held information sessions and meetings at their organization's office. As mentioned previously, Escalante and the CWRO also published numerous articles that were published in Chicano Movement, Chicana feminist, and community publications. In their articles they articulated and advocated the CWRO's positions on legislation such as the Talmadge Amendment, denounced the existence of inhuman treatment in the welfare system, and economic and social injustices that existed in society. Along with writing articles and holding information sessions, the CWRO organized protests, demonstrations and marches, held community events, wrote letters to politicians, conducted research and surveys, confronted members of the State of California Social Service Board, the County Board of Supervisors, and the director of the Los Angeles County Department of Public Social Services. The CWRO also successfully helped create a Chicano community relations board and organized for the implementation of cultural awareness training for social workers and staff. This represented a significant victory for the CWRO given that recipient participation in the policy-making process was among their demands for a more just welfare system. Escalante was honored in *Ms. Magazine* in early 1973 for her work in the community and her commitment to the advancement of women. In December of 1973, the CWRO launched a telethon titled "*Operación Navidad*" with the purpose of collecting toys and funds for less fortunate families in the Chicano community. The CWRO teamed up with Channel 34 KMEX, the station that aired the telethon. By 1974, the CWRO were successful in the implementation of translated welfare documents into Spanish. They were also instrumental in the establishment of new welfare offices within the Chicano community. As per their demands, bilingual and bicultural social workers and office workers staffed these offices. Their efforts opened up entry-level positions for welfare recipients within the welfare system. Lastly and most importantly, the activism of Alicia Escalante and the members of the CWRO gave welfare recipients newfound dignity and hope.[64]

Alicia Escalante: Closing One Door and Opening Another

Alicia Escalante officially resigned as director of the Chicana Welfare Rights Organization on March 29, 1974. Escalante informed the public of her resignation in a letter to the editor of the *Eastside Sun*, on April 18, 1974. The following month in another letter to the editor, Escalante explained that she had been traveling and writing, arguing, "I really believe I will be able to reach more people this way."[65] Escalante's leadership had led to several crucial gains for the Chicana welfare recipient. Her decision to resign was based on something much more tangible than the desire to reach more people. According to Escalante, "[t]he bottom line was I needed a job first of all. I also felt that there were already sufficient women leaders within the area that could continue . . . my kids were still young you know so I needed to work." The reality of survival, of taking care of yourself, your family, and your future is something that we all understand. Escalante relocated with her family to Sacramento where she looked for a job. After working in a few jobs that involved migrant workers that she enjoyed, but didn't pay much she landed a position that seemed promising. Escalante had applied for a step one staff services analyst position with the Department of Public Social Services in Sacramento. While in this position Escalante made sure that she would work in an area that aligned with her strengths, "community programs."[66]

She worked in the farm workers unit for a couple years and then moved up to work in the Indian Health Services program in the department. From there, she worked in the civil rights unit. Each time she moved on to a new position, she moved up the ladder. In the civil rights unit she was promoted to level three staff services analyst. She enjoyed working in this area but also found that her days of being controversial were not over. She was assigned a case that involved the Pitt River Tribe of northern California. The case involved the removal of five children from a mother who lived on the reservation. Escalante conducted a thorough investigation of the removal of the children and found that the children had been illegally removed. Although she was doing her job, she found herself in hot water due to the fact that the Department of Public Social Services wanted her to change the report she was going to submit. She refused to do so, and despite being threatened, she stood her ground and submitted her report as it was. Following her time in the civil rights unit she obtained a position with the Equal Employment Opportunity Office. Escalante worked for the state of California for 23 years, until she retired in 1999, and still lives in the Sacramento area.[67]

Notes

1   Alicia Escalante, "Canto de Alicia" *Encuentro Femenil* 1:1 (1973).
2   *Encuentro Femenil* was established in 1973 by Anna Nieto Gómez, and several other women who were former student activists at California State University, Long Beach (CSULB). Nieto Gómez and these women were initially members of UMAS/ MEChA at CSULB and had founded a Chicana student organization called Hijas de Cuauhtémoc which produced a newspaper under the same name. Nieto Gómez would later go on to work closely with Francisca Flores producing articles for *Regeneración*, and working with the Chicana Service Action Center. Nieto Gómez was also very involved with the Chicana Welfare Rights Organization's (CWRO) battle against the Talmadge Amendment, and produced several articles in both *Regeneración* and *Encuentro Femenil* on the amendment and on Escalante and the CWRO.

3   The East Los Angeles Welfare Rights Organization (ELAWRO) was also known as
    the National Chicano Welfare Rights Organization, La Causa de los Pobres, and the
    Chicana Welfare Rights Organization.
4   Escalante lived in the Ramona Gardens housing project in East Los Angeles and was
    raising five children alone. I use the terms Chicana/Mexicana interchangeably
    throughout because it is not completely clear what the ethnic backgrounds were of
    the membership. I am only aware of the ethnic background of Alicia Escalante who
    was Chicana.
5   There is a much literature on this topic, for recent literature see: Karen Seccombe,
    "So you think I drive a Cadillac?": Welfare Recipient Perspectives on The System and Its Reform
    (Boston: Allyn & Bacon, 2011); Carly Haden Foster, "The Welfare Queen: Race,
    Gender, Class and Public Opinion," *Race, Gender, Class* 15:3/4 (2008), 162–179; Rose
    Ernst, "Localizing the 'Welfare Queen' Ten Years Later: Race, Gender, Place and
    Welfare Rights," *Journal of Gender, Race, and Justice* 11:2 (2007), 181–208; Angie-Marie
    Hancock, *The Politics of Disgust: The Public Identity of the Welfare Queen* (New York: New
    York University Press, 2004); Ruth Sidel, "The Enemy Within: The Demonization of
    Poor Women," *Journal of Sociology and Social Welfare* 27:1 (2000), 73–84.
6   For histories of the Civil Rights movement and the Black Power Movement see: Joseph
    E. Peniel, Ed., *The Black Power Movement: Rethinking the Civil Rights–Black Power Era*
    (New York: Routledge, 2006); Judson L. Jeffries, Ed., *Black Power in the Belly of the
    Beast* (Urbana: University of Illinois, 2006); Renee Romano and Leigh Raiford, *The
    Civil Rights Movement in American Memory* (Athens: University of Georgia Press, 2006);
    Bruce J. Dierenfield, *The Civil Rights Movement* (New York: Pearson Longman, 2004);
    Clayborne Carson, et al., *Civil Rights Chronicle: the African-American Struggle for Freedom*
    (Lincolnwood, IL: Legacy Press, 2003); Peter B. Levy, *The Civil Rights Movement*
    (Westport, CT: Greenwood Press, 1998).
7   For histories of the Chicano movement see: Maylei Blackwell, *¡Chicana Power!:
    Contested Histories of Feminism in the Chicano Movement* (Austin: University of Texas
    Press, 2011); Lee Bebout, *Mythohistorical Interventions: the Chicano Movement and Its
    Legacies* (Minneapolis: University of Minnesota Press, 2011); Mario T. García and
    Sal Castro, *Blowout!: Sal Castro and the Chicano Struggle for Educational Justice* (Chapel
    Hill: University of North Carolina Press, 2011); David Montejano, *Quixote's Soldiers:
    A Local History of the Chicano Movement, 1966–1981* (Austin: University of Texas Press,
    2010); Rodolfo Acuña, *Occupied America: A History of Chicanos* (New York: Pearson
    Longman, 2007); Enriqueta Vásquez, et al., *Enriqueta Vasquez and the Chicano
    Movement: Writings from El Grito del Norte* (Houston, TX: Arte Público Press, 2006);
    Lorena Oropeza, *Raza Sí!, Guera No!: Chicano Protest and Patriotism During the
    Vietnam War Era* (Berkeley: University of California Press, 2005); George Mariscal,
    Brown-eyed Children of the Sun: Lessons From the Chicano Movement, 1965–1975
    (Albuquerque: University of New Mexico Press, 2005); Ernesto Chávez, *"Mi Raza
    Primero!" Nationalism, Identity, and Insurgency in the Chicano Movement in Los Angeles,
    1966–1978* (Berkeley: University of California Press, 2002); Reies López Tijerina and
    José Angel Gutiérrez (Eds.), *They Called Me "King Tiger": My Struggle for the Land and
    Our Rights* (Houston, TX: Arte Público Press, 2000); Ernesto B. Vigil, *The Crusade
    for Justice: Chicano Militancy and the Government's War on Dissent* (Madison: University
    of Wisconsin Press, 1999); José Angel Gutiérrez, *The Making of a Chicano Militant:
    Lessons From Cristal* (Madison: University of Wisconsin Press, 1998); Arturo F.
    Rosales, *¡Chicano!: The History of the Mexican American Civil Rights Movement* (Houston,
    TX: Arte Público Press, 1996); Ignacio M. García, *United We Win: The Rise and Fall
    of La Raza Unida Party* (Tuscon: The University of Arizona Press, 1989); Carlos Muñoz
    Jr., *Youth, Identity, Power: The Chicano Movement* (New York: Verso, 1989); Juan
    Gómez-Quiñones, *Mexican Students por la Raza: The Chicano Student Movement in
    Southern California, 1967–1977* (Santa Barbara, CA: Editorial La Causa, 1978).

8   For histories of the welfare rights movement see: Premilla Nadasen, *Rethinking the Welfare Rights Movement* (New York: Routledge, 2012); Premilla Nadasen, *Welfare Warriors: The Welfare Rights Movement in the United States* (New York: Routledge, 2005); Felicia Kornbluh, *The Battle for Welfare Rights: Politics and Poverty in Modern America* (Philadelphia: University of Pennsylvania Press, 2007); and Guida West, *The National Welfare Rights Movement: The Social Protest of Poor Women* (New York: Prager, 1981).

9   Blackwell, *¡Chicana Power!*; Oropeza, *¡Raza Sí!, Guera No!*; Vicki L. Ruiz, *From Out of the Shadows: Mexican Women in Twentieth-Century America* (New York: Oxford University Press, 1998); Rodolfo Acuña, *Occupied America: A History of Chicanos* (New York: Harper & Row, 1988) to name a few.

10   The recent work of Maylei Blackwell has been the most extensive in treating Escalante and the ELAWRO. For other studies that focus on the work of Chicana activists during the Chicana/o movement see: Blackwell, *¡Chicana Power!*; José Ángel Gutiérrez, Michelle Meléndez and Sonia Adriana Noyola, *Chicana in Charge: Texas Women in the Public Arena* (Lanham, MD: AltaMira Press, 2007); Vásquez, et al., *Enriqueta Vasquez and the Chicano Movement*; Elizabeth Martínez, *500 Years of Chicana Women's History* (New Brunswick, NJ: Rutgers University Press, 2008); Virginia R. Espino, "Women Sterilized as They Give Birth: Population Control, Eugenics and Social Protest in the Twentieth Century United States" (Ph.D. diss., Arizona State University, 2007); Marisela R. Chávez, "Despierten Hermanas y Hermanos! Women, the Chicano Movement, and Chicana Feminisms in California, 1966–1981" (Ph.D. diss., Stanford University, 2004); "'We Lived and Breathed and Worked the Movement': The Contradictions and Rewards of Chicana/Mexicana Activism in el Centro de Acción Social Autónomo-Hermandad General de Trabajadores (CASA-HGT), Los Angeles, 1975–1978," in Vicki L. Ruiz, Ed., *Las Obreras: Chicana Politics of Work and Family*, (Los Angeles: Chicano Studies Research Center, 2000); Maylei Blackwell, "Contested Histories: *Las Hijas de Cuauhtemoc*, Chicana Feminisms and Print Culture in the Chicano Movement, 1968–1973," in Gabriela Arredondo, et al., Eds., *Chicana Feminisms: A Critical Reader* (Durham, NC: Duke University Press, 2003); Dionne Espinoza, "'Revolutionary Sisters': Women's Solidarity and Collective Identification Among Chicana Brown Berets," *Aztlán* 26:1 (Spring 2001), 17–58; Dolores Delgado Bernal, "Grassroots Leadership Reconceptualized: Chicana Oral Histories and the 1968 East Los Angeles School Blowouts," *Frontiers: A Journal of Women Studies* 19:2 (1998), 113–142; Vicki L. Ruiz, Ed., "La Nueva Chicana: Women and the Movement," in *From Out of the Shadows*, 99–126; Alma M. García, *Chicana Feminist Thought: The Basic Historical Writings* (New York: Routledge, 1997); Alma M. Garcia "The Development of Chicana Feminist Discourse, 1970–1980," in Ellen Carol DuBois and Vicki L. Ruiz, Eds., *Unequal Sisters: A Multicultural Reader in Women's History* (New York: Routledge, 1990), 418–431.

11   Alicia Escalante, interview by author, Sacramento, California, 10 November 2012.

12   Ibid.

13   Escalante found out who Tillmon and Jermany were through their participation at the organizing meetings against the Medi-Cal cuts.

14   Escalante, interview, 10 November 2012.

15   It is unclear how long ELAWRO maintained its incorporation status. Escalante does make clear that ELAWRO was the only name the organization incorporated under.

16   Escalante, interview, 10 November 2012.

17   Ibid. Escalante did not recall whether the conference she attended was a national convention or a regional conference. She recalls going to a few conferences with members of the NWRO. She remembers going to Jackson, Mississippi and to Washington D.C.

18   Alicia Escalante, "The Los Angeles Chicana Welfare Rights Organization" Speech delivered at California State University Northridge, Spring 1974. Acquired from the personal archive of Maylei Blackwell, July, 2008.

19   There were several community-based complaint centers. There was also an
     Educational Issues Complaint Center, a Consumer Fraud Complaint Center, and a
     Health Services Complaint Center. The police malpractice center was located across
     the street from Dr. Carlo's medical office. The ELAWRO shared this office with the
     police malpractice center. Initially Dr. Carlo paid for the rent and the phone line for
     the organization.
20   Escalante, "The Los Angeles Chicana Welfare Rights Organization."
21   Ibid.
22   For more on the Poor People's Campaign see: Gordon K. Mantler, *Power to the Poor:
     Black-Brown Coalition and the Fight for Economic Justice, 1960–1974* (Chapel Hill:
     University of North Carolina Press, 2013); Michael K. Honey, *Going Down Jericho
     Road: The Memphis Strike, Martin Luther King's Last Campaign* (New York: W.W.
     Norton & Co., 2007); Gerald McKnight, *The Last Crusade: Martin Luther King, Jr.,
     the FBI, and the Poor People's Campaign* (Boulder, CO: Westview Press, 1998).
23   Escalante, interview, 10 November 2012.
24   Mantler, *Power to the Poor*, 201. Escalante's daughter had been given a scholarship for
     college because of her stellar academic record. In response to her attending the Poor
     People's Campaign with her mother her scholarship was revoked. Escalante, interview,
     10 November 2012.
25   Alicia Escalante, untitled article, *La Raza* 1:12 (May 11, 1968), 7.
26   García and Castro, *Blowout!*; Delgado Bernal, "Grassroots Leadership Reconceptual-
     ized."
27   *La Raza*, Special Issue, "Chicanos Liberate Board of Education," 2:1 (October 15,
     1968).
28   "Los 35 arrested for Liberation," *La Raza*, Special Issue, "Chicanos Liberate Board
     of Education," 2:1 (October 15, 1968), n.p.
29   Maylei Blackwell provides a strong critique of histories that have been written on the
     Chicano movement stating, "its historiography has been organized around a
     cosmology of male heroes that reifies the 'great man' narrative and interpretive
     structure." *¡Chicana Power!*, 28.
30   "Chicana Symposium," *La Raza* 2:10 (1969), 4.
31   Alicia Escalante, "Around the World to Expose Hunger in the U.S.A." *La Raza* 2:9
     (1969), 12.
32   Lorena Oropeza, *¡Raza Sí! ¡Guerra No! Chicano Protest and Patriotism During the Viet
     Nam War Era* (Berkeley: University of California Press, 2005), 141–142; *People's World*,
     27 December 1969.
33   Escalante's children were often present at historical events such as the Chicano
     Moratoriums. "Chicano Moratorium," film, directed by Victor Millan, n.d.; Alicia
     Escalante, interview conducted by María E. Cotera for the Chicana Por Mi Raza Oral
     History Project, Sacramento, California, 23 & 24 February 2012. For more on
     Escalante's experience as an activist mother see, *A Crushing Love: Chicanas, Motherhood
     and Activism*, Dir. Sylvia Morales. DVD, 58 min., 2009.
34   Mario T. García, "Religion and the Chicano Movement: Católicos por la Raza" in
     Gastón Espinosa and Mario T. García, Eds., *Mexican American Religions: Spirituality,
     Activism, and Culture* (Durham, NC: Duke University Press, 2008), 125–152; Mario
     T. García, *Católicos: Resistance and Affirmation in Chicano Catholic History* (Austin:
     University of Texas Press, 2008); Mario T. García, *Chicano Liberation Theology: The
     Writings and Documents of Richard Cruz and Católicos Por La Raza* (Dubuque, IA:
     Kendall/Hunt, 2009); Lara Medina, *Las Hermanas: Chicana/Latina Religious-Political
     Activism in the U.S. Catholic Church* (Philadelphia: Temple University Press, 2004).
35   García, *Católicos: Resistance and Affirmation*, 134.
36   Escalante, interview by Maria E. Cotera, February 2012.

37   Luckily her son Alex was found by one of Escalante's *comadres* who took him home with her and celebrated Christmas. Escalante, interview, 10 November 2012.

38   Ibid.

39   Ibid.

40   Escalante, interview, 10 November 2012.

41   Ibid.

42   Escalante explains that there were multiple names for the organization and that they simultaneously identified as ELAWRO, The National Chicano Welfare Rights Organization, La Causa de los Pobres, and the Chicana Welfare Rights Organization. Escalante, interview 10 November 2012.

43   Ibid.

44   Eddie Pardo, "Talmadge law hurts poor and women most," *Eastside Sun*, December 7 (1972), 1.

45   Alicia Escalante, "A Letter From the Chicana Welfare Rights Organization," *Encuentro Femenil* 1:2 (1974), 16.

46   "Alicia Escalante Welfare Rights Organizer" *La Raza* 1:1 (1968).

47   Francisca Flores was a life-long activist in Los Angeles. She was involved with the founding of the G.I. Forum, and the Mexican American Political Association. She was also one of the founders of the League of Mexican American Women and the Comisión Femenil Mexicana Nacional. Flores was the director of the Chicana Service Action Center which was an employment center for Chicanas that was developed by Comisión Femenil. Flores also served as an editor to the East Los Angeles community newsletter, *Carta Editorial* which became *Regeneración* when Flores became the sole editor.

48   Francisca Flores, "A Reaction to Discussions on the Talmadge Amendment to the Social Security Act," *Encuentro Femenil* 1:2 (1974): 13–14.

49   Alicia Escalante, "A Letter from the Chicana Welfare Rights Organization," *Encuentro Femenil* 1:2 (1974): 15–19.

50   Blackwell, *¡Chicana Power!*, 8.

51   Escalante, "A Letter from the Chicana Welfare Rights Organization," 17.

52   "Are Welfare Recipients Human?" *La Raza* 1:9 (February 10, 1968), 4.

53   B.N. Estar, "Are Welfare Recipients Represented?" *La Raza* 1:10 (March 1, 1968), 2.

54   B.N. Estar, "Welfare doesn't help people" *La Raza* 1:11 (March 31, 1968), 2.

55   Clemencia Martínez, "Welfare Families Face Forced Labor," *La Raza Magazine* 1:7 (1972), 41; Sandra Ugarte, "Welfare: If Nixon Can Create Jobs For Welfare Recipients, Why Can't He Create Jobs To Get Them Off Welfare," *La Raza Magazine* 1:8 (April 1972), 16–17.

56   For more on the Chicano Press Association see: Blackwell, *¡Chicana Power!*, 138; Raúl Ruiz, "The Chicanos and the Underground Press," *La Raza Magazine* 3:1 (1977), 8–10. For more on *La Raza* Newspaper and Magazine see: Francisco Manuel Andrade, "The history of La Raza newspaper and magazine, and its role in the Chicano community from, 1967–1977," (M.A. Thesis, California State Univeristy, Fullerton, 1979).

57   Alicia Escalante, "ELA Chicana Welfare Rights Report," *Eastside Sun*, November 1 (1973), 1.

58   Poverty Status of People by Family Relationship, Race, and Hispanic Origin: 1959 to 2006. U.S. Bureau of the Census, Annual Social and Economic Supplements. www.census.gov/hhes/www/poverty/histpov/hstpov2.html., accessed January 2010.

59   Escalante, "A Letter from the Chicana Welfare Rights Organization," 17.

60   Anna Nieto Gómez, "madres por JUSTICIA," *Encuentro Femenil* 1:1 (1973), 17.

61   Escalante, "Canto de Alicia," 10.

62   Blackwell, *¡Chicana Power!*, 26.

63   Escalante, interview, 10 November 2012.
64   Escalante, 1973, 1974; Escalante, Speech, Spring 1974.
65   Escalante, *Eastside Sun*, June 27, 1974.
66   Escalante, interview, 10 November 2012.
67   Ibid.

5

CHICANA/O MOVEMENT GRASSROOTS LEFTIST AND RADICAL ELECTORAL POLITICS IN LOS ANGELES, 1970–1980

José G. Moreno

Introduction

In 2005, Antonio Villaraigosa became the second Latino mayor of the city of Los Angeles, California.[1] Why did it take over 130 years before another Latino was elected mayor of Los Angeles? During the post-World War II era, an increase of grassroots politics occurred within the Los Angeles Latino population.[2] The outcome of this influenced the establishment of new social and civil organizations, which emphasized political reform by working within the U.S. political structure.[3] The League of United Latin American Citizens (LULAC), the Community Services Organization (CSO) and the Mexican American Political Association (MAPA), emerged from this grassroots political endeavor. In 1965, the modern U.S. political climate changed in a tremendous fashion. For instance, Chicanas/os formulated radical and leftist consciousnesses, by creating mass political movements for social justice and equality that became the Chicana/o Movement. The expansion of Chicana/o radicalism in the Los Angeles Basin utilized organizational methodologies to exercise mass protests, walkouts, sit-ins, street riots, and occupy public buildings. This chapter examines electoral grassroots politics, spotlighting the foundation of the Los Angeles La Raza Unida Party (LRUP) from 1970 to 1980, focusing on the LRUP chapters in East Los Angeles, City Terrace, and San Fernando, and their organizational applications, political campaigns, and grassroots strategies. This historical narrative demonstrates how LRUP formulated a social and political movement to increase Latino electoral representation throughout the past three decades. Furthermore, it combines social history and political history to contextualize the significance of this independent political party.

The Origins and the Development of the La Raza Unida Party

The increase in post-World War II grassroots Latino electoral politics led to the historical origins of the Mexican American generation and the first wave of the middle-class sector.[4] This new type of activism and leadership made a historical impact in the struggle for political and social reform within the various U.S. mainstream institutions. However, it failed to improve the living wage and economic conditions for the Latino population. Even with this disappointment, they gained a further understanding on organizational methodologies and practical applications of the U.S. electoral process. The construction of Chicana/o radicalism changed their grassroots political direction and provided new ideologies to promote social justice and electoral equality in low-income communities.[5] The expansion of leftist politics influenced the development of an independent third political party, which attempted to represent the working-class population. But, concerned by the mass violence in the aftermath of August 29, 1970 of the Chicano Moratorium March and other historical events, various Chicana/o organizations were forced to consider alternative organizational methodologies to continue their social movements.[6] For instance, these collectives were determined to further formulate an independent third political party to confront the status quo for political control of their communities. As a result, they argued that the Democratic and Republican Parties were a two-party dictatorship, which controlled the majority of the U.S. political power structure.

In April of 1970, key members from the Mexican American Youth Organization (MAYO) formulated the La Raza Unida Party in Crystal City, Texas. The final outcome of this process led to the establishment of LRUP electoral candidates for public office in four areas of South Texas.[7] By 1971, this chapter of LRUP had replaced most of the MAYO chapters due to concentrating on grassroots electoral politics and limiting their work to university campuses. From 1971 to 1979, political collectives focused their organizing efforts on building political and community bases. As a result, the LRUP of Texas attained mass support and built a significant powerful grassroots foundation, which impacted the political construction of this social movement at the national level.[8] By late March 1970, the LRUP had formulated chapters in the Colorado region that were critical of the two-party dictatorship. For instance, at the Second Annual Chicano Youth Liberation Conference, the Crusade for Justice and various Chicana/o civil rights leaders announced that various political candidates had accepted their invitation to develop an electoral campaign under the LRUP banner. After making the official announcement, they organized a press conference to attain public support from the local and regional Chicana/o population. These LRUP chapters conducted a radical and militant ideological framework in their organizational applications and political campaigns. They exercised the general concept for self-determination, rather than a reformist political perception.[9]

Moreover, the political construction of the La Raza Unida Party in Texas and Colorado sparked chapters in California, New Mexico, Arizona, Washington, and in the Midwestern states.

The Construction of LRUP in California

The popular increase of radical grassroots electoral politics around the nation influenced the construction of the La Raza Unida Party in the state of California. In late 1970, the LRUP formulated its first California chapter in the Oakland/Berkeley area. This first historical gathering passed a motion stating: "La Raza Unida Party will not support any candidate of the Democratic or Republican Party or any individual who supports these parties."[10]

With this suggestion, the LRUP Oakland/Berkeley chapter clarified its distance from the two mainstream parties. It encouraged individuals to join the La Raza Unida Party in order to generate an alternative political voice for the local working-class Latino population. As a result, they spent the next few months building their community bases all over Northern California.

In early 1971, the LRUP Oakland/Berkeley chapter published a founding document of the Oakland chapter:

> We the people of La Raza, have decided to reject the existing political parties of our oppressors and take it upon ourselves to form LA RAZA UNIDA PARTY which will serve as a unifying force in our struggle for self-determination. We understand that our real liberation and freedom will only come about through independent political action on our part. Independent political action, of which electoral activity is but one aspect, means involving La Raza Unida Party at all levels of struggle in action which will serve to involve and educate our people. We recognize that self-determination can only come about through the full and total participation of La Raza in the struggle.[11]

This manuscript became the preamble that most new LRUP California chapters emphasized in their political platform. The historical significance of this document positioned the ideological and organizational character for the establishment of future chapters during the years of 1971 to 1974. However, they utilized the LRUP Texas chapter practical grassroots applications and frameworks across the state of California. In addition, the initiative of establishing this LRUP chapter occurred due to the outcome of the 1969 National Chicano Youth Liberation Conference (NCYLC), which took place in Denver, Colorado, and the call for an independent Chicana/o political party.

By the beginning of 1971, La Raza Unida Party had formulated new chapters throughout the state of California. On February 21, 1971, the LRUP chapters from Northern California held a conference to construct an organizational and practical strategy to establish various new chapters in their region. Over 14 Northern California LRUP units and 1,300 people attended this historic gathering in Stockton, California. La Raza Unida Party leader José Ángel Gutiérrez traveled from South Texas to present the keynote address, with a particular focus on the political significance of increasing future chapters throughout the west coast. After Gutiérrez's speech, conference participants passed a critical resolution to construct new regional and local LRUP chapters. Furthermore, the outcome of this gathering influenced the establishment of La Raza Unida Party in the Southern California region.

In early 1971, the LRUP conducted various meetings in the Los Angeles area to formulate new local chapters. On February 27, 1971, over 200 people attended an organizational conference at California State University, Los Angeles (CSULA). The outcome of this historic gathering was the foundation of LRUP in San Diego County, the Inland Empire, Ventura County, Orange County, and various other areas of Los Angeles County.[12] A few months later, a variety of Chicana/o civil rights movement organizations and activists in the San Bernardino/Riverside region hosted a La Raza Unida Party Conference at Chaffey College. Over 500 people attended this event, and contributed in creating an organizational and practical methodology to establish new LRUP chapters throughout San Bernardino and Riverside counties. The result of this assembly was affirmative due to the encouragement of Chicanas/os to join their political party and formulate new local and regional chapters. In May of 1971, several new LRUP Southern California chapters conducted an organizational conference at the Euclid Community Center in Boyle Heights. The general purpose for this meeting was to construct a sensible guide for new local LRUP chapters and invent public relations strategies to promote their political party to the Chicana/o population. In addition, these organizational conferences were significant in increasing the Southern California La Raza Unida Party chapters and politically motivating new membership and leadership.

The Historical Foundation of LRUP in Los Angeles

During the late 1960s and early 1970s, the Los Angeles area became a primary urban location for the construction of Chicana/o Power Movement organizations and activities.[13] By mid-1971 a variety of new chapters had materialized throughout the Los Angeles area. For instance, new chapters were organized in East Los Angeles, City Terrace, and the San Fernando Valley.[14] In the coming months, they conducted a series of practical meetings to construct: 1) organizational strategies, 2) an electoral campaign format, 3) a voting registration campaign, 4) a financial operation procedure, and 5) a grassroots media outlet. The enhancement of this new process changed their local and regional political and practical direction. As a result, these LRUP chapters spent a decade attempting to utilize this organizational structure in their grassroots electoral campaigns.

East Los Angeles Chapter

During the height of the Chicana/o Power Movement era, East Los Angeles was a major regional center due to having a massive Latino population.[15] This location is one of the largest U.S. Latino communities that remains unincorporated. However, with this circumstance the East Los Angeles area has had a long historical significance in the struggle for political representation and social justice. For instance, in early 1971, various Chicana/o civil rights organizations and activists from this local community established the first active Los Angeles LRUP chapter.[16] By the summer of 1971, they had conducted a series of planning meetings which led to the foundation of an organizational structure and ideology. This process assisted the development of a political base and an action plan which led to the recruitment of additional general members and the development of new local chapters. In addition, the outcome of this progression was significant in strengthening their organizational framework and political strategy.

During the summer and fall of 1971, the East Los Angeles chapter organized a series of local voter registration clinics to formulate strategies to register over 66,000 people by the end of the year,[17] with the outcome of a field report constructed to help new LRUP chapters further comprehend their political ideology and organizational format. This document was significant to the future progress of local LRUP electoral campaigns as they utilized the field report to outline and formulate a community grassroots outreach and media strategy. For example, the East Los Angeles chapter worked on the two 1971 Raúl Ruíz electoral campaigns, which allowed them to adopt this new organizational application.[18] These electoral campaigns were successful in gaining community support and registering new voters to their political party. With this new focus, the East Los Angeles chapter spent the first part of 1972 continuing to develop their organizational strategies for the next electoral campaign cycle. By the summer, this LRUP chapter had a major growth of new members and local community confirmation. As a result, most of the California LRUP chapters asked them to host the statewide convention. This gathering was held at East Los Angeles Community College with the objective of discussing the first national convention and developing political resolutions.[19] Moreover, from September 1–4, 1972, they sent political delegates to El Paso, Texas to make an impression during the LRUP National Convention.

Following the national convention, they joined a new grassroots Ad Hoc Committee aimed at constructing a political initiative to incorporate East Los Angeles from the county of Los Angeles.[20] This was not the first time that local residents and civil organizations had attempted an incorporation campaign; two unsuccessful prior attempts in 1961 and 1963 had failed due to the lack of community and financial support from the taxpayers in the corporate area. In early 1973, the former director of The East Los Angeles Community Union (TELACU) Esteban Torres was elected chairperson of the Ad Hoc committee.

After the first gathering, the Ad Hoc Committee decided to commission the James F. Hays and Associates law firm to develop a field description to promote the social and political benefits of being an incorporated city.[21] Three months later, they filed a general proposal to the Local Agency Formation Commission (LAFCO) to begin the political process to incorporate East Los Angeles.[22] LAFCO sent a general statement to the Ad Hoc Committee on June 13, 1973, providing further details on the outcome of this incorporation attempt. Following this letter the Committee filed a new proposal which provided more information on the incorporation campaign. The second proposal provided a plan of political development for police protection and a general directory of local residents that supported their electoral initiative.[23] A new economical budget of 4.7 million dollars was proposed to operate the incorporated city. In early August of 1973, LAFCO allocated the authorization for the Ad Hoc Committee to petition local community members for this measure. For the next 7 months, they collected over 8,000 signatures to turn into the County Registrars Office. Furthermore, in June of 1974, the Los Angeles County Board of Supervisors (LACBS) voted to have the political measure of incorporation on the 1974 California election ballot.[24]

Further to the LACBS authorization, the Ad Hoc Committeee had a 2-month deadline to seek possible East Los Angeles residents to run for the future 5 city council seats, and 5 months to advocate this incorporation initiative.[25] During the late summer of 1974, the East Los Angeles LRUP chapter determined to run a political slate of five candidates. The five LRUP members were Daniel Zapata, Raúl Ruíz, Jorge García, Arturo Sánchez, and Celia Rodríguez. These individuals were selected due to their strong historical and cultural roots in the local area. After finalizing their political slate, each LRUP candidate adopted five critical platform positions, which included 1) community control of the local government; 2) grassroots community development; 3) quality health care and facilities; 4) community control of local law enforcement; and 5) relevant public education.[26] The East Los Angeles chapter had the only electoral candidates that strived for a political voice outside the two dominant political parties.

On November 5, 1974, this political attempt for incorporation of East Los Angeles was defeated by the local voters with over 7,000 out of 12,000 people voting against this measure.[27] However, the cityhood election was successful due to LRUP candidates finishing in the top 14 out of 39 candidates. For instance, Ruíz finished first with 2,440 votes; he would have become mayor if the incorporation initiative had passed; candidate Rodríguez finished seventh with 1,557 votes, and Zapata was eleventh with 1,395 votes. Sánchez and García received over 1,000 votes to finish twelfth and fourteenth respectively on the city council candidate list. If this incorporation attempt had passed, the East Los Angeles chapter would have had a historic function in the foundation of this new city. However, in the aftermath of this electoral campaign there were political divisions within the membership that forced people to leave the organization.[28]

This outcome led to a lack of economic resources and the closing of their office space. By 1975, the East Los Angeles chapter members had made the critical decision to merge with the City Terrace chapter to continue stressing independent grassroots political representation.[29] Even with these circumstances, they made a major historical and political impression by establishing an organizational trend for the rest of the Los Angeles Basin LRUP chapters.

City Terrace Chapter

City Terrace is located in the East Los Angeles area and has a massive Chicana/o population.[30] However, this population group was marginalized and powerless due to the status quo controlling the local electoral process. In 1971, various Chicana/o grassroots civic organizations and activists established the second local LRUP chapter in the Los Angeles Basin.[31] *La Raza* magazine editor Raúl Ruiz became a key individual due to his local political engagement and involvement. City Terrace was the ideal location for the construction of a LRUP chapter because of CSULA which existed as a major recruiting base for future members and organizers. Having access to the *La Raza* magazine staff and office space assisted in the advancement of social media strategies for future grassroots electoral campaigns. In addition, staff writers published articles and tabloid flyers that promoted the City Terrace chapter.

During the summer of 1971, they decided to run Raúl Ruiz for the 48th assembly district seat in a replacement special election.[32] This special election occurred when incumbent David Roberti assumed a seat in the California State Senate. The City Terrace chapter considered this as a major political and historic opportunity to challenge the local status quo candidates. For instance, Ruiz ran against Democratic Party candidate Richard Alatorre, Republican Party candidate Bill Brophy, and the Peace and Freedom Party candidate John C. Blaine.[33] This special election took place on October 19, 1971 and Ruiz received 1,378 of the total votes. The LRUP organizational effort prevented any of the candidates from accomplishing over 50 percent of the required votes to attain the assembly seat. This outcome forced a November 16, 1971 run-off election, with a Brophy triumph attaining 46 percent of the total electoral votes. Ruiz and the rest of the general membership took the credit for the unexpected political defeat of Democrat Alatorre. This was a historic political election, being the first time since the nineteeth century that two Latino candidates had confronted each other to attain electoral representation.[34] However, the political platform stressing an independent Chicana/o political party was the major factor in defeating Alatorre, and served as practical model for future LRUP electoral campaigns. In addition, this electoral campaign was the first LRUP organizational task in the Los Angeles Basin.

In 1972, Ruiz ran for the 40th State Assembly District in the East Los Angeles area.[35] This time he ran against incumbent Democratic Party Assemblyman Alex

García and only received 13 percent of the votes.[36] The electoral victory for the incumbent García made various City Terrace chapter members discouraged about the voting patterns and behavior of their local working-class community.[37] At the same time, both political campaigns to elect Ruiz for State Assembly were successful in influencing other LRUP chapters to run political candidates for public office.[38] A few months later, the City Terrace chapter played an important role at the 1972 La Raza Unida Party National Convention due to Ruiz chairing the convention. After this historic gathering, the City Terrace was forced to spend most of 1973 reorganizing its political and practical methodologies and rebuilding its local community base.[39] In 1974, the chapter decided to join the East Los Angeles incorporation attempt and agreed to have Ruiz run for a city council seat. A year later, they merged with the East Los Angeles chapter due to the decline of local general membership and campaign organizers.[40] By 1977 the majority of the general leadership and membership had disbanded the LRUP chapter due to the lack of economic resources and the changing political climate. However, the City Terrace chapter had a historical significance on the foundation of the LRUP in the Los Angeles region, due to organizing major local grassroots electoral campaigns during the height of the Chicana/o Power generation.

San Fernando Chapter

The San Fernando Valley was a major political center during the Chicana/o Power Movement era.[41] The local Chicana/o population had a rich and long history in the Valley that went back to the Spanish colonial period. Most of the San Fernando Valley is part of the city of Los Angeles, but three independent areas are the cities of Burbank, Glendale, and San Fernando. The city of San Fernando is the oldest historical section in the Valley, and has the largest Chicana/o population. In 1971, the San Fernando chapter became the third chapter to be established in the Los Angeles Basin.[42] Most of the founding membership of the chapter were involved in various grassroots Latino organizations prior to joining the LRUP.[43] The general idea of establishing this chapter developed from California State University, Northridge (CSUN), Chicano Studies Department Student Political Committee.[44] After conducting a series of meetings, they made the critical decision that the city of San Fernando would become their political hub. There were three major factors for building an electoral base in San Fernando: 1) the rich Latino historical roots in that area; 2) it was an independent city; and 3) some of the membership and leadership had personal contacts within the local Chicana/o population.[45] These organizational factors were critical in the construction of this LRUP chapter.

In early 1972, the San Fernando chapter ran Richard Corona and Jess Margarito for the San Fernando city council, and supported the re-election of city treasurer E.C. Orozco.[46] Corona and Margarito were university students who had historical and political roots in this community. The major enthusiasm for the San Fernando chapter to develop an electoral campaign was due to the electoral monopoly that the Anglo-American population had in the local political arena.[47] Corona and Margarito, in their political platform, called for: 1) better housing conditions; 2) quality health care; 3) relevant public transportation; 4) bilingual and relevant education; 5) the provision of drug abuse centers for the Chicana/o population; and 6) the offer of free health education to low-income residents.[48] During this electoral campaign, the traditional Anglo-American political sector started to critically question the intentions of the San Fernando chapter. For example, they claimed that the LRUP candidates were a bunch of radicals and had no business in city's political and public affairs.[49] LRUP responded to the red-baiting by challenging this subjective perspective and focusing on their electoral campaign.

On April 11, 1972, in this election in the city of San Fernando, Corona and Margarito attained over 1,000 votes each, but failed to win the two city council seats.[50] This grassroots electoral campaign was somewhat successful in challenging the status quo for community grassroots political control and struggling for a paradigm shift in their local government. After the San Fernando city council election, they decided to run Guadalupe Ramírez for the 41st assembly district during the 1972 presidential election.[51] Ramírez lost this election by a large margin due to the lack of economic resources and concrete grassroots strategic planning. However, it was a great organizational experience for the San Fernando chapter to fully learn about their weaknesses and the community at large. In late December of 1972, it ran Andrés Torres for the 22nd State Senator district, with a small amount of funding from the various Los Angeles Basin LRUP chapters.[52] During the electoral campaign, the San Fernando chapter struggled in their organizational efforts due to political harassment from the Los Angeles Police Department (LAPD).[53] The LAPD pestering affected the chapter membership and forced them to lose concentration on the Torres campaign. However, on February 27, 1973, Torres received 2,636 votes, which forced Democrat candidate Alan Robbins to spend almost $400,000 to win the special election.[54]

In January of 1974, the San Fernando chapter hosted the Southern California La Raza Unida Party Conference.[55] The general purpose of this conference was to conduct discussions on new organizational strategies and the political importance of unity between each LRUP Southern California chapter. After this historic gathering, San Fernando LRUP spent most of 1974 building its local chapter and assisting the East Los Angeles chapter with the incorporation campaign.[56] In 1975, it decided to run Xenaro Ayala and Marshal Díaz for the San Fernando city council.[57] The election result was not successful for the LRUP candidates and they failed to attain sufficient electoral votes and grassroots community confirmation. However, they both finished in the top five, out of seven candidates, and were able to challenge the Anglo-American candidates with a low financial budget. A year later, the chapter ran Torres and José Gonzales for the 39th and 63rd assembly districts respectively.[58] Torres finished the election in third place with 3,292 votes and Gonzales also ended in third place after receiving almost 3,000 votes.[59] Torres and Gonzales failed to win their elections due to the lack of financial resources and the decline of chapter general membership. In 1977, the San Fernando chapter continued to reorganize their political and social methodology and focused on saving the LRUP in the state of California. In early 1978, it decided to give electoral politics another chance by running Torres for the San Fernando city council.[60] On March 7, 1978 Torres lost this election by only 54 votes and it was the first time that a local LRUP chapter had come so close to winning a political election.[61] Moreover, after this election, the chapter moved away from electoral politics to focus on local grassroots issues and struggles.

Conclusion

The political construction of La Raza Unida Party politically and ideologically changed the Chicana/o Power Movement in the 1970s. For instance, the strong establishment of the party chapters in the states of Texas, Colorado, New Mexico, and Arizona and in the Midwest challenged the two major political parties for political control of their communities. The radical leftist social climate and political interest in the Latino community was a major factor in the increase of LRUP membership and chapters at the national level. This political party formulated the construction of the LRUP in the Los Angeles Basin though the ideological and political problems in their electoral campaigns caused the decline of this social movement. Finally, the lack of political and organizational experience within the electoral arena became a major obstacle for the Los Angeles Basin chapters. As a result, they failed to attain the required 66,000 registered voters and were forced to write in their political candidates for the state and national electoral offices.

The ideological divisions within the Los Angeles Basin core leadership and membership also led to their political decline by the end the 1970s. The changing political climate was the major factor in the collapse of this social organization. The conservative mood of the 1980s influenced the birth of U.S. Latino mainstream politics, which had been developing over the last three decades. The Los Angeles LRUP chapters made a historical and political impact in the new wave of modern professional Latino politics due to former general members becoming major power brokers in the U.S. electoral arena. They opened the doors for future grassroots electoral campaigns during the post-civil rights movement era. As a result, an increased number of Latino electoral candidates have been elected to public office since the decline of the LRUP in 1980. To answer the critical question: How did Antonio Villaraigosa attain the city of Los Angeles mayor position? Villaraigosa's mayoral victory occurred due to two generations of Latino grassroots social movements for political representation. The Mexican American generation struggled for political reform and the Chicana/o Movement generation pushed independent representation outside the two-party dictatorship. So Villaraigosa was elected as the city of Los Angeles mayor as a result of the grassroots campaigns of the second half of the twentieth century.

Notes

1   Lisa García Bedolla, *Fluid Borders: Latino Power, Identity, and Politics in Los Angeles* (Berkeley: University of California Press, 2005); Kenneth C. Burt, *The Search for a Civic Voice: California Latino Politics* (Claremont, CA: Regina Books, 2007).

2   Ignacio García, *Hector P. Garcia: In Relentless Pursuit of Justice* (Houston, TX: Arte Publico Press, 2002), Rodolfo Rosales, *The Illusion of Inclusion: The Untold Political Story of San Antonio* (Austin: The University of Texas Press, 2000); Mario T. García, *The Making of a Mexican American Mayor: Raymond L. Telles of El Paso* (El Paso: Texas Western Press at the University of Texas El Paso, 1998); Richard A. Garcia, *Rise of the Mexican American Middle Class San Antonio, 1929–1941* (College Station: Texas A&M University Press, 1991); and George J. Sánchez, *Becoming Mexican American: Ethnicity, Culture, and Identity in Chicano Los Angeles, 1900–1945* (New York: Oxford University Press, 1993).

3   Mario T. García, *Mexican Americans: Leadership, Ideology & Identity, 1930–1960* (New Haven, CT: Yale University Press, 1989); Juan Gómez-Quiñones, *Chicano Politics: Reality and Promise, 1940–1990* (Albuquerque: University of New Mexico Press, 1990).

4   Ibid.

5   Ibid.

6   Lee Bebout, *Mythohistorical Interventions: The Chicano Movement and Its Legacies.* (Minneapolis: University of Minnesota Press, 2011).

7   Charles Chandler, "The Mexican American Protest Movement in Texas", (Ph.D. diss., The University of Tulane, 1968).

8   Ignacio M. García, *Chicanismo: The Forging of a Militant Ethos Among Mexican Americans* (Tucson: University of Arizona Press, 1997); José Ángel Gutiérrez, *The Making of a Chicano Militant: Lessons From Cristal* (Madison: The University of Wisconsin Press, 1999).

9   Ibid.

10   Oakland Area Raza Unida Party Program, Personal Collection of Armando Navarro.

11   Ibid.

12   Raúl Ruiz, interview by author, minidisc recording, Northridge, CA, February 2004.

13   David Rodríguez, interview by author, tape recording, Northridge, CA, 12 December 2003.

14   Ruiz, interview; Rodríguez, interview.

15   Jorge García, "Forjando Ciudad: The Development of a Chicano Political Community in East Los Angeles," (Ph.D. diss., University of California at Riverside, 1986).

16   Jorge García, interview by author, minidisc recording, Northridge, CA, 17 December 2003.

17   El Partido De La Raza Unida Report on Registration Clinic, 24 October 1971, Personal Collection of Jorge García.

18   Ruíz, interview.

19   Rodríguez, interview.

20   García, interview.

21   James F. Hayes and Associates, Feasibility Study for the Proposed Incorporation of E.L.A., February 23, 1973, Personal Collection of Jorge García; Richard Santillán "East Los Angeles: The Politics of Incorporation 1961–1974," unpublished paper, Personal Collection of Jorge García.

22   Richard Santillán, "East Los Angeles: The Politics of Incorporation 1961–1974," unpublished paper, Personal Collection of Jorge García.

23   Ibid.

24   Gloria Santillán, "An Analysis of the Incorporation of East Los Angeles," unpublished paper, Personal Collection of Jorge Garcia; Ray Zeman, "Supervisors OK Election on Incorporation of East Los Angeles," *Los Angeles Times*, 14 June 1974.

25   Frank del Olmo "5 Raza Unida Candidates to Run as Slate for East L.A. Offices in Cityhood Election," *Los Angeles Times*, 16 August 1974; and "Vote Yes on Incorporation, Vote Raza Unida Party" Flyer, 1974, Personal Collection of Jorge García; Vote Nov. 5 "Make E.L.A Your City, For East L.A." Incorporation Special Campaign Tabloid, 1974, Personal Collection of Jorge García.

26   Ruiz, interview; García, interview.

27   Richard Santillán, "Incorporation of East Los Angeles," *La Raza*, 2, no. 3 (1974); Pedro Arias, "East Los Angeles y Las Elecciones En USA," *La Raza*, 2, no. 4 (January, 1975).

28   Pedro Arias, "East Los Angeles y Las Elecciones En USA," *La Raza*, 2, no. 4 (January, 1975).

29   Ruíz, interview; Rodríguez, interview.

30   Miguel Pérez, interview by author, minidisc recording, Northridge, CA, 16 December 2003.

31   Ibid.

32   Ruíz, interview.

33   Olga Rodríguez, "Raza Unida Builds Strong Campaign in L.A.," *The Militant*, 22 October 1971; and Richard Bergholz "10 Scramble for Votes in Bid for Assembly Seat," *Los Angeles Times*, 12 October 1971.

34   García, interview.

35   Frank del Olmo, "3 Mexican-American Seeking 40th Assembly District Seat, *Los Angeles Times*, 2 November 1972; Ruiz, interview.

36   Gilbert M. López, "La Raza Unida Party the 40th Assembly Race," *La Raza*, 1, no. 10 (February 1973).

37   Ruíz, interview; and Raúl Ruíz, "An Analysis of a Campaign," *La Raza*, 1, no. 10 (February 1973): 4–5.

38   Richard Santillán, "Obstacles to Chicano Political Power," unpublished paper, Personal Collection of Jorge García; and López, "La Raza Unida Party the 40th Assembly."

39   Ruíz, interview.

40   Ibid.

41   Rodríguez, interview.

42   Xenaro Ayala, interview by author, minidisc recording, San Fernando, CA, 15 December 2003.

43   Ibid.

44   Pérez, interview; Rodríguez, interview.

45   Ayala, interview; Rodríguez, interview; Pérez, interview.

46   Richard Corona, interview by author, minidisc recording, Northridge, CA, 15 December 2003; Ayala, interview.

47   Corona, interview; Ken Fanucci, "Chicanos Challenge Two San Fernando Incumbents," *Los Angeles Times*, 9 April 1972.

48   Ricardo Loa, "The Establishment of La Raza Unida Party in San Fernando Valley," unpublished paper, East Los Angeles Public Library, Chicano Resource Center; Corona, interview.

49   Corona, interview; Pérez, interview.

50   Pérez, interview

51   San Fernando Chapter of the La Raza Unida Party, Press Release, 23 October 1972, on the Candidacy of Guadalupe Ramírez, Personal Collection of Jorge García.

52   Ayala, interview; Rodríguez, interview; Pérez, interview.

53   Frank del Olmo, "Chicano in Senate Race Raps Police," *Los Angeles Times*, 25 January 1973.

54   Kenneth Reich, "Robbins Election Expenditure Sets Record," *Los Angeles Times*, 5 May 1973.

55   Ayala, interview.

56   Ibid.
57   Ibid.
58   Pérez, interview; Ayala, interview.
59   Eugene Hernández, "La Raza Unida Party Runs in Local Elections," *El Sembrador*, 1, no. 1 (April, 1977); and Steve Warshell, "Raza Unida Parties Assess November 2 Voting," *The Militant*, 26 November 1976.
60   Gayle Johnson, "Four Candidates Join in Race for SF Council Posts," *The San Fernando Valley Sun and Sylmar Breeze*, December 1977; Ayala, interview.
61   Pérez, interview; Ayala, interview.

6

¡YA BASTA! THE STRUGGLE FOR JUSTICE AND EQUALITY

The Chicano Power Movement in Oxnard, California

Luis H. Moreno

We are marching in protest so that our youth's lives will not be used as pawns in a political game.

Roberto Flores[1]

We live and work with the poor. We are the poor. We don't have to prove anything.

Citizens Against Poverty[2]

Introduction

The political and social movements within the United States and throughout the world in the late 1960s and early 1970s would play an important part in raising the political consciousness of the masses of Chicana/os living within the United States, including in Oxnard, California.[3] This awareness led Chicana/os to demand political and social changes through protests that included sit-ins, walkouts, and demonstrations.[4] In March of 1968, Chicana/o students challenged the educational system in East Los Ángeles, California by calling for a mass walkout (blowout). This call led to more than 10,000 Chicana/o students walking out of their high schools demanding educational changes.[5] With the support of Sal Castro, a teacher and outspoken critic of the public school system, and United Mexican American Students (UMAS), the walkout called attention to the unequal educational system Chicana/o students faced everyday.[6]

A month earlier, César Chávez went on a fast in Delano, California to reaffirm the United Farm Workers Organizing Committee's grape strike and boycott commitment to non-violence.[7] Throughout the fast, Chávez received support from numerous congressmen, senators, and union and religious leaders, such as Martin Luther King Jr. and Robert Kennedy. The fast lasted 25 days and ended on March 11, 1968 with a mass attended by more than 4,000 farm workers. A letter written by Chávez was read; it expressed his further commitment to non-violence. He stated "I am convinced that the truest act of courage, the strongest act of manliness is to sacrifice ourselves for others in a totally non-violent struggle for justice."[8] The fast brought national attention to the farm worker movement.

In March 1969, Chicana/o youth from throughout the United States, especially the Southwest, attended the Crusade for Justice's National Chicano Youth Liberation Conference in Denver, Colorado.[9] The week-long conference produced *El Plan Espiritual de Aztlán*, a key *movimiento* document calling for the liberation of all Chicana/os.[10] With the concept of self-determination, Chicana/os left the conference with the mission to educate and unite their communities.[11] A month after the conference, Chicana/o students, activists, and professors met at the University of California, Santa Barbara (UCSB) to participate in a conference organized by the Chicano Coordinating Council on Higher Education (CCHE).[12] The participants focused on developing a stronger link between the community and university by issuing *El Plan de Santa Barbara*. The plan called on the university to provide the space for Chicana/os to organize and develop strategies to empower the community through educational programs and centers.

Those events influenced Chicana/o youth in Oxnard (also referred to as the Oxnard Plain) during the late 1960s and 1970s. Within the city of Oxnard, Chicana/os took to the streets to demand an end to police brutality and the Viet Nam War. In the midst of a political struggle, the battlefield moved from the streets to the agricultural fields of Ventura County as Chicana/os joined the farm worker movement. The struggles for justice and equality on the Oxnard Plain would leave many social and political memories on the Chicana/o working-class community.

This chapter focuses on the rise of the Chicano Power Movement on the Oxnard Plain between 1965 and 1975. Before examining the Chicano Power Movement, it is very important to mention that the daily lives of the Chicana/o community in Oxnard were connected to the billion-dollar agriculture industry of the Oxnard Plain.[13] Not just connected, but the backbone. Throughout the previous decades, the Chicana/o community had attempted to organize themselves through unions, civic, and political organizations. This legacy of resistance sparked the Chicano Power Movement in Oxnard as the children of farm workers demanded justice and equality.

Within the last decade, numerous Chicana/o scholars have expanded our understanding of the Chicano Power Movement by focusing on the *movimiento* outside of the key urban locations in California and Texas.[14] In this chapter, I chose to examine the *movimiento* in Oxnard, especially *La Colonia*, one of the oldest Chicana/o neighborhoods, by focusing on the local events, organizations, and activists. As I examined the activities of Chicana/o youth in Oxnard, it became apparent that the *movimiento* in Los Ángeles had played an important part in developing their political consciousness. The majority of the Chicana/o youth who were involved with the *movimiento* on the Oxnard Plain had attended the universities or participated in marches, events or meetings in Los Ángeles.[15] Moreover, the experience of participating with other Chicana/o youth outside of Oxnard would play an important part as they took on the struggle for justice and equality into the streets and agriculture fields of their hometown.

The Legacy of Resistance

The legacy of resistance and the termination of the Bracero Program in 1964 left physical markers among the Chicana/o working-class communities on the Oxnard Plain. As a key agriculture location it also had been a site of resistance as Chicana/o workers organized a series of strikes in 1903, 1933, and 1941 for better wages and work conditions.[16] Years after being a stronghold of the Bracero Program, Ventura County, where Oxnard is located, still ranked tenth among farm counties in California, fifteenth nationwide, and earned $147 million in value of farm products in 1966. Agriculture continued to be big business in the coastal landscape of Ventura County. It was connected to every aspect of life through culture, history, and politics. The growers controlled the power structure by influencing civic and educational policies of the residents of the Oxnard Plain, especially the Chicana/o working-class community.

The rise of community activism in Oxnard called on the sons and daughters of Chicana/o workers to re-examine their connection to the capitalist power structure that controlled every aspect of society. Their reaction can be seen in the rise of civic engagement within city politics. The voter registration drives of the Ventura County Community Service Organization (VCCSO) between 1958 and 1959 involved a series of political campaigns in the 1960s. In 1960 and 1962, community organizer John Soria ran for an Oxnard city council seat.[17] The political landscape of the city of Oxnard changed on April 12, 1966 with the support of the local Mexican American Political Association (MAPA), when local businessman Salvatore Sánchez was elected to the city council with 2,400 votes, winning all of the precincts of the *La Colonia* neighborhood.[18]

During the 1960s, President Lyndon B. Johnson took on the challenge to eliminate poverty and racial injustice in the United States with the Great Society initiative. The Great Society's programs addressed education, medical care, urban problems, and transportation among the working-class communities. Within Oxnard, city officials and community members utilized the Urban Renewal and War on Poverty programs to target the Chicana/o working-class community. On the other side, the Chicana/o community responded by organizing against urban renewal and utilizing the War on Poverty funding to empower and organize the overall working-class community.

Through numerous War on Poverty programs, the Chicana/o working-class community of Oxnard were able to empower themselves to demand social and political changes. The community connection to VCCSO, United Packing-house Workers of America Local 78, and the Agricultural Workers Organizing Committee led a number of individuals and organizations to seek War on Poverty funding for a series of programs dealing with agriculture workers and the Chicana/o working-class community. As city officials targeted *La Colonia* for urban renewal, two key projects formed in 1965 attempted to provide leadership and empower the working-class community: Operation Buenaventura and the Farm Workers Opportunity Project.

Both played an important part in organizing farm workers, but also giving a voice to the overall Chicana/o working-class community in *La Colonia* and surrounding areas. For instance, Operation Buenaventura focused on building community leadership by "seek[ing] out men and women among the community of migrants and seasonal farm workers in Ventura County who have potential leadership qualities and through intensive training, develop these qualities."[19] Likewise, the Farm Workers Opportunity Project pushed to improve the lives of farm workers through increasing their education and job placement. They both had positive effects on the empowerment and organizing of the Chicana/o working-class community.[20] Clearly, the growers wanted to maintain the system as it was, calling both projects a waste of government funds and, in the words of one grower, "if the two federally funded organizations are giving people the opportunity to become dependent on the government, then I think that is bad."[21]

In spite of criticism, the projects sparked the creation of new civic organizations, such as the Citizens Against Poverty (CAP). CAP grew out of the "ashes of Committee of the Poor" in April 1965; they "consider themselves veterans in the war against poverty because they are poor."[22] CAP had been criticized for its actions in defending the working-class community, and in response to their critics, they stated, "we live and work with the poor. We are the poor. We don't have to prove anything [to anyone]."[23]

Their legacy of resistance and the commitment to political and social changes led a new generation of Chicana/os to organize against police brutality, the Viet Nam War, and the unionization of farm workers in Oxnard.

The Struggle to End Police Brutality

Throughout the *barrios* in California and elsewhere, the Chicana/o community faced decades of police brutality.[24] In response, Chicana/os organized numerous community organizations and groups to expose the tension between the working-class community and the police. By 1968, Chicana/o youth, influenced by the black civil rights movement, had formed the Brown Berets in Los Ángeles to defend the community from police brutality, but also to empower the community through educational and community programs. The Brown Berets motivated other

Chicana/o youth to form chapters or similar organizations throughout the Southwest and elsewhere.

In the summer of 1968, local Chicana/os formed the independent chapter of the Brown Berets. The local Brown Berets were organized under the leadership of Roberto Flores, Fermín Herrera, Andrea Herrera, Armando López, and José Ontiveras and took on the issue of police brutality in Oxnard, especially *La Colonia*.[25] All the members brought years of organizing experience into the Brown Berets, especially Roberto Flores who had spent many years organizing around local issues in *La Colonia*.[26] Armando López had previously worked with the Farm Workers Opportunity Project and had run for the city council that past April.[27] Furthermore, the majority of the members were born on the Oxnard Plain and raised in *La Colonia*.[28]

On August 13, 1968, the Brown Berets challenged the city council on the issue of police brutality by requesting an investigation on the matter. Spokesperson Fermín Herrera stated that they had sworn documents of several cases of police brutality and a petition from the Chicana/o working-class community for an investigation.[29] In response to the request, the city council voted unanimously to forward a request to investigate the alleged acts of police brutality against the residents of *La Colonia* to the California Attorney-General's Office.

Following the first appearance of the Brown Berets at the city council meeting, the editors of *The Press-Courier* raised the following question, "Who are the Brown Berets?" In their editorial, they stated "the Brown Berets are nothing but a few young college men out to brew a tempest in a teapot before skipping off to campus."[30] In a sharp criticism, the newspaper stated "the real problems of Colonia of which there are many will not be solved by impossible demands and exaggerated and shrill appeals for mass protest."[31] The Brown Berets pointed out that their key purpose was "to see better living conditions, better education, and better working conditions for the Mexican-Americans."[32]

With this mission, the Brown Berets moved to circulating a petition for a community police review board from their shared office with the American Friends Service Committee in *La Colonia*. A controversy occurred as a campaign flyer labeled the Oxnard Police Department (OPD) as "white racist cops" and "white helmeted dogs."[33] Within the Chicana/o working-class community, the Brown Berets had supporters and non-supporters. One non-supporter stated, "they do not represent the greater Mexican feeling."[34] A supporter of the Brown Berets stated, "I favor a police review board as a forward step in this community and not just for the Colonia but for all of us" and "I think a civilian advisory review board is needed to increase respect for law and improve the quality of justice."[35] The Brown Berets continued organizing against police brutality, as they waited for a final report.[36]

On December 28, the Brown Berets organized a 1-day community conference in *La Colonia*, which brought out more than fifty individuals from local community organizations such as the Circulo Social Mexicano, Los Amigos, the

Mexican American Political Association, and the Association of Mexican American Educators to discuss solutions for community problems.[37] Out of the conference, a new group was formed, the Mexican-American Unity Council. Raul Maynez of Circulo Social Mexicano was elected chairperson. He stated that the goal of the new group was "a united Mexican-American community, preservation of the Mexican culture, a better understanding between the Spanish speaking and English speaking communities."[38]

In the struggle against police brutality and discrimination, the local Brown Berets participated in or organized numerous protests to expose those issues. On January 23, 1969, at the county's courthouse, thirty Brown Berets and supporters picketed, in the rain, the hearing of 15-year-old Robert Estrada, who faced a 1-year sentence for burglary. The Brown Berets and others charged racial discrimination in the handling of Estrada's case.[39] Spokesperson Andrea Herrera stated, "this is just another example of the way Mexican brown people and black people are treated. We don't get justice."[40] The following day, forty Brown Berets and supporters picketed in front of the OPD headquarters protesting the shooting of Lorenzo Hernández Torres by the police. Herrera stated, "the shooting was coldblooded," and claimed that the officers did not fire any warning shots.[41] Torres survived the shooting and was charged with burglary.

A battle of words on the incident continued between the Brown Berets and the police at the city council meeting, where they criticized the OPD and Chief Al Jewell for continuing the harassment of *La Colonia* residents. Chief Jewell responded by calling the Brown Berets' accusations "completely ridiculous."[42] Such tensions between the Oxnard working-class communities and the police were not new. Several years before, twelve black and Chicana/o residents filed a complaint of police brutality against Chief Jewell.[43] The city council called for an investigation on the complaint. It exposed how racially divided the city was between whites and the communities of color by clearing the chief and police department from any wrongdoing.[44]

On January 28, 1969 more than 200 Brown Berets and supporters flooded the city council meeting to demand the firing of Chief Jewell, the suspension of three police officers involved with the shooting of Torres, and the development of a police review board. The city council agreed to form a committee composed of Mayor William Soo Hoo, Councilman Sal Sánchez, and City Manager Paul Wolven to investigate the shooting, but refused to suspend any of the police officers involved with the shooting. Alberto Ordóñez of the Brown Berets accused Chief Jewell of "formatting a policy of shooting to kill suspects."[45] Chief Jewell responded to the Brown Berets, "I've done everything possible for the Mexican-Americans and will continue to do it but not for your group . . . because you're militants."[46]

The Brown Berets continued to organize and defend the rights of Chicana/os in Oxnard. Due to their position on police brutality, they were criticized throughout the pages of *The Press-Courier*. One non-supporter stated, if the Brown

Berets "are genuinely interested in helping the community as they profess to do so, their past actions have belied their sincerity by being only concerned and associated with the welfare of the criminals of society."[47] The editors of *The Press-Courier* stated, "it is possible to say that the [Brown Berets'] case against the police consists of ineffective and unsupported claims."[48]

On January 31, Councilman Sánchez announced he did "not feel a review board would be bad for the city."[49] He was criticized for this position, but he responded to his critics by stating

> whether the Oxnard Police are guilty today of discrimination or the abuse of power or applying a double standard, I do not know, but I do know that a large percentage of Americans of Mexican descent believe that it exists today.[50]

On February 11, the city council found no wrongdoing in the shooting of Torres, but called for the creation of a community relations representation linked to the Community Relations Commission "to act as liaison between administrate officials, department heads, the police, and the people."[51]

The Brown Berets disagreed with the decision but continued to organize and empower the Chicana/o community through their tutoring and education programs.[52] As the local Brown Berets organized against police brutality, other organizations in Oxnard and elsewhere focused on exposing the unjust war in Viet Nam.

¡Raza Si! Guerra No!

In 1967, Ralph Guzmán published his article "Mexican American Casualties in Vietnam," exposing Chicana/os to the high number of people of color dying in the unjust war in Viet Nam.[53] In this groundbreaking article, Guzmán compared the Chicana/o population of the United States Southwest with the number of Chicana/o dead in Viet Nam. The results stated that Chicana/o only made up 13.8 percent of the population in the Southwest but were 19.4 percent of the dead from the region. This article raised the political consciousness of Chicana/os to the need to organize and join the struggle against the Viet Nam War.

With the military draft in place, Chicana/os began to be recruited into the war. The Chicana/o community was divided over the issue, with some entering the draft and others becoming draft resisters. In 1969, Rosalio Muñoz, Ramses Noriega, and other individuals founded what became the National Chicano Moratorium Committee (NCMC). The purpose of the NCMC was to expose the Chicana/o community to the unjust war in Viet Nam and to raise the issues (i.e. irrelevant education, police brutality) Chicana/os faced every day.[54] The NCMC called for a series of demonstrations against the Viet Nam War leading to a mass demonstration in East Los Ángeles during the summer of 1970.

On February 28, 1970, more than 3,000 Chicana/os marched in the rain in East Los Ángeles against the Viet Nam War.[55] Following this march, other small demonstrations took place in San Francisco, San Diego, Santa Barbara, and other cities in the Southwest.[56] On August 29, more than 20,000 Chicana/os gathered at Belvedere Park to march down Atlantic and Whittier Blvd in the heart of East Los Ángeles ending at Laguna Park. At Laguna Park, the peaceful crowd listened to music and speakers.[57]

Outside the park, a so-called dispute happened at a nearby liquor store, which brought a response by the Los Ángeles Sheriff Department (LASD) when they called for the end of the rally at Laguna Park. It turned the peaceful rally into a violent attack against the Chicana/os in the park. The LASD entered the park with riot gear and shot tear gas into the crowd. In response to the attack, the crowd defended themselves by throwing the tear gas back at the LASD and moving into the surrounding community to find safety. The rally ended with the death of Ángel Díaz, Lyn Ward, and *Los Ángeles Times* reporter Rubén Salazar.[58]

On the Oxnard Plain, the Chicana/o community responded to the Viet Nam War and the NCMC by organizing their own moratorium event, the La Raza Moratorium Peace March in September 1970. To avoid violence, the police met with march organizers from MAPA and MEChA (*Movimiento Estudiantil Chicano de Aztlán*). John Soria of MAPA stated, "we don't want any difficulties, only an effective and peaceful march."[59] As part of the march activities, Roberto Flores, one of the march organizers, reported that fifteen members of the Oxnard Chicano Moratorium Committee would begin a fast on September 16 at Our Lady of Guadalupe Church in *La Colonia* to highlight the 8,000 Chicana/os killed in the Viet Nam War, which included 30 from Ventura County. Focusing on one key point of the march, Flores stated, "we are marching in protest so that our youth's lives will not be used as pawns in a political game."[60]

More than 1,000 Chicana/os marched from Colonia Park to Oxnard Community Center on September 19, in protest over the Viet Nam War. The crowd heard speeches from a number of local and national speakers. Ricardo Carmona of the Oxnard Chicano Moratorium Committee told the crowd, "we must band together and change our course by fighting for all of our rights." Another local speaker, Roberto Aliasa stated, "we just want to be liberated" and "we have been raped of our land and heritage."

Joey García, a member of *Teatro de la Esperanza*, a Chicano theater group from UCSB, read a powerful poem to the crowd on police brutality: "with a gun on your side/you walk so tall./But I know you're afraid/'cause you can't kill us all./So just go away, until another day,/When we shall meet face to face/once again,/at the moratorium."[61] Rosalio Muñoz of the NCMC reminded the crowd, "we are a nation of people rising on our home front to fight for justice and we must organize to pressure the issues of police brutality and working conditions." And finally, Reverend Blasé Bonpane pointed out that Chicana/os "were the largest single race sent [to Viet Nam], but they receive the least from society and face hunger, injustices, and racism."[62] The march ended with no violence and left a historical marker within the Chicana/o community in Oxnard, which called on organizing for social and political justice.

After the march, numerous organizations and individuals continued to organize in *La Colonia*. Tensions between the Chicana/o working-class community and the police continued. In 1971, a series of civil unrest events occurred in *La Colonia* between the police and Chicana/o youth.[63] Police Chief Robert Owens dismissed this by stating that it "was just attack by frustrated youth against the establishment and police."[64] The OPD and city officials did not publicly pinpoint the unrest on the Brown Berets, Chicano Moratorium Committee, or key organizers, but those organizations and individuals became key targets of police harassment.[65]

By November of 1972, numerous Brown Berets chapters throughout California had disbanded but others continued.[66] As for the members of the local Brown Berets, the majority of them moved into other struggles on the Oxnard Plain and throughout California. Furthermore, the political struggle moved from the streets into the agriculture fields, as the children of farm workers supported or joined the ranks of the farm worker movement.

¡Viva La Huelga!

The United Farm Workers Organizing Committee (UFWOC) entered Ventura County in 1967 and by 1970 had set up shop in the heart of *La Colonia*.[67] On October 22, 1970, the VCCSO organized an event in *La Colonia* with César Chávez and the UFWOC to discuss the organizing of agricultural workers in Ventura County.[68] In his speech to the crowd, Chávez stated that "the giants have been defeated in other places and they can be defeated here."[69] Those words would motivate a decade of struggles against the growers ending with some victories and defeats.

In 1973, the *Ventura County Star-Free Press* reported that agriculture was the number one industry in Ventura County with $220 million earned by local growers.[70] Strawberries were the third top-ranking crop with $19 million earned.[71] The UFW (United Farm Workers) had targeted the strawberry industry in Salinas Valley to organize strawberry pickers.[72] One of the key growers in Salinas was Dave Walsh, who also grew strawberries on the Oxnard Plain.

On May 24, 1974, 200 strawberry pickers in Oxnard walked off their job in a sympathy strike in support of Salinas's strawberry pickers strike against grower Walsh.[73] The strawberry strikers called on the local UFW to negotiate better wages with the growers. A key issue was the differences in wages being paid in Salinas and on the Oxnard Plain.[74] The walkout led to mass picketing at Walsh's property the day after, which turned violent. The Ventura County Sheriff's Department (VCSD) responded to a call by Cecil Martínez, who reported that the UFW organizers and supporters were intimidating strawberry pickers and destroying farm equipment. The VCSD arrested four individuals on charges of arson, trespassing, and malicious mischief.[75] Roberto Flores, a local activist, stated that he "deplored the violence by some pickers but maintained the union had been invited to the fields by dissatisfied workers."[76] Furthermore, Flores charged the VCSD with attempting to intimidate the UFW with "arbitrary arrests."

The strawberry strike was over low wages, poor working conditions, and general dissatisfaction with growers. Flores added that, "the strawberry pickers are the lowest paid in California."[77] The walkout turned into a majority strike of 2,000 strawberry pickers against the local strawberry growers of Walsh, Driscoll, Oxnard Berry Farms, and the American Food Company.[78] The local growers, under the direction of the Western Growers Association (WGA), refused to raise wages and negotiate with the strawberry pickers or the UFW.[79] The strikers continued to encourage other strawberry pickers to join the strike by utilizing the tactic of going from field to field. Again, the growers called the VSCD, which warned the strawberry strikers to leave the fields or be arrested for trespassing.

As reported by UFW spokesperson Lorenzo Moreno, the strawberry strike was "spontaneous and not directed by the union." The strawberry pickers sought the support of the UFW after they walked out.[80] At the same time, the growers were seeking legal action. On May 27, Cecil Martínez filed a legal action in Oxnard Superior Court seeking a preliminary injunction and restraining order against the UFW and strawberry strikers to keep them off his field, with a claim of $1 million in damages.[81]

The next day, more than 400 strawberry strikers and supporters demonstrated at the Ventura County Jail calling for the release of the arrested strikers and the end of arbitrary arrests and harassment by the VSCD.[82] In the evening, Chávez spoke to a crowd of more than 2,000 strikers and supporters in Oxnard, stating, "the union will protect workers. We will fight the unfair injunctions."[83] He continued by stating that "striking is the most important and effective weapon in showing ranchers of the needs of the campesino."[84] Local UFW supporter, Jesús Madrigal agreed with the UFW: "Chávez says we ought to unite ourselves to fight the boss for what is just . . . and I think that is right, that's why I support Chávez's union."[85]

The following day, Oxnard Superior Court Judge Donald Pollock issued a temporary injunction limiting the picketing of the UFW. The strawberry strikers and supporters were limited to five individuals per field and two individuals at each entrance. Debra Peyton, UFW attorney, stated that "the court order was one of most oppressive ever issued and one which is illegal and unconstitutional."[86] Furthermore, Peyton pointed out that the temporary restraining order "denies the basic rights of the 1st Amendment and prevents the farm workers from effectively expressing his grievances with other workers."[87]

Violence erupted between strawberry strikers and supporters, the OPD, and VCSD as they attempted to serve the injunction papers. The VCSD escalated the situation by using helicopters to disperse the strawberry strikers and supporters on the picket line.[88] An exchange between the OPD and Roberto Flores led to six individuals including himself being arrested over a rock-throwing confrontation.[89] Before being arrested, Flores accused the VCSD of harassment as they labeled the picket line an unlawful assembly of strawberry strikers and supporters.[90] The VCSD and OPD continued the arrests of non-violent strawberry strikers and supporters, which only increased the number of individuals on the picket line.

The local growers continued with legal action by suing the UFW for damages per day for the loss of strawberries, which included $4 million in punitive damages.[91] As local growers took legal action, Leo Hubbard of the WGA bragged that the growers could beat the strike, even though it was costing the growers hundreds of thousands of dollars a day. On May 30, Superior Court Judge Richard Heaton issued a new temporary restraining order that covered several more local growers. Attorneys of the UFW and the growers were able to reach an agreement on a new restraining order, which permitted no more than 50 picketers, each 50 feet apart on the picket line, and prohibited picketers from entering the field.[92]

The UFW increased its organizing leadership with the arrival of Manuel Chávez to strengthen the organizing drive of local strawberry pickers.[93] Both sides claimed gains in the strike. Hubbard stated, "90 percent of the pickers are back in the fields" and the "UFW does not, as it has claimed, represent local workers."[94] Manuel Chávez responded by stating that the strike was "85 percent successful" and the "strike is working and the ranchers are scared."[95]

The growers continued to use the VCSD, OPD, the Ventura County Tactical Squad, and armed security guards to harass the strawberry strikers and supporters on the picket line.[96] The harassment moved from the picket line to the community when UFW organizer Roberto García was arrested when leaving the UFW office in *La Colonia* on charges of preventing the transporting of the strawberry pickers to the fields.[97] On May 31, the VCSD and OPD continued their harassment by arresting thirty strawberry strikers and supporters for violating the temporary restraining order. García pointed out that the "growers know how effective our strike is, and they're using the sheriffs and police department the same way they used the judge to break our strike."[98]

The VCSD and OPD continued their harassment of Roberto Flores, as he was arrested again for the third time. Flores stated "they're arresting me for anything they can think of."[99] UFW attorney Peyton said that the VCSD had gone crazy and arrested strawberry strikers and supporters on trumped-up charges.[100] It was reported that Daryl Arnold, executive vice president of the WGA was party to the harassment. It was very clear that the WGA's mission was "to disorganize, demoralize, and terrorize the striking workers back into the field."[101]

In the midst of the bitter struggle between strawberry strikers and growers, the Teamsters announced that they were ready to start organizing agricultural workers in Ventura County.[102] To inform the overall Chicana/o working-class community of the strawberry strike, the UFW planned a march and rally in

Oxnard. UFW representative, Sister Pearl McGivney stated "[the] purpose of the march is to bring the people together and protest the injustices and attitudes of the Ventura County Sheriff's Department and Oxnard Police Department in their handling of the berry strike."[103]

On June 1, more than 2,000 supporters from the local community, throughout Ventura County and California, joined César Chávez and the strawberry strikers in a march through the streets of *La Colonia* protesting the extreme law enforcement harassment. Chávez told the crowd, "Sheriff Hill has taken it upon himself to be the judge, prosecutor, and sheriff . . . we're going to picket because of our god given rights and no one . . . can take those rights away from us."[104] He continued, "we are going to submit to arrest non-violently" and "we are going to go to jail by the thousands to demonstrate that we are not going to be kicked around."[105] At the end the crowd shouted, "*Huelga, Huelga,*" and "Chávez sí, Teamsters no."[106] Local UFW organizer, Jesús Villegas pointed out "the support of our brothers and sisters here in the community is a sign of the justice of our cause."[107] García reported that there were more than 2,000 individuals available for picketing duty.[108]

Hubbard continued to preach that the "growers would break the UFW activities, claiming the UFW does not represent local workers."[109] Teamster Jim Hanson reported that organizers were on the ground in the Oxnard Plain assessing the situation with growers and strawberry pickers. As the strike continued, the strawberry strikers and the UFW received support from the ACLU, the Oxnard Federation of Teachers, and the American Federation of Teachers.[110] Violence erupted again, however, on June 2, as a farm labor bus, which transported strawberry pickers to Oxnard from Santa Paula, was set on fire.[111]

On June 3, the Ventura County Board of Supervisors (VCBS) announced that they would form a committee composed of Supervisors John Flynn and Frank Jewett to investigate UFW charges of harassment by the VCSD.[112] Isedillia Quirez of the UFW informed the Board of Supervisors about her harassment by the VCSD. She stated that "the wind created by the helicopters was so strong I . . . was knocked down . . . the helicopter over me I thought it was going to kill me."[113] Sheriff Hill responded to allegations of harassment in a written statement by "acknowledging the rights of UFW and supporters to voice their concerns through orderly picketing and freedom of speech but also it's their job to enforce the injunction."[114]

On June 5, 100 strawberry pickers and supporters attended the Oxnard city council meeting to protest OPD's tactics and harassment on the picket line. UFW attorney Ellen Lake called on the city council to "pull the Oxnard Police off the strike lines outside of the city limits."[115] The following day, growers and their supporters jam-packed another city council meeting to oppose any move to decrease the police efforts to enforce the court injunctions. Police Chief Robert Owens reported that "the police are not antifarm workers . . . we had frequent relatively peaceful encounters even though incidents went somewhat beyond permissive bounds."[116] The UFW attempted to put more pressure on the city of Oxnard as they filed a 250,000 dollar claim in court for the injuries that occurred when the police were arresting UFW strawberry strikers and supporters.[117]

Both sides continued in their battle of words, as the Ventura County Agricultural Association (VCAA) maintained that the strawberry strike was over and the UFW hinted about a call for a nationwide strawberry boycott.[118] Violence continued as the result of the labor dispute between growers and the UFW with reports of arson on strawberry pickers' homes and growers' properties.[119] On June 14, Superior Court Judge Heaton issued a preliminary injunction limiting the picketing by the UFW at eighteen strawberry fields. The preliminary injunction changed the previous temporary injunction to no more than 2 picketers every 50 feet.[120] UFW attorney Peyton called the injunction, "an incredible infringement on the first amendment rights."[121] Growers' attorney William Hair stated, "this is exactly what I've asked for. Now we have an order so we can keep the peace."[122]

The injunction put an end to the strawberry strike and the picketing of the UFW. UFW organizer Villegas connected all the dots regarding how powerful the local growers were by stating, "[it is] my opinion . . . the courts work hand to hand with the growers by approving such an injunction."[123] The strawberry strike reconnected many Chicana/os to their working-class history. Also, it provided the opportunity for them to gain or use their organizing skills for the struggle for justice and equality. Lastly, the *movimiento* in Oxnard connected the urban and rural experiences of Chicana/os as they crossed between the battles in the streets and fields of the Oxnard Plain.

Conclusion

The Chicano Power Movement shaped the drive for equality on the Oxnard Plain. The *movimiento* sparked the establishment of the local Brown Berets, the Chicano Moratorium Committee, and the UFW. Those organizations played an important part in the political education of generations of local activists, organizers, and community members. Yet, after years of battles with the growers and city officials, the Chicana/o working-class community on the Oxnard Plain would face more battles in the 1980s and beyond.

As the Chicano Power Movement activities decreased in the mid-1970s, local activists continued their mission to empower the working-class community and advocate for farm worker rights. For instance, in 1975 local activists formed the *El Concilio del Condado de Ventura*, as an umbrella organization to provide information in the areas of education, farm labor, and health.[124] As the community confronted the issues of criminalization, discrimination, and segregation, they gained the courage to resist by demanding better wages or calling for an end to police brutality. In closing, I have shared with you an unofficial history of political unrest on the Oxnard Plain, but it is just a brief introduction to the historical memory of the Chicana/o working-class community; there are many more stories to be told.

Notes

1 "Peace march leaders issue conduct code for paraders," *The Press-Courier*, 17 Sep 1970.
2 "CAP tells about itself," *The Press-Courier*, 4 Oct 1965.
3 Huey P. Newton, *Revolutionary Suicide* (New York: Writers and Readers, 1973); Clayborne Carson, *In Struggle SNCC and the Black Awakening of the 1960s* (Cambridge, MA: Harvard University Press, 1981); Bobby Seale, *Seize The Time: The Story of the Black Panther Party and Huey P. Newton* (Baltimore: Black Classic Press, 1970); Kwame Ture and Charles V. Hamilton, *Black Power: The Politics of Liberation* (New York: Vintage Books, 1967); Rodolfo Acuña, *A Community Under Siege: A Chronicle of Chicanos East of the Los Ángeles River 1945–1975* (Los Ángeles: Chicano Studies Research Center Publications, University of California, Los Ángeles, 1984); Carlos Muñoz, Jr., *Youth, Identity, Power: The Chicano Movement* (New York: Verso, 1989); Rodolfo "Corky" Gonzales and Antonio Esquibel, Eds., *Message To Aztlán: Selected Writing Rodolfo "Corky" González* (Houston, TX: Arte Publico Press, 2001); Ernesto Vigil, *The Crusade For Justice: Chicano Militancy And The Government's War On Dissent* (Madison: University of Wisconsin Press, 1999); Ernesto Chávez, *My People First! Mi Raza Primero: Nationalism, Identity, and Insurgency in the Chicano Movement in Los Ángeles 1966–1978* (Berkeley: University of California Press, 2002).
4 Rodolfo Acuña, *Occupied America: A History of Chicanos, Fifth Edition* (New York: Longmen, 2004), 298–337.
5 Ibid., 319–320.
6 Mario T. García and Sal Castro, *Blowout!: Sal Castro and the Chicano Struggle for Educational Justice* (Berkeley: University of California Press, 2011).
7 Richard Griswold del Castillo and Richard A. García, *César Chávez: A Triumph of Spirit* (Norman: University of Oklahoma Press, 1995), 84–88.
8 Ibid., 87–88.
9 Founded in Denver, Colorado in 1966 by Rodolfo "Corky" Gonzales; see Gonzales and Esquibel, Eds., *Message To Aztlán*; Vigil, *The Crusade For Justice*.
10 El Plan Espiritual de Aztlán, www.panam.edu/orgs/mecha/aztlan.html (accessed 29 Nov 2011).
11 Muñoz, *Youth, Identity, Power*, 75–78.
12 According to Juan Gómez-Quiñones, the main organizers of the conference were René Núñez, Armando Valdez, Jesús Chavarria, Fernando de Nicochea and himself; see Juan Gómez-Quiñones, "To Leave to Hope or Change: Propositions on Chicano Studies, 1974," in *Parameter of Institutional Change: Chicano Experiences in Education* (Hayward, CA: Southwest Network, 1974), 154; for information on CCHE, see Muñoz, *Youth, Identity, Power*, 134–141.
13 The Oxnard Plain is composed of the following cities: Oxnard, Ventura, Camarillo, Port Hueneme, Santa Paula, and including unincorporated areas of El Río, Saticoy, and Somis.
14 Lorena Márquez, "Sacramento en el Movimiento: Chicano Politics in the Civil Rights Era" (Ph.D. diss., University of California, San Diego, 2010); Oliver Rosales, "Mississippi West: Race, Politics, and Civil Rights in California's Central Valley, 1947–1984" (Ph.D. diss., University of California, Santa Barbara, 2012); Gordon K. Mantler, *Power to the Poor: Black-Brown Coalition and the Fight for Economic Justice, 1960–1974* (Chapel Hill: University of North Carolina Press, 2013); Leonard G. Ramírez, Ed., *Chicanas of 18th Street: Narratives of a Movement from Latino Chicago*

(Chicago: University of Illinois Press, 2011); Dionicio Nodín Valdés, *Barrios Norteños: St. Paul and Midwestern Mexican Communities in the Twentieth Century* (Austin: University of Texas Press, 2000); Marc Simon Rodríguez, *The Tejano Diaspora: Mexican Americanism and Ethnic Politics in Texas and Wisconsin* (Chapel Hill: The University of North Carolina Press, 2011).

15 Roberto Flores, interviewed by author, Oxnard, CA, 14 Jan 2012.

16 Tomás Almaguer, *Racial Fault Lines: The Historical Origins of White Supremacy in California* (Berkeley: University of California Press, 1994), 183–204; Frank P. Barajas, "Resistance, Radicalism, and Repression on the Oxnard Plain: The Social Context of the Betabelero Strike of 1933," *The Western Historical Quarterly*, Vol. 35, no. 1 (Spring 2004): 27–51; Frank P. Barajas, *Curious Unions: Mexican American Workers and Resistance in Oxnard, California, 1898–1961* (Lincoln: University of Nebraska Press, 2012).

17 "3 Women, 9 Men in Oxnard Race," *Oxnard Press-Courier*, 11 Apr 1960; "Ten Candidates in Race For 3 Oxnard Council Seats," *Oxnard Press-Courier*, 5 Apr 1962; "Council Vote Running High," *Oxnard Press-Courier*, 12 Apr 1960; "Chart Shows Voting Precincts in Oxnard Election," *Oxnard Press-Courier*, 13 Apr 1960; "Incumbent Nason beaten; record 52 percent vote," *Oxnard Press-Courier*, 11 Apr 1962; he received 413 votes in 1960 and 636 in 1962.

18 "Nielsen Fourth in Tight Race," *Oxnard Press-Courier*, 13 Apr 1966.

19 Katherine Peake, A Report on Operation Buenaventura, Prepared for the Board of Directors of the Emergency Committee to Aid the Farm Workers, 7 Jun 1965, Mont Collection, Box 9, Folder 9–16, Urban Archives Center, Oviatt Library, California State University, Northridge.

20 "Farm worker program—success and waste?," *The Press-Courier*, 12 May 1966; "Follow-up study of the farm workers graduates," *The Press-Courier*, 13 May 1966; "Imported trio heads county's farm labor efforts," *The Press-Courier*, 13 May 1966; "Not all comments are critical," *The Press-Courier*, 15 May 1966.

21 "County farmers critical of two federal projects," *The Press-Courier*, 16 May 1966.

22 Founding members were Albert Rojas, Manuel Alva, Encarnación Flores, and Jesús Gonzales (Flores and Gonzales were original members of the Committee of the Poor); see "CAP tells about itself," *The Press-Courier*, 4 Oct 1965.

23 CAP tells about itself," *The Press-Courier*, 4 Oct 1965.

24 Ian Haney López, *Racism on Trial: The Chicano Fight for Justice* (Cambridge, MA: Harvard University Press, 2004); Edward J. Escobar, *Race, Police, and the Making of a Political Identity: Mexican Americans and the Los Ángeles Police Department, 1900–1945* (Berkeley: University of California Press, 1999).

25 "Who are the guys in Brown Berets?" *The Press-Courier*, 21 Aug 1968.

26 Roberto Flores, interviewed by author, Oxnard, CA, 14 Jan 2012.

27 "Oxnard's Council Race," *PC: The Weekly Magazine of Ventura County*, 7 Apr 1968.

28 Roberto Flores, interviewed by author, Oxnard, CA, 14 Jan 2012; Armando Lopez, interviewed by author, Oxnard, CA, 13 Sep 2011.

29 "Plea for Police Probe Granted," *The Press-Courier*, 14 Aug 1968.

30 "Who are the Brown Berets?," *The Press-Courier*, 20 Aug 1968.

31 Ibid.

32 "Brown Berets aggressive in spirit, energetic," *The Press-Courier*, 29 Aug 1968.

33 Ibid.

34 "Plenty to do," *The Press-Courier*, 2 Sep 1968.

35 "Backers for review board," *The Press-Courier*, 10 Sep 1968; "Review board would help," *The Press-Courier*, 14 Sep 1968.

36 "Brutality report delayed," *The Press-Courier*, 14 Sep 1968.

37 "Brown Berets plan meeting in Oxnard," *The Press-Courier*, 25 Dec 1968; "Unity Group planned for Oxnard," *The Press-Courier*, 29 Dec 1968.

38 "Brown Berets plan meeting in Oxnard," *The Press-Courier*, 25 Dec 1968.

39 "Mexican pickets protest hearing," *The Press-Courier*, 24 Jan 1969; "Brown Berets picket youth's court hearing," *Ventura County Star-Free Press*, 24 Jan 1969.

40 "Mexican pickets protest hearing," *The Press-Courier*, 24 Jan 1969.

41 "Brown Berets picket youth's court hearing," *Ventura County Star-Free Press*, 24 Jan 1969.

42 "Pickets protest at police," *The Press-Courier*, 25 Jan 1969.

43 "Oxnard Council Votes Censue of City Police," *Los Ángeles Sentinel*, 5 Apr 1962; "Oxnard in Uproar over Police Brutality Charges," *Los Ángeles Sentinel*, 12 Apr 1962; "Brutality probe asked by council," *The Press-Courier*, 5 Apr 1962.

44 "Oxnard Police Whitewashed," *Los Ángeles Sentinel*, 26 Apr 1962.

45 "Brown Berets demand firing of Oxnard Chief," *Ventura County Star-Free Press*, 29 Jan 1969.

46 "Soo Hoo, Sánchez to probe burglary suspect shooting," *The Press-Courier*, 29 Jan 1969.

47 "Berets Booed," *The Press-Courier*, 29 Jan 1969.

48 "Oxnard council misses cue," *The Press-Courier*, 30 Jan 1969.

49 "Review board urged to help in probe of police," *The Press-Courier*, 31 Jan 1969.

50 "Councilman Speaks," *The Press-Courier*, 1 Feb 1969.

51 "City to name expert as tie with public," *The Press-Courier*, 12 Feb 1969.

52 "Berets give service," *The Press-Courier*, 3 Feb 1969.

53 Ralph Guzmán, "Mexican American Casualties in Vietnam," *La Raza*, Vol. 1, no. 1, 1969.

54 Lorena Oropeza, *¡Raza Si! Guerra No!: Chicano Protest and Patriotism During the Viet Nam War Era* (Berkeley: University of California Press, 2005), 118–182; Chávez, *My People First*, 61–79.

55 See the film, *Chicano Moratorium: March in the Rain* by Victor Millan.

56 Chávez, *My People First*, 66.

57 Oropeza, *¡Raza Si! Guerra No!*, 118–182; Chávez, *My People First*, 61–79.

58 See the film, *Requiem 29*.

59 "Mexican-American slate peace march," *The Press-Courier*, 10 Sep 1970.

60 "Peace march leaders issue conduct code for paraders," *The Press-Courier*, 17 Sep 1970.

61 George Mariscal, *Aztlán and Viet Nam: Chicano and Chicana Experiences of the War* (Berkeley: University of California Press, 1999), 201.

62 "Chicanos urged to unite," *The Press-Courier*, 20 Sep 1970.

63 "Office quell disturbance in Colona area," *The Press-Courier*, 12 Jul 1971; "Mob cut destructive swath through Colonia," *The Press-Courier*, 19 Jul 1971; "Colonia disorders explored," *The Press-Courier*, 20 Jul 1971; "Major disturbance averted in Colonia," *The Press-Courier*, 26 Jul 1971.

64 "Colonia disorders explored," *The Press-Courier*, 20 Jul 1971.

65 Roberto Flores, interviewed by author, Oxnard, CA, 14 Jan 2012.

66 "Brown Berets Disbansing Leader Says," *The Press-Courier*, 2 Nov 1972.

67 Ignacio García was listed as Oxnard's UFWOC representative in the issue of *El Malcriado*, No. 51, 2 Dec 1966; Report #1, 9 Oct 1971, United Farm Workers: Office of the President Collection, Part II, Box 36, Folder 1, Walter P. Reuther Library of Labor and Urban Affairs, Wayne State University, Detroit, Michigan.

68 "Chávez to speak in Oxnard," *The Press-Courier*, 22 Oct 1970; "Chávez predicts growers' defeat," *The Press-Courier*, 23 Oct 1970.

69 "Chávez predicts growers' defeat," *The Press-Courier*, 23 Oct 1970.

70 "Agriculture—our no. 1 industry," *Ventura County Star-Free Press*, 11 Jan 1974.

71 "4 pickets arrested at berry field," *The Press-Courier*, 26 May 1974.

72 Miriam Wells, *Strawberry Fields: Politics, Class, and Work in California Agriculture* (Ithaca, NY: Cornell University Press, 1996), 74–96.

73 "Strawberry strike erupts in Oxnard," *El Malcriado*, 24 Jun 1974.

74 "Berry harvesting halted by violence," *Ventura County Star-Free Press*, 25 May 1974.
75 "4 pickets arrested at berry field," *The Press-Courier*, 26 May 1974.
76 Ibid.
77 "Growers sue UFW over berry picketing," *The Press-Courier*, 28 May 1974.
78 "Strawberry strike erupts in Oxnard," *El Malcriado*, 24 Jun 1974.
79 Wells pointed out that, "Berry growers regarded the WGA as their most powerful political representative on union issues," see Wells, *Strawberry Fields*, 88.
80 "César Chávez to aid Oxnard berry strike," *Ventura County Star-Free Press*, 28 May 1974.
81 Ibid.
82 "Strawberry strike erupts in Oxnard," *El Malcriado*, 24 Jun 1974.
83 Ibid.
84 "Violence erupts in berry dispute," *The Press-Courier*, 29 May 1974.
85 "Strawberry strike erupts in Oxnard," *El Malcriado*, 24 Jun 1974.
86 "Violence erupts in berry dispute," *The Press-Courier*, 29 May 1974.
87 Ibid.
88 "Strawberry strike erupts in Oxnard," *El Malcriado*, 24 Jun 1974.
89 "Violence erupts in berry dispute," *The Press-Courier*, 29 May 1974; "Picketers, deputies clash in berry strike," *Ventura County Star-Free Press*, 29 May 1974.
90 "Picketers, deputies clash in berry strike," *Ventura County Star-Free Press*, 29 May 1974; "Chávez to resist strike-breaking," *Ventura County Star-Free Press*, 29 May 1974;
91 "Strawberry strike erupts in Oxnard," *El Malcriado*, 24 Jun 1974; "30 more arrested in labor dispute," *Ventura County Star-Free Press*, 31 May 1974.
92 "Berry pickets hit by new court order," *The Press-Courier*, 30 May 1974; "County growers seek legal block," *Ventura County Star-Free Press*, 30 May 1974.
93 Manuel Chávez is the cousin of César Chávez; "County growers seek legal block," *Ventura County Star-Free Press*, 30 May 1974.
94 "Both sides in berry dispute, claim gains," *The Press-Courier*, 31 May 1974; "UFW vows $500,00 to win strike," *Ventura County Star-Free Press*, 31 May 1974.
95 "UFW vows $500,00 to win strike," *Ventura County Star-Free Press*, 31 May 1974.
96 "Strawberry strike erupts in Oxnard," *El Malcriado*, 24 Jun 1974; "Both sides in berry dispute, claim gains," *The Press-Courier*, 31 May 1974.
97 "County growers seek legal block," *Ventura County Star-Free Press*, 30 May 1974.
98 "30 more arrested in labor dispute," *Ventura County Star-Free Press*, 31 May 1974.
99 Ibid.
100 "Chávez returning for rally tonight," *Ventura County Star-Free Press*, 1 Jun 1974.
101 "Strawberry strike erupts in Oxnard," *El Malcriado*, 24 Jun 1974.
102 "Chávez returning for rally tonight," *Ventura County Star-Free Press*, 1 Jun 1974.
103 "Candlelight march scheduled by UFW," *The Press-Courier*, 1 Jun 1974.
104 "Strawberry strike erupts in Oxnard," *El Malcriado*, 24 Jun 1974; "Chávez urges mass arrests in county," *Ventura County Star-Free Press*, 2 Jun 1974; "UFW's Chávez pledges to put strikers in jail," *The Press-Courier*, 2 Jun 1974.
105 "Chávez urges mass arrests in county," *Ventura County Star-Free Press*, 2 Jun 1974.
106 Ibid.
107 "Strawberry strike erupts in Oxnard," *El Malcriado*, 24 Jun 1974.
108 "UFW's Chávez pledges to put strikers in jail," *The Press-Courier*, 2 Jun 1974.
109 "Candlelight march scheduled by UFW," *The Press-Courier*, 1 Jun 1974.
110 "Supervisors to probe UFW harassment," *The Press-Courier*, 4 Jun 1974.
111 "Strawberry pickers vehicle set on fire," *The Press-Courier*, 3 Jun 1974.
112 "Supervisors to probe UFW harassment," *The Press-Courier*, 4 Jun 1974.
113 "Flynn, Jewett to confer with strikers, sheriff," *Ventura County Star-Free Press*, 5 Jun 1974; "Hill responds to allegation of ACLU head," *Ventura County Star-Free Press*, 6 Jun 1974.

114 "Flynn, Jewett to confer with strikers, sheriff," *Ventura County Star-Free Press*, 5 Jun 1974.

115 "Strikers protest tactics of Oxnard's police force," *Ventura County Star-Free Press*, 6 Jun 1974.

116 "Police role changes in UFW dispute," *The Press-Courier*, 7 Jun 1974.

117 "Berry growers oppose restraining police," *The Press-Courier*, 6 Jun 1974.

118 "UFW may ask nationwide berry boycott," *Ventura County Star-Free Press*, 6 Jun 1974; "UFW feels capable of lengthy holdout," *The Press-Courier*, 9 Jun 1974

119 "5 pickers OK as house set on fire," *The Press-Courier*, 5 Jun 1974; "Arson blamed for fires," *The Press-Courier*, 7 Jun 1974; "Fire bomb thrown into home of pickers but fails to explode," *The Press-Courier*, 10 Jun 1974; "Fire bomb hurled into Oxnard home," *The Press-Courier*, 11 Jun 1974; "Non-violent tactics," *The Press-Courier*, 8 Jun 1974.

120 "Injunction issued on UFW pickets," *The Press-Courier*, 14 Jun 1974.

121 "Picket injunction condemned by UFW, praised by growers," *The Press-Courier*, 15 Jun 1974.

122 Ibid.

123 Ibid.

124 "Bylaws draft meeting slated," *The Press-Courier*, 4 Oct 1975; "Chicano group meets tonight," *The Press-Courier*, 9 Jan 1976.

PART TWO

The Student Movement

7

THE IDEOLOGICAL STRUGGLE FOR CHICANA/O UNITY AND POWER

A Short History of California MEChA

Gustavo Licón

In the late 1960s, *Chicanismo* (Chicano cultural nationalism) captured the hearts and minds of thousands of Chicana/o student activists in California, who formed the student branch of the Chicano Movement. This philosophical drive for self-determination and cultural pride led these students to adopt the ethno-political identity labels "Chicana" and "Chicano" and to create a confederation of Chicana/o student organizations called *Movimiento Estudiantil Chicano de Aztlán* (Chicano Student Movement of Aztlán, or MEChA) in 1969. Although movement leaders promoted *Chicanismo* as a common denominator to facilitate Chicano and Chicana political unity and action, creating actual political cohesion proved itself easier said than done. Uniting under the movement's banner was a constantly contested, evolving, dynamic, and permanently incomplete process. MEChA members brought their own unique experiences, perspectives, and identities to the organization and used these to frame their activism and their participation in the organization and within the larger Chicano Movement. In my writing, I highlight and analyze the contested processes by which Chicana/o student activists in California MEChA attempted to create political cohesion for action despite members' heterogeneous identities, perspectives, and experiences.

In this chapter, I document, contextualize, and analyze one aspect of this process: the struggles over organizational and movement leadership between self-proclaimed adherents of *Chicanismo* and those who promoted Marxism-Leninism within California MEChA chapters between the early 1970s and the early 1990s. Struggles over ideological beliefs played a major role in shaping the direction and political evolution of MEChA and Chicana/o student activism in general during the late twentieth century. Although ideological proponents from competing camps held great sway over the organization and its members at different points in time, at no point did any one camp achieve uncontested political dominance within the organization or among its membership. As I attempted to understand this aspect of the larger process of creating political unity, I found four significant and identifiable periods that define shifts in the history of MEChA. This chapter primarily contributes to the historiography of the Chicano Movement by defining the quest for political unity as a perpetually incomplete process, by identifying and defining four periods of ideological struggle within MEChA, and by expanding the focus and periodization of Chicana/o Movement Studies. I recognize that attempts to use ideology to shape and direct Chicana/o political action began before and continued after the periodization of this study, and that these attempts include ideological camps additional to the groups I focus on in this paper. Nevertheless, I focus on these two ideological camps and set my periodization as such because many scholars have delineated the early 1970s as the height and decline of *Chicanismo*, while I have identified the early 1990s as an era defined by the end of the successful infiltration of MEChA by a national multiracial and multiethnic Marxist-Leninist organization, which engendered a concurrent demand for *Chicanismo* to be the central philosophy of the organization.

In this article I characterize, delineate, and document what I will argue are four phases of cultural nationalist and Marxist-Leninist struggle within the California MEChA network. This is important because these periods coincide with and influence other aspects of MEChA's ideological and organizational evolution, thus facilitating our historical understanding of this dynamic organization and its membership. The early 1970s encompass the first phase, which I characterize as the climax and decline of Chicano cultural nationalism (*Chicanismo*) and the start of a growing shift towards Marxist-Leninist thought among many Chicana and Chicano student activists. I identify the second phase of struggle with the rise of Chicana/o Marxist-Leninist organizations, the higher profile of Marxist-Leninist thought and rhetoric employed within MEChA and the Chicano Movement, and the struggle between two prominent Chicano Marxist-Leninist organizations to become the vanguard of the Chicano Movement in the mid-1970s. The third phase runs from the late 1970s through the mid-1980s, and is characterized by the rise of the League of Revolutionary Struggle (LRS), a national multiethnic and multiracial Marxist-Leninist organization, and its successful bid to infiltrate California MEChA's statewide network. The last and final period runs from the late 1980s through the early 1990s and is characterized by the climax and decline of influence of the LRS within the California MEChA, as well as the successful rise and institutionalization of a MEChA autonomy movement that stressed the centrality of *Chicanismo* to MEChA.

I have stated what I am arguing, and now I would like to clarify what I am not arguing. First, although there are inherent ideological tensions between cultural nationalists and Marxist-Leninists due to their political analyses, organizational structures, and tactics, a nationalist versus Marxist-Leninist binary did not emerge within MEChA or within the Chicano Movement. The illusion of a binary was a tactic used by groups competing for power; in reality, Marxist-Leninist groups fought one another more intensely and consistently than they fought nationalist groups, and ideological combatants were not limited by such labels. Second, even in the early years of the Chicano Movement there was a wide variety of political thought and tactics that coexisted and clashed; thus, I am not arguing that the Chicano Movement was united under Chicano nationalism and that this unity was disrupted by Marxist-Leninism. Third, recognizing this diversity of thought from the start, I do not argue that *Chicanismo* is organic to the Chicano community or that Marxist-Leninism is a foreign entity. I recognize the rich and long-standing history of Marxist-Leninist thought and activism among Latina/os and Latin Americans. Finally, when I discuss infiltration I am referring to organizational infiltration and not ideological infiltration, although attempts to infiltrate MEChA were framed as ideological by many of those who were involved.

My work fills in gaps within twentieth-century United States social movement historiography by going beyond the black/white and north/south binaries of the field and also by analyzing the Chicano Movement past its peak and beyond its traditional periodization. Late twentieth-century United States social and student movement studies tend to focus on either the primarily white "New Left" organization Students for a Democratic Society, or black power organizations such as the Black Panthers and the Student Non-Violent Coordinating Committee.[1]

Latino organizations are overlooked in this activist tradition despite the significant legacies they left behind both in *barrios* and university campuses across the country. Nevertheless, recent studies that have analyzed organizations within the Chicano Movement such as the United Farm Workers, *Centro de Acción Social Autónoma-Hermandad General de Trabajadores* (CASA), the Brown Berets, the Chicano Moratorium Committee, and La Raza Unida Party (LRUP), articulate an activist history that proved politically pivotal for all Americans of Mexican descent at that time and posed a challenge to the racial status quo shaped by the white/black binary.[2] Although several of these studies argue that youths played a significant role in the Chicano Movement, few studies have focused on student organizations such as MEChA (or the Mexican American Youth Organization) of Texas.[3] Despite MEChA's presence as the largest student organization to emerge from the Chicano Movement and the fact that its members continue to advocate for educational reform, civil rights, and immigration policy favorable to the Latino community, its historical significance has been largely neglected by scholars of social movements.

To begin to grasp the historical significance of Chicano student activism I will shift the focus to students and expand the periodization of my study to go well beyond the peak of the Chicano Movement in the 1970s and its traditional periodization by scholars. Thus, in this study I analyze the ideological trends of thought—and specifically the struggles that shaped them—within MEChA from the early 1970s through the early 1990s. Countering the image of a conformist generation that followed the activists of the 1960s and 1970s, my study documents that Chicana/o student activists continued to fiercely debate and attempt to improve the conditions of the Chicano community through ideological analysis, structural reform, and activism well past the peak of the Chicano Movement. I argue that these ideological struggles for political unity and action, which primarily took the shape of efforts within MEChA to either spread or contain the influence of Marxist-Leninism, are better understood when broken up into the four phases and periods that I characterize and demarcate in this article. My argument is based on a textual analysis of archival sources such as student newsletters, newspapers, political plans of action, and conference programs, as well as oral histories of participants.

Phase 1: The Climax of Chicanismo and Marxist-Leninism at the Gates

The Chicano Movement emerged in the mid-1960s from labor struggles in Central California and land-tenure struggles in New Mexico, both of which inspired mass urban Chicano youth activism across the Southwest, along with large contingents in California, Texas, and Colorado. The United Farm Workers' struggle to unionize predominantly Chicano and Asian American farmworkers, combined with the more militant tactics taken by the Spanish/Mexican land grant recovery movement, Alianza Federal de Mercedes, inspired Chicano students to actively demand community liberation and greater access to quality education. Chicano youth, aided by community leaders and campus faculty, organized action committees and espoused *Chicanismo* (pride in Chicano heritage, culture, and people) as a tool with which to face a society and an educational system that sought to eliminate their culture. Similar to the contemporaneous black power movement, Chicana/o student activists believed that their community was oppressed by a racist colonial system that exploited their community resources and deprived them of social mobility and political power. Thus, their demands and political manifestos condemned racism and colonization while emphasizing the virtues of their own peoples' culture, wisdom, and history.

In 1969, several California Chicano student organizations merged to form the MEChA and dedicated themselves to influence institutions of higher education to produce knowledge, leadership, and resources geared towards liberating the Chicano community from exploitation, discrimination, and oppression. Activists codified MEChA's ideology, tactics, structure, and purpose in the organization's founding document, *El Plan de Santa Bárbara* (EPSB), a Chicano activist blueprint for reforming higher education in California to meet the needs of students of Mexican descent.[4] The EPSB, grounded in the political philosophy of *Chicanismo*, outlined the need for Chicano-centered and community-run programs within universities. The founding of Chicano Studies programs was chief among the goals espoused by the EPSB, and this document assigned MEChA the responsibility of holding such programs accountable to the community.[5]

Although *Chicanismo* played a prominent role in shaping the political thought of Chicano student activists, they were also exposed to and cognizant of the potential use of other ideologies for social change and community liberation. Domestic and international forces made an impression on Chicano student activists, who began as a result to take note of Marxist-Leninism. Chicanos recognized that the Vietnamese, Chinese, Cubans, and other Third World peoples had successfully used Marxist-Leninism to defy and gain independence from First and Second World colonial powers.[6] Domestically, Chicano student activists admired organizations such as the Black Panthers, whose leadership was heavily influenced by Marxist-Leninism. Furthermore, Chicano activists were courted by overtly Marxist-Leninist organizations such as the Socialist Workers Party and the Progressive Labor Party, and Marxist literature was readily accessible to college students.[7] A former member of the University of California Los Angeles (UCLA) chapter of the United Mexican American Students, a student organization that changed its name to MEChA, recalled that in the late 1960s Mao Zedong's "Little Red Book" was in "everybody's hand" because thousands of free copies were distributed to UCLA students.[8] The teachings of Mao Zedong applied Marxist-Leninist thought to the struggle of Third World people of color and advocated grassroots community-based tactics. Thus, many Chicana/o activists found these teachings appealing since they saw their own communities as internal colonies of the United States.[9]

As early as 1970, Chicano Movement media sources took note of Chicano Marxist-Leninists collaborating with white leftist organizations in attempting to recruit and challenge Chicano Movement participants. Chicano Movement leaders and their media openly criticized these Chicanos and their Marxist-Leninist allies for attempting to influence the movement and recruit other Chicana/o activists. For example, in its 1970 coverage of the second National Chicano Youth Liberation Conference in Denver, an *El Popo* editorialist wrote: "A few radical gabachos [whites] and Chicanos on their own trip soon found out that's [sic] what the Chicano party is all about—'independent' [sic]. The [sic] only 'ismo' about the Chicano movement and party will be Carnalismo and Chicanismo!"[10] *El Popo* was the self-proclaimed newsletter of the Chicano and Chicana community at San Fernando Valley State College (now known as California State University Northridge) from 1970 through the 2000s. The editorialist in this article implied that conference participants rejected the advances of white and Chicano Marxist-Leninists and affirmed their desire to form a Chicano political party independent of both the mainstream two-party system and non-Chicano leftist organizations. Furthermore, the writer is clear about his/her conviction that what the Chicano political party conference-goers were attempting to establish would be based on only two "*ismos*," Chicano cultural nationalism, known as *Chicanismo*, and brotherhood, known as *Carnalismo*.[11]

Some movement leaders recognized the brewing ideological conflict within the ranks of Chicana/o student activists, but they underestimated its serious nature.

José Ángel Gutiérrez, co-founder of the Mexican American Youth Organization and LRUP in Texas, gave a speech at San Fernando Valley State College in the spring of 1970. He called on California Chicana/o student activists to stop their "petty" infighting over who was a sellout and who had the right ideology and instead unite to fight "the gringos" who ran the racist colonial system that oppressed Chicanos.[12] That a nationally recognized Chicano activist visiting from Texas knew about the ideological infighting in California and thought it a priority to address reflects the visibility of these ideological struggles among Chicana/o youth and the concern that it raised among national leaders of the Chicano Movement. It also highlights the point that the ideological unity that the El Popo editorialist claimed existed was more of a desire than a reality.

Ideological disunity within the movement only increased, particularly due to the perceived inability of the Chicano Moratorium to stop police brutality and due to the inability of LRUP to gain electoral success beyond South Texas or form a national leadership that all could agree upon. In 1970, most Chicano Movement organizations supported the Chicano Moratorium Committee's (CMC) anti-Vietnam War efforts. Nevertheless, its campaign ended in failure due to intense police repression, loss of community support, and infighting.[13] MEChA members and alumni actively participated in the CMC and its series of anti-war marches, which culminated in the approximately 30,000 people-strong Chicano Moratorium protest march on August 29, 1970.[14] Although Chicanismo seemed to be at its peak with such a large turnout, the police riot and government repression of Chicana/o activists that followed this march hurt the legitimacy of the movement among the greater Chicano community and diminished the ability of leaders to employ Chicanismo as a tool to inspire activism. For some Marxist-Leninist Chicanos the extent of this police repression only served to confirm their conviction that reforming existing institutions was futile and that it was time to organize the Chicano community for a socialist revolution.[15] Thus, Marxist-Leninist Chicanos were emboldened by police violence to reorganize the Chicano community according to Marxist-Leninist protocol; their first step to make this a reality was to take over or influence Chicano Movement organizations to take up this cause.

Another major setback to those that espoused Chicanismo as the basis of political unity was the failure of LRUP to produce political unity at the national level. LRUP first emerged in Texas, where it replaced the Mexican American Youth Organization in 1970 and won several local elections under the leadership of José Ángel Gutiérrez. Gutiérrez believed that the winning strategy to achieve Chicano political empowerment was to create a Chicano third party with a voting block that could produce electoral victories, especially in places where Mexicans made up a majority of the electorate. LRUP chapters soon sprang up across California, primarily run by students. These chapters exhibited a wide spectrum of ideological diversity that prevented them from uniting at the state level or producing a statewide leader. On the other hand, Rodolfo "Corky" Gonzales, a prominent Chicano activist and co-founder of the Crusade for Justice in

Denver, became the leader of LRUP chapters in Colorado. He contended that the party should primarily be geared toward political campaigns meant to educate and radicalize the Chicano community, rather than attempting to produce electoral victories. A national power struggle ensued between Gonzales and Gutiérrez at the 1972 LRUP national convention in El Paso, Texas; this competition over leadership of the national party produced a split that the party and the Chicano Movement overall proved unable to overcome. The inability of LRUP leaders to unite Chicana/o activists, and the subsequent series of electoral losses the party experienced, made even more activists question the ability of cultural nationalism to serve as the common denominator that would unite the community and sustain a movement.

The ideological fragmentation and relative decline of cultural nationalism within the California MEChA network became more and more evident at the chapter level, but also manifested itself at the statewide level. At California State University, Northridge (CSUN) the local MEChA chapter used their newsletter, El Popo, to lecture Chicana/o students about their debt to their community and to the students who came before them, who had made possible the large number of Chicano students enrolled in the university and the very existence of the CSUN Chicano Studies Department. The number of individuals in MEChA and in the movement overall declined after the first cohort of students graduated; CSUN MEChA's calls for political action now fell flat and caused resentment among the greater Chicana/o student community, who felt judged by the Mechistas (MEChA members).[16] At the 1973 California MEChA statewide conference, held at the University of California, Riverside, Marxist-Leninist Mechistas insisted that they had adopted the right ideology and that the lack of enthusiasm among the greater Chicana/o community for MEChA stemmed from the inadequacy of cultural nationalism as a sole basis for unity, as well as from problems in MEChA's organizational structure. Marxist-Leninist Mechistas argued that Chicanismo was a type of capitalist separatism that did not take into account the interconnectedness of world problems and incorrectly regarded racism, instead of capitalism, as the true source of Chicana/o oppression. Furthermore, Marxist-Leninist Mechistas labeled MEChA a bureaucratic and reactionary organization. While still at the conference, they declared their immediate resignation from the organization and proceeded to walk out in protest.[17]

This episode marked the end of the first period of ideological struggle for political unity and leadership within MEChA and led to the rise of Chicana/o Marxist-Leninist organizations. Although cultural nationalism declined in popularity and continued to be critiqued and challenged by different sectors of the community, it was not completely discarded by Chicana/o student activists, even those that adopted other "ismos." In fact, most Marxist-Leninist and feminist Chicana/o organizations that emerged in the mid-1970s continued to see themselves as part of the Chicano and Chicana Movement and they continued to draw from cultural nationalist concepts to frame their political projects.

Phase 2: Rise of Chicana/o Marxist-Leninist Organizations

In the 1970s, Chicana/o youth and student activists played a more visible role in the direction and creation of Marxist-Leninist organizations in California. They joined multiracial and multiethnic Marxist-Leninist organizations such as the Communist Labor Party, the October League, the Socialist Workers Party, and the Communist Party USA. Chicana/o activists also created primarily Chicana/o Marxist-Leninist organizations such as the August Twenty-Ninth Movement (ATM) and converted primarily Chicano organizations into Marxist-Leninist ones, such as CASA.[18] Although some of the non-Chicano Marxist-Leninist organizations attempted to woo the Chicano community, I focus on the feud between ATM and CASA because these groups had a more direct and broader impact on Chicana/o student activism in California in the mid- to late-1970s.[19]

Los Angeles area activists formed CASA in 1968 to provide social services and legal defense to urban Chicana/o workers, but in the mid-1970s CASA became a Marxist-Leninist organization and shifted its focus to study groups and conciousness-raising. In its early years, CASA's dues-paying membership grew into the thousands, prompting organizers to form chapters across the Southwest and in Chicago.[20] CASA's national headquarters in Los Angeles changed leadership in 1974 and the new administration cut down social services and focused on Marxist-Leninist study groups, political advocacy, and community/labor organizing, causing CASA's membership to dramatically decline.[21] Some of the students that left MEChA in 1973 joined the Marxist-Leninist student group *El Comité Estudiantil del Pueblo* (The Peoples' Student Committee), an organization that then merged with the new CASA.[22] Although the new CASA was Marxist-Leninist, it espoused a type of Mexican transnationalism, claiming that Mexican nationals and people of Mexican descent born in the United States constituted a single people. This claim put them at odds with Chicana/o activists who believed in the notion of an Aztlán nation and Chicana/o peoplehood that was separate and unique from Mexico due to their historical experience of conquest and contemporary marginalization within the United States that most Mexicans did not experience until immigrating. Nevertheless, their concept of transnational *Mexicanidad* and their tenet of *Sin Fronteras* (without borders) caught on within many Chicana/o circles, including MEChA. Yet it was their advocacy work in defense of undocumented immigrants and immigration reform at a time when immigration became a hot-button issue that helped them gain national prominence despite a dwindling membership base.[23]

ATM emerged as a new organization from the merger of several predominantly urban Chicana/o Marxist-Leninist study groups and collectives from across the Southwest, including sections of Chicano Movement organizations such as the Los Angeles LRUP's Labor Committee. ATM criticized *Chicanismo* as short-sighted, and emphasized the potential strength of multiracial working-class solidarity, but its membership still considered itself part of the Chicano Movement, and they named their group in the spirit of resistance to government repression demonstrated at the August 29, 1970 Chicano Moratorium protest march.[24]

ATM delineated its position on key issues and differentiated itself from political rivals in *Fan the Flames*, the most prominent single written document ATM produced. Based on Vladimir Lenin's views about ethnic minorities within the Soviet Union, ATM made the case that Americans of Mexican descent were an oppressed nation within the U.S. with the right to "self-determination."[25] The document urged communists to redouble their efforts in building a revolutionary communist party to, "*lead* the Chicano national movement and the movements of other oppressed nationalities and to unite these struggles *under* the leadership of the multinational proletariat of the U.S."[26] ATM thought Marxist-Leninists needed to curb the sexism and isolationism within *Chicanismo* by further developing the most democratic cultural aspects of Americans of Mexican descent.[27] The group criticized other Marxist-Leninist organizations for denying Chicanos' right to self-determination, for not giving the Chicano community deep enough thought, and for providing reformist solutions to Chicanos' problems.[28]

Although CASA was visibly more influential in MEChA and in the Chicana/o Movement than ATM, it is misleading to use visibility as the sole unit of measuring their relative importance. In the approximately 100 issues of CSUN's Chicana/o student newsletter *El Popo* that I read for this study, ATM was only mentioned once. Its name appeared in an obscure announcement for a talk by the Iranian Student Movement that ATM co-sponsored. ATM's presence in MEChA and in the Movement is more difficult to detect from a primary source such as *El Popo* because of the organization's secrecy and the similarities between their views and that of *Mechistas* at the time. It is also possible that ATM may not have been as active at CSUN as it was in other MEChA chapters.

On the other hand, CASA's presence and influence over MEChA is easy to detect because of its overt relationship with individual MEChA chapters and the visibility of its catchphrases in MEChA. For example, California State University, Los Angeles (CSULA), MEChA hosted a 2-day Chicana/o student conference in February 1975 with over 500 activists in attendance. CASA's influence over participants is undeniable: attendees passed resolutions to support CASA's "National Campaign of Solidarity with the Immigrant Workers" and conference organizers filled the speakers' list with CASA's known allies, such as the Socialist Puerto Rican University Students, la *Alianza Unidad Obrero-Estudiantil* (Student-Worker Unity alliance), *Comité Estudiantil del Pueblo*, and the National Committee to Free *Los Tres*.[29] Aspects of CASA's *Sin Fronteras* trend of thought also appeared on the pages of *El Popo* with regularity throughout the mid-1970s. Juan Cárdenas, a CSUN *Mechista*, stated in an *El Popo* article: ". . . it takes Chicanos and Mexicanos both to make up La Raza. . . . It doesn't make any difference what side of the border you're born on. We are still the same people."[30] In another example, writer Rudy Cardona titled his *El Popo* article "Estudiantes: luchas *sin fronteras*," (Students: struggles without borders) in which he emphasized the similarities between student and working-class movements in Mexico and the U.S., and demanded student-worker unity.[31]

International models, professors, domestic issues, and feuding among Chicana/o Marxist-Leninist organizations to become the vanguard of the Chicano Movement all help explain the increased popularity of Marxist-Leninist thought and rhetoric among Chicana/o student activists in MEChA in the mid-1970s. In 1975, influential Chicano Studies professor Raúl Ruiz spent 2 weeks traveling in Cuba; upon his return to CSUN, Ruiz praised the virtues of the Cuban Revolution and Marxist-Leninism to students.[32] Ruiz argued that Americans of Mexican descent should follow the Cuban model of liberation: "It was a colony and we have been colonized. It suffered American imperialism and we have also. The language and Latin American culture is the same. It's our model."[33] Although Ruiz oversimplified the similarities between the Chicano and Cuban experiences within U.S. imperialism, the fact that he and other faculty members endorsed these views influenced student activists.

Chicana/o activism experienced a resurgence in the second half of the 1970s due to national struggles to influence immigration reform and to defend affirmative action from the repercussions of the 1978 Bakke decision.[34] Chicana/o Marxist-Leninist organizations embraced these struggles as their own, and while they were at it also promoted internationalism, working-class solidarity, and multiracial/multiethnic alliances, while critiquing *Chicanismo* as narrow and counterproductive to achieving victory in these struggles. Due to these two national issues, activists once again swelled the ranks of MEChA and other Chicana/o Movement organizations. Nevertheless, their attempts to forge a widescale united front based on these issues succumbed to continued infighting.[35]

An ATM document provides a glimpse of this infighting and the feud for power within the Chicano Movement. In a position paper from the summer of 1977, ATM characterizes CASA as a reformist, manipulative, and divisive force within the Chicano Movement and MEChA, and describes itself as a legitimate revolutionary force and the defender of MEChA's right to autonomy and democratic decision-making. The document purports that the ATM-CASA feud was part of a broader international struggle between Marxist-Leninist groups that supported the policies and direction of the Soviet Union, such as CASA, and those groups that supported the policies and direction of China, such as ATM.[36] In this position paper, ATM explains that the battle to influence MEChA was ultimately a battle to direct the Chicano and working-class movements.[37] ATM accused CASA and its allies of attempting to convince CSULA *Mechistas* that they should expel suspected ATM members, and also of interfering with CSULA MEChA's decision-making process by crowding meetings with CASA supporters from other campuses. Furthermore, ATM claimed that CASA and its supporters resorted to threats and physical intimidation to get their way, including starting fights, following people after meetings, and making sexist remarks to female

Mechistas. Both organizations claimed to treat women as equals to men while attributing sexist attitudes to their Marxist-Leninist and cultural nationalist adversaries in an attempt to recruit female activists to their respective organizations.

In the position paper, ATM blamed CASA for the setbacks experienced in building unity among progressive and revolutionary groups, and for making *Mechistas* wary of working with other groups. On the other hand, ATM asserted its own right to take a position on issues that impacted MEChA, as well as their right to democratically urge *Mechistas* to adopt ATM's position. They denied CASA's charges of infiltration, claiming: "ATM (ML) upholds the right of every MECHA to its organizational independence and integrity. Every MECHA has the right to decide its internal affairs by majority vote, free from coercion, unprincipled *movidas* [actions or tricks], and stacking by non-members."[38] Furthermore, ATM alleged that CASA had attempted to replace MEChA with the *Comité Estudiantil del Pueblo*, and that CASA did not believe in the right to self-determination for Americans of Mexican descent.

Two things stand out to me from this position paper that may need further analysis and contextualization: ATM's denial of the accusation of infiltration and the paper's implication that ATM was the true defender of MEChA's structural and decision-making integrity. CASA and some *Mechistas* accused ATM of infiltrating MEChA and other organizations, partly because ATM's membership was kept secret and partly because their organizing efforts included joining other organizations to recruit new members and influence the direction of those organizations. ATM justified its secrecy as an attempt to avoid government suppression, but it is not surprising that ATM's efforts would be regarded with suspicion within both the movement and MEChA because both had already experienced and probably continued to experience government infiltration and sabotage. The second matter of contention here is that both ATM and CASA claimed the right to influence MEChA, covertly or overtly, and the right to criticize the other group for their efforts to do the very same thing. This contradiction stems from both groups' desires to be the revolutionary vanguard of "the people" and from the belief that they alone held the "correct" formula for liberation. Lost in their desires, beliefs, and conflicts was the voice of non-affiliated *Mechistas* and the organization's right to autonomy.

This period came to an end when CASA's leadership was unable to sustain the organization beyond 1979, due to years of conflict with other groups and the ideological gap between its leadership and its membership. Soon after CASA became a Marxist-Leninist group, its national membership plummeted from an estimated 4,000 to 300, with only 50 active members. CASA's decision to adopt democratic centralism, which forced chapters across the country to accept decisions made by the Los Angeles national headquarters, their dogmatic adherence to ideology, and their struggle to develop and defend the "correct political line" alienated CASA's mass membership and destroyed its relationship with the community.[39] Historians Ernesto Chávez and David Gutiérrez argue that Marxist-Leninism had limited appeal to working-class Americans of Mexican descent, causing CASA's membership to decline. They also argue that Marxist-Leninism had a greater appeal among a small professional class in the community that included students. This argument helps explain why a mass organization like CASA failed, while a cadre-driven organization like ATM sustained itself—and why both organizations prioritized influencing and recruiting student activists, particularly *Mechistas*.[40]

Phase 3: The Rise of LRS in MEChA

In the third period of ideological struggle within MEChA, ATM merged with other people-of-color, Marxist-Leninist-Maoist organizations across the country to form the LRS (League of Revolutionary Struggle), and as LRS they successfully infiltrated the California MEChA statewide structure. By infiltrate I mean that LRS members were able to join MEChA, influence the decision-making of individual chapters and the statewide structure, and recruit *Mechistas* to join LRS, all while keeping their membership in LRS a secret from most *Mechistas* and the general public. This period ended with the rise of ideological opponents to LRS within and outside of MEChA who claimed nationalism as their philosophy and decried what they saw as LRS's usurpation of MEChA's autonomy, leading *Mechistas* within this "nationalist" camp to leave the California MEChA statewide network.

In the late 1970s, ATM merged with an Asian-American organization (I Wor Kuen) and an African-American organization (the Revolutionary Communist League) to form LRS.[41] The goal of LRS was the formation of a single united communist party in the United States, but they believed that first they had to achieve political unity among themselves and develop the "correct" ideological analysis "based on the integration of Marxism-Leninism-Mao Zedong Thought with the concrete conditions of the U.S. . . . ."[42] LRS continued ATM's policy of maintaining a secretive membership base and clandestine operations to avoid government repression.[43] A few high-ranking LRS members revealed their membership to the public in order to communicate with media outlets, gain the public's trust, and recruit new members.[44] LRS had a prolonged, secretive, and selective recruitment process that involved identifying potential neophytes, inviting them to LRS study groups and public events, and finally having the neophytes solicit membership through a written personal statement.[45] The organization was based on democratic centralism and party discipline, thus once a decision was reached by the central committee all had to fall in line.

LRS argued that Chicanos constituted an oppressed nation with the right to self-determination, and that it was in the best interest of Marxist-Leninists to support this struggle. Nevertheless, LRS made it clear that while it supported Chicana/o self-determination it did not support nationalism itself. Their support for Chicano self-determination was thus self-interest in that they believed that a

Chicano victory over the United States government would be a blow to their common enemy that would strengthen the possibility of a successful Marxist-Leninist revolution. According to LRS, the group engaged itself with Chicano liberation struggles in order to eliminate nationalistic chauvinism and racism among the white working-class, to challenge and eliminate "narrow nationalism" among Chicanos, and to help Chicano leaders adopt Marxist-Leninist-Maoist trends of thought.[46] The label "narrow nationalism" was commonly used to construe *Chicanismo* and cultural nationalism as a gateway philosophy to ethnocentrism and isolationism, and as a sociopolitical analysis devoid of broader contextual understanding of the oppressive system at large. In 1982, LRS central committee member and nationally acclaimed poet Amiri Baraka stated, "We support nationalists to the extent to which they fight imperialism, but there is no support whatsoever for nationalism, per se!"[47] Baraka delineated the limitations of nationalism and called on Marxist-Leninists to challenge nationalists at every turn for the leadership of national liberation movements. He wanted Marxist-Leninists to convince people in mass liberation movements that only an alliance between the multinational working-class and oppressed peoples would result in the defeat of their common enemy.

LRS became a dominant force within the California MEChA statewide structure in the 1980s, but individual chapter autonomy prevented it from controlling all chapters; some *Mechistas* also began a campaign to purge LRS from MEChA. Through their clandestine methods of organization and recruitment, LRS systematically took over positions of power within MEChA chapters in California, convincing MEChA members to vote their way and incorporating willing MEChA leaders into LRS. Nevertheless, some MEChA members and community groups resisted the advances of LRS and challenged individuals whom they suspected were part of that organization within MEChA. The struggle between these competing camps split several MEChA chapters and the state-wide structure as a whole in the mid-1980s. Although each MEChA chapter was autonomous, MEChA formed city, county, region, state, and national committees and entities to facilitate communication and collective activism, but also to exchange ideas and to formulate collective positions on important issues. Nevertheless, before the 1990s, decisions made above the chapter level were not binding, and chapters individually decided whether to accept or reject such decisions. At a 1985 LRUP summit, for example, UCLA and University of California Berkeley (UCB) MEChA chapters denounced LRS activities within MEChA.[48]

That same year, a new group called Unión del Barrio produced a position paper tracing the divisive history of ATM and LRS in the Chicano Movement, and demanding that LRS respect the autonomy of MEChA.[49] According to this document, Unión del Barrio was founded in 1981 by "veteran" grassroots activists formerly involved in the Brown Berets, MEChA, LRUP, UFW, the Mexican American Political Association, the Chicano Park Steering Committee, and the

Committee on Chicano Rights. Their mission was to: "halt the colonization of our gente" and "bring the day of Aztlán's self-determination that much closer" by promoting the Chicana/o community's history, culture, and movement; establishing community control of institutions that serve them; addressing the concerns of *barrio* residents; and educating and organizing the youth of the community. Part of the reason why a series of organizations came to the "defense" of MEChA's autonomy at different points in time was that these groups saw *Mechistas* as young and impressionable students; on the other hand these organizations included relatively older adult members who saw it as their responsibility to defend MEChA "kids" from the manipulation of other adult organizations and steer them in the "right" direction.

UCB MEChA hosted the National Chicano Student Conference in the spring of 1986, and some *Mechistas* went on the offensive against LRS. According to Carlos Muñoz: "The conference was plagued with ideological struggle between two factions of MEChA. . . . The conference was disrupted by the nationalist faction and ended on a divisive note."[50] These "disruptive" MEChA chapters were all from Southern California and they claimed to be "defending the self-determination of all *Mechistas* de Corazon [sic] [of the heart]. . . ."[51] They argued that LRS was using MEChA, manipulating its democratic decision-making process, and suppressing freedom of speech and information in a quest to achieve "unity" at any cost. Demonstrating the extent of LRS's influence in MEChA by 1986 was the relatively marginal status of *Chicanismo* within MEChA. This is evident in the fact that it was nationalist *Mechistas* who resorted to disruptions and walking-out protest tactics to make their position known at the 1986 conference, while in 1973 it was Marxist-Leninist *Mechistas* who had walked out of a MEChA conference and left the organization to make their position known.

Pro-LRS MEChA chapters used their numerical voting advantage to institutionalize their perspective within MEChA's California statewide structure over a 3-year period. These chapters developed a California statewide MEChA constitution and guidelines in 1986, and a new guiding document, *El Plan de MEChA* (EPM) in 1989.[52] Like previous MEChA documents, the EPM recognized MEChA's commitment to educational reform, described *Chicanismo* as "the clearest expression of national consciousness," and stated that *Mechistas* will "continue to fight for political power and for the self-determination of our oppressed nation, Aztlán."[53] Nevertheless, the EPM placed a new emphasis on MEChA's "tradition" of supporting workers' causes and the gains that MEChA had made through alliances with African Americans and Asian Americans.[54] Furthermore, the EPM described the Socialist Workers Party and the Revolutionary Communist Party as "racist white groups who refused to respect the goals, purpose and autonomy of MEChA as an integral part of the Chicano movement for self-determination," and accused them of attempting to infiltrate MEChA.[55] The EPM also argued that California MEChA had adopted guidelines and a constitution to counter "a minority of ultra-nationalistic *Mechistas*" that had attempted to push their own agenda and ideology on MEChA by using threats, red-baiting, and other disruptive tactics. The creators of the EPM contended that MEChA should be open to all people working for the betterment of the Chicano community regardless of their political ideology or outside affiliations.[56] The EPM provided LRS members working within MEChA with a shield against red-baiting; it also marginalized its "ultra-nationalist" detractors, and played up the role of labor struggles and multiracial alliances within MEChA's history to further align MEChA with LRS's trajectory. As was the case since the 1970s, it was not ATM's or LRS's style to visibly push their ideology on MEChA from within; instead they relied on clandestine infiltration and on "influencing" the organization.

Phase 4: MEChA Summit and Decline of LRS

The MEChA chapters that caused the disturbance in 1986 continued to work on purging LRS from MEChA by creating their own set of position papers and forming an alternative MEChA statewide structure called MEChA Summit. Unlike the Marxist-Leninist Chicana/os who had left MEChA in 1973 and formed or joined other organizations, these Summit *Mechistas* planned to officially reintegrate into the MEChA statewide structure. Additionally, they believed that it was they who were the "real" *Mechistas* and not those who remained in the organization. These chapters identified their allies as those involved in summit meetings and those chapters "loyal" to MEChA's founding document, *El Plan de Santa Bárbara*.[57] MEChA Summit chapters produced several position papers on MEChA's philosophy, structure, relationship to outside organizations, goals, and objectives, all of which they merged into a single document, the Philosophy of MEChA (PoM), in 1992.[58] In the PoM, MEChA Summit chapters asserted the centrality of *Chicanismo* to MEChA through references to *El Plan de Santa Bárbara, El Plan de Aztlán*, and the early years of the Chicano Movement.[59] They believed that this ideology was key to countering infiltration:

> Recently and historically, opportunistic outside organizations have utilized the legitimacy of MEChA as a voice of the Chicano/Chicana Movement to promote their own agendas inside of our movement. Such groups . . . began to promote class-wide multi-nationalism that sought to displace Chicano nationalism as the central focus for our Movement.[60]

With the PoM and other documents, Summit *Mechistas* planned to set up a decision-making system within the California MEChA statewide conferences that limited participation to *Mechistas* from MEChA chapters that were "recognized" by their local and regional MEChA networks as being active and following the tenets of the PoM and the EPSB. They believed that these measures would eliminate any further infiltration of MEChA and help avoid ideological splits.[61]

MEChA Summit chapters embarked on a campaign to "reclaim" the California MEChA statewide network by: 1) taking over Southern California MEChA networks and restructuring them according to the PoM, and 2) finding allies within Northern California MEChA networks (which they suspected were heavily infiltrated by LRS) that could help them achieve the same restructuring there.[62] On December 1, 1990, seven MEChA Summit chapters gained a voting majority at the Los Angeles County MEChA central meeting held at the CSUN. Through their voting majority they implemented aspects of the PoM and forced all MEChA chapters present to discuss their connections and loyalties to other organizations.[63] CSULA MEChA representatives attempted to block the MEChA Summit takeover by quoting stipulations from the EPM and the MEChA statewide constitution, but their protests fell on deaf ears.[64] Summit MEChA chapters then fortified their network by restructuring the Southern California county-level MEChA committees known as *Centrales*, improving communication among MEChA Summit chapters, and identifying MEChA chapters outside of Southern California who were willing to join their program.[65] These MEChA chapters used EPSB as their flag and banner: Their goal was to expel LRS members, eliminate the EPM, and implement PoM documents.

Summit MEChA chapters made their first attempt to retake the statewide structure on May 5, 1991 at the California MEChA statewide conference hosted by the CSU Fresno chapter. Four hundred and fifty students attended the conference, representing sixty-three MEChA chapters. Summit chapters engaged other chapters in heated debates over the EPSB and the California MEChA statewide structure. As a result, CSU Fresno MEChA called campus security to end the conference and escort participants out of the building before any resolutions could be voted on. Once outside, *Mechistas* formed two camps, and it was at this moment that Summit MEChA chapters realized that they were now the numerical majority.[66]

Summit MEChA chapters continued their offensive at the following California MEChA statewide conferences, where they finally gained control and MEChA officially adopted the EPSB and the PoM. By the fall of 1991, Summit MEChA chapters were better organized and more confident, and the UC Davis MEChA chapter had become their ally and the host of the next California MEChA statewide conference. At this conference, an overwhelming majority of MEChA chapters passed a resolution to officially adopt the EPSB and to annul the EPM at the statewide level. They restructured their conferences to be more exclusive and set out to implement the aspects of EPSB that called for the establishment of Chicano Studies programs and departments where they did not exist, and to demand that more resources be directed to these programs where they did. *Mechistas* also agreed to advocate for greater student feedback and decision-making power within these programs and departments.[67] For many at the conference, passing these resolutions was "a victory for the resurgence of Chicana and Chicano nationalism within the student movement."[68] The final nail in the coffin for LRS as a force in MEChA was the adoption of the PoM at the spring California MEChA statewide conference held at CSU Fullerton on January 18, 1992.

Part of the turnaround of events that facilitated this Summit MEChA takeover of the California MEChA statewide structure was the implosion of LRS during the late 1980s and early 1990s. International events had caused LRS members to have second thoughts about the viability and desirability of a Marxist-Leninist revolution. In 1989, for example, the Chinese government resorted to violence and media censorship to stifle a pro-democracy and pro-economic liberalization movement among students across the country. The most infamous episode of this repression was the Tiananmen Square massacre, during which the Chinese army slaughtered an estimated hundreds or thousands of protesters. The actions of the Chinese government were a heavy blow to Marxist-Leninists around the world, and particularly to those who followed the teachings of Mao and regarded the Chinese government as a real-life model of what they wanted to establish. Further dampening the allure of Marxist-Leninist revolution among international adherents was the fall of the Berlin Wall in Germany, the economic liberalization reforms in many socialist countries, and the collapse of the Soviet Union. All of these international events cast doubts on the feasibility of the socialist alternative to capitalism.

LRS members voted to disband at their national conference on September 8, 1990. According to LRS's official statement of dissolution, a large majority of LRS members had decided to move beyond the Marxist-Leninist framework and organizational form, due to personal experience and world events.[69]

> In reviewing the developments in the world, a large majority of us feel that there are aspects of Marxism-Leninism and the practice carried out in its name that are inappropriate, unsuitable, and even antithetical to the vision we hold of a democratic and just society.[70]

Beto, a former member of LRS, recalled that as an ATM member he was uneasy about the elitism of Marxist-Leninists who proclaimed that they possessed the sole knowledge of the right ideology and thus had the right to infiltrate and attempt to lead other peoples' struggles. These concerns were assuaged, however, by his faith in the good intentions of ATM's membership, as well as that group's unorthodox approach. Nevertheless, Beto's concerns re-emerged as ATM became LRS and the organization's membership, influence, and orthodoxy grew exponentially. Beto believed that by the late 1980s, LRS was more concerned about winning power struggles and implementing central committee orders than with addressing the needs of the communities it claimed to be liberating.[71] These concerns, combined with international events and infighting within LRS, caused its membership to doubt the need for their own organization, and they reached a majority decision to dissolve. Thus, the well-organized Summit MEChA chapters defeated the disoriented remnants of an organization that no longer existed.

The Summit MEChA victory did not eliminate the legacy of LRS within MEChA, but it did mark the last large-scale attempt by a Marxist-Leninist organization to infiltrate MEChA. The struggle over ideology and power in MEChA led to the annulment of EPM and the adoption of the PoM and the EPSB, as well as the restructuring of the California MEChA statewide network. While *Chicanismo* enjoyed a renewed prominence in the early 1990s, the next cohort of *Mechistas* in California challenged the reactionary aspects of the PoM and used anti-infiltration policies against outside organizations that ideologically identified as Chicano nationalist.[72] The Soviet Union and China were pushed aside by most *Mechistas* as models of Marxist-Leninist resistance, but the prominence of Latin American models such as the government of Cuba, Mexico's EZLN, Venezuela's Hugo Chávez, and Bolivia's Evo Morales, as well as the material conditions in Latin America and United States *barrios* kept Marxist-Leninist thought alive within MEChA and the Chicano Movement.

Conclusion

Although it was created by the fervor of the late-1960s Chicano Movement and anchored in its *Chicanismo* and *Carnalismo* ideological premises, MEChA was in practice defined by the outcome of internal and external struggles. In this study I have delineated four phases of ideological struggle for political cohesion and leadership of the California MEChA network from the early 1970s through the early 1990s. These four distinct periods help us understand the shifting ideological trends within the organization and the struggles between different ideological camps and organizations to achieve political unity under their own leadership. As demonstrated in this study, political unity through ideological hegemony is an ever-changing and always contested incomplete process. Recognizing this helps us understand the political infighting within MEChA and the Chicana/o Movement and why major ideological trends among student activists and the leadership of MEChA continue to shift and change over time.

Notes

1   For representative examples, see Maurice Isserman and Michael Kazin, *America Divided: The Civil War of the 1960s* (Oxford: Oxford University Press, 2000); Clayborn Carson, *In Struggle: SNCC and the Black Awakening of the 1960s* (Cambridge, MA: Harvard University Press, 1995).
2   See George Mariscal, *Brown-eyed Children of the Sun: Lessons From the Chicano Movement, 1965–1975* (Albuquerque: University of New Mexico Press, 2005); Lorena Oropeza, *¡Raza Si! ¡Guerra No! Chicano Protest and Patriotism During the Vietnam War Era* (Los Angeles: University of California Press, 2005); Ernesto Chávez, *My People First! "¡Mi Raza Primero!" Nationalism, Identity, and Insurgency in the Chicano Movement in Los Angeles, 1966–1978* (Los Angeles: University of California Press, 2002).
3   For MEChA, see María Eva Valle, "MEChA and the Transformation of Chicano Student Activism: Generational Change, Conflict, and Continuity." (Ph.D. diss., University of California at San Diego, 1996) and Carlos Muñoz, *Youth, Identity, Power:*

The *Chicano Movement* (London: Verso, 1989). For MAYO, see Armando Navarro, *Mexican American Youth Organization: Avant-garde of the Chicano Movement in Texas* (Austin: University of Texas Press, 1995).

4   *El Plan de Santa Bárbara: A Chicano Plan for Higher Education* (Oakland, CA: La Causa Publications, 1969).

5   For more on the early years of the Chicano Student Movement in California and the founding of MEChA, see Muñoz, *Youth, Identity, Power*, 1989; and Ignacio M. García, *Chicanismo: The Forging of a Militant Ethos Among Mexican Americans* (Tucson: University of Arizona Press, 1997).

6   Oropeza, *¡Raza Sí! ¡Guerra No!*, 80–111.

7   Ibid., 133, 154, 156.

8   Beto, interview by author, 16 January 2007, South Pasadena, CA, digital recoding. Mao Zedong, leader of communist China, took Marxist-Leninist theory and amended it to fit the conditions of China. His theories are commonly referred to as Mao Zedong Thought. Outside of China, the combination of Mao Zedong Thought and Marxism-Leninism is commonly referred to simply as Maoism and its adherents as Maoists. Mao's "Little Red Book" was meant to spread and teach key principles of Maoism. Maoists translated the manual into several languages and distributed it around the world.

9   For an analysis of the internal colony model as it has been applied to Latina/os and ethnic Mexicans in the United States, see Armando Navarro, *Mexicano Political Experience in Occupied Aztlán: Struggles and Change* (Oxford: Altamira Press, 2005), 1–29; for a contemporary source see Rodolfo Acuña, *Occupied America: The Chicano Struggle Toward Liberation* (San Francisco: Canfield Press, 1972).

10 *El Popo* 1, no. 2 (7 April 1970): 6, The *El Popo* Newspaper Collection, Urban Archives, California State University, Northridge.

11 According to Ignacio M. García, the Socialist Workers Party was present at this conference; I believe this reference was directed at them. See Ignacio M. García, *United We Win: The Rise and Fall of La Raza Unida Party* (Tucson: University of Arizona Press, 1989), 96.

12 *El Popo* 1, no. 3 (5 May 1970): 5, The *El Popo* Collection, Urban Archives, California State University, Northridge.

13 Oropeza, *¡Raza Sí! ¡Guerra No!*, 187.

14 Ibid., 155.

15 Beto, interview, 2007.

16 See, *El Popo* 3, no. 2, 3, 6–7; *El Popo* 4, no. 2, 4–5; *El Popo* 4, no. 3, 2, 10–11; *El Popo* 5, no. 1, 2, 4–5, The *El Popo* Collection, Urban Archives, California State University, Northridge.

17 Muñoz, *Youth, Identity, Power*, 91–92.

18 Laura Pulido, *Black, Brown, Yellow, and Left: Radical Activism in Los Angeles* (Los Angeles: University of California Press, 2006), 25.

19 According to Armando Navarro, the Socialist Workers Party was also battling to become the "main influence" in MEChA and the Chicano student movement. Armando Navarro, *Mexicano Political Experience in Occupied Aztlán: Struggles and Change* (Walnut Creek, CA: Alta Mira Press, 2005), 385.

20 David G. Gutiérrez, "CASA in the Chicano Movement: Ideology and Organizational Politics in the Chicano Community, 1968–1978," *Working Paper Series* 5 (Stanford Center for Chicano Research, 1984): 10.

21 Ibid., 13

22 Muñoz, *Youth, Identity, Power*, 94. For more on the CEP-CASA merger and their ideology, see Mario T. García, *Memories of Chicano History: The Life and Narrative of Bert Corona* (Los Angeles: University of California Press, 1994), 308–315; Chávez, *My People First! "¡Mi Raza Primero!"*, 106–108.

23 Pulido, *Black, Brown, Yellow, and Left*, 129.

24 August Twenty-Ninth Movement, "CASA ATTACKS THE CHICANO MOVE-MENT: AUGUST 29th MOVEMENT (M-L) RESPONDS," Chicano Moratorium Vertical Files Collection, Chicano Studies Research Center, University of California, Los Angeles.
25 August Twenty-Ninth Movement, "Fan the Flames," 1976, Mike Conan Collection: The New Communist Movement, Southern California Library for Social Studies and Research, Los Angeles.
26 I italicized words in the quote for emphasis. August Twenty-Ninth Movement, "Fan the Flames," 1976.
27 It was implicit that they believed Chicano cultural nationalism was sexist and isolationist, but that by combining it with a dominant Marxist-Leninist perspective these limitations could be eliminated.
28 August Twenty-Ninth Movement, "Fan the Flames," 1976.
29 The latter two merged with CASA. "Student Conference Supports CASA Campaign," *El Popo* 8, no. 3, 3, The *El Popo* Collection, Urban Archives, California State University, Northridge.
30 Juan Cárdenas, "Don't Insult Yourselves," *El Popo* 12, no. 2 (May 1978): 11, The *El Popo* Collection, Urban Archives, California State University, Northridge.
31 I italicized for emphasis. Rudy Cardona, "Estudiantes: luchas sin fronteras," *El Popo* 13, no. 1 (Sept.-Oct. 1978): 4, The *El Popo* Collection, Urban Archives, California State University, Northridge.
32 Ruiz had a known track record of community activism. He was a political candidate for *La Raza Unida* Party in East Los Angeles; in 1970 he photographed the post-Chicano Moratorium police siege of the Silver Dollar Café during which police officers murdered *LA Times* reporter Ruben Salazar. Ruiz's influence among Chicano student activists at CSUN at the time may have been second only to CSUN Chicano Studies Department founder professor Rudy Acuña.
33 John Cárdenas, "Ruiz Reflects on Cuba," *El Popo* 8, no. 4: 6, 8, Southern California Periodicals Collection, Southern California Library for Social Science and Research, Los Angeles.
34 *The Regents of University of California v. Bakke* (1978) decision banned racial quotas in college admissions, making it illegal to set aside a certain number of spaces for students of underrepresented backgrounds. This case served as a rallying cry for Chicana/o activists who perceived the case and the court decision as a setback and backlash against many of the goals and achievements of the Chicano Movement.
35 August Twenty-Ninth Movement, "CASA ATTACKS THE CHICANO MOVEMENT: AUGUST 29th MOVEMENT (M-L) RESPONDS," Chicano Moratorium Vertical Files Collection, Chicano Studies Research Center, University of California, Los Angeles; Union del Barrio, "Self-determination for the Chicano Movement: A Critique of the League of Revolutionary Struggle," Mike Conan Collection, Southern California Library for Social Science and Research, Los Angeles.
36 August Twenty-Ninth Movement, "CASA ATTACKS THE CHICANO MOVEMENT: AUGUST 29th MOVEMENT (M-L) RESPONDS," Chicano Moratorium Vertical Files Collection, Chicano Studies Research Center, University of California, Los Angeles.
37 Ibid.
38 Ibid.
39 Gutiérrez, "CASA in the Chicano Movement," 15, 27.
40 For more on the decline of CASA, see Chávez, *My People First! "¡Mi Raza Primero!"*, 107–116; and Gutiérrez, "CASA in the Chicano Movement," 27.
41 Michael Friedly, "Nationwide organization active here, students say," *Stanford Daily* (18 May 1990): 10.

42   League of Revolutionary Struggle, "Interview with William Gallegos of the League of Revolutionary Struggle on some question of party building," *Unity*, (18 Jan. 1980): 4, Mike Conan Collection: The New Communist Movement, Southern California Library for Social Studies and Research, Los Angeles.

43   Friedly, "Nationwide organization active here, students say," 10.

44   Beto, interview, 2007

45   Michael Friedly, "League recruitment deterred many: Secretive process alienated dozens who were approached," *Stanford Daily* (30 May 1990): 12.

46   League of Revolutionary Struggle, "The Struggle for Chicano Liberation," *Forward: Journal of Marxism-Leninism-Mao Zedong Thought*, no. 2 (August 1979).

47   Amiri Baraka, *Unity*, Mike Conan Collection: The New Communist Movement, Southern California Library for Social Studies and Research, Los Angeles.

48   Ibid.

49   See Union del Barrio, "Self-determination for the Chicano Movement: A Critique of the League of Revolutionary Struggle," Mike Conan Collection, Southern California Library for Social Science and Research, Los Angeles.

50   Muñoz, *Youth, Identity, Power*, 185.

51   All the MEChA chapters involved in the disruption were from Southern California: five from San Diego county, four from Orange County, and two from Los Angeles County. They were from UCLA, CSUF, SWC, OCC, Mesa College, SAC, UCI, UCSD, UCCC, SDSU, and LaRUE. See untitled manuscript (15 March 1986), author's personal collection.

52   Support for LRS was more abundant among Northern California MEChA chapters, while resistance to LRS primarily came from Southern California chapters. California MEChA Statewide, *El Plan de MEChA* (Apr. 1989): 24–25, 28; Milo Alvarez, "MEChA: A Recent History of Conflict and Change, 1986–1991," 7, author's personal collection.

53   Álvarez, "MEChA: A Recent History of Conflict and Change, 1986–1991," 7.

54   Ibid., 4, 5, 9.

55   California MEChA Statewide, *El Plan de MEChA*, 15.

56   Ibid., 16–17.

57   Alvarez, "MEChA: A Recent History of Conflict and Change, 1986–1991," 3.

58   The MEChA Philosophy Papers were merged, revised, and adopted by California MEChA at the Spring MEChA statewide conference at CSU Fullerton on 18 January 1992 and were renamed Philosophy of MEChA (PoM). The PoM went through more revisions to make it more inclusive and less reactionary from 1997–1999 and was adopted by National MEChA on 21 March 1999 at the Phoenix College MEChA National Conference. The PoM is still commonly referred to as the MEChA Philosophy Papers.

59   Chicano youth activists drafted the *El Plan de Aztlán* in 1969 at the National Chicano Youth Liberation conference hosted by the Crusade for Justice in Denver. It declared Chicanos' wish to unite as a people and liberate Aztlán, the United States Southwest, from those who oppressed the Chicano community. *El Plan de Aztlán* had a radical and separatist tone, but its goals were pragmatic, such as using *Chicanismo* to unite Chicanos across the Southwest and forming a Chicano third party. For more information on this document and the conference, see Muñoz, *Youth, Identity, Power*, 1989; Ignacio M. García, *Chicanismo*, 1997; MEChA Summit, "The Philosophy of Movimiento Estudiantil Chicano de Aztlán," (18 Jan. 1992): 2.

60   MEChA Summit, "The Philosophy of Movimiento Estudiantil Chicano de Aztlán," 13–14. In the early 1990s MEChA reasserted its right to autonomy and self-determination not only from LRS, but also from the National Chicano Moratorium Committee, which was Chicano Nationalist and anti-LRS. In 1996 MEChA did the same against one of the remaining branches of the Brown Berets after it was accused

of infiltrating the Michigan State University MEChA chapter and taking over the 1996 MEChA National Conference held at Michigan State University.

61   MEChA Summit, "The Philosophy of Movimiento Estudiantil Chicano de Aztlán" (18 Jan. 1992): 5, 7.
62   Alvarez, "MEChA: A Recent History of Conflict and Change, 1986–1991," 7, 10.
63   Ibid., 11. According to Alvarez, during the meeting a known LRS member in MEChA claimed that LRS had disbanded but few actually believed him.
64   CSULA MEChA, untitled manuscript (1991): 1–2.
65   Ibid., 11–12.
66   Ibid., 12–13.
67   Alvarez, "MEChA: A Recent History of Conflict and Change, 1986–1991," 13–14.
68   Ibid., 14.
69   LRS, "Statement on the Dissolution of the League of Revolutionary Struggle," 1.
70   Ibid., 3.
71   Beto, interview, 2007
72   I analyze efforts to reform the Philosophy of MEChA in the 1990s in "Sexo en Aztlán: Gender, Sexuality, Sexism, and Homophobia in MEChA" and "Chicanismo, Solidarity, and Immigration: MEChA 1970–1999," in Gustavo Licon "'¡La Union Hace La Fuerza!' (Unity Creates Strength!): MEChA and Chicana/o Student Activism in California, 1967–1999." (Ph.D. diss., University of Southern California, 2009).

8

UNDERSTANDING THE ROLE OF CONFLICT, FACTIONALISM, AND SCHISM IN THE DEVELOPMENT OF THE CHICANO STUDENT MOVEMENT

The Mexican American Student Association and La Vida Nueva at East Los Angeles College, 1967–1969

Marisol Moreno

At the height of the March 1968 East Los Angeles blowouts,[1] Mike de la Peña reprimanded the Mexican American Student Association (MASA), the organization he presided over as president a few months earlier, for failing to endorse and assist in the week-long walkouts spearheaded by Lincoln High School teacher Sal Castro and a cadre of college and high school student leaders. Days prior to the walkouts, de la Peña and other MASistas who had attended community meetings to organize the protests had repeatedly warned the group's leadership that the eastside schools were "about to explode." In response to de la Peña's criticism, executive committee member Ramón Olayo defended MASA's decision and argued instead for protestors to pursue educational reform by procuring additional meetings with school officials. Frustrated with a leadership he perceived to be out of touch with the politics of the emergent Chicano Movement, de la Peña angrily shouted, "all you ever do is talk!," as he and two female members stormed out of the meeting.[2] De la Peña's frustration stemmed from a growing factionalism that had been brewing between moderate and radical students since the beginning of the Chicano student movement.[3]

In 1970 Mexican Americans represented about 12 percent of California's population, and yet by 1972, Chicana/o students numbered approximately 3 percent of the student population at the University of California, 5 percent in the California State College (later University) system, 3 percent at California private colleges, and nearly 8 percent of day students in the junior college system.[4] Alarmed by the lack of educational opportunities, a small but significant number of Mexican American students from the Los Angeles area came together, as early as 1966, to form campus and community groups aimed at reforming educational inequity in higher education and local K-12 public schools.[5] In 1967, MASA from East Los Angeles College (ELAC), along with its sister organization the United Mexican Americans Students (UMAS), helped to pioneer the Chicano student movement in California. Armed with a noble mission and a strong sense of civic duty, MASA—founded by military veterans in their twenties—set out to improve the educational experience of Mexican American children. It was therefore ironic that from the outset of the blowouts, MASA's leadership refused to participate in the mass walkouts aimed at pressuring the Los Angeles School Board to enact meaningful institutional reform at eastside schools. Eager to partake in the Chicano student movement's entry to 1960s radical protest politics, individual MASA members nonetheless joined the 10,000 Mexican American high school and college student protestors.

Without an internal mechanism from which to resolve conflict over divergent views on goals and tactics, discontented members gave up trying to change MASA from within, and opted instead to exit the organization. Factionalism leading to schism, however, did not mark the end of Chicano student activism at East Los Angeles College. Unable to persuade their older MASA peers to adopt militant politics, a group of younger MASistas created a new organization called La Vida Nueva (the new life). La Vida Nueva soon surpassed MASA as the leading Chicano organization on campus, as it aligned itself with the Los Angeles-based Chicano Movement, adopting its cultural nationalism and use of direct action in their struggle to establish a Chicano Studies Department and a Chicano Movement newspaper serial at ELAC. Its contribution to social movement politics also extended to its alliance with the Brown Berets and to its participation in local movement events such as the defense for the East L.A. Thirteen and the 1969 Nueva Vistas educational conference held at the Biltmore Hotel in downtown Los Angeles.[6]

This study's focus on the role of factionalism and schism in the development of the Chicano student movement borrows from Deborah B. Balser's scholarship on social movement conflict. According to Balser,

> Factionalism refers to the conflict that develops between groups, belonging to the same organization, who formerly held common beliefs but who experience a growing divergence in their views and interests. Rather than focusing on the conflict of individuals within an organization, factionalism concerns groups that come into conflict as they pursue different goals, strategies, and tactics, stemming from their diverging interests. Schism occurs when a faction formally breaks its membership ties to the organization.[7]

Whereas social movement literature traditionally considers factionalism to be a "result of poor internal management of conflict and as a source of organizational decline," Balser seeks to develop a "process theory showing how conflict between factions develops and how the conflict leads to schism."[8] By taking into account how external environment and internal organizational dynamics converge to create conflict, Balser postulates on the potential consequences of factionalism and schism to expand a social movement's range of tactics.

Scholarship on the Chicano Movement regularly features the phenomenon of conflict, though few studies explain the process and impact of factionalism and schism on social movement growth.[9] For example, Ernesto Chávez's study on the East Los Angeles chapter of the Brown Berets references a power struggle between two male leaders vying for control over organizational identity and direction, yet does not explain the process by which conflict escalated to the point where an aggrieved party left the cultural nationalist organization to create a Marxist one.[10] In contrast, Dionne Espinoza's study of the Berets explains how internal dynamics contributed to a gendered conflict for organizational authority and legitimacy.[11] Her analysis of masculinist practices and policies within the organization, however, minimizes the process by which the external environment impacted the behavior of female members. In this case, it is not entirely clear how an extended women's social network present in the Chicano Movement influenced female Berets to exit the organization and join a Chicana anti-war group, nor is it readily apparent how interaction with other social movements contributed to the formation of a feminist consciousness and solidarity among Beret women. As these studies suggest, there is much to learn about the ways that conflict shapes movement trajectories and outcomes.[12]

Indeed intra-organizational conflict can result in potentially constructive changes to a social movement. For example, it can help to sharpen or construct new collective identities as "people create conflict as part of their search for meaning, as part of their definition of themselves and of the groups to which they belong, and to achieve what they need to survive and develop."[13] Speaking on the role of discord within the women's liberation movement, Jo Freeman adds that a "political group without any conflict is a stagnating group. Conflict is necessary and valuable, as it is the means by which we debate our ideas, resolve our differences, test our theories, and come to conclusions."[14] Distinguishing between constructive and destructive forms of conflict in the Chicano student movement, Juan Gómez-Quiñones argues that factionalism "is a part of development, positive or negative; if positive it strengthens progressive ideological clarity and organizational coherence. Negative factionalism causes confusion and weakens organization."[15] Likewise, this study demonstrates that conflict over tactics, ideas, and goals of the Chicano student movement were present at all stages of its development, and functioned as critical moments for collective assessment on the meaning, significance, and direction of the larger Chicano Movement. This essay also seeks to expand the scholarship on community college student activism and on the organizational dynamics and social networks making up the Chicano student movement during the late 1960s.

As noted by Rodolfo Acuña, community colleges such as East Los Angeles College served as a "frontline of the Chicano Studies movement," as most Chicana/o high school graduates were likely to attend a 2-year college due to structural educational inequities and limited social and financial capital.[16] Of those Chicanas/os pursuing a higher education in California during the academic year of 1971–1972, 70 percent attended junior colleges,[17] yet historical studies on the Chicano Movement have largely overlooked community colleges as part of the tapestry of Chicana/o youth activism. The few historical references to East Los Angeles College are usually limited to broad narratives mapping the activist landscape of the Los Angeles Chicano Movement.[18]

One such study is the 1978 publication *Mexican Students Por La Raza* authored by Juan Gómez-Quiñones, an eyewitness and former UMAS member at UCLA. Gómez-Quiñones offers a political framework for understanding the developmental stages and political tendencies of the Southern California Chicano student movement from 1967 to 1977. Though his account is limited to a broad generalization of movement trends and organizations, Gómez-Quiñones' analysis highlights the ebbs and flows of the Chicano student movement. In his brief account of MASA, Gómez-Quiñones credits the organization with helping to jumpstart the Chicano student movement in Los Angeles, but notes that after the summer of 1967, MASA's moderate politics placed it outside the vanguard of a radical student movement.

Building on Chicano Movement scholarship and Social Movement theory, this essay examines the process by which conflict leading to factionalism and schism expanded the Chicano student movement's collective identity, goals, and tactical repertoire.[19] In the case of MASA, I argue that the 1968 East L.A. blowouts contributed an external strain to an ongoing process of internal conflict over organizational identity, tactics, and goals. The walkouts represented the breaking point between moderate and radical students. MASA's refusal to officially support the protest politics of the walkouts widened the fissure between pre-existing factions, prompting disgruntled members to exit MASA and to form an alternative militant organization. In doing so, Chicana/o students created La Vida Nueva, in Balser's words, to "pursue their own goals using desired tactics, drawing in new adherents, raising new resources, and expanding the scope of the social movement as a whole."[20] While sustained internal dissension can weaken an organization, the group conflict experienced within MASA suggests that factionalism and schism can broaden the range of a social movement's tactics and goals. For instance, the creation of La Vida Nueva resulted in the recruitment and indoctrination of a new core of radicals into the Chicano student movement, who, unlike MASA, employed direct action to pressure the ELAC administration and its student body to fund a Chicano Studies Department. This study is guided by the following questions: how did student activists create and negotiate meanings central to the student movement's collective identity and action? What social ties did student activists forge with other Chicano Movement organizations, and how did social networking assist Chicana/o youth in mobilizing a student movement? How did internal and external factors interact to create factionalism among Chicana/o student activists at ELAC? How did factionalism and schism contribute to the development of the Chicano student movement in Los Angeles?

Social Movement theory stressing cognitive and structural processes behind movement mobilization and development informs my methodological practice. This study defines the Chicano student movement as a political social movement made up of "(1) informal networks, based on (2) shared beliefs and solidarity, which mobilize about (3) conflictual issues, through (4) the frequent use of various forms of protests."[21] Accordingly, the Chicano student movement of the late 1960s and early 1970s was composed of a network of Chicana/o college and university student organizations and informal social ties with other campus and community individuals and groups, bound together by a shared sense of injustice toward structural inequalities, cultural values, and ideologies sustaining oppressive social relationships. While educational inequity lay at the forefront of its grievances, the student movement defined its struggle as part of a broader attack against racism, sexism, capitalism, and imperialism, and regularly employed various forms of non-violent direct confrontational tactics, including sit-ins, marches, rallies, and boycotts.[22]

This study applies a constructionist framework to explain how collective identity—a group's shared sense of itself—is forged in the process of negotiation and conflict between movement actors.[23] Robert D. Benford and David A. Snow explain identity construction to be "the process through which personal and collective identities are aligned, such that individuals regard engagement in movement activity as being consistent with their self-conception and interests."[24] Collective identity becomes a salient component in the recruitment and sustenance of a social movement, as it offers a sense of solidarity and commitment. Adherents are more likely to join or stay in a Social Movement Organization (SMO) or a social movement that reflects similar goals, beliefs, and values as their own. Collective action, defined as "joint action by protest groups in pursuit of common ends," is equally important to the mobilization of a social movement and SMOs as it offers movement adherents a shared sense of mission and projected outcomes.[25]

Social networks also factor in as key to movement mobilization, as they promote "the circulation of essential resources for action (information, expertise, material resources) as well as a broader system of meaning."[26] Interpersonal social ties accompanying social networks additionally function as a stimulus for movement recruitment. Movement theorists interested in answering questions such as "why do individuals join movements?" and "what makes some individuals more predisposed to join a movement?" posit the importance of pre-existing networks where "links to one or more movement members" play a major factor in movement participation.[27] Taken together the analytical tools of collective identity, collective action, and social networks underscore the interactionist nature of movement work, demonstrating how movement participation tends to yield some level of personal transformation in individual identities.[28] Why and how factions emerged between radical and moderate members in MASA has much to do with how internal organizational dynamics and external environment such as social networks influenced a student's identity, political consciousness, and political commitments. This study subsequently explores conflict between factions as a process of internal organizational factors and external environment, namely the influence of Chicano Movement SMOs on the behavior of individual members of MASA and La Vida Nueva.

Given the paucity of secondary sources on the Chicano student movement, this essay relies extensively on print media and oral histories to construct an analysis of MASA and La Vida Nueva. Whereas archival collections on the Chicano student movement are more commonly abundant and available at the research libraries of the University of California, and less so within the California State University system, limited archival records at community colleges made it difficult to construct this historical narrative. With some minor exceptions, most of the print media utilized in this study came from the East Los Angeles College Library and the East Los Angeles Library Chicano Resource Center.[29] Extensive interviews with three male and two female movement activists from MASA and/or La Vida Nueva helped to fill in any informational gaps on organizational histories and provided the study with the necessary political biographies to sketch out personal motives for joining and exiting a social movement organization.[30]

An Emerging Social Movement: The Origins of MASA and the Transitional Politics of the Mexican American Community in Los Angeles, 1967–1968

ELAC served as one of the primary agents of higher education for Mexican American Angelinos during the 1960s. In 1967, the year in which MASA was founded, Mexican Americans made up approximately 40 percent of the campus's student population.[31] MASA's founding members—a group largely made up of male veterans and married students in their early to mid-twenties—proudly embraced their Mexican cultural heritage as a significant collective identity marker. Though individual MASA members helped to establish UMAS, a key student movement network that would help to launch the 1968 blowouts, by-and-large the organization remained committed to pursuing reform through conventional politics.

On the eve of the walkouts, as UCLA and Cal State L.A. UMAS chapters moved closer toward adopting Chicano militancy as personified by Reies López Tijerina and Rodolfo "Corky" Gonzales, MASA members looked to accomplished Mexican-American political leaders, such as Dr. Julian Nava, a World

War II veteran, Harvard graduate, and newly elected member to the Los Angeles Unified School District Board of Education, as viable role models from which to emulate their own personal success.[32] As one student, Alberto Juárez, told a campus newspaper in the spring of 1967, "Dr. Nava is one of us who made it because there was a helping hand at the time he needed it most. There are more Dr. Navas around us today, but we must help them."[33] Upon returning to ELAC for a second time, Juárez, who had just completed his service in the United States Navy, noticed the growth of the Mexican-American student population on campus in 1967. Reflecting on his father's union activities and on his own childhood experiences in a tight-knit Presbyterian community where he often addressed Spanish and English speaking church congregations, Juárez aspired for a student group that would encourage Mexican-American students to collectively work toward graduation while serving the Mexican-American community. Sharing his idea over lunch with classmates Raúl Henderson, Roy Acevedo, and John Castillo, also veterans of the armed forces, Juárez wondered "wouldn't it be great if we had something like a national Chicano fraternity like the [way] Black kids have their Kappas?"[34]

Taking their cue from older Mexican-American political organizations such as the Mexican American Political Association (MAPA) and the American G.I. Forum, students envisioned MASA as a self-help group made up of model American citizens.[35] In the words of Juárez, MASA's first president, "When we came together as a group . . . [we] really didn't have any real ideological underpinnings . . . if anything it was extremely conservative . . . and very orderly."[36] Influenced by the recent military service of its founding members, MASA's "conservative" and "orderly" orientation extended to a hierarchical and centralized organizational structure comprising a bi-annually elected executive board made up of a president, vice-president, secretary, and treasurer, and four committees housing its tutorial, education, political, social functions, and scholarship programs.[37] As was common for the time, males dominated elected leadership positions while women chaired and staffed community service committees. Within the span of 1 year in 1967, MASA succeeded in creating a support network for Mexican-American college students.[38] On campus, MASA's social events, scholarship fundraisers, and student support services helped to garner positive recognition from the campus newspaper's editorial staff and from sympathetic faculty.[39]

In spite of its "conservative" origins and its liberal mission—"the advancement of the Mexican-American student on campus and in the community"—the organization was accused by some Anglo-American faculty and Anglo-American and Mexican-American students of being divisive and exclusionary.[40] In defense of its organizational mission and goals, MASA's fall 1967 president Mike de la Peña submitted a letter to the editor of the Campus News where he refuted charges of MASA's alleged radicalism and challenged critics to support its community service mission:

> Since the inception of the Mexican American Student Association (MASA)
> last semester, there has been some question as to the exact nature and purpose
> of this new club. The very name of the club has given rise to some
> misconception such as whether or not the club is a group of ethnocentric
> subversives . . . the association is staunchly dedicated to the educational
> mobility of those proud Americans of Mexican descent. In essence the group
> is a student initiative for community and campus interaction . . . For those
> students who by this time haven't noticed; there are traumatic socio-
> economic and especially educational problems in the neighborhood which
> this college is named after. I would like to see a better cross-section of
> Elans involved in this most worthwhile endeavor.[41]

De la Peña's attempt to raise the social consciousness of his fellow ELANS echoed
the organization's primary purpose: "To make the Mexican-American student
aware of the educational problems within his community."[42] Exactly how and
for what purpose the group would go about accomplishing this task would soon
contribute to a growing sense of tension among fomenting factions.

As its membership ranks swelled to over fifty dues-paying students in its second
semester,[43] MASA mobilized a cadre of volunteers to tutor at local elementary
schools Marianna, Sheridan, and Griffith,[44] and organized a speakers' bureau to
address Chicana/o student assemblies at Eastmont Junior High, Roosevelt High
School and Garfield High, and other eastside schools.[45] Student speakers regularly
discussed the value of a college education and instructed eastside students on good
citizenship behavior, warning them to avoid engaging in criminal action and drug
experimentation. So while MASA aimed to increase student success by boosting
academic achievement, it did not seek to indoctrinate eastside students to the
emerging politics of the Chicano Movement. Its tutoring committee openly
discouraged its volunteers from talking of race, color, and controversial issues
during their school site visits.[46] At one point, Juárez, soon to be elected as UMAS
Central's first chairperson, defended MASA's position in a campus publication
stating that, "We are not trying to correct the image of the Mexican American,
we are only trying to stress the positive points about him as an American of
Mexican descent."[47]

MASA aimed to correct "educational deficiencies" in the eastside schools by
boosting the individual self-esteem and academic skills of Mexican-American
youth.[48] Though volunteers readily recognized that *barrio* children suffered
from an inadequate education, having been products of the same eastside schools,
their volunteer work did not necessarily lead them to interpret low academic
performance as a structural failure of the educational system. Instead, MASA tutors
generally perceived underachievement to be the result of troubled students or
apathetic parents and teachers.[49]

While this conventional view echoed American individualism, it had already
begun to lose credibility among some Mexican Americans such as teacher Sal

Castro. Speaking on the grievances that would give rise to the 1968 walkouts, Castro recalls that the roots of social discontent leading to protest politics lay in a growing critical awareness among youth and their parents on how institutional inequalities and racism translated to limited material resources and narrow educational opportunities for working-class Mexican-American students in the eastside schools.[50] Parent groups and professional organizations had long attempted to address their educational concerns with Los Angeles political officials. According to Dolores Delgado Bernal, in the 1950s the Education Committee of the Council of Mexican American Affairs used conventional politics to enact reforms on behalf of Mexican schoolchildren. "They met with legislators, school officials, and community members and attended hearings, press conferences, and symposia to no avail."[51] Again in 1963, business and professional leaders, organized under the Mexican American Education Committee, approached the Los Angeles Board of Education with a proposed series of reforms that highlighted the need for a culturally relevant curriculum. As quoted in Bernal's study on the blowouts, "Few of those recommendations were accepted and even fewer reached the community," yet the Board agreed to form an advisory body, called Urban Affairs. Along with the Los Angeles County Commission on Human Relations, Urban Affairs co-sponsored an annual Mexican American Youth Leadership conference held at the Hess Kramer camp in Malibu.[52]

Castro credits the initial politicalization of the walkout leaders to the annual leadership conference held at the Hess Kramer camp. In spite of the camp's assimilationist outlook aimed at aiding the Mexican youth's successful integration to an Anglo-American society, Castro and other adult camp mentors regularly encouraged students to discuss their educational experiences for the purpose of creating a shared social consciousness and set of grievances.[53] Soon conference participants openly embraced the emergent politics of the Chicano Movement as they set out to resolve their educational grievances through direct action.[54] According to camp participant and high school walkout leader Paula Crisostomo, students left the 1967 leadership conference with a determination to change the poor schooling conditions in their eastside schools. Students distributed surveys at their schools to gather evidence in support of their grievances against the L.A. Unified School District. After directly encountering the School Board's stonewalling tactics, students were primed for using protest politics to enact social change. It was around this time that Castro turned to this newly radicalized group of high school and college students to organize a series of walkouts in the hopes of pressuring the Board of Education to address the long-standing grievances of the Mexican-American community.[55] So while progressive segments of the Mexican-American community in Los Angeles began to undergo a process of radicalization, MASA remained stagnant in its prognosis of educational inequality and in its preference of using tutoring as a conventional strategy for improving education at eastside schools.

Forging a Chicano Student Movement: The Role of Social Ties and Networks in the Radicalization of Chicana/o Students, 1967

During late 1967, as Chicano student organizations flourished throughout California, noticeable divisions between moderates and radicals emerged within campus groups. Factions often centered on tactics and movement identity: "accommodation versus self-determination, Mexicano (Chicano) versus Mexican American."[56] At times, internal differences escalated into conflict, with factions perceiving each other as adversaries vying for control of organizational goals and strategy.[57] Months before the spring walkouts, MASA experienced a similar split between its older and younger members. Conflict and factionalism emerged from a convergence of internal and external factors that, with time, led aggrieved parties to believe that their differences lay in divergent interests and organizational objectives.[58] Between 1967 and 1968, MASA members underwent various levels of radicalization, with some developing a greater sympathy for militancy than others. Divisions between those who favored moderate politics and those who embraced militancy became readily apparent on the eve of the 1968 blowouts. Interaction with other social movement organizations, activists, and adversaries influenced a member's political consciousness and politics. As demonstrated by Doug McAdams and Ronnelle Paulsen's study of Freedom Summer volunteers, students embedded in various movement organizations and networks were more likely to link their personal identity with a movement's collective identity and action.[59]

Mexican-American students at ELAC shared the development of a political and social consciousness occurring at other college campuses. They, like their college peers, were introduced to the politics of the emerging Chicano Movement by seminal works that included Carey McWilliams' book on the history of Mexican Americans in the United States entitled *North From Mexico* (1949) and Eliézer Risco's local Chicano Movement newspaper *La Raza*. Drawing from an informal social network of family and friends from high school, college, church, neighborhood, and county sponsored leadership programs, ELAC students collaborated with other student groups to create UMAS and to sponsor the initial statewide Chicano student conferences that would give birth to the Chicano student movement.

On Saturday May 13, 1967 an estimated 150 to 200 college and high school students representing 14 Southern California campuses gathered at Loyola University in West Los Angeles to discuss "the role of the Mexican-American college student in the school and in the community."[60] Co-sponsored by the Los Angeles Human Relations Office, the Mexican-American Collegiate Conference organized a day-long program of workshops on racism, the farm workers' struggle, education, tutoring, and college recruitment.[61] The conference drew Chicana and Chicano students, many of which were old school acquaintances, from Southern California campuses including UCLA, Loyola University, the University of Southern California to Cal State L.A., Long Beach State, Cal State Dominguez Hills, San Fernando Valley State College, Los Angeles Community College, and East Los Angeles College.[62] Inspired by the day's events and by a desire to consolidate their shared interests, conference participants passed a resolution to create a new regional student organization which was UMAS. An ad hoc committee of students were charged with the duty of drafting a constitution stressing the central ideas of the conference: "education," "community involvement," and "social activity."[63]

After a series of summer meetings, the ad hoc committee reconvened with the general student assembly in late September to present its newly written constitution. By the end of the gathering, students had elected representatives to the UMAS coordinating committee known as *El Central* and appointed volunteers to begin UMAS chapters at their respective colleges. Within a few weeks, UMAS had expanded to include seven chapters.[64] Perhaps in recognition of his experienced leadership, oratory skills, and social ties with campus and community networks, students elected Alberto Juárez, now a UCLA transfer student, to serve as the first UMAS *Central* chair. While UMAS *Central* encouraged campuses to adopt the UMAS structure and name, it was not a requirement for admission and representation to the UMAS *Central*. MASA was one of the few groups that maintained its previous organizational identity while still participating in UMAS *Central* meetings as an affiliate. According to Juárez, this agreement did not initially pose a problem for UMAS because "the whole idea was that there would be autonomy on each of the campuses but that we would all take [similar] positions and support [common] issues."[65] Throughout the fall of 1967, UMAS *Central* coordinated activities among local chapters and organized a follow-up leadership conference for all Chicano student groups in California.

The December 16–17, 1967 statewide Mexican-American collegiate convention, originally scheduled at East L.A. College and later moved to the USC campus, highlighted the divergence between the middle-class and moderate politics of the Southern California component and the more politically radicalized and counterculture elements of the Bay area. According to Gómez-Quiñones, "Northern students at the time had a richer experience, more carefully delineated goals, and a coherent concept of the student role."[66] At the urging of the northern component, members at the convention voted to hold a demonstration with picket signs, leaflets, and chants outside a Rams and Colts football game at the Los Angeles Coliseum in an attempt to attract media attention to the link between poor schooling conditions, low college admission rates, and the fate of Chicano youth drafted to the Vietnam War. Although the television cameras remained focused on the game going on inside the stadium, students chose this venue as the occasion from which to publicly announce the birth of a Chicana/o student movement as they marched in unison shouting "Chicano Power."[67]

While some UMAS *Central* students were immediately attracted to the military fatigues, beards, long hair, black berets, anti-imperialist rhetoric, and confrontational approach of the northern California Mexican American Student Confederation (MASC) and the Student Initiative (SI) organization from San Jose State College, others were not so impressed. Southland students who had already begun to explore the Black Panthers' cultural nationalism and direct-action confrontation tactics welcomed the radical northern California group because they brought a level of energy and new analysis to the student movement that had been missing from groups such as UMAS and MASA.[68] Carlos Montes, MASA's political chairman, was one of those students receptive to such a change.

During his first year and a half at ELAC (1966–1967), Montes successfully ran for vice-president of the Associated Men's Student Government and later served as parliamentarian chair of the Associated Student Council. However, his sense of injustice grew out of his work with "rowdy street kids" as a Teen Post director at Lincoln High School. It was talking with these young people about police abuse, drugs, and street violence that drove Montes to critically analyze the consequence of racism and poverty in the barrios. In his second year at ELAC, Montes' War on Poverty job with the local Teen Post opened a window for him to befriend Fr. John Luce, the rector of the Episcopalian Church of the Epiphany who mentored Chicana/o youths, and Eliézer Risco, editor of *La Raza*, a publication that offered a critical perspective of city officials and the War on Poverty. Soon after, Montes started to attend meetings of the Young Chicanos for Community Action (YCCA) held at the East Los Angeles Piranya coffee house.[69] More a hang out than an actual coffee house, the Piranya served as a key movement nexus where Chicana/o high school and college students' political interests and social grievances coalesced into the creation of the Brown Berets, a paramilitary organization made up of Mexican-American youth advocating direct confrontational action and Chicano cultural nationalism. Once he "hooked up with *La Raza* and the Berets," early in the fall semester of 1967, Montes was introduced to the ideas of Stokely Carmichael, H. Rapp Brown, Malcolm X, Ernesto "Che" Guevara, and later Ho Chi Minh.[70] Within a year, Montes' personal identity and political consciousness had merged with the identity politics of the Chicano Movement.

Montes' concurrent participation in movement networks off campus contributed to his radicalization process. It was therefore hardly surprising that Montes would form a strong affinity with the militancy he perceived coming from the northern California student component at the USC fall conference.[71] The convergence of the northern and southern student groups also prompted fellow MASA member Luis Carrillo to reassess what he perceived to be the middle-class niceties in the dress code, behavior, and speeches of East Los Angeles students and barrio youths. "These *vatos* [dudes]," states Carrillo of the northern activists, ". . . they dressed differently, *más tirado* [more poor looking] . . . and with *más coraje* [more angry], and [they were] not too concerned about their personal appearances . . . [whereas] the East L.A. kids were profiling [dressed to impress]. It made me think that maybe we were a little slower . . . I respected them."[72]

In addition to class identity and an affinity for militancy, age seemed to have been among the factors that determined which students found the northern component appealing and those that thought them to be strange. In recalling the December meeting, Juárez noted that MASA was "really saying to the status quo 'Move over. We're coming in with our own institutions and . . . we're going to break into the country club,' [whereas] the other kids were saying 'Screw your country club.'"[73] Juárez was among the older generation of students that did not embrace the counterculture elements of the north, yet recognized that the future course of the student movement lay with the radical rhetoric of the Berkeley, San José, and other Bay area delegates. Whatever militant advantage northern groups possessed in late 1967 would soon dissipate as southland students experienced a whirl of radical activism with the outbreak of the 1968 East Los Angeles blowouts.[74]

Mobilizing Collective Action: Understanding the Impact of Conflict, Factionalism, and Schism in the Expansion of Movement Tactics and Goals, 1968–1969

Conflict centering on differences over an organization's direction does not always result in the splintering of a group, as "differences may co-exist rather harmoniously."[75] In the case of student activism in ELAC, however, conflict emerged from incompatible differences over collective action (shared goals and tactics), which in turn solidified into a factionalism that ultimately resulted in an aggrieved party splitting from MASA. The March 1968 East Los Angeles High School blowouts represented a defining moment between those students attached to the liberal and conventional politics of the Mexican-American generation and those students eager to embrace the radical protest politics of the emergent Chicano Movement. As noted by Gómez-Quiñones in his study of the Southern California student movement, "Direct support and participation in the blowouts were the demarcation lines between militants and non-militants."[76] So while the blowouts served as the climatic event leading to conflict between moderates and radicals, the process leading to factionalism and schism stemmed from an increasingly divergent view among MASistas on how best to mobilize collective action in the Chicano student movement. Unsuccessful attempts to change MASA from within inspired a small group of radical members to leave the group shortly after the walkouts. Free from the constraints of MASA, former members created a decentralized social movement organization that openly advocated direct confrontational action, such as strikes and demonstrations. Accordingly, La Vida Nueva helped to broaden the Chicano student movement's tactical repertoire by expanding its range of tactics. Equally significant, the creation of La Vida Nueva at ELAC facilitated the student movement's goal to establish Chicano Studies programs and departments at 2- and 4-year colleges; a goal explicitly expressed in the 1969 *Plan de Santa Barbara*, a manifesto for Chicano Studies.[77]

On the fateful afternoon when de la Peña and his associates walked out of MASA's weekly Thursday meeting to protest at the executive board's opposition to the blowouts, Carlos Montes had already suspended his participation in MASA. When Montes, a graduate of Garfield High School, first joined MASA in his freshman year, he shared the organization's commitment to improving the lives of Mexican-American students. Younger than most of the founding members, Montes often found himself at odds with the moderate ethnic politics and reforms favored by his fellow MASistas. After months of trying to prod the executive board into inviting Movement guest speakers, Montes succeeded in bringing labor leader Bert Corona to speak on the Vietnam War. Hoping that the organization would adopt an anti-war resolution, Montes soon found himself embroiled in a conflict between MASA's veterans, who overwhelmingly supported America's foreign policy, and MASA's younger members, who were more critical of the nation's involvement in Vietnam. An earlier attempt to persuade MASA to support the United Farm Workers strike failed to convince MASA's conservative base into championing Chicano Movement issues and causes as their own. This led Montes and other like-minded members to believe that militant leaning members would need to run for an executive board position, if organizational change were ever to happen. After a close but unsuccessful run for MASA's presidency, Montes concluded that his activist energies would probably be better served at other places. After leaving MASA, just a short few weeks before the blowouts, Montes would soon go on to launch a prolific activist profile as the Brown Berets' Minister of Information and co-founder of La Vida Nueva.[78]

The East Los Angeles blowouts were the first large-scale urban protests of the Chicano Movement. Prior to the walkouts, the movement had been primarily a rural movement among farm workers in California and agrarians in the land grant movement of New Mexico. The blowouts, as referred to by student demonstrators, brought the civil rights movement to the backyard of many urban youth, who up to this point had watched its development on television and had supported its ideological stance, but had yet to personalize it to fit their own daily experience. Protesting a long list of grievances that included ending corporal punishment, hiring Mexican-American teachers and staff, and implementing classes in Mexican-American history, an estimated 10,000 students walked out of their eastside junior high and high schools during the first 2 weeks of March 1968. The blowouts succeeded in raising national and local attention to the urban problems of working-class Mexican Americans. In addition to the impressive number of striking students, the police violence directed at some of the youth protesting in front of their schools mobilized the Los Angeles Unified School District Board of Education and eastside community members to immediately address the inequities in Mexican-American public education.

The walkouts radicalized and indoctrinated many eastside students and their parents into the Chicano Movement.[79] During the planning and execution of the walkouts, MASA's executive leadership had been reluctant to join other UMAS college students in assisting the high school students to walk out of their schools. From its inception in January 1968, Lincoln High School teacher Sal Castro sought out the cooperation of college students in his effort to mobilize students, teachers, and parents into action. Unsure if the walkouts would actually be carried out, as he had hoped to use its threat to garner political capital for pressuring the Board of Education to enact educational reform, Castro nevertheless worked diligently to recruit college students. Key among those who aided Castro and his "Kitchen Cabinet," the name he assigned to his closest co-organizers, was Alberto Juárez, who had recently transferred to UCLA and joined its UMAS chapter. Fearing possible police violence, especially in light of the 1965 Watts Riot, Castro recruited college students and the newly created Brown Berets to serve as buffers between high school student protestors and police officers. ELAC was among the various local college campuses he visited to garner support for the walkouts.[80] Though details on the dialogue of the meeting are absent, it appears that MASA passed on his offer. Drawn by a shared sense of grievances and goals with those of the walkout organizers, individual members such as Mike de la Peña, Luis Carrillo, and Olivia Velásquez joined Castro's cadre of college volunteers, but not as MASA representatives. Having exited MASA earlier in the spring semester, Carlos Montes drew from his Brown Beret membership as the basis for group participation in the walkouts. While MASA continued to prioritize tutoring and education as an appropriate strategy for social reform, militant-leaning students such as Velásquez, believed that direct confrontational action was needed if the East L.A. community was to ever uproot the structural problems of racism and poverty plaguing the barrio. Upon graduating from Roosevelt High School in June 1966, Olvia Velásquez recognized that only a "handful" of her peers had gone on to college, with the majority of young men drafted to Vietnam, married, or working for the county of Los Angeles. Wanting to experience life outside her Boyle Heights neighborhood, Velásquez enrolled at Los Angeles City College (LACC) and soon joined a campus organization made up of Mexican and Central American students who later went on to publish *El Machete*, one of the first student movement newspapers on a college campus. Tired of the long bus commute, Velásquez transferred to East Los Angeles College in early 1968, where she joined MASA and began a courtship with fellow member Carlos Montes. Upon arriving, she immediately contrasted the political activities of the Latin American group and the Black Student Union (BSU) at LACC with what she perceived to be the "complacent" attitude of many Mexican-American students at ELAC. Convinced that Mexican-American students needed to be more critical of their educational experience, the walkouts provided the occasion by which she personally witnessed the power behind student activism.[81]

In the wake of the blowouts, 1968 spring semester MASA president Richard Ávila publicly denounced the walkouts and its unintended outbreak of violence, in the daily campus newspaper. Blaming apathetic teachers and parents for failing to "inspire" Mexican children "to strive towards academic success," Ávila went on to say in the *Campus News* editorial that:

> If the above mentioned parties contributed to the students' frustration, then one must also consider one element which wholeheartedly supports the cynical ideas that 'might makes right' and that 'any means justify the ends.' It was this party that inspired the mentioned demoralized students to take some form of radical action. And since the 'more responsible' members of the community had refused to show concern for these students the radical group moved to fill the vacuum and was successful.[82]

Luis Carrillo took issue with Ávila's claim that MASA had acted responsibly and in the best interest of the high school students whereas college and community radicals had manipulated their younger peers into engaging in violence. In an editorial rebuttal featured in the same campus newspaper, Carrillo wrote:

> Because MASA failed to act, failed to respond, they are left out of discussions now held by the Board of Education . . . MASA was also excluded from a meeting between Congressman Roybal and UMAS. . . . MASA was the irresponsible party for failing to do anything but talk. At this stage it should become more receptive to the feelings of the grass roots and the core of Mexican-American students everywhere. It's time MASA realizes they should become a part of these roots.[83]

In the aftermath of the walkouts MASA appeared to have earned a damaged reputation among activists in student movement networks. Recalling her return to ELAC in late 1968, Rosie Martínez received telling advice from her younger brother, a Cal State L.A. UMAS member: stay clear of MASA. Recognizing her interest in joining the student movement, Martínez's brother recommended that she instead connect with the activists from the newly formed group La Vida Nueva.[84]

For those militant-leaning students who had already perceived significant differences with their moderate peers, the walkouts convinced them that MASA was out of touch with the developing ideas and tactics of the emergent Chicano Movement. Montes' increasing involvement in the eastside community and his subsequent arrest and indictment for his role in aiding students in carrying out the walkouts led him to contrast this experience with what was going on at ELAC.[85] "MASA never got to another level," he later recalled. "It was really frustrating knowing that the walkouts had already happened and they said the answer was tutoring. . . . That's not what a group of us wanted to do."[86] In Montes' words, "it got to the point that you just couldn't work within MASA" anymore.[87] Left with little recourse, disenchanted members gave up trying to steer the organization towards a militant path and individually exited the organization at the end of the

1968 spring semester. By the following fall semester, former MASA members, joined by a newly radicalized Chicano student base, came together to create a new Chicano student movement organization at ELAC.

La Vida Nueva differed from most student groups on campus. The organization formed as a result of a series of open-air meetings held on the campus lawn at the peak of noon. By meeting outside where all students could listen and participate in the talks, the open-air sessions succeeded in attracting a large crowd. The former MASA members hoped to generate a discussion on the role of Mexican-American students in their communities and the Chicano Movement.[88] Meetings resembled "rap sessions" where students discussed a wide variety of topics such as the walkouts, Chicano Studies, police brutality, poverty, the Vietnam War, Fidel Castro, Che Guevara and Cuba, Black Power, the United Farm Workers union, Reies López Tijerina, and the Crusade for Justice.[89]

In aligning its collective identity and collective action with the larger Chicano Movement, La Vida Nueva did not blindly adopt the patriarchal privilege that was already being reproduced in the organizational structures and practices of nearby organizations such as the Brown Berets.[90] Having directly witnessed gender hierarchy in MASA and the Brown Berets, in the latter of which her boyfriend Montes held a leadership position, Velásquez recalls that women in La Vida Nueva insisted on a policy of shared governance and duties after witnessing the secondary roles assigned to women in the Brown Berets:

> The leadership of the Berets was men, [but] . . . the real work and the strategy and the organizing were done by the women. I never was a Brown Beret, but because we went to different things together, I observed this and other women that I was with observed this. So our take right away was that if we were going to form an organization . . . [we had] to make sure there was equal gender leadership.[91]

In a conscious attempt to further distinguish itself from the Berets and MASA, La Vida Nueva favored a decentralized structure headed by one female and one male co-chair elected by majority decision. Women and men actively participated in all aspects of La Vida Nueva, ranging from staffing its newspaper publication to planning events, organizing demonstrations to representing the group at picket lines, conferences, and rallies throughout Los Angeles, the state, and the southwest.[92]

Membership was contingent on shared responsibilities and active engagement in the surrounding Chicano Movement. When and if a person did not carry out their duties, the other members would hold him or her responsible. This pointed to the organization's emphasis on direct action and not just rhetoric. For those individuals who had perceived MASA to be "all talk and no action," La Vida Nueva was to be an organization that went beyond just talking about what needed to be done. Instead it would participate in the mobilization of collective action.[93]

La Vida Nueva members subsequently partook in key movement events throughout 1969, including the St. Basil's Christmas Eve protest in Los Angeles, the Denver Youth Liberation Conference, the Plan de Santa Barbara Conference, and the Nuevas Vistas conference held at the Biltmore Hotel that would later lead to the arrest of La Vida Nueva's newspaper editor Tomás Varela and La Vida Nueva co-founder and Brown Beret, Carlos Montes.[94]

By the spring of 1969, La Vida Nueva had become the leading Chicano organization on campus and had successfully developed into one of the most active and recognizable movement organizations in East Los Angeles. In less than a year, the organization secured student council funding for a Chicano Movement-centered newspaper named *La Vida Nueva*. The publication functioned as a means of communication for students and eastside community members with staff writers, featuring articles and poetry dealing with cultural identity, bilingual education, art and music, indígenismo, cultural nationalism, and often publicizing Chicano Movement events such as the 1969 National Youth Liberation Conference and Chicana/o student activities such as *Semana de la Raza*. In its effort to relate to the eastside Mexican communities, *La Vida Nueva's* news staff also published articles about the effects of poverty on the Chicano family, barrio discrimination, police brutality, local politics, and the Vietnam War's impact on Chicano communities. *La Vida Nueva* newspaper serial, which continued into the early 1970s, contributed to the formation and expansion of Chicano Movement and Chicana/o student movement political and cultural networks in Los Angeles.[95]

Confident that a Chicano Studies Department would educate students about structural and cultural inequities and informally recruit potential adherents to the Chicano Movement, La Vida Nueva formed a valuable alliance with the Black Student Union and turned to their movement networks to mobilize campus and community support for Chicano Studies at ELAC.[96] La Vida Nueva's use of direct confrontational tactics on campus, including walkouts and rallies, unintentionally attracted the attention of the Los Angeles Police Department and the East Los Angeles Sheriffs, who were intent on breaking up the momentum of the Chicano Movement through violent harassment, surveillance, and infiltration.[97] Despite harassment by local law enforcement, La Vida Nueva continued to advocate Chicano Studies; to participate in Anti-Vietnam War moratoriums in East L.A.; and to sponsor some of the earliest celebrations of Cinco de Mayo and Mexican Independence day at Southern California college campuses.[98]

Conclusion

This study seeks to expand scholarship on the formative stage of the Chicano student movement from 1967 to 1969, a period pre-dating the student movement's institutionalization into El Movimiento Estudiantil Chicano de Aztlán (MEChA) in the spring of 1969. The origins of the Chicano student movement at East Los Angeles College is an important story because so little has been written about student activism in community colleges. As such, factionalism's potential to create constructive change and growth within the Chicano student movement has yet to be fully appreciated and examined as a key ingredient in the emergence and development of the larger Chicano Movement's collective action and collective identity.

This essay also adds to the scholarship focusing on the micromobilization of social movements. As noted by Deborah Balser, factionalism leading to schism is an under-researched phenomenon in social movement scholarship. This study responds to Balser's assertion that theory explaining the processes leading to factionalism "must take a historical perspective. It must look at the story of the SMO [Social Movement Organization] to understand the interplay of people and events over time. It should portray conflict and schism as a process rather than an isolated event."[99] When placed within a framework of internal factors and external environment, this study on factionalism in MASA offers empirical evidence from which to examine the process by which Chicana/o student activists constructed and negotiated movement strategies, goals, and identity.

Internal organizational differences are not a phenomenon unique to MASA. My previous research on the Chicano student movement in Southern California reveals that student groups almost always comprised members with varying levels of political consciousness. Yet, internal conflict becomes significant to an organization's dynamics when it escalates into factionalism and schism. In the case for MASA, incompatible differences over strategies (i.e., tutoring versus political agitation) reflected divergent goals between moderate and radical members. For example, moderate members favored MASA's tutor and speaker panel program because it reflected the organization's identification as a self-help group, and because it served as the means from which to help individual Mexican-American youth excel at education for the purpose of successful integration into an Anglo-American society. In sharp contrast, radical members' preference for protest politics was tied to a view that conventional politics had been unresponsive to the Mexican-American community's grievances, and that substantive change was needed to uproot the structural problems leading to inferior schooling conditions and to the annihilation of a Mexican cultural identity in the eastside schools.

Failed attempts by radical students to successfully run for office and to persuade their moderate colleagues to support popular movement causes, all in the hope of aligning MASA to the emergent Chicano Movement, instead contributed to a growing factionalism on the eve of the March 1968 walkouts. De la Peña's condemnation of the executive board, for its refusal to support the walkouts, revealed the radical faction's frustration with its inability to negotiate MASA's organizational identity, strategy, and goals. While the executive board could have served as a mechanism for conflict resolution, given its delegated responsibility to represent the entire membership, it failed to do so largely because the moderate faction's domination of the board insured that its interests would prevail.[100] MASA's absence in the blowouts was troubling for those MASistas who had wanted the organization to share in the collective risks and benefits of protest politics, especially since Sal Castro had assigned college students the primary responsibility for protecting high school students from potential police violence. Members who were sympathetic to Chicano militancy concluded that MASA's status and legitimacy within the local Chicano student movement had been permanently damaged by its absence in the walkouts. The scale and historical significance of the East Los Angeles High School blowouts, at last, convinced the radical faction that internal differences over organizational goals and strategy indeed mattered.

Internal conflict also stemmed from the impact of external factors, such as Chicano Movement networks, on the organizational behavior and political identities of MASA members. Overlapping participation in one or more movement networks led a small faction of members to rethink MASA's approach for solving the problem of educational inequity. Drawing from the emergent Chicano Movement's framework on race and class, MASA's radical faction came to view the systematic marginalization of Mexican Americans in education as part of a longer historical process of racism and economic exploitation of racial minorities in the United States. Regular interaction with UMAS, and other movement actors and groups, influenced some MASistas to embrace militancy. Upon realizing that MASA's goals and strategies were incompatible with their newly adopted Chicano Movement identities, aggrieved members left the group and formed La Vida Nueva in late 1968 and early 1969. Free to pursue its desired goals and tactics, La Vida Nueva subsequently mobilized a series of strikes and demonstrations in support for the establishment of a Chicano Studies Department at East Los Angeles College. In so doing, its direct action strategy helped to expand the range of strategies and tactics used by Chicano student organizations throughout California's college and university campuses.

MASA continued to exist after its schism, though not without some changes. Two years after its founding in early 1967, a new cohort of students refashioned MASA into a chapter of UMAS. Still, even as students attempted to reinvent MASA by linking it more directly to the local Chicano student movement, UMAS at ELAC appeared to remain out of step with the developing Chicano student movement. For example, as MASA transitioned into UMAS in the spring of 1969, student delegates at the *El Plan de Santa Barbara* conference simultaneously voted to consolidate the various student groups throughout California into a newly unified umbrella organization called MEChA. Forced to compete with La Vida Nueva for movement legitimacy and resources (i.e.,volunteers, funds)—a challenging task given La Vida Nueva's successful mobilization of campus and communitywide support for ethnic studies and a movement-themed newspaper serial—UMAS at ELAC remained outside the vanguard of the Chicano student movement at East Los Angeles College and in the Los Angeles Metropolitan area.[101] As the larger Chicano Movement contracted during the 1970s, so did its student component. With fewer campus resources and youth volunteers from which to staff the two student organizations, UMAS and La Vida Nueva merged in the mid-1970s to form a MEChA chapter at East Los Angeles College.

Notes

1 The "East Los Angeles" blowouts refers to a number of eastside Los Angeles communities including the unincorporated neighborhood known as East Los Angeles, as well as other eastside areas including Boyle Heights, City Terrace, Lincoln Heights, and Belvedere. For a history of Mexican settlement in eastside Los Angeles, see George J. Sánchez, *Becoming Mexican American: Ethnicity, Culture, and Identity in Chicano Los Angeles, 1900–1945* (New York: Oxford University Press, 1993) and Ricardo Romo, *East Los Angeles: History of a Barrio* (Austin: University of Texas Press, 1983).

2 "MASA 'Unprepared' for Garfield High Violence," *Campus News* 13 Mar. 1968: 1 spec. coll. Helen Miller Bailey Library, East Los Angeles College (hereinafter spec. coll. HMBL).

3 I use the term "Chicano" to refer to the collective identity created by movement adherents. In the process of building a movement identity, Chicana/o activists differentiated their political consciousness, tactics, goals, and racial identity from an older Mexican-American generation of the 1930s through mid-1960s. In an effort to acknowledge the overlooked contributions of women in a cultural nationalist movement dominated by masculine imagery and male leadership, I will use the terms "Chicana" or "Chicana/o" to highlight and nuance the gender dynamics of the movement. Unless otherwise noted, the term "Mexican American" will be used when specifically referring to U.S. citizens and residents of Mexican ancestry, while the term "Mexican" will be used as an ethnic label inclusive of U.S. native and foreign born persons of Mexican ancestry.

4 For Chicana/o student population statistics see Ronald W. López and Darryl D. Enos, comp. *Chicanos and Public Higher Education in California prepared for the Joint Committee on the Master Plan for Higher Education California Legislature* (Sacramento, CA, 1972), appendix G-2. For 1970 California population estimates see chart 7 "Ethnic Diversity in California, 1970–2020" in Elías López, Major Demographic Shifts Occurring in California. California State Library, California Research Bureau Note, 6:5 (October, 1999), 8. www.library.ca.gov/crb/99/notes/v6n5.pdf (accessed July 17, 2013).

5 Juan Gómez-Quiñones dates the origins of the Southern California student movement at colleges and high schools to "the summer and fall of 1966 and the spring of 1967." See Juan Gómez-Quiñones, *Mexican Students Por La Raza: The Chicano Movement in Southern California 1967–1977* (Santa Barbara, CA: Editorial La Causa, 1978) 16.

6 The *Nueva Vistas* conference was hosted in downtown Los Angeles by an association of Mexican American Educators in spring 1969. *La Vida Nueva* news editor Tomás Varela and Brown Beret Minister of Information, and former MASista, Carlos Montes were among a group of students, teachers, and community activists indicted for the April 24, 1969 Biltmore Hotel fire that broke out during the conference. The conference demonstration, in which a predetermined group of activists stood up to interrupt a speech delivered by Governor Ronald Reagan, was partially planned during meetings of La Vida Nueva to protest the Governor's cutbacks to minority state programs such as EOP. However, when minor fires broke out in the conference room and on various floors of the hotel, the testimony of Brown Beret undercover Sheriff Fernando Sumaya incriminated six individuals, including Montes, on false charges of conspiracy to commit arson. Carlos Montes, personal interview, 20 Feb. 1999 (hereinafter C. Montes). Also see Pánfilo de la Muerte, "The Nuevas Vistas Defendants," *Chicano Student Movement* (1969) reprinted in *La Raza* Summer, 1969:

39. For information on the Biltmore fires, see "No hay ningún detenido en los incendios del Biltmore," *La Opinion* 26 April 1969: 1; and Tom Newton, "Demonstration Disrupt Talk by Governor," *Los Angeles Times* 25 April 1969: 1 in Chicano Studies Research Center Library, UCLA (hereinafter CSRCL, UCLA).

7 Deborah B. Balser, "The Impact of Environmental Factors on Factionalism and Schism in Social Movement Organizations," *Social Forces*, Sept. 7, 76(1): 200.

8 Ibid., 199–200. For studies on the decline of 1960s social movement organizations and social movements see: Frederick D. Miller, "The End of SDS and the Emergence of Weatherman: Demise through Success," (303–324), Doug McAdam, "The Decline of the Civil Rights Movement" (325–348) and Emily Stoper, "The Student Nonviolent Coordinating Committee: Rise and Fall of a Redemptive Organization" (349–364) in *Waves of Protest: Social Movements Since the Sixties*, Eds. Jo Freeman and Victoria Johnson (Lanham, MD: Rowman & Littlefield, 1999).

9 For example see Carlos Muñoz, *Youth, Identity, Power: The Chicano Movement* (London: Verso, 1989); Ignacio M. García, *United We Win: The Rise and Fall of La Raza Unida Party* (Tucson: University of Arizona Press, 1989); Armando Navarro, *Mexican American Youth Organization: Avant-Garde of the Chicano Movement in Texas* (Austin: University of Texas Press, 1995); Lorena Oropeza, *¡Raza Sí! ¡Guerra No!: Chicano Protest and Patriotism during the Viet Nam War Era* (Berkeley: University of California Press, 2005); David Montejano, *Quixote's Soldiers: A Local History of the Chicano Movement, 1966–1981* (Austin: University of Texas Press, 2010); Maylei Blackwell, *Chicana Power!: Contested Histories of Feminism in the Chicano Movement* (Austin: University of Texas Press, 2011).

10 Ernesto Chávez, *¡Mi Raza Primero! (My People First!): Nationalism, Identity, and Insurgency in the Chicano Movement in Los Angeles, 1966–1978* (Berkeley: University of California Press, 2002). The Brown Berets were a paramilitary barrio youth organization modeled on Black nationalist organizations such as the Black Panthers. According to Chávez, factionalism centered on dissonant views between David Sánchez, co-founder and leader of the Berets who advocated cultural nationalism and limited the Berets' role to community protectors against police abuse and Cruz Olmeda, who advocated the group to adopt Maoist revolutionary politics.

11 Dionne Espinoza, "'Revolutionary Sisters': Women's Solidarity and Collective Identification among Chicana Brown Berets in East Los Angeles, 1976–1970," *Aztlán* 26 (2001).

12 The origins of El Centro de Acción Social Autónomo (CASA) offers additional evidence of factionalism leading to schism in the Chicano Movement. See Chávez, *¡Mi Raza Primero!* and Muñoz, *Youth, Identity, Power.*

13 Patrick G. Coy and Lynne M. Woehrle, Eds. *Social Conflicts and Collective Identities* (Lanham, MD: Rowman and Littlefield, 2000) 2.

14 Jo Freeman, "Crises and Conflicts in Social Movement Organizations," *Chrysalis: Magazine of Women's Culture*, No. 5, 1978, pp. 43–51. www.jofreeman.com/social movements/crisis.htm. (accessed April 4, 2013).

15 Gómez-Quiñones, 5.

16 Rodolfo F. Acuña, *The Making of Chicana/o Studies: In the Trenches of Academe* (New Brunswick, NJ: Rutgers University Press, 2011) 47.

17 According to a 1972 state commissioned report, 55 percent of Californians enrolled in higher education in 1971–1972 attended junior colleges compared to 77 percent of Mexican-American/Chicano students. López and Enos, *Chicanos and Public Higher Education in California*, appendix F-4.

18 See Acuña, *The Making of Chicana/o Studies* and Gómez-Quiñones, *Mexican Students Por La Raza.*

19 Charles Tilly, *From Mobilization to Revolution* (Reading, MA: Addison-Wesley, 1978) and William A. Gamson, *The Strategy of Social Protest*, 2nd ed. (Homewood, Ill.: Dorsey

Press, 1990). As defined by Verta Taylor, tactical repertoires of contention refers to "the strategies used by collective actors to persuade or coerce authorities to support their claims. The tactical repertoires of social movements include conventional strategies of political persuasion such as lobbying, voting, and petitioning; confrontational tactics such as marches, strikes, and public demonstrations that disrupt day-to-day life; violent acts such as bombing, rioting, assassination, and looting that inflict material and economic damage and loss of life; and cultural forms of political expression such as ritual, music, art, theater, street performance, and practices of everyday life that inspire solidarity and oppositional consciousness." *Blackwell Encyclopedia of Sociology*, s.v. "Contention, Tactical Repertoires of," by Verta Taylor. www.blackwellreference.com/public/tocnode?id=g9781405124331_yr2012_chunk_g97814051243319_ss1-129 (accessed July 19, 2013).

20 Balser, 199–200.
21 Donatella della Porta and Mario Diani, *Social Movements: An Introduction* (Oxford: Blackwell, 1999) 16.
22 Marisol Moreno, "'Of the Community, For the Community'": The Chicana/o Student Movement in California's Public Higher Education, 1967–1973" (PhD diss., University of California, Santa Barbara, 2009).
23 Nancy Whittier and Verta Taylor, "Collective Identities in Social Movement Communities: Lesbian Feminist Mobilization," *Frontiers in Social Movement Theory*, Eds. Aldon D. Morris and Carol M. Mueller (New Haven, CT: Yale University Press, 1992); Scott A. Hunt, Robert D. Benford, and David A. Snow, "Identity Fields: Framing Processes and the Social Construction of Movement Identities," *New Social Movements: From Ideology to Identity*, Eds. Enrique Laraña, Hank Johnson, and Joseph R. Gusfield (Philadelphia: Temple University Press, 1994); Scott A. Hunt and Robert D. Benford, "Collective Identity, Solidarity, and Commitment," *The Blackwell Companion to Social Movements*, Eds. David Snow, Sarah A. Soule, Hanspeter Kriesi (Malden, MA: Blackwell, 2004)
24 Robert D. Benford, and David A. Snow, "Framing Processes and Social Movements: An Overview and Assessment," *Annual Review of Sociology*, 26 (2000): 49.
25 Charles Tilly (1978) quoted in Aldon Morris, "Black Student Sit-in Movement: An Analysis of Internal Organization. *American Sociological Review*, 46 (6) (1981): 746.
26 Doug McAdam, John D. McCarthy, and Meyer N. Zald, Eds. *Comparative Perspectives on Social Movements: Political Opportunities, Mobilizing Structures, and Cultural Framings* (Cambridge, UK: Cambridge University Press, 1996) 14. For another example of network analysis see Roberto M. Fernández and Doug McAdam, "Social Networks and Social Movements: Multiorganizational Fields and Recruitment to Mississippi Freedom Summer," *Sociological Forum*, 3 (1988): 357–382.
27 David A. Snow, Louis A. Zurcher, Jr. and Sheldon Ekland-Olson, "Social Networks and Social Movements: A Microstructural Approach to Differential Recruitment," *American Sociological Review*, 45 (1980): 798.
28 David A. Snow and Doug McAdam, "Identity Work Processes in the Context of Social Movements: Clarifying the Identity/Movement Nexus," in Sheldon Stryker, Timothy J. Owens, and Robert W. White, Eds. *Self, Identity, and Social Movements* (Minneapolis, MN: University of Minnesota Press).
29 As noted in Maylei Blackwell's *¡Chicana Power!*, a study on feminist print media and the formation of a Chicana feminist consciousness, underground newspapers engaged in critical movement work by creating a common framework and identity from which to recruit potential participants and to strengthen a shared set of beliefs, ideas, and grievances among social movement organizations and adherents.
30 Personal interviews included in this study include Luis Carrillo (MASA/La Vida Nueva), Alberto Juárez (MASA), Rosie Martínez, (La Vida Nueva), Carlos Montes (MASA/La Vida Nueva), and Olivia "Velásquez" Montes (MASA/La Vida Nueva).

31 Helen Miller Bailey, *East Los Angeles College History, 1945–1974* in spec. coll. HMBL. Ref. 378.7949, [c.1976] N. pag. It is doubtful that this historical paper was ever published. The sole edition in the library is incomplete and missing the section on the Chicano Movement.

32 According to Gómez-Quiñones, in 1967 a small group of students at UCLA were simultaneously gathering into an informal group to discuss their alienation on campus and their desire to promote Mexican interests on campus. Unlike their MASA peers at ELAC, these UCLA students "were nearly all in their late teens, rejected adult political groups and vented freely a dislike for traditional politics though their concerns also focused on education and community involvement. Significantly, they looked to the United Farmworkers for a model and inspiration and not to MAPA or Kennedy politics," Gómez-Quiñones, 20.

33 Alberto Juárez, qtd. in José Mauro Vejar, "Hands of Compassion," *ELAN* May 1967: 13 in Chicano Resource Library, East Los Angeles Public Library (hereinafter CRC, ELAPL).

34 Alberto Juárez, personal interview, 29 April 2002. (hereinafter A. Juárez). As a participant of Camp Hess Kramer and Teen Post, Juárez participated in two important county and federally funded community organizations that served as a stepping stone in the politicalization of several Mexican American youth in Los Angeles during the mid-1960s. Moreover, his sense of egalitarianism and familiarity with integrated environments were reinforced by his frequent interactions with English-speaking congregations, his days as a boy scout, his attendance at the ethnically diverse Franklin High School in Highland Park, where he participated in student government and athletic sports, and his recent experience in the Navy.

35 "Mexican American Students Association, East Los Angeles College (An Affiliate of United Mexican American Students), September 1968," *Calisphere*, http://content. cdlib.org/ark:/13030/hb6000106f/?&brand=calisphere (accessed May 24, 2013). Bailey, *East Los Angeles College History.*

36 A. Juárez, personal interview, 29 April 2002.

37 "Four Committees Formed," *Campus News* 21 Feb. 1968: 6 in spec. coll. HMBL.

38 There is one recorded instance in May 1968 where the *Campus News* lists a woman as a candidate for MASA President. In an election for fall semester 1968, Rachel Galan received three votes compared to Roger Holguin's twenty-four votes and Milton Rolan's twenty votes. See "MASA Proxy Elected," *Campus News* 22 May 1968: 6 in spec. coll. HMBL.

39 "A Little Praise for MASA," editorial, *Campus News* 25 Oct. 1967: 2 in spec. coll. HMBL.

40 For example, see Joe Blackstock, "Unity Brews Trouble, Threatens Society," editorial, *Campus News* 3 April 1968: 2 in spec. coll. HMBL. Also see "Mexican American Students Association, East Los Angeles College (An Affiliate of United Mexican American Students), September 1968," *Calisphere*, http://content.cdlib.org/ark:/ 13030/hb6000106f/?&brand=calisphere (accessed May 24, 2013). According to Juárez, the Proud Americans, an ELAC student group that included Mexican American members were among the ELAC student body that rejected MASA's ethnic moniker. Juárez also recalls MASA's advisor, Dr. Helen Miller Bailey expressing concern that the group's ethnic title suggested a self-imposed segregation from the general student body. A. Juárez, personal interview 13 July 2002 and 23 June 2013.

41 Mike de la Peña, letter, "MASA Needs Support to Serve Purpose," *Campus News* 15 Nov. 1967: 2 in spec. coll. HMBL.

42 "Mexican American Students Association, East Los Angeles College (An Affiliate of United Mexican American Students), September 1968," *Calisphere*, http://content. cdlib.org/ark:/13030/hb6000106f/?&brand=calisphere (accessed May 24, 2013).

43 A. Juárez, personal interview, 13 July 2002; and Olivia "Velásquez" Montes, personal interview, 5 Feb. 1999 (hereinafter O. "Velásquez" Montes).
44 Irene García, "Tutors Help Poor Children to Read, Adjust to Society," *Campus News* 15 May 1968: 3 in spec. coll. HMBL.
45 Irene García, "MASA Speakers Push Education," *Campus News* 15 May 1968: 3 in spec. coll. HMBL; and "MASA Will Visit," *Campus News* 18 Oct. 1967: 3 in spec. coll. HMBL.
46 Irene García, "MASA Tutors," *Campus News* 16 Oct. 1968: 3 in spec. coll. HMBL.
47 Alberto Juárez, qtd. in José Mauro Vejar, "Hands of Compassion," *ELAN* May 1967: 13 in Chicano Resource Library, East Los Angeles Public Library (hereinafter CRC, ELAPL).
48 Richard Avila, letter, "Constructive Achievements Noted as MASA Moves Ahead," *Campus News* 7 Feb. 1968: 2 in spec. coll. HMBL.
49 Richard Avila, "Neglect Cause of Exodus," *Campus News* 13 Mar. 1968: 1,6 in spec. coll. HMBL.
50 Mario T. García and Sal Castro, *Blowout!: Sal Castro and the Chicano Struggle for Educational Justice.* (Chapel Hill: University of North Carolina Press, 2011).
51 Dolores Delgado Bernal, "Grassroots leadership reconceptualized: Chicana oral histories and the 1968 East Los Angeles school blowouts." *Frontiers: A Journal of Women Studies.* 19, no. 2 (1998): 117.
52 Ibid.
53 Ibid.
54 García, *Blowout!*, 138.
55 Ibid., 138–140.
56 Gomez-Quiñones, 23
57 Louis Kriesberg, *Constructive Conflicts: From Escalation to Resolution* (Lanham, MD: Rowman & Littlefield, 1998).
58 Balser, p. 224–25
59 Doug McAdam and Ronnelle Paulsen. "The Relationship Between Social Ties and Activism." *Journal of Sociology.* 99 (1993): 640–667.
60 "Mexican-American Students Organize," *La Raza* 15 Oct. 1967:4 in Chicano Studies Resource Center Library, UCLA (hereinafter CSRCL, UCLA), Gómez-Quiñones, *Mexican Students Por La Raza* 20–21, A. Juárez, personal interview, 13 July 2002.
61 Gómez-Quiñones, 21.
62 A. Juárez, personal interview, 13 July 2002.
63 Gómez-Quiñones, 21.
64 Ibid., 22
65 Ibid.
66 Ibid., 24. According to Gomez-Quiñones, the Cal State Long Beach chapter refused to participate in the picket because it did not approve of militancy.
67 Ibid.; A. Juárez, personal interview, 29 April 2002; and "Time of Studies & Statistics Over, Time For Action & Revolution Now!," *La Raza* 25 Dec., 1967: 3 in CSRCL, UCLA. Between 200–300 students came together to discuss the role of students in alleviating the problems of their local communities and to coordinate action programs. Speeches delivered by Alberto Juárez and Armando Valdez, a northern California student leader, in the morning assembly gave way to afternoon workshops focusing on politics, education, leadership, and forming brown and black alliances. The latter workshop was by far the most attended, as students crowded into the conference room to hear two representatives of the Black Student Union talk about revolution. Other issues discussed at the convention included the New Mexico land movement, bilingual and bicultural education, the high drop-out rate of Mexican American high school students, the disproportionate rate of Mexican Americans drafted into the military and killed in combat, political gerrymandering, the farm workers struggle,

and employment and housing discrimination. The successful turnout at the USC convention was a testament to the social network developed by southland students.
68 In *Mexican Students Por la Raza*, Gómez-Quiñones identifies four general tendencies present at the conference: the "traditional youth 'model leadership' of . . . a few years back"; the "liberal moderate view" of UMAS founders; the "radical community-oriented militancy;" and the "extremist juvenile left (25)." According to Gómez-Quiñones, the "radical liberals and militants were to be the dominant and gain the consensus" of the assembly.
69 For a discussion on the Brown Berets see chapter two in Chávez's *¡Mi Raza Primero! (My People First!)*; and chapter eight in Ian Haney-López, *Racism on Trial: The Chicano Fight for Justice* (Cambridge, MA: Belknap Press of Harvard University Press, 2003).
70 Carlos Montes, personal interview, 22 Oct. 1998 (hereinafter C. Montes).
71 Ibid.
72 Luis Carrillo, personal interview, 1 Mar. 2003 (hereinafter L. Carrillo).
73 A. Juárez, personal interview, 29 April 2002.
74 Gómez-Quiñones, 24.
75 Coy and Woehrle, 2.
76 Gómez-Quiñones, 26.
77 Chicano Coordinating Council on Higher Education. *El Plan De Santa Barbara: A Chicano Plan for Higher Education: Analyses and Positions*, (Oakland, CA: La Causa Publications, 1969).
78 C. Montes, personal interview, 8 Sept. 1998 and 20 Feb. 1999. Montes dropped out of college by the end of 1969 to fully dedicate himself as the Berets' Minister of Information. No longer a student, Montes risked being drafted to war. Moreover, his involvement in the Brown Berets organization soon placed him in direct confrontation with law enforcement, leading to surveillance, intense police harassment, several arrests, and eventually exile.
79 See Delgado Bernal, "Grassroots Leadership Reconceptionalized," and Henry Joseph Gutiérrez, "The Chicano Education Rights Movement and School Desegregation Los Angeles, 1962–1970," diss., UC Irvine, 1990.
80 García, *Blowout!*. Castro names the following college students as part of "the kitchen cabinet": Al Juárez (UCLA), Vicki Castro (Cal State L.A.), Moctesuma Esparza (UCLA), Carlos Vásquez (UCLA), Susan Racho (UCLA), Juan Gómez-Quiñones (UCLA), Hank López (San Fernando State), and Monte Pérez (Golden West College).
81 Olivia "Montes" "Velásquez" Montes, personal interview, 5 Feb. 1999.
82 Richard Ávila, "Neglect Cause of Exodus," *Campus News* 13 Mar. 1968: 6 in spec. coll. HMBL.
83 Luis Carrillo, "Walkout Explained," *Campus News* 20 Mar. 1968: 1,6 in spec. coll. HMBL.
84 Rosie Martínez, personal interview, 27 Feb. 1999 (hereinafter R. Martínez).
85 For an account on the arrests and indictment of walkout leaders on charges such as disturbing the peace and disrupting public schools see chapter two in Muñoz, *Youth, Identity, Power*.
86 O. "Velásquez" Montes, personal interview, 5 Feb. 1999.
87 C. Montes, personal interview, 22 Oct. 1998.
88 Gerald Hansen, "Open-Air Chicano Meeting on Role Draws Big Crowd," *Campus News* 16 Oct. 1968: 6 in spec. coll. HMBL.
89 For an extended discussion see Moreno's "Of the Community, For the Community."
90 For a discussion on sexism in the Brown Berets see Espinoza's "Revolutionary Sisters."
91 O. "Velásquez" Montes, personal interview, 5 Feb. 1999.
92 In addition to Olivia Velásquez, who served as one of the first La Vida Nueva co-chairs, women activists in La Vida Nueva included Rosie Martínez, Donna Plank,

Terri Gonzáles, Margaret Luna, Isabel Gómez. According to Velásquez, at this point of the movement La Vida Nueva women did not identify themselves as Chicana feminists, however my preliminary research suggests that their organizational behavior and individual identities exhibited a feminist consciousness. O. "Velásquez" Montes, personal interview, 5 Feb. 1999; 12 Feb. 1999; 9 April 1999.

93 Ibid., 12 Feb. 1999.

94 Sponsored by Católicos Por La Raza, a Chicano/a youth organization, Mexican Americans ranging from children to the elderly participated in the St. Basil's Christmas Eve midnight mass demonstration, held on the evening of December 24, 1969 to protest issues such as Cardinal McIntyre's cutbacks on Catholic schools in the barrios. In their attempt to enter the St. Basil's Church, a Los Angeles parish famous for its wealthy congregation, protestors were met with police violence. The Los Angeles Thirteen was a group of male activists, including UMAS leaders and Carlos Montes, who were arrested and indicted on felony charges of conspiracy to commit misdemeanors, such as disturbing the peace and trespassing on school grounds, during the East Los Angeles High School Walkouts. College students and community youth from the Eastside formed a defense committee to raise funds for legal expenses and to sponsor a series of events to gather support for the accused. The "L.A. Thirteen" became a rallying call for social justice for Chicanas/os. The Denver Chicano Youth Liberation Conference of March 1969 represented the first national Chicana/o youth event where students and community activists gathered to discuss issues such as identity, history, political mobilization, and social justice. The conference also produced a key document, El Plan de Aztlán, a Chicano manifesto that would later be distributed throughout college and high school campuses. The Santa Barbara Conference was a three-day event that took place at UC Santa Barbara in April 1969. Over one hundred Chicana/o college students, faculty, and staff from California assembled to create a statewide model for Chicano Studies known as El Plan de Santa Bárbara.

95 La Vida Nueva bimonthly circulation was later published on a monthly basis during 1970 and reappeared in April 1973. Gerald Hansen, "A.S. Council Okays Brown Newspaper for February 26," Campus News 19 Feb. 1969: 1, 6; Gerald Hansen, "'We'll Come Out By Force' Scares Council into Decision," Campus News 5 Mar. 1969: 1 in spec. coll. HMBL. Visual artist Gronk contributed illustrations to later editions of La Vida Nueva while he was enrolled at East L.A. College. Gronk would later become part of the East L.A. performance group ASCO.

96 La Vida Nueva activists were interested in developing a curriculum that specifically focused on the Mexican American historical and contemporary experience in the United States as well as courses embracing the counter-hegemonic politics of the Chicano Movement, and classes addressing Chicano cultural identity. While MASA may not have shared the same vision for what a Mexican American curriculum at ELAC should look like, fall 1968 MASA president Roger Holguin, nonetheless, reaffirmed La Vida Nueva's grievance by announcing to the Student Council the results of his research on the status of Mexican American Studies at Los Angeles City College (LACC). According to Holguin, there were "150 Spanish surname students in LACC's files. Yet there are [sic] already providing [an introductory course on Mexican Americans] but ELAC with over 4,000 Mexican Americans does not." See Roger Holguin, quoted in "Chicanos Not Using Courses Here Now," Campus News 23 Oct. 1968: 6 in spec. coll. HMBL.

97 By this point, Carlos Montes had dropped out of ELAC to join the Brown Berets full time. See Pánfilo de la Muerte, "The Nuevas Vistas Defendants," Chicano Student Movement (1969) reprinted in La Raza Summer, 1969: 39. For information on the Biltmore fires, see "No hay ningún detenido en los incendios del Biltmore," La Opinión 26 April 1969: 1; and Tom Newton, "Demonstration Disrupt Talk by Governor," Los Angeles Times 25 April 1969: 1 in CSRCL, UCLA. C. Montes, personal interview,

20 Feb.1999; O. "Velásquez" Montes, personal interview, 12 Feb. 1999; R. Martínez, personal interview 27 Feb. 1999; and L. Carrillo, personal interview, 1 Mar. 2003.

98 See "East Los Angeles College Strike," *La Raza*, Sept. 1971: 20 in CRC, ELAPL. Also see, "Chicano Moratorium Committee Plans War Protest for Feb. 28," *Campus News* 11 Feb. 1970: 1 in spec. coll. HMBL; Kerry Sayler, "Students, Faculty Members Gather at Rally," *Campus News* 13 May 1970: 5 in spec. coll. HMBL; "Board Decision Questioned Seriously," *Campus News* 30 Sept. 1970: 2 in spec. coll. HMBL; "Cinco de Mayo Festivities Include Full Week of Events," *Campus News* 6 May 1970: 1 in spec. coll. HMBL; "Cinco de Mayo is Fiesta Time," *Campus News* 5 May 1971: 1, 2 in spec. coll. HMBL; David Aviles, "Labor Issue Kills Burger," *Campus News* 3 Mar. 1971: 1 in spec. coll. HMBL; "General Strike Scheduled on Campus as Chicano Press for 19 Demands," *Campus News* 17 Mar. 1971: 1,6 in spec. coll. HMBL; "The Chairman of Mexican-American Studies," *La Vida Nueva* April 1971: 2–4 in spec. coll. HMBL; and "The Strike," *La Vida Nueva* April 1971: 6 in spec. coll. HMBL.

99 Balser, 225.

100 Montes' unsuccessful run for MASA's 1968 spring term president had been a close election with a two to five vote margin difference between him and president-elect Richard Ávila.

101 Mayer N. Zald and John D. McCarthy, "Social Movement Industries: Competition and Cooperation among Movement Organizations." *Research in Social Movements, Conflict and Change*, 3 (1980): 1–20. Zald and McCarthy liken the scene of a social movement to a free market where social movement organizations compete for limited material and non-material resources for survival. Zald and McCarthy refer to "movement resources" as material and non-material resources such as volunteer labor, loyalty, and money to fund and support activities, events or organizational labor.

PART THREE

Geographic Diversity and the Chicano Movement

9

SAN ANTONIO CHICANO ORGANIZERS (SACO)

Labor Activists and *El Movimiento*

Max Krochmal

In November 1969, a group of several hundred protestors assembled in San Antonio's upscale King William neighborhood, marched *en masse* down Durango Street on the edge of downtown, and rallied at the headquarters of the San Antonio Independent School District (SAISD). Blocked from reaching the building's front door by a specially erected cyclone fence, the protestors wedged a picket sign through the mesh and scotch-taped their list of demands to it. The bulk of the marchers were ethnic Mexican school janitors who had recently joined Local 84 of the Service Employees International Union (SEIU). But the demonstration was not only part of a run-of-the-mill labor conflict, nor was it simply a brash expression of racial solidarity or cultural nationalism amid the then-flowering Chicano/a movement. Rather, a polyglot group of labor and civil rights activists joined the janitors in denouncing the city's low-wage economy and the school board's hostility to unionism. One photograph of the march paints an unusual picture of its participants and message: in it, SEIU representative Arnold Flores leads the procession alongside Bexar County Commissioner Albert Peña, several renowned African American civil rights leaders, the officers of a wide range of Mexican American and Chicano/a movement organizations, and a white Catholic priest known for his advocacy on behalf of the United Farm Workers (UFW). A group of black children from the Early Breakfast Club—an anti-poverty initiative—flanks this diverse leadership, while a single man in front pushes a coffin bearing a sign reading, "Rest in Peace Mr. Low Wages." Members of several unions carry picket signs in the rear.[1]

The janitors' protest announced the arrival of a new force in San Antonio's Chicano/a movement as well as in the city's political life writ large. Far from an aberration, the march instead represented the tip of a much larger iceberg—the emergence of a powerful Chicano/a labor movement that flourished alongside, and in dialogue with, the better-known Chicano/a youth movement. At its core was a group of union activists who came to call themselves SACO, or San Antonio Chicano Organizers.[2]

SACO represented a network of full-time, paid Chicano/a union and political activists through which members could ask one another for help in the day-to-day work of union organizing and representation. It doubled as a caucus within the white-dominated labor movement and helped to create and mobilize a political constituency for firebrand Chicano/a politicians such as Albert Peña. SACO also served as the institutional bridge between organized labor and the youthful Chicano/a movement, with member unions and staffers providing the younger activists with training and resources and in turn receiving broader community support for their own campaigns thanks to the *movimiento*. SACO welded together adult activists and the younger militants through a variety of inter-generational and organizational connections. It also built close ties with like-minded African American civil rights leaders.

Most importantly, SACO allowed Chicano/a organizers from diverse unions to come together to exchange ideas and develop strategies. It served as the incubator of a distinct and innovative but long-forgotten Chicano/a labor movement, a coordinated effort with a mass base that combined the civil rights demands of the *movimiento* and earlier ethnic Mexican activism with the fight for economic justice and independent political power.[3]

In fact, the goals of the campus-based youth and labor-based adult Chicano/a struggles closely paralleled one another, and the personnel often overlapped. By organizing at the worksite, SACO members expanded the base of the Chicano/a movement and broadened its commitment to economic justice issues. Organizing unions meant bringing together ordinary working people to build political and economic power, just as mobilizing the college campuses and *barrio* youth aimed to create Brown Power. Moreover, building solidarity at the worksite meant fighting against the historical oppression inherent in the low wages that were still assigned to "Mexican jobs," that is, the positions in which ethnic Mexicans predominated. It also meant combating the rampant employment discrimination still facing ethnic Mexican working people in this period. Finally, organizing unions translated seamlessly into expanded electoral power for ethnic Mexican working people—another goal of the Chicano/a youth movement. Whereas politicians such as Peña had previously managed to build their own precarious power bases through civil rights organizations based in the city's *barrios*, Chicano-led labor unions offered the possibility of vastly expanding a militant political constituency. SACO thus took the Chicano/a movement to innumerable working adults in an effort to inexorably transform the city's economic and political structure— just as Chicano/a youth activists had long sought to organize the latent revolutionary masses of the *barrios*. In short, SACO brought labor to the movement and the movement to organized labor.

A closer look at the history of this other Chicano/a movement suggests that distinctions of class and political philosophy and tactics at times mattered at least as much as did ties of ethnicity or race, while similarities in strategy and ideology often meant more than simple generational divides. While many middle-class Mexican Americans mobilized uplift strategies that emphasized their whiteness, leading them to oppose the more radical, nationalist youth struggle, many working-class ethnic Mexicans in contrast harbored no such illusions about their racial identity. In fact, they experienced discrimination on a daily basis and readily supported the goals of the Chicano/a movement. They also consistently elected both politicians and union officials who supported the African American freedom struggle.[4]

Of course, union organizing among ethnic Mexicans was hardly new in the 1960s and 70s, nor have all connections between labor and the student-led movement been obscured. In fact, it is now commonplace to assert that the urban Chicano/a movement in Texas, as in California, gained inspiration and even traced its own beginnings to the struggle of rural ethnic Mexican farm workers in the UFW (United Farm Workers). In Texas, moreover, many analysts of the movement trace its origins back further still, to the early 1960s, to the first "Chicano revolt" in Crystal City, when the Political Association of Spanish-Speaking Organizations (PASO) joined with the Teamsters union and a group of students led by José Ángel Gutiérrez to elect a slate of working-class *mexicanos* to govern the small town, the self-styled "Spinach Capital of the World." In both cases, rural labor uprisings provided the spark that set off the powder kegs of urban college campuses and *barrios*.[5]

Yet both the unions and adult working-class struggles for racial and economic justice tend to take a back seat in the historiography of the late 1960s and 1970s, when the leadership of the ever-radicalizing urban Chicano/a movement seemingly passed into the hands of a younger generation of recently politicized, relatively well-educated brown nationalists. Of course, Davíd Montejano's excellent new book ably shifts attention to poor and working-class urban *barrio* youth, arguing that a unitary cultural nationalism did not alone provide a common collective identity for the movement in San Antonio. Rather, multiple individual identities overlapped and shifted, producing a kaleidoscope of "group-specific" associations designed to meet the needs of particular groups of Chicanos/as instead of subsuming all participants into a single, univocal movement organization. Still, the members of the adult working class and their own organizations—namely, Chicano/a labor unions—remain largely absent from the larger historiography of the movement.[6]

At the same time, studies of the "Mexican American Generation" that preceded the rise of the Chicano/a youth movement have tended to flatten and even distort the elder group's diverse ideologies, constituencies, organizations, and tactics. While Mario García's original use of the term included a wide range of activists, workers, and intellectuals engaged in a broad array of organizing, the bulk of the subsequent literature focuses on a narrow band of middle-class professionals who tended to advocate assimilation, opposed radical politics and labor unions, and pursued a strategy of uplift that emphasized the group's whiteness. Neil Foley, in an extreme version of this line of thinking, further argues that Mexican American civil rights leaders internalized a white racial identity and in so doing actively cast their lots with white supremacy in opposition to the black freedom struggle.[7] Legal scholars have responded that Mexican American strategists used the "class apart" argument only instrumentally, as a tool in a racist courtroom, while other historians have noted the fissures of Mexican American activism based on divisions of gender and class.[8] Most notably, historian Carlos Blanton has shown that George I. Sánchez— in many ways the archetypal Mexican American professional activist—partnered with African American leaders, put forth a broad vision of civil rights for all Americans, and understood well the trade-offs of a "citizenship sacrifice" that accepted immigration restriction as part of the fight against racism in the U.S.[9]

This story of Chicano/a unionists in San Antonio builds on these works, suggesting the need for scholars to extend the periodization and expand the constituencies of a broader, longer Chicano/a freedom struggle. Paying attention to labor reveals intimate inter-generational and organizational connections between the familiar youth-led movement and the less publicized, ongoing activism of their parents. It underscores the diversity of opinions among both generational cohorts, the possibility of interracial collaboration with African Americans, and above all, the centrality of economic justice issues in *el movimiento*.

The story begins in 1968, when Arnold Flores, an otherwise obscure 32-year-old civilian worker at one of the city's four Air Force bases, was transformed into a sort of local celebrity by leading the fight against systematic employment discrimination and widespread racism at Kelly Field. A political activist and "unofficial aide" to Albert Peña since the early 1960s, Flores gathered evidence from his co-workers, convinced them to file complaints, and brought their grievances to an aggressive middle-class group called the Federation for the Advancement of Mexican-Americans (FAMA). Aided by several prominent FAMA members—attorney (and future state representative) Matt García, State Senator Joe Bernal, and Father Henry Casso—Flores publicly testified against the base's military leadership at hearings of both the state and federal civil rights commissions. His own equal opportunity complaint culminated in a month-long trial in which the same trio of FAMA leaders represented him, taking turns assailing the base's routine ethnic favoritism. The case became a *cause célèbre* that inspired multiracial demonstrations at the base and angry editorials in the booming Chicano/a press. The cat was out of the bag. Decades of occupational segregation came to a screeching halt when the trial ended in Flores's favor, and countless ethnic Mexicans across the base immediately gained promotions and other upgrades.[10]

For his part, Flores faced ongoing retaliation by base supervisors and ended up quitting his job to pursue full-time activism. After a stint working for FAMA and the Mexican American Unity Council, which he co-founded, Flores became an organizer for SEIU Local 84 in August 1969. The union had been founded to some fanfare in 1937 but had since deteriorated into a *"compadre* [old boys] club" of only thirty or forty "head janitors" who all worked as foremen in the SAISD. Working with a stipend from the international union's organizing department, Flores was charged with resuscitating the moribund local by making new entreaties to the predominately ethnic Mexican rank-and-file service workers in the schools.[11]

For Flores, a veteran of countless electoral campaigns alongside Albert Peña and more recently the poster-child for the Mexican American civil rights struggle, growing the union was synonymous with organizing in the community and building political power. He quickly got to work. Aided by City Councilman John Alaníz, who served as the union's attorney, Flores rapidly recruited enough new members to replace the stodgy old leaders of the union's *compadre* club. By the fall of 1969, over 500 workers at SAISD—virtually all of its janitors and maids— had added their names to the local's membership rolls. The school district responded to the union's growing power by ending its long-standing practice of deducting union dues from workers' paychecks. Flores and the members, in turn, staged the previously mentioned multiracial "March Against Low Wages," took the district to court over the matter, and expanded their organizing efforts to include the schools' cafeteria workers and bus drivers. Local 84 later grew into the Edgewood and Harlandale school districts, reaching as many as 1,800 paid members by 1977.

Their strategy was straightforward. Flores and Alaníz organized around the pre-existing grievances of the mostly-Chicano/a workers in each of the various school districts. In many cases, concerns about respect at the worksite mattered as much as did bread-and-butter, wage-related issues. At SAISD, for example, the janitors demanded that the district allow them to sit and eat their meals in the schools' teacher lounges, rather than in the boiler rooms where they had been traditionally relegated. The union also insisted that only principals could approach the head custodian with work requests, forbidding the predominately Anglo (and presumably condescending) teachers from doing so directly. The janitors desired treatment as professionals rather than unskilled, "Meskin" workers (as they were routinely called), and they sought training programs and upward mobility. Their demands, in short, were not too dissimilar from those of the Chicano/a student movement.[12]

Shop-floor militancy carried over into larger issues of equity as the union aggressively fought against discrimination based on race, national origin, or gender. Throughout the 1960s and 1970s, his case at Kelly Field and then union organizing brought Flores into sustained contact with the most aggressive wing of San Antonio's African American civil rights movement, led since the late 1940s by Reverend Claude Black Jr. of Mt. Zion First Baptist Church, funeral home director G. J. Sutton, and photographer and publisher Eugene Coleman. Like

Flores and the FAMA leaders, these activists demanded immediate social change and did not shy away from engaging in sit-ins, rallies, and other contentious tactics. Since the 1930s Sutton and company had formed temporary coalitions with the more militant ethnic Mexican civil rights activists, and by the mid-1960s leaders of both groups came to depend upon one another for support. In 1967, for example, Sutton joined Flores on a picket line outside the Kelly Air Force Base Anniversary Ball. The duo carried signs denouncing "50 Years of Discrimination" at the base. Coleman's *SNAP News* publicized Sutton's and Black's civil rights activism directly alongside a front-page column written by county commissioner and civil rights leader Albert Peña. Flores joined all of these men and a wide range of white liberal activists at informal monthly meetings of the "lunch bunch," sessions of planning and coordination that began in the mid-1960s and continued into the twenty-first century.[13]

Flores drew upon his relationship with African American leaders to build multiracial solidarity both within and beyond the union. Although ethnic Mexicans constituted the vast majority of the local's membership, Flores had been working with Rev. Black to bring African American workers into the local as well. School district supervisors at times attempted to play the racial groups off one another, telling ethnic Mexican men that the black janitors wanted to seduce their wives, or vice versa. In other cases, black or brown workers complained about working under the supervision of a member of the other race. Flores invited Rev. Black to come to a monthly membership meeting to urge inter-racial cooperation, and his oratory proved effective at helping the two groups better understand one another as well as their common cause in the union. Still, the newly elected officers of the local initially resisted when Flores suggested that they create new posts on the board of directors in order to include an African American and a woman. Though they had recently rejected the old "*compadre* club," Flores feared that the new officers now stood in danger of replacing it with an equally unrepresentative monocultural clique. Flores noted that he had no formal power to make demands on the board, but he threatened to resign publicly and to denounce the union's bigotry if they did not comply. Again Rev. Black spoke in support of the measure, and the two then left the meeting. Soon after Flores returned to his house, the new chairman called him and said that they had elected as directors both a black janitor and a white woman cafeteria worker. The San Antonio chapter of the NAACP, of which Rev. Black was an officer, later honored Flores for taking this stand in support of racial inclusion.[14]

A single issue of the Local 84 newsletter likewise listed numerous cases of the union fighting entrenched inequalities at the worksite. One blurb noted that cafeteria managers were "trying to impose dress length restrictions on some of the 'not to favorite' [sic] employees." It continued, "We guarantee that this will come to a screeching halt . . ." An entire section was devoted to the issue of "Equal Pay for Women." The article noted that Flores had worked with the U.S. Department of Labor's Wage and Hour Division to win over $9,000 in total back pay for nine maids working in the Harlandale district, women who had received unfair compensation based solely on their gender. At present, the article continued, the local was working to get SAISD "to adjust their unequal pay schedules" and protest the district's evasive reclassification of "maids" to the gender-neutral but still underpaid position, "custodian II." The union planned to use the provisions of the Equal Pay Act and Title VII of the Civil Rights Act to contest this subterfuge and pledged to take the matter to court if necessary.[15]

Dynamism on the shop floor and in the community carried over into the union hall, where Local 84 developed an internal "movement culture." While most contemporary unions had little rank-and-file participation except in times of strikes, contract negotiations, and other crises, Flores drew upon the community-based organizing tradition of the UFW to foster activism within Local 84. For example, monthly membership meetings featured one of a rotating set of keynote speakers from the black and brown civil rights movements, including Albert Peña, Matt García, Joe Bernal, and Eastside African American activists G. J. Sutton and Rev. Claude Black. Using the service centers established by the UFW as a model, Flores also created classes and recreational programs for women and children. Thus, even if a man did not want to come to a union meeting, his wife and kids would still want to go to their respective activities and would drag the man along with them. The meetings concluded with tamales, a keg of beer, and a fiesta for the entire family.[16]

The social movement atmosphere inside the union paralleled the feeling of the streets. Indeed, the city's Chicano/a movement and Chicano-led unions increasingly overlapped, with the Local 84 hall becoming an epicenter of the larger *movimiento*. Flores, of course, had been in the Mexican American civil rights struggle for nearly a decade. More recently, in March 1969, Flores participated in the march of more than 3,000 Chicanos/as in support of the "Del Rio Manifesto," a demonstration in a nearby small town led by members of the Mexican American Youth Organization (MAYO) that protested funding cuts to the Minority Mobilization component of the federal VISTA program. (In all likelihood, Flores emulated the march when his union chose to nail its demands to the front door of the SAISD later that year.) In early 1970, Flores, while on the union payroll, traveled to Crystal City to speak in support of José Ángel Gutiérrez and MAYO's school boycott and voter mobilization effort—the town's second Chicano/a revolt. The union's inter-generational ties were particularly clear in the case of the boycott of the San Antonio Savings Association (SASA). In June 1970, Mayor William McAllister questioned the ambition of ethnic Mexicans in a racially charged interview on national TV. The Chicano/a movement responded by calling for a boycott of the SASA, a community bank owned by the mayor. On September 10, at one particularly contentious rally during the protracted conflict, police detained dozens and arrested some thirty pickets, including not only many of the so-called "young Turks" and other Chicano/a youth, but also numerous older activists, including Flores, Albert Peña, and veteran African American activist G. J. Sutton. Flores was not booked, but he returned to the city jail as part of a delegation of Mexican American activists who met with the police to secure the release of the demonstrators.[17]

It wasn't simply that Flores and some union members showed up at Chicano/a movement protests. Rather, many student activists hung out at the union hall, including Gutiérrez and Willie Velásquez, another one of the five co-founders of MAYO and an enduring leader among young Chicano/a activists and what Montejano terms "second-generation" movement organizations in San Antonio. Velásquez and other younger activists learned some of the basic get-out-the-vote and block-walking strategies from Peña, Flores, and other union organizers, and in so doing, they expanded the youth movement's constituency to include working-class adults. Biographer Juan Sepulveda writes that Velásquez's ". . . work . . . with Arnold Flores brought him directly in contact with various San Antonio unions—representing workers, negotiating on their behalf, drafting propaganda for them, and getting drunk with them . . ." Velásquez and Flores together served as the critical links between the youth struggle and the Chicano/a labor movement, so much so that the two arenas of activism, in Flores's words, "became one and the same."[18]

The fusion reached its apogee in the founding of SACO as early as 1969. Chaired by Flores until 1977, SACO over time brought together an evolving membership consisting of staffers from the United Auto Workers (UAW), the International Union of Radio, Machine, and Electrical Workers (IUE), the Amalgamated Meat Cutters (AMC), the Amalgamated Clothing Workers of America (ACWA), the Laborers, the American Federation of Government Employees (AFGE), Flores's SEIU, and others. As noted above, SACO served as the institutional bridge between organized labor and the youthful Chicano/a movement leaders. The unions provided resources for demonstrations, from activist training, picket signs and copies of leaflets to direct financial support. When movement activists needed such aid for a particular march, a voter registration campaign, or even a protest in front of a local Catholic church, one of them approached Flores or another SACO member, who in turn took the request to his fellow union organizers for fulfillment. Velásquez, José Ángel Gutiérrez, and other student activists benefited—in various ways—from the money, the mentorship, and the institutional homes provided by SACO unionists.

Of course, SACO remained at its core a collection of Chicano-led labor unions. As noted above, SACO also served as a sort of mutual benefit society for full-time, paid Chicano/a union organizers whose members came together to share technical expertise regarding negotiations or grievances, provide assistance to one another in turning out workers to support a picket or rally, and mobilize large numbers of union members for political or social action. It allowed its members to share ideas and take collective action. In other words, it helped to transform a collection of separate unions and activists into a Chicano/a labor movement.

While Flores organized SACO and served as its chairman, the group also included a number of veteran union organizers whose activities shed additional light on the rising movement's meaning, potential, and limitations. For example, more than a decade before the service employees' "March Against Low Wages," back in 1957, the IUE had successfully organized about a thousand mostly-ethnic Mexican workers at Friedrich Refrigerator. Initially led by a *mexicana* chief steward, Local 780 at Friedrich encouraged militant shop-floor activism and wide rank-and-file participation in union affairs, including the promotion of ordinary workers into full-time staff positions. One worker, one of a group of Polish-Americans in the plant, proved invaluable to the union because he could speak three languages, including Spanish, making him uniquely able to communicate with and unite the factory's major ethnic groups. This former farmer, Paul Javior, helped lead the local through a 2-month strike in the winter of 1964–65—the first successful work stoppage since the infamous busting of the Tex-Son garment workers union several years before. Javior soon took over as the IUE staff director in San Antonio and aligned himself and the union with SACO, Peña, and the black and Chicano/a civil rights movements. Javior was "the token Anglo" in SACO, but his colleagues never doubted his sincerity. Moreover, Javior hired several new organizers—all ethnic Mexicans who joined SACO—and set out to organize a number of new factories in the city. The IUE grew rapidly throughout the late 1960s, making it the envy of San Antonio's other unions. It proved able to stage mass pickets on short notice as well as mobilize thousands of (mostly) ethnic Mexican voters in the electoral arena. The union also became the local labor movement's most dedicated supporter of civil rights and *chicanismo*, providing institutional and financial support and routinely turning out members for movement marches and other activities. The IUE brought diversity, militancy, and numbers to organized labor. In 1967, Javior recruited "C. J." Littlefield, a long-time civil rights activist who worked at Chromalloy Metals, to serve as the city's first African American union president. Later, Javior recruited Jaime Martínez, a Chicano/a youth movement activist who went on to serve as an international vice-president of the IUE (and recently ran for the national presidency of the League of United Latin American Citizens, or LULAC).[19]

Likewise, Franklin "Tortillas" García of the Amalgamated Meat Cutters, another SACO member, brought trade unionism to countless ethnic Mexican workers and brought them into electoral politics and the civil rights movements. A native of Garland, near Dallas, García in 1961 quit his job at a Ford Factory and began a decade of organizing in the viciously anti-union Rio Grande Valley. There, 5 years prior to the UFW's first strike in the region, García dug in deep and implemented a strategy similar to Peña's—building industrial unions in various sectors, organizing in the community, and mobilizing members into electoral politics, PASO, and later the Chicano/a movement. When he came to San Antonio in the early 1970s, he continued doing much of the same. Like Flores and Javior, García organized thousands of workers and made ties between them and the black civil rights and Chicano/a movements. He served on the steering committee for numerous local Chicano/a organizations and, notably, he also led the local branch of the national campaign to free African American political prisoner Angela Davis in 1975. Two years earlier, García was elected third vice-president at the founding of the Labor Council for Latin American Advancement (LCLAA), a national constituency group within the AFL–CIO (American Federation of Labor and Congress of Industrial Organizations) modeled on SACO and other similar local groups. Arnold Flores was likewise one of LCLAA's founding directors. Both men also served as board members and advisors to two key "second-generation" Chicano/a movement organizations, the Southwest Voter Registration and Education Project and the National Council of La Raza.[20]

Each of the SACO organizers connected the labor movement to ordinary *mexicanos* and tied the local unions they led to the larger Chicano/a movement and, at times, the African American freedom struggle. They covered a tremendous amount of ground and popped up in a wide range of labor, civil rights, and political settings. Yet the larger meaning of their work remains difficult to pin down. Unlike student leaders, most working people left neither a treatise nor a unified *plan* that reflected their thoughts.

In contrast, County Commissioner Albert Peña generated a paper trail that offers a clearer view of the strategies and ideologies behind SACO's day-to-day organizing praxis. Peña, recently deemed the "Dean Emeritus of Chicano Politics" by a prominent scholar-activist, had long considered himself a "friend of labor," and for decades he had advocated on behalf of union workers. He had walked precincts with union activists in Houston since attending law school there in the late 1940s. He then organized the *barrios* of San Antonio as the political action chair of LULAC Council #2, building a powerful local electoral base that landed him on the Bexar County Commissioners Court in 1956. In 1959, Peña came to the aid of striking *mexicana* garment workers at the Tex-Son plant, spoke at the convention of the Texas AFL–CIO, and worked his way up to a position of leadership in statewide liberal Democratic clubs. In the early 1960s, he served as the chair of PASO, the state's leading ethnic Mexican political organization, and led a liberal/labor faction of ethnic Mexicans that allied with the Teamsters in the Crystal City revolt. Key staffers circulated among positions that included Peña's county patronage appointments, his endless political campaign, and the local Teamsters union. Of course, Peña had also recruited and proved critical to the rise of one of his protégés, SACO Chairman and founder Arnold Flores. By the end of the 1960s, Peña had served as a behind-the-scenes coordinator of the city's and state's most militant Chicano/a politicians, an advisor to the Chicano/a youth movement, and an honorary member of—and organic intellectual—within SACO.[21]

Peña was thus anything but a neophyte at labor organizing when he received a call in 1969 from the UAW, offering him a job directing a new organizing campaign in San Antonio as part of its nationwide effort to build "community unions" across the country. Peña accepted the offer and approached his task in the same way that Flores had revived the SEIU: build the union by organizing in the community. In late 1969 or early 1970, drawing on 15 years in the trenches of the interwoven labor, political, and civil rights struggles, Peña penned "A Program for Organizing in South Texas," a document that makes plain the theory behind his organizing praxis—and by extension, the approach of many of the other SACO members. His experientially-derived, broad vision for the future of labor among *mexicanos* in the region underscores the importance of unions in the burgeoning Chicano/a struggle, opening a new front in the movement's history.

The "Program" opens with a survey of the problem at hand and the recent successes and failures of traditional union organizing efforts. One and a half million Mexican Americans currently live in Texas, Peña began, with most of them concentrated south of what SACO member Franklin García called the "Mexican-Dixon Line," a parallel that runs across the state from El Paso through San Antonio to Houston. Their "plight" was by then well-known to the country, yet no solutions had been forthcoming. "We beleive [sic] that union organizing is part of the answer," he wrote. With an "industrial base [that] is ever growing," unions in San Antonio had in the past 5 years increased their organizing activities, with mixed degrees of success, it continued. The IUE had organized over 2,000 workers in the city in the previous 3 years, "primarily through the efforts of two local representatives out of a San Antonio plant." Meanwhile, in the Rio Grande Valley in 1966, "a home-grown Chicano organizer," Franklin García, had built a local union of 2,500 members in the shrimping and fishing industry. "These unions have succeeded, where others have failed," Peña noted. In contrast, the International Association of Machinists (IAM) had notably botched a campaign to organize 20,000 workers at Kelly Air Force Base, despite sending in some fifteen professional organizers who "invaded" the city from across the country while spending "untold thousands of dollars." The problem, Peña argued, was that the IAM staffers "knew their stuff, but regretably [sic] for the Kelly employees they didn't know the people involved. And they were all 'Anglos.'" Meanwhile, a rival union, the American Federation of Government Employees (AFGE), arrived on the scene. After giving the IAM a 2-year head start, the AFGE "hired local organizers, including several Chicanos, in the last two months of the campaign [and] pulled off the election." [sic] The latter union focused its efforts on blue collar workers and "developed solid leadership within the local union." It provided "representation the employees trust because [the leadership] is for the most part Mexican American . . ." A national union using professional organizers did not "understand" the workers, while local knowledge and local staffers did. "That then is the lesson that we feel we have learned and want to teach," Peña concluded. "We want to organize unions in South Texas! That means, primarily, that we want to organize Mexican Americans."[22]

If Peña's target for the organizing drive cut against labor's historic focus on white workers in the region, his plan for how to do so bucked the conventional wisdom of the post-war House of Labor. He began, "We propose that a local all-inclusive local be chartered [to] some international union and that jurisdiction be unlimited." Whereas unions had traditionally organized along strict craft lines or been separated by industry, Peña argued for the creation of One Big (Mexican) Union. Further, he demanded that the sponsoring union pay for all of the new effort's organizing and service activities for 3 years and continue to share costs for 5 additional years. Peña also demanded that all organizers be hired locally, including a director, and that most if not all of the organizers should be Mexican Americans. For training, he offered a compromise. The international union would instruct the newly hired organizers, but they had to do so at a location in South Texas "surrounded by the area's unique problems." Legal matters would likewise be handled locally by Peña's network of ethnic Mexican civil rights lawyers (he had aided the founding of the Mexican American Legal Defense and Education Fund, or MALDEF, in 1968). "Finally we propose that the jurisdiction of this local be so broad as to include not only industrial workers, retail and wholesale sales employees, and farm workers, but also public employees," he added. "We feel this is a necessary condition, because it is in the last area that we hope to establish our initial base. Because of the political influence that we already exert this is the area where we feel we could make our quickest showing to instill confidence in other workers."[23]

Here, then, was his initial strategy—use the decades of political base-building to expand the labor movement into the still relatively uncharted territory of the public sector, including the school districts and public hospitals. Arnold Flores's union was a model, one which Peña had helped see to fruition (Peña would also become Local 84's general counsel in 1973). So too was the Laborers' union that had successfully organized city garbage collectors. ". . . We know this from past experience," Peña wrote in the Program, that "all that need be done is find the leaders within the units, develop their role, isolate and define the issues, call meetings and sign up members." Flexing political muscle and utilizing age-old techniques of organizing around worksite grievances would thus produce powerful unions. But ethnic or racial solidarity would also be key. "With a little effort and leadership, plus the cohesion which we feel can develop through La Raza, there is little doubt that this segment of the work force can be organized in South Texas," Peña concluded. Yet the strategy was also proven to work in industrial settings. In another case, he added, striking industrial workers abandoned by the IAM eagerly joined a new effort that emphasized "the value of unity among brown brothers." Peña indicated that doing so also meant following the lead of SEIU, a union that used unnamed "unorthodox techniques" to win a bitter contract dispute—including the marches, political pressure tactics, and direct action protests that had become commonplace in the larger Chicano/a movement.

The "Program" concluded by mapping out the proposed One Big Local's long-term strategy. It called for Chicano/a organizers such as those in SACO to start with the "easiest marks" in the public sector, then move on to industrial, construction, and "wholesale-retail sales," and finally reach out to farm workers.

The latter had suffered tremendously and should not be last, Peña noted, but pragmatism suggested that the union must first establish a mass base. He promised that sufficient financial support would allow the new union to organize and win contracts for three to five thousand workers in the first 3 years and countless more down the road. The city's population of 800,000 included only 40,000 union members, but the biggest industrial concerns remained untouched. So too did the 8,000 heavily *mexicano/a* garment workers in the 4 largest factories. The question was not whether the workers wanted a union but whether a union that understood them would commit to the region and service the workers adequately. The lessons were clear, Peña concluded, the implications vast. "We know that this route can be traveled time and time again until some day South Texas will have sufficient unions to give the area a standard of living that will support the population . . ."[24]

For Peña, then, it was simple: send Chicano/a organizers to reach out to the city's mostly ethnic Mexican workers, beginning at the sites where most of them were already working. Start with the thousands of government employees, the "low-hanging fruit" whose elected bosses could be subject to political pressure tactics. Appeal to the solidarity of La Raza and use the disruptive tactics of *el movimiento*. Then move on to garment workers and other industries.

Unfortunately for SACO, Peña's "Program" never got off the ground. When the UAW called in 1969, Peña had agreed to organize workers under the union's banner and eventually create a "community union under the ALA," the Alliance for Labor Action. He made a commitment to Walter Reuther, the union's international president, and expected that the UAW would hold up its end of the bargain. Among other conditions, Peña had sought to make it clear that the campaign would include political action, would be locally run and controlled, would need outside financial assistance, and most importantly, "that UAW and [the] Chicano movement would complement each other."[25] But the very next day, Peña met in person with two Anglo UAW staffers who shared neither his and Reuther's joint vision, nor their passion for organizing ethnic Mexican workers. Peña jotted down that the two union men believed that they "could do it better," that they had experience organizing "all kinds of people" and didn't need to be told how to organize *mexicanos*, and finally, one suggested that he had been given the assignment of working with Peña "without wanting it." They also told him that "word is out that you are on the UAW payroll [and] it would look bad if you quit now."[26]

Despite these initial flare-ups, Peña continued with the effort and soon hired Juan Flores and Roy Hernández, two stalwart precinct-level activists from his local electoral machine, and the campaign got underway. But the UAW brass soon objected on several grounds. First, Peña had overlooked experienced union men whom the UAW believed were more likely to succeed at winning conventional union recognition elections. The union remained skeptical of Chicano/a nationalism and desperately wanted Peña to hire an Anglo to serve as the third organizer. In the end, Peña hired Juan Díaz, a young Chicano/a movement activist and fellow precinct worker. Second, Peña's broad vision of organizing violated traditional jurisdictional boundaries, lines that were often sacrosanct in labor circles. In November 1969, at a meeting with Paul Russo, one of the Anglo UAW regional organizers forcibly assigned to the effort, Peña argued that the new campaign should first seek to organize the city's publicly-owned utility and transit districts. He told Russo that he had already organized an association of 100 workers at the City Public Services Board, a workplace known for "job discrimination" that he believed had "potential," and he added that the new UAW organizers could easily expand the group to 300 members. The UAW's Russo replied that the campaign should focus exclusively on workers within the union's jurisdiction of automobile, aircraft, and other related industries. Throughout the meeting, Russo seemingly talked down to Peña, explaining in minute detail and with great condescension the UAW's internal structure, chain-of-command, and multi-layered hierarchy. Community organization was fine, Russo said, but UAW manpower could not work outside of the union's jurisdiction without "word from upstairs." It would be better to contact the unions assigned to those areas, he added. Peña noted that he had already done so and that he had a good relationship with the local branch of AFGE—in other words, he had the connections to launch a joint campaign to organize the public sector. Russo changed the subject.

A third area of disagreement centered on the fact that Peña's plans called for a long-term commitment to organizing all *mexicanos* in pursuit of a larger vision of social and economic justice, while the union sought immediate gains in membership through low-commitment tactics and surface-level appeals. At the same meeting, Russo contended that Peña should begin the campaign by sending each of the three new organizers into the field, instructing each to talk to workers at three plants in the UAW's jurisdiction, a total of nine potential targets. Then, he added, Peña should wait and see which workers responded to their appeals and then choose one plant to focus on and maintain only minimal contact with the other eight factories. Russo also suggested that the organizers should "throw some cards" at workers at the unorganized Gary Aircraft plant in town and "Let them holler. Let's find out" whether the workers wanted to join the union, he added. Such strategies may have produced a plant that was hot and ready for a union, but they probably would not have led to the targeted organizing of *mexicanos* that Peña sought as part of his commitment to the Chicano/a movement and his larger political project. Peña replied instead about the many garment workers and others in San Antonio that he believed needed and wanted to form unions: "There are lots of people to organize in this town . . . It's a rough deal but it can be done." Russo and Peña thus talked past each other, leaving the campaign on uncertain footing from the start.[27]

Peña's implicit vision, and his explicit "Program for Organizing in South Texas" penned around the same time, simply could not be reconciled to the status quo of a distant, and indifferent, international labor union. For the county commissioner, the distinction between his daily work at the courthouse and in the community and his new job in the union was artificial and nearly imperceptible. For the UAW brass, Peña's expansive but unfocused vision was intolerable.

When the campaign finally got underway, Peña's staff ended up combining traditional UAW union organizing with support for the larger Chicano/a movement as well as the broad Chicano/a-oriented labor movement called for by the "Program" and already being enacted by SACO. The new union drive narrowly lost a contested representation election at Gary Aircraft, held another at U.S. Gypsum, another major San Antonio employer, and won a third at the city's small Fruehauf plant.[28] The new UAW organizers—Flores, Díaz, and Hernández—joined SACO and participated in local Chicano/a movement demonstrations. For example, on February 27, 1970, they joined Willie Velásquez, Rosie Castro, and other MAYO members who walked out during a speech by Congressman Henry B. González at St. Mary's University, a small Catholic school on the Westside. The young activists charged that the Congressman had become "irrelevant" in the city's *barrios*, but González used his bully pulpit to blast the protestors in the press. The demonstrators included "Paid organizers for Albert Peña . . . racial fanatics . . . a known felon . . . MAYO hot-heads," he said. "They were all sitting there like a row of coiled rattlesnakes, poised to strike." Specifically, Peña's "hirelings were there and they were the ring leaders." González was quick to add that several of the Peña protégés in the crowd were employees of the UAW. Peña responded by standing behind the MAYO militants and his organizers and noting that González had aligned himself with the Chamber of Commerce and no longer understood the problems facing "Chicanos in South Texas," the subject of the latter's planned address. Paul Thompson, an *Express-News* columnist who had long been a detractor of Peña's, gleefully proclaimed that long-simmering tensions between the two politicos had finally evolved into "open war." Indeed, the battle lines were soon drawn, as Peña, SACO, and the Chicano/a movement all stood together in opposition to the Congressman.[29]

Bad press, mixed results in union elections, and above all a sharp contrast in visions doomed the UAW campaign in San Antonio from the outset. Walter Reuther's death in May 1970, further eroded Peña's faith in the union's top leadership. Peña left the position at the end of the year, though he continued to serve intermittently as a consultant. Hernández and Díaz remained on the UAW payroll, deepened their commitment to SACO, and continued (in a more traditional manner) to bring ethnic Mexican workers into both the labor movement and electoral politics.[30]

Although Peña's individual campaign sputtered, his "Program" took shape in reduced form in the ongoing actions of SACO, which continued to promote solidarity, collaboration, and mutual support among the city's separate local and international labor unions. At times, the group served as a Chicano/a caucus within the city's white-dominated labor movement. Although they never obtained an absolute majority within the larger, Anglo-dominated San Antonio AFL-CIO Council (a federation of local unions), SACO members did collectively command enough votes to influence the Council's endorsement of political candidates— one of the body's most important functions. SACO wielded this power in 1972 when it forced a routine endorsement meeting to continue late into the night, withholding the votes of its affiliated unions until the labor movement's craft-oriented, generally conservative Anglo leaders agreed to support Albert Peña's bid for reelection.[31] The Chicano/a caucus's power continued to grow. In 1973, Arnold Flores and other SACO members were among the founders and initial officers of the LCLAA, a predominately Chicano/a caucus within the national AFL-CIO. Three years later, in 1976, Flores rode SACO support to gain a seat on the executive board of the previously stodgy San Antonio AFL-CIO Council.[32]

More generally, while the individual stories of the SEIU, UAW, IUE, and Meat Cutters varied, SACO remained more than the sum of its parts. Peña's "Program for Organizing South Texas" stemmed from the successes of other organizers and helped to engender a spirit of collaboration between SACO-affiliated unions. As the decade wore on, SACO facilitated cooperation among its members and helped create a distinct "movement culture" among Chicano/a working people, bringing together members from a wide variety of unions and cutting across occupational and jurisdictional lines. Most notably, in 1973 SEIU Local 84 launched the Industrial and Service Employees Service Center, a gathering place for not only the local's members but also unorganized workers and members of all of the city's Chicano-led unions. It immediately became a SACO project—representatives of eight unions, all SACO members, comprised the Service Center's board of directors, Flores served as chairman, and Willie Velásquez was its first and only staff person. Employees of future organizing targets such as the Bexar County Hospital and the City Public Services Board figured prominently in the Center's operations, but so too did workers in smaller manufacturing firms, distribution and retail industries, and other *barrio* worksites.[33] Velásquez appealed to and attracted unorganized *mexicano* workers from throughout the Westside and Southside, seeking to "mobilize large numbers of people to support the union cause." The Center gained funding from church sources as well as unions and sought to develop a "membership at large" able to "physically support the member locals on picket lines" and through "monetary support, and boycotts."[34] Flores noted that "the service center [intended] to educate the public at large concerning the need to improve the wages conditions of the working man here in San Antonio."[35]

The infrastructure provided by SACO and the creation of the Service Center allowed the Chicano/a union organizers and allied Chicano/a activists to quickly swing into action as a series of strikes involving *mexicano* workers reached a fever pitch in the summer of 1973. The most significant occurred at Farah Manufacturing beginning in May 1972, when members of the ACWA at the company's flagship plants in El Paso and several satellite factories walked off the job to win recognition of their union and a first-ever collective bargaining agreement. Workers at Farah's San Antonio plant joined the campaign, led by ACWA organizers and SACO members Joan and Joe Suárez. The company-wide strike quickly begot a national boycott of Farah slacks sanctioned by the AFL-CIO, with "Don't Buy" notices appearing in union publications across the country. In San Antonio, SACO members raised money for and provided direct assistance to the local strikers, and worked individually to inform rank-and-file members and the public at large about the boycott. At the same time, less-publicized strikes at other SACO-affiliated plants were also dragging on. By July 1973, IUE members at Longhorn Machinery had been on strike for 14 months, the same span as the Farah workers, and members of García's Meat Cutters at L&H Packing had been out for more than a year. IUE members at nearby Ingram Steel Manufacturing had also struck 3 months earlier.[36]

SACO and its Service Center were perfectly positioned to coordinate these myriad battles and to weave them together into a broader Chicano/a struggle for economic justice. At a press conference in support of the Farah workers, Flores and Velásquez announced that the Center would sponsor a July 7 rally in support of all of the local strikers. Newspapers recognized the common theme of the various industrial conflicts: in a town in which Anglos had made most of the headlines, including in the annals of organized labor, Mexican American workers stood at the forefront of that summer's overlapping fights. Organizers in SACO and the members of their unions likewise identified the parallels between the struggles at Farah, L&H Packing, Longhorn Machinery, and Ingram Steel, and they understood that the larger war against low wages and for union recognition also included an ethnic or racial dimension. For example, at a "pre-rally rally" on the evening of Friday, July 6, UFW founder and national vice-president Dolores Huerta "drew several standing ovations from more than 100 strikers and supporters when she said, 'Mexicans don't know when to give up. They can't keep us down.'"[37]

On the day of the rally, at least 1,000 ethnic Mexican union members, workers, and allied activists joined an Archbishop and other high-ranking Catholic clergy in denouncing the city's low-wage, anti-union economy. Led by SACO organizers, the crowd assembled and held a rally at Milam Plaza downtown, marched along Houston and Main streets to the city's historic San Fernando Cathedral, and celebrated a 2-hour mass filled with liberation theology. Auxiliary Bishop J. Patrick Flores, the nation's first Mexican American prelate who was better known in San Antonio as "Patricio," told the crowd that the problem facing workers in the *barrio* was one of "subemployment" rather than unemployment. "Even with full-time work, almost half the people living on the West Side are living in poverty," he noted. "It's insulting to people to depend on alms and welfare while working full-time. San Antonio does not need alms and welfare. San Antonio only needs just wages." Amid cries of "¡*Viva la huelga!*" ("Long live the strike!"), an international representative of the IUE told the strikers that his union would be "behind you forever," while Henry Santiestevan, a former UAW staffer who now led the Southwest Council of La Raza, promised to extend the Farah boycott throughout the U.S. and across Europe. Dolores Huerta of the UFW again drove home the protest's larger meaning. "They want to continue exploitation of the Mexican-Americans in Texas," she said. "They want to keep us down economically and politically." Carrying placards from their various unions and an oversized banner of the UFW eagle, the marchers concluded by observing a somber mass "to pray for the cause of unionism."[38]

SACO thus brought striking members of three unions together, first with each other and then with sympathetic members of the other SACO-affiliated unions, unorganized *mexicano* workers, and the influential Catholic clergy to build a movement in support of economic justice for all Chicanos/as. They continued the theme of Flores' and the school district employees' 1969 "March Against Low Wages," contending that San Antonio's anti-union climate was not the cause of economic development but the culprit for persistent poverty in the *barrio*. And they won the support of the symbolically important and inspirational UFW and Catholic Church, gaining a moral imprimatur for "*la huelga*."

In December, 1973, Farah management announced that it would close its San Antonio plant just in time for Christmas, dealing a lethal blow to the ACWA strike. The Service Center remained at the epicenter of rallying the city's larger ethnic Mexican community to support of relief efforts for the displaced clothing workers. In collaboration with the union, Velásquez brought together a Workers Support Coalition comprising hundreds of local Mexican American community organizations, labor unions, and Catholic groups as well as two state representatives. The Center moved to a new location from which counselor members of the coalition offered former Farah workers assistance in job placement, retraining, legal services, and emergency financial aid. Velásquez noted that the company had hired *mexicano* strikebreakers in "concerted attempts" to isolate the *mexicano* union members and divide the ethnic community. Instead, he said, the strike had ironically resulted in a "united effort by Mexican-American organizations 'to do something about this situation.'"[39]

Even in defeat, then, SACO members had enlarged the cause of a few workers in a single union into a larger community-based, civil rights campaign. Members of other SACO unions rallied behind the Farah strikers, as did the Westside's religious and political leadership. Such support was anything but unusual. Throughout the 1970s, the travails of one *mexicano* union quickly became the cause of other Chicano-led unions and the broader ethnic Mexican community. Likewise, published photographs of union rallies, Chicano/a movement protests, and even some African American civil rights marches frequently included placards, banners, and speakers representing a broad spectrum of SACO-affiliated unions.

Through SACO and its member unions, then, Chicano/a labor activists challenged racism at the worksite and in the white-dominated labor movement and created an ambitious agenda for transforming the status of *La Raza* in South Texas through a community-based union movement. In so doing, Chicano/a labor activists shifted the locale of the larger Chicano/a movement beyond college campuses, and deepened its agenda to include not only nationalist pride but also economic justice and real political power.

The Chicano/a movement thus looks different through the eyes of SACO organizers, and, by extension, the thousands of ethnic Mexican workers they quite literally represented. From their vantage point, the youth stage of the struggle was less a departure from previous activism than an extension of it. For workers such as Flores and García, the struggle began more than a decade earlier, and it started at the worksite and in the door-to-door work of building independent political power in the *barrios*. For workers, organizers, and politicos such as Albert Peña, worksite grievances, union organizing, and other economic justice issues remained inseparable from the struggle for Chicano/a power. The opposite was also true: the movement always included the fight for access to good jobs. For Velásquez and other students and youth activists, the technical expertise, financial backing, and institutional resources of Chicano/a unions and SACO organizers provided much-needed support for the demonstrations and campaigns of the more recognizable Chicano/a liberation movement. The *movimiento* in turn aided and meshed with the Chicano/a labor movement. SACO and the organizers and union members that comprised it served as connective tissue that linked older activists to younger militants, liberal Mexican American generation advocates to Chicano/a generation leaders, and all of them to the masses of *barrios* and occasionally the African American freedom struggle. Seen from their vantage point, the Chicano/a movement appears longer, broader, class-specific, and at times even multiracial.

Notes

1   Cy Luna, "S.A. Marchers Hit Low School Wages," *San Antonio Express/News*, November 30, 1969, 2–A; "Sherrill Smith Returns to Help Marchers," n.d. [1969], unknown union-printed publication [probably *Texas AFL-CIO Labor News*], copy in author's possession, courtesy Arnold Flores. See also "Union Eyes Court Action, Strike Over SAISD Proposal," *San Antonio Express*, November 13, 1969, 12–H; and other daily newspaper coverage. All Chicano/a history articles begin with a statement on terminology. I use "ethnic Mexican" or "*mexicano/a*" to include the all people of Mexican descent, "Chicano/a" to denote those who self-identified with the movement, and "Mexican American" to delineate those who self-identified as an ethnic community but not necessarily as activists.

2   I first learned about SACO during an informal conversation with José Ángel Gutiérrez in Arlington, Texas, in the fall of 2008. Ángel also told me about Arnold Flores and provided me with an introduction and phone number. For that, I am eternally grateful. *Gracias*. The group did not include "Chicana" in its title, and there was only one woman member throughout its existence. I thus self-consciously use "Chicano" and "Chicano-led" in some descriptions of SACO, omitting the "/a" to indicate that it was a male-gendered formation.

3   The only scholarly reference I have located related to SACO is a brief, gross misrepresentation in Juan Sepúlveda, *The Life and Times of Willie Velásquez: Su Voto Es Su Voz* (Houston, TX: Arte Publico Press, 2003).

4   I expand on these arguments and offer a corrective to the generational approach in Max Krochmal, "Chicano Labor and Multiracial Politics in Post–World War II Texas," in *Life and Labor in the New New South*, Ed. Robert H. Zieger (Gainesville: University Press of Florida, 2012), 133–76.

5   See, for example, Ignacio M. García, *Chicanismo: The Forging of a Militant Ethos Among Mexican Americans* (Tucson: University of Arizona Press, 1997); Armando Navarro, *Mexican American Youth Organization: Avant-garde of the Chicano Movement in Texas* (Austin: University of Texas Press, 1995); John S. Shockley, *Chicano Revolt in a Texas Town* (South Bend, IN: University of Notre Dame Press, 1974); Marc Simon Rodríguez, *The Tejano Diaspora: Mexican Americanism & Ethnic Politics in Texas and Wisconsin* (Chapel Hill: University of North Carolina Press, 2011); David Montejano, *Anglos and Mexicans in the Making of Texas, 1836–1986* (Austin: University of Texas Press, 1987).

6   David Montejano, *Quixote's Soldiers: A Local History of the Chicano Movement, 1966–1981* (Austin: University of Texas Press, 2010). One exception has been a growing examination of the role of Chicano/a movement activists and less-known grassroots leaders in the War on Poverty beginning in 1964. See William S. Clayson, *Freedom Is Not Enough: The War on Poverty and the Civil Rights Movement in Texas* (Austin: University of Texas Press, 2010). Other recent community studies of the movement include Lorena Oropeza, *¡Raza Sí!, ¡Guerra No!: Chicano Protest and Patriotism During the Viet Nam War Era* (Berkeley: University of California Press, 2005); and Ernesto Chávez, *"¡Mi Raza Primero!" (My People First!): Nationalism, Identity, and Insurgency in the Chicano Movement in Los Angeles, 1966–1978* (Berkeley: University of California Press, 2002).

7   Neil Foley, "Becoming Hispanic: Mexican Americans and the Faustian Pact with Whiteness," *Reflexiones* (1997): 53–70; Neil Foley, *Quest for Equality: The Failed Promise of Black-Brown Solidarity* (Cambridge, MA: Harvard University Press, 2010); Mario T. García, *Mexican Americans: Leadership, Ideology, & Identity, 1930–1960* (New Haven, CT: Yale University Press, 1989); Brian D. Behnken, *Fighting Their Own Battles: Mexican Americans, African Americans, and the Struggle for Civil Rights in Texas* (Chapel Hill: University of North Carolina Press, 2011).

8   Ariela A. Gross, "'The Caucasian Cloke': Mexican Americans and the Politics of Whiteness in the Twentieth Century Southwest," *Georgetown Law Journal* 95 (2007): 337–392; Ariela J. Gross, *What Blood Won't Tell: A History of Race on Trial in America*, Amazon Kindle Edition (Cambridge, MA: Harvard University Press, 2008); Thomas A. Guglielmo, "Fighting for Caucasian Rights: Mexicans, Mexican Americans, and the Transnational Struggle for Civil Rights in World War II Texas," *Journal of American History* 92, no. 4 (March 2006): 1212–1237; Ian Haney-López, *Racism on Trial: The Chicano Fight for Justice* (Cambridge, MA: Harvard University Press, 2003). On gender and class, see for example, Emma Pérez, *The Decolonial Imaginary: Writing Chicanas into History* (Bloomington: Indiana University Press, 1999); Cynthia Orozco, *No Mexicans, Women, or Dogs Allowed: The Rise of the Mexican American Civil Rights Movement* (Austin: University of Texas Press, 2009); Vicki Ruíz, *From Out of the Shadows: Mexican Women in Twentieth-century America* (New York: Oxford University Press, 1998).

9   Carlos K. Blanton, "The Citizenship Sacrifice: Mexican Americans, the Saunders-Leonard Report, and the Politics of Immigration, 1951–1952," *Western Historical Quarterly* 40, no. 3 (Autumn 2009): 299–320; Carlos K. Blanton, "George I. Sánchez, Ideology, and Whiteness in the Making of the Mexican American Civil Rights Movement, 1930–1960," *Journal of Southern History* 72, no. 3 (August 2006): 569–604. Blanton's biography of Sánchez is forthcoming from Yale University Press.

10 Author's oral history interviews with Arnold Flores, San Antonio, October 18, 2008; September 1, 2009; and March 11, 2010 (tape logs and digital audio recordings in author's possession). "Discrimination Hearing of Mr. Arnold Flores," hearing transcript

and attached exhibits, Boxes 91 and 92, Joe J. Bernal Papers, Benson Latin American Collection, University of Texas Libraries, the University of Texas at Austin (hereinafter "Bernal Papers"); FAMA advertisement in *Inferno*, October 5, 1967, copy in author's possession, courtesy of Arnold Flores; Texas State Advisory Committee to the U.S. Commission on Civil Rights, "Employment Practices at Kelly Air Force Base, San Antonio, Texas," June 1968, reporting on hearings held November 7 and 8, 1967 (U.S. Government Printing Office). For a longer version of this story, see Krochmal, "Chicano Labor and Multiracial Politics."

11   Flores interview (2008), file 1, 1:02:05–1:04:50, 1:19:25–end; Flores interview (2009), file 1, 30:15, file 2, 25:40–28:05; "Officers are Elected by FAMA," *San Antonio Light*, January 23, 1969, 2; "100 Hospital Employes Study Union," *San Antonio Light*, July 21, 1969, 15; Sharon Lumm, "Custodians, Union Discuss Job Woes," *San Antonio Light*, August 17, 1969.

12   "100 Hospital Employees Study Union"; Lumm, "Custodians, Union Discuss Job Woes"; "Maids, Janitors of SAISD Plan Meet," *San Antonio Light*, August 28, 1969, 63; Doris Wright, "Working Together Would Help," *San Antonio Light*, August 31, 1969, 7–A; Doris Wright, "Tempers Flare at Grievance Session," *San Antonio Light*, October 24, 1969, 6; Anne Pashkoff, "SAISD Votes to Halt Union Dues 'Checkoff,'" *San Antonio Express*, November 14, 1969, 8–F; "Court Next Stop for Custodians," *San Antonio Light*, November 14, 1969, 1; "SAISD Janitors Plan Protest," *San Antonio Express/News*, November 23, 1969, 2–C; Luna, "S.A. Marchers Hit Low School Wages"; "Sherrill Smith Returns to Help Marchers"; Doris Wright, "Edgewood School Harmony is Sought," *San Antonio Light*, January 20, 1970, 4; Anne Pashkoff, "School Janitors, Maids Press for Dues Deductions," *San Antonio Express*, May 15, 1970, 16–D; Flores interviews by author. The membership numbers cited above are from the Flores interviews by author; incomplete records from the international union reflect somewhat smaller numbers of members with fully-paid per-capita taxes. Otherwise the international union records agree with Flores's testimony. See, for example, letter from Val Cox to George Hardy, January 19, 1973, Service Employees International Union (SEIU) Executive Office Files: George Hardy Collection, Walter P. Reuther Archives of Labor and Urban Affairs, Wayne State University (hereinafter "SEIU Hardy Papers"), Box 71, Folder 14. Also see Box 12. Flores's numbers are probably more accurate in terms of on-the-ground participation. For a snapshot of the union's shop-floor activities, also see its "March 1973 Newsletter," in Albert A. Peña, Jr. Papers, MS 37, University of Texas at San Antonio Libraries Special Collections (hereinafter "Peña Papers"), Box 15, Folder 5.

13   Flores interview (2008), file 2, 1:17:50–end and file 3; copy of clipping, *Inferno*, October 5, 1967, featuring a photograph of Flores and Sutton at Kelly AFB with caption, in author's possession; author's interview with Rev. Claude William Black, Jr., San Antonio, October 27, 2008; author's interview with Eugene Coleman, San Antonio, September 2, 2009; Claude W. Black and Taj I. Matthews, *Grandpa Was a Preacher: A Letter to My Grandson* (Bloomington, IN: AuthorHouse, 2007). A vast but incomplete run of *SNAP News* can be found within the San Antonio Black History Collection, 1873–1996, MS 139, Archives and Special Collections, University of Texas at San Antonio Library. For more information, see Krochmal, "Chicano Labor and Multiracial Politics"; Max Krochmal, "Labor, Civil Rights, and the Struggle for Democracy in Texas, 1935–1965" (Ph.D. diss., Duke University, 2011).

14   Flores interview (2008), file 2, 25:30–29:15, 38:05–41:30, and especially 56:25; Flores interview (9/9/2009), file 1, 57:45–1:03:35.

15   "March 1973 Newsletter," Peña Papers.

16   Flores interview (2008), file 2, 25:30–28:20, 51:25; Albert Peña, handwritten "Report to S/Employees General Meeting," March 11, 1973, Peña Papers, Box 15, Folder 5; Letter from Arnold Flores to Auxiliary Bishop Patrick Flores, December 23, 1970,

Peña Papers, Box 8, Folder 1; "March 1973 Newsletter," Peña Papers. The phrase "movement culture" underscores the fact that group identity is constructed through social and cultural practices rather than coming automatically from racial, class, or other identifications. I borrow it and the insights from Lawrence Goodwyn, *The Populist Moment: A Short History of the Agrarian Revolt in America* (New York: Oxford University Press, 1978). For additional examples of the cultural practices of organized labor in other contexts, see, among others, Elizabeth A. Fones-Wolf, *Selling Free Enterprise: The Business Assault on Labor and Liberalism, 1945–60* (Urbana: University of Illinois Press, 1994), chapters 4–5; Daniel Katz, *All Together Different: Yiddish Socialists, Garment Workers, and the Labor Roots of Multiculturalism* (New York: New York University Press, 2011); Keona Ervin, "'Interracial Good Will': Black Women Unionists and the Educational Department of the ILGWU's Southwestern Region, 1935–1957" (conference paper presented at the Southern Labor Studies Association, New Orleans, 2013).

17   Flores interview (2008), file 1, 1:12:00–1:17:10, file 2, 23:30–25:30; Flores interview (2009), file 1, 1:23:10; "Don's Bagatelles," *San Antonio Light*, March 22, 1970, 10–D; Leo Cardenas and R.B. Fields, "10 Arrested After Melee At Frost National Bank," *San Antonio Express*, September 11, 1970, 14–A; clippings in Peña Papers, Box 9, Folder 4; clippings in Bernal Papers, Box 98; author's interview with Eugene Coleman, San Antonio, September 2, 2009 (in author's possession); author's interview with Rosie Castro, San Antonio, September 8, 2009 (in author's possession). According to Flores interview (2010), the police initially detained many more people than the thirty-one who were officially booked. Arnold was surprised to learn recently that he was not officially booked and therefore no record exists of his arrest in court or newspaper records.

18   Sepúlveda, *The Life and Times of Willie Velásquez*, 162; Flores interviews by author.

19   Author's interviews with Paul Javior; author's interview with C. J. Littlefield; author's interview with Eddie Felán; "Struck Firm Looking For Workers," *San Antonio Light*, December 20, 1964, 11-A; "Solon Sees 'Low-Wage Conspiracy,'" *San Antonio Light*, December 23, 1964, 21; "Friedrich Harassment is Claimed," *San Antonio Express*, January 13, 1965, 1, 11; "Friedrich, Union, Okay Pact," *San Antonio Light*, January 24, 1965, 1; Jim Price, "Priest Banning Protested: Chancery Faces Picketing," *San Antonio Light*, February 4, 1967, 1; "Electric Union Pact Signed," *San Antonio Light*, July 22, 1968, 14. Flores, Javior, and the IUE all receive sympathetic treatment in Phyllis Palmer, *Living as Equals: How Three White Communities Struggled to Make Interracial Connections During the Civil Rights Era* (Nashville, TN: Vanderbilt University Press, 2008).

20   The term "second-generation" belongs to Montejano, *Quixote's Soldiers*. I am still piecing together Franklin García's biography. This summary draws upon all of my oral history interviews in San Antonio; Samuel A. Twedell Papers, 1915–1963 and 1954–1968, Texas Labor Archives, Special Collections Library, University of Texas, Arlington, AR44 and AR124, Box 9; Richard A. Twedell Papers, Texas Labor Archives, UTA, AR 264, Box 8, Folder 7; and a bunch of fragmentary sources from BLAC and the Peña Papers—all of which are cited in my dissertation, Krochmal, "Labor, Civil Rights, and the Struggle for Democracy in Texas." Also see note 12. For an overview, see his best obituary: Ruperto García and Frances Barton, "Franklin García: A Union Man," *Texas Observer*, February 10, 1984.

21   This short biographical sketch highlights Peña's ties to organized labor, but it should be noted that he was also a pioneer among ethnic Mexicans who sought to build alliances with African Americans. In 1960, for example, Peña allied with black activist G. J. Sutton and labor leaders to gain significant power in the local and state units of the Democratic Party. As a result, Peña became the state's first *mexicano* delegate to the Democratic National Convention in Los Angeles in that year, while Sutton was the county's first black delegate. In 1963, Peña served as a co-chair of the state-wide Democratic Coalition. See Krochmal, "Labor, Civil Rights, and the Struggle

for Democracy in Texas." For the seminal, long-overdue biography, see José Angel Gutiérrez, *Dean Emeritus of Chicano Politics: Albert A. Peña, Jr. of San Antonio, Texas, 1917–2006* (Fall 2013 manuscript in author's possession).

22   "A Program for Organizing in South Texas," Peña Papers, Box 9, Folder 1, 1–2. The document lists no author but was almost certainly written by Peña. It matches the tone and style of other similar treatises in his archive and includes, in the first person, experiences of which only Peña would have first-hand accounts. Still, he regularly uses the pronoun "we" in proposing the program. Thus it can also be read as a collective statement from his circle of collaborators, including legal and political colleagues, movement activists, and undoubtedly SACO members.

23   Ibid, 2–3.

24   Ibid, 3–5.

25   Peña's handwritten notes, October 8, 1969; and "My Agreement," n.d.—both in Peña Papers, Box 7, Folder 9.

26   Peña's handwritten notes, October 9, 1969; and notes beginning "J. Vincent trying to pull the same thing," n.d.—both in Peña Papers, Box 7, Folder 9.

27   "Meeting at La Posada," November 5, 1969, Peña Papers, Box 7, Folder 9.

28   "Potpurri," *San Antonio Express/News*, February 8, 1970, 5–H; Paul Thompson column, *San Antonio Express/News*, February 14, 1970; "Union Vote Decision Is Awaited," *San Antonio Express*, July 17, 1970, 6–C; Paul Thompson column, *San Antonio Express/News*, July 19, 1970, 1; "The Don's Bagatelles," *San Antonio Light*, December 6, 1970, 14–F; "Firm Workers Vote for Union," *San Antonio Light*, December 15, 1970, 4; "Freuhauf Group Votes for UAW," *San Antonio Express*, December 16, 1970, 4–D; "Trailer Firm, Union Reach Agreement," *San Antonio Express*, 5–A.

29   Doris Wright, "González Clash Resounds," *San Antonio Light*, March 1, 1970, 7–C; Paul Thompson column, *San Antonio Express/News*, March 7, 1970; "Miss Castro Sets Meeting On 'Attacks,'" *San Antonio Express*, March 12, 1970, 8–B. The cleavage got worse, with González denouncing Arnold Flores of SEIU as a "Communist-trained" organizer who had "infiltrated the labor movement." The Congressman ultimately allied himself with a rival public sector union, the local branch of the American Federation of State, County, and Municipal Employees (AFSCME) led by Henry "The Fox" Muñoz, Jr., and Linda (Ramírez) Chávez-Thompson. Flores helped to reconcile Peña and González in the late 1970s. See Flores interviews by author; SEIU Hardy Papers, Box 12, Folders 47–48; American Federation of State, County and Municipal Employees (AFSCME) Office of the President: Jerry Wurf Collection, Walter P. Reuther Archives of Labor and Urban Affairs, Wayne State University, Box 116, Folder 12.

30   Letter from Shelton Tappes, June 23, 1970, Peña Papers, Box 7, Folder 9; "The Don's Bagatelles," *San Antonio Light*, December 6, 1970, 14–F; Jim Price, "Pena Lists Financial Status, Asks Same of All Politicos," *San Antonio Light*, January 29, 1971, 18; author's interview with Roy Hernández (in author's possession). Strangely, the union got more bad press when it was revealed that a private investigator hired by unknown parties installed a wiretap on the phones of Peña's UAW office. "Wiretap Testimony," *San Antonio Light*, November 29, 1971, 1; Wilson McKinney, "Former Valley Police Chief Linked to UAW Wiretap," *San Antonio Express*, November 30, 1971, 2–C.

31   Flores interview (2008), file 2, 57:55–1:17:50 and file 3, 6:40; Flores interview (2009), file 1, 38:40–46:35, 57:15, 1:10:05; Flores interview (9/9/2009), 1:03:35; photograph of SACO members with Senator Ralph Yarborough, n.d., in author's possession; copy of open letter motion from SACO to San Antonio labor council, March 23, 1972, in author's possession; letter to Joe Hernández signed by SACO members, n.d., p. 2 (in author's possession); author's interview with Paul Javior, San Antonio, September 4, 2009, esp. 37:15; author's interview with Roy Hernández, San Antonio,

September 8, 2009; author's interview with Jaime Martínez, San Antonio, March 10, 2010; author's interview with C. J. Littlefield, San Antonio, September 2, 2009. The informal group became the model for the national AFL-CIO when it created the Labor Council for Latin American Advancement, and Flores served on the national body's board. See "A New Awakening," n.d. [1975] and "Franklin García (Left) Talks to LCLAA Committee," 1975, both in author's possession. On the Angela Davis rally, see Mario Marcel Salas Papers, 1968–2009, MS 142, University of Texas at San Antonio Libraries Special Collections, Box 15.

32 "Council Elects Six," *San Antonio Light,* November 25, 1973, 23–D; Frank Trejo, "Frank Talk Around the Plaza," *San Antonio Light,* February 4, 1976, 3–B; Letter from Arnold Flores to George Hardy, October 6, 1973, SEIU Hardy Papers, Box 12, Folder 44.

33 Flores interview (2008), file 2, 25:30–28:20, 51:25; Peña, "Report to S/Employees General Meeting," March 11, 1973, Peña Papers; "March 1973 Newsletter," Peña Papers. "The Cock Pit," *San Antonio Express/News,* March 4, 1973, III-3; Nell Fenner Grover, "New Center Aims to Aid Laborers," *San Antonio Express,* June 12, 1973, 2–A.

34 "The Cock Pit," March 4, 1973, III-3 (both quotations).

35 Grover, "New Center Aims to Aid Laborers."

36 Ibid.; Ann B. Robinson, "Women Demand 'Rights,'" *San Antonio Light,* July 2, 1973, 7–B; Gaylon Finklea, "Strikers to Get Rally Aid," *San Antonio Light,* July 7, 1973, 2–A. The exact union present at Longhorn Machinery remains unclear, but it's probable that its workers were represented by the IUE, a union staffed by SACO members. It appears that "Ingram Steel" and "Ingram Manufacturing" are, in fact, the same plant. It is clear that workers at Ingram were members of IUE Local 1013 prior to the strike, and IUE and Meat Cutters staffers are identified as leaders of the strikers' planned rally. See Doris Wright, "1,000 Rally for Unionism," *San Antonio Light,* July 8, 1973, 5–B; "Churchmen to March in Strike Rally," *El Paso Herald-Post,* July 7, 1973, 1; and Letter from SACO to Joe Hernández, March 9, 1973, Peña Papers, Box 15, Folder 5.

37 Finklea, "Strikers to Get Rally Aid."

38 Wright, "1,000 Rally for Unionism" (all quotations except "*Viva la huelga*" and the final quotation); "Chicano March Held to Support Strikes," *Sun-News* (Las Cruces, New Mexico), July 8, 1973, 2 ("*Viva la huelga*" and final quotation only). On Santiesteven, see Kenneth C. Burt, "Henry Santiestevan '40, Mexican American Activist," *Occidental* 22, no. 4 (Fall 2000), available online, www.kennethburt.com/santiestevan.html (accessed July 19, 2013).

39 Nell Fenner Grover, "Center Set for Jobless," *San Antonio Express,* December 19, 1973, 2–A.

10

"WE ARE A DISTINCT PEOPLE"

Defending Difference in Schools Through the Chicano Movement in Michigan, 1966–1980

Nora Salas

The Chicano Movement in Michigan sought bilingual/bicultural education because it contributed to building *La Raza* as a national construct and rejected assimilation they associated with whiteness. Chicanos challenged meritocracy, a key component of American Exceptionalism, that is the assumption that upward mobility awaited those who assimilated and worked hard in school. Instead, they focused on building a distinct cultural identity. Taken together, Chicano activists' criticism of the schooling they received as rooted in white supremacy and their focus on combatting erasure by reinforcing their difference constituted a fundamental part of Chicano anti-colonial thought.

Michigan schools were places where future Chicano and Chicana activists experienced dissonance between the rhetoric of American Exceptionalism and American reality on a daily basis. Michigan growers sought to maintain Chicano families as a group subject to labor stratification whose reproductive costs were born outside the local economy in a lower cost area. To this end Michigan growers, agricultural capital, and their political allies, promoted a colonial binary which defined *domestic* workers as whites who belonged in rural areas and *migrants* as Mexicans and foreigners regardless of their actual residence, race or citizenship status. Although many Chicanos instead traced their presence in Michigan to industrial wage labor, the domestic/migrant binary was pervasive. As with many another colonial project, promulgators of the domestic/migrant binary effaced a multitude of differences among Chicanos in "making up (the) people" who could be defined as "migrants" and therefore "foreign."[1] Thus, Michigan Chicanos saw schooling as promoting an American national identity that denied and denigrated them while simultaneously demanding their allegiance. Migrant children in Michigan's rural areas during the 1950s and 1960s were routinely treated as a group to be separated or excluded from public schooling. The exclusion of migrant children, punishment for speaking Spanish, and incorrect assignment to classes for the "mentally retarded" alienated not only migrant children, but resident Chicano children and their families from cities to countryside.

In their pursuit of a bilingual education that reinforced cultural differences, Chicanos in Detroit shared much with their peers in the Southwest. Yet, the schooling of Chicanos in Detroit also differed. Though certainly neglected, Chicanos were not systematically segregated from whites in Michigan's largest city as they were in many parts of the Southwest. Nevertheless, their treatment in urban areas fit with dominant school practices of excluding migrant children and the discourse of foreignness that permeated the Chicano experience in Michigan.

Though Chicanos were physically excluded from rural schools, they were excluded in Michigan's largest urban district discursively, not only from academic success, but from reality. Throughout the long court battle for desegregation in Detroit, Chicanos were routinely labeled "white" and seen as a demographic resource to desegregate black schools. Chicanos opposed desegregation when it compromised bilingual education because they believed it endangered the success of their children and because reinforcing their children's difference as part of *La Raza* was more important to them than an abstract American ideal of "integration." Furthermore, they rejected the white identity supported by school policies and legal actions in Detroit.

Schooling as Alienation

> It was a rare day indeed if, in those days, I didn't hear a teacher say,
> "Don't speak Spanish. If you do, you will be punished!"[2]

The exclusion of migrant children from schooling in Michigan grew out of structural factors that facilitated child labor and a discourse that defined Mexican migrant children as a temporary part of the community, as long as they remained in the fields. Local farmers and grower interests organized in the Michigan Farm Bureau and the Women for the Survival of Michigan Agriculture resisted efforts to enforce school attendance for migrant children throughout the 1960s and 70s. They often asserted that anti-child labor laws only further impoverished vulnerable farm workers and "deprived" their children of work experience. Seemingly unconcerned with lessons which might have been learned in a formal school setting, the secretary of the Michigan Association of Cherry Producers defended child labor in 1963 saying, "There are valuable lessons of responsibility to be gained from the employment of children, as well as the importance of keeping them occupied."[3] Mrs. Robert Neumann struck a similar note in 1966 writing in opposition to new child labor restrictions in her local newspaper, "denying our children the privilege of working at the harvest of our vast fruit crop" while leaving the "migrant families . . . who depend upon the little money their children bring home . . . denying them this work could mean disaster."[4] In this way grower allies such as Neumann claimed credit for providing migrant worker children with the "privilege" they had of working in the fields while eschewing any responsibility for their need to work. Growers and their organizations often claimed to be protecting the livelihood of farm worker families when defending child labor.

Resistance to other programs whose purpose was to "help" migrants called upon a similar discourse that defined migrant workers as not belonging if they were anywhere but the fields. It was under this logic that the Shelby migrant school had its water service cut off and was subject to what the school supervisor Jane Moog called "harassment and hostility" when the school first opened in 1967. School Board member and newspaper editor Elwood Huggard asserted that the school's employees were overpaid and that "local opinion is running real strong against it."[5] It seems unlikely the parents of the 57 children attending the two schools were accounted for in Huggard's description of "local opinion." In this same vein the superintendent of the Benton Harbor public schools opposed the efforts of United Migrants for Opportunity to "recruit" migrants to settle in the area because there was no room in the public schools for them.[6] Yet school staff who characterized individual students as "migrants" and thus "not from here" when they began school in the fall were not simply observing a child's history, but making a prediction as to the child's future residence and engaging in a process by which the "community" was socially constructed.

As migrant advocates turned toward Chicano Movement strategies schooling remained a primary concern. The newly formed Concerned Citizens for Migrant Workers, led by Rubén Alfaro, headed the turn toward public protest in 1967. Alfaro's group grew out of the more moderate Latin Americans United on Political Action (LAUPA). Though it was not the first march for migrants in Michigan, LAUPA and Alfaro's shift in tactics was a turning point for Michigan Chicanos.[7] Alfaro's decision to use public protest, not just voter registration and lobbying as LAUPA had, was initially controversial among his peers.[8] At the Easter Sunday 1967 culmination of the march from Saginaw to Lansing, between 800 and 1000 people denounced child labor.[9] They inverted the growers' colonial discourse in their official "Declaration of Grievances" maintaining, "The children of migrant workers must sacrifice the privilege of an adequate education in order to accompany their families to Michigan to help harvest our crops. This sacrifice is a deterrent to their ability to pursue other means of employment or to continue their education."[10] Unlike growers who argued that work in the fields was a "privilege," mobilized migrants asserted that field work was instead a "sacrifice" that trapped them and their children, unable to pursue other jobs and educational opportunities. Both in their words and actions the marchers contested the colonial order that defined migrant workers as a subordinate people for whom both public schools and the public sphere were out of reach.

Chicano activists and educators noted continued resistance to schooling for migrants even as dedicated summer schools and school-year programs expanded during the late 1960s and early 1970s. The La Raza Citizens' Advisory Committee reported that twenty school districts eligible for migrant program funding had refused to create summer programs for migrants.[11] Many were in southwest Michigan, near Dowagiac and Hartford, sites of heated conflict between growers, farm workers, and their Chicano allies.[12] The committee attributed this situation to local sentiments that viewed migrants as outsiders for whom their communities had no responsibility.[13] Jesse Soriano, who worked on bilingual education for the Ann Arbor school district, asserted,

> it's not uncommon to hear that "We can't have a summer school program for the Mexican kids because recreation program funds were cut for our kids." The townspeople would be very upset if we had a program for the Mexican kids.[14]

In this way teachers and school district personnel relied upon the existence of the migrant/domestic binary that defined Chicanos as not "our kids" to avoid programs that would have weakened the colonial order. Conversely, migrant advocates rejected the idea that agricultural workers who resided in Texas for a part of the year ought to be categorized differently than "locals." The chairman of the Saginaw area Bishop's Committee for the Spanish Speaking asserted, "We profit from the work of migrants and we can't send them back to Texas and call the whole thing a 'Texas problem.'"[15]

The lack of belonging communicated to Chicano and Chicana students who spoke Spanish paralleled the exclusion of migrant children precisely because "migrant" was a social construct that encompassed Spanish-speakers and others of Mexican descent. Andres Fierro, who graduated from Holland High School in 1968, recalled how his treatment as a Spanish-speaker affected his identity:

> I really lost 99 percent of my language going through the school system here . . . that's part of being robbed of my language . . . of being robbed of identity . . . when you're told that to speak another language is a sign of ignorance, you begin to be very self-conscious of what your roots are.[16]

Fierro's comments reveal his alienation, not only from the schools that "robbed" him of his Spanish language, but also from his Mexican heritage. Soriano asserted that in the Midwest there was "a greater isolation from his cultural and linguistic environment than . . . his counterpart in Texas or California. . . . The pressures to ignore or reject his culture exerted upon him by the school are correspondingly greater."[17] Soriano believed that the Midwest was actually more difficult for Spanish-speaking children because of increased alienation. Reformers responded to the problem by emphasizing in the state manual for teachers in Migrant Programs that teachers should "remember that Spanish is a respectable language which these children have demonstrated their ability to learn. Spanish is not 'wrong.' Do not penalize children because they speak it."[18] Although a positive step, the need to provide this type of advice to teachers of migrant children reveals just how common the problem continued to be in the 1970s.

Urban Mexican children had greater access to the public schools, but they experienced a high dropout rate and sporadic attendance. It was an acute problem in Detroit, where the Webster Elementary School principal noted that as the 1968 school year began, forty-seven new Mexican students matriculated at Webster, but only eight of those remained at the beginning of 1969. Gustavo Guynett, director of the first Latino community service organization in Detroit, La Sed, decried Detroit's high Chicano dropout rate. White school administrators disputed Guynett's claims about a 90 percent dropout rate, but they acknowledged they could not establish a dropout rate for Mexican or Latino students because they only kept statistics on white or black students.[19] Alfaro also linked the high dropout rate to poor treatment, "The Mexican child, who in many cases speaks only Spanish, is at a disadvantage in the school," he said. "Most of these children don't drop—they are forced out."[20]

The erroneous assignment of Latino and "Spanish-speaking" children to classes for the "mentally retarded" was another mechanism for subordinating Chicanos through the school system. The inaccurate assignment of these students emerged as a particular concern later than the attention paid to services for migrant children and punishment for speaking Spanish. This issue received greater attention as bilingual/bicultural education programs were instituted in the mid-1970s. A comprehensive 1974 report by the La Raza Citizens' Advisory Committee protested that Spanish-speaking students were being erroneously placed in special education courses due to their score on English language IQ tests. For instance, only 15.4 percent of students in the Holland Public Schools were Spanish-speaking, but 43.5 percent of all students in the special education program were Latino.[21] As a result of parents' complaints, Detroit's La Sed became involved in a class action lawsuit against the state Department of Education and local school districts on behalf of Guadalupe Hernández. Hernández was first assigned to classes for the "mentally retarded" in 1970, but when La Sed and Hernández' parents had her re-evaluated by a Latino psychologist in 1975, she was reclassified as a "normal child." Her parents, and others involved in the suit, claimed the erroneous assignment of their children had actually caused them to be "deficient" in their education.[22] In this way, those involved in this suit asserted, quite literally, that the very state institution ostensibly charged with remedying their children's under-development was causing the condition it was supposed to cure.

Schooling and American Nationalism

> Many Americans proudly said that our army's victory was like the one the
> conquistadors had won in the 1500s. Scott rode into the center of the city
> . . . the band played . . . "Yankee doodle" and at the end "Hail to the
> Chief." It was such a splendid sight that it is said even the Mexicans cheered.[23]

Perhaps, as a 1968 high school history textbook claimed, Mexicans applauded
General Winfield Scott's invasion of Mexico City in 1847 and fondly reminisced
about the welcome their ancestors had given the Spanish conquistadores of 1520.
The Free and the Brave, from which this passage is taken, was one of the most
popular history texts in Michigan schools in 1970.[24] As embodied in this passage,
white supremacist American nationalism in the curriculum combined with other
forms of discriminatory treatment to alienate Chicanos. The history of educational
policy towards Mexicans in the United States is beyond the scope of this work,
but suffice to say that Chicano movement participants increasingly noted that the
schooling they received reproduced their subjugation. Much like the perpetual
subjects who welcomed the American invasion of Mexico City, Chicanos in
Michigan schools learned there was indeed a place for them within the American
national project, as a conquered people.

Chicanos who managed to be enrolled in Michigan colleges and universities
despite their inferior schooling were few, but increased during the 1970s. On
campus, Chicano students, faculty, and staff worked together to increase
enrollment and make college more accessible. In their efforts they directly
confronted the domestic/migrant binary because many of the state's institutions
of higher education defined "migrant students" as non-resident out-of-state
applicants subject to higher tuition rates. In 1970 the University of Michigan,
Ann Arbor, was still designating migrant students as "non-residents," though it
was under pressure from the federally funded state agency United Migrants for
Opportunity to change its policy.[25] Members of Chicanos Organized for Progress
and Action (COPA) demonstrated on Central Michigan University's (CMU)
campus on February 15, 1972, demanding that CMU give migrant students
residency status. Their demands were met beginning in the fall of that year.[26]

These few Chicano college students, those most able to adapt and survive the
schooling they received, often reflected on their early school experiences and
identified how this conveyed a second-class status. Members of the student group,
Chicanos at Michigan (CAM), criticized their K-12 schooling in their "Historical
Background of Chicanos in Michigan":

> Not only do they have to spend one or two years learning the language,
> but they tend also to look at it as the only acceptable, and "American"
> form of speaking. Somehow it has been forgotten that one-third of the
> United States once belonged to Mexico. But there is more damage done

than this. The child soon also begins to feel that there is something "foreign" and different about their parents and their background, and because of the demeaning attitude the white power structure has toward Chicanos, become ashamed of their own culture. Nothing he learns in school or anything he reads in his books has anything at all in common with this home and his background. He learns to be bilingual, he learns to be bicultural, he knows how to speak English but his language is Spanish. He knows how to be Anglo but he *is* Mexican.[27]

In this passage CAM members, led by their president, Linda Guzmán, clearly identified the alienation they experienced in the schools. They objected to the Anglocentric view of the American national project when they reminded readers of the lands formerly a part of Mexico now included in the territory of the United States. Yet, their rhetorical focus was not on the effects of the schooling they received as Mexicans as a group, but on the effects on the individual's sense of self, shifting from the plural "they" to the masculine singular, "he." The authors asserted that as individuals Chicanos learned in school that they did not belong because they were "foreign" and that the nature of their non-belonging was inferior, a cause for shame. Finally, they asserted that this experience instructed students how to perform in Anglo society, "how to be Anglo," yet, no matter the teaching that took place, the Mexican was forever excluded, because on an essential level "he *is* Mexican." In this way the authors both named their fundamental alienation from the American national project and rejected the position they were assigned within it. They opposed the supposedly "shameful" nature of their group and instead claimed not their identity, but emphatically stated their nature as Mexicans. In this way they posited their place as individuals who were a part of a cohesive, separate group, outside the reach of any colonial project.

When Chicanos took an active role in bilingual curricula their condemnation of white supremacist American nationalism was especially evident. In 1972, four Chicano students at Eastern Michigan University collaborated with a University of Michigan student to modify a sensitization exercise they had witnessed in migrant classes. In this exercise, designed to portray the punishment received by Spanish-speaking students, Chicano presenters were introduced to a college class and proceeded to run the class in Spanish. In the middle of the exercise students were asked in Spanish to repeat not the U.S. Pledge of Allegiance, but a "Pledge to Aztlán" written for this purpose.

We are children of the sun, we are children of the race. Our race is brave and noble. We are citizens of Aztlán. We would die for Aztlán. We come from a noble heritage. Viva la Raza, Viva Aztlán.[28]

The "Pledge to Aztlán" is reflective of how the Pledge of Allegiance was perceived by Chicano students, as well as the emergence of Aztlán as a competing national construct. The "Pledge to Aztlán" reflected a view of the nation, be it the U.S. or Aztlán, as a distinctly racialized entity, one that demanded loyalty, and one whose fate was intimately tied to racial survival. In the "Pledge to Aztlán" there was no nation without a coherent group who were the descendants, or "children" of a great people with a "noble heritage." In this way the authors asserted that the U.S. Pledge of Allegiance similarly spoke to a distinct group with a common heritage whose well-being was essential to the survival of the United States. The English-speaking students who participated in the exercise were compelled to follow rules they could not understand, punished for the violation of those rules, shamed for speaking their native language, and then forced to pledge loyalty to the group that created these alienating conditions because they were superior by virtue of their descent. Together with the rest of the exercise, meant to communicate the othering and subordination Chicanos experienced in schools, the "Pledge to Aztlán" described how American schools alienated them from the American national project. In this way the "Pledge to Aztlán" spoke to both Chicanos' experiences of American nationalism and Aztlán.

Another area where Chicanos made the links between their schooling in the United States and the alienating effects of an exclusionary American nationalism was in the materials produced by educational professionals active in the Chicano Movement. Such materials often critiqued the absence of Chicanos from United States history courses and the prevalence of an ideology of Anglo superiority while they presented alternate national visions. Adelfa Arredondo's 1976 booklet "The Miseducation of Chicano Students: Recommendations for Confronting It" was designed for teachers and used in teacher education workshops. First published by the Michigan Department of Education, where Arredondo was employed, the booklet includes a self-assessment, discussion of common misconceptions and solutions as well as a selected bibliography.[29] Arredondo emphasized the internal diversity among Chicanos, opposed assimilation as a route to success in the U.S. and offered practical suggestions about resources. She also portrayed a number of standard historical narratives presented as a part of an exclusionary American nationalism in her list of forty items entitled "Miseducation of Chicanos":

1. Telling a Chicano child that Columbus discovered America.
2. Teaching that George Washington is the father of the U.S.
3. Teaching that the English settlers were the "founders" of America.[30]

In these first three items Arredondo directly confronted imperial historical narratives that portray the Americas as unpeopled prior to European colonization, as well as those that place the roots of the American national project exclusively in its Anglo heritage. Furthermore, she characterized this sort of nationalism as responsible for the "miseducation" of Chicano students. Her list also addressed more predictable points such as "not teaching the Chicanos about their culture, heritage and language," and "Teaching Chicanos that they must conform to white society's ways." Arredondo chose first to address ideas considered "common sense": Columbus' discovery of America, the importance of Washington, and the founding of the United States.[31] In this way she asserted the poor educational attainment of Chicano students was not only due to the exclusion of information about them, of their "culture, heritage and language," but also a result of Anglocentric America as an ideological project.

The Conflict Between Desegregation and Bilingual Education

> Do not group, categorize or lump us with anyone—we are a distinct people, with a real and unplastic culture . . . Call it anything you like, our children have been segregated for generations. Not only from Whites and Blacks, but from achievement, from success and from the academic system.[32]

Though people of Mexican descent had lived in Detroit since the 1910s, Chicano students in this urban area were subject to the same discourse of foreignness that excluded migrant children from rural schools. The idea of Mexicans, many of whom were born in the United States, as "migrants" and thus foreign was pervasive, influencing even sympathetic portrayals of their educational challenges. In 1969 journalist John Peterson entitled his report on the efforts of Detroit Latino advocates seeking bilingual education "a tragic lesson" but when describing the origins of Detroit's "Latin-American" population in migrant farm work, he asserted, "Most of the newcomers are refugees from the grinding misery of the southwestern barrios."[33] When applied to Latino families in Detroit, distancing language such as "newcomers" and "refugees" played into the narrative that "migrant" families whose labor contributions had been critical to Michigan agriculture for decades were nonetheless outsiders in Michigan. One would scarcely know these "refugees" were fellow Americans. In addition to being defined as "migrants," urban Chicanos were excluded from educational advancement by a legal system that erased them from Detroit's racial reality. When activists from La Sed spoke before the school board in 1975, they vigorously asserted their existence as a "distinct people" with a history of inequality. Most importantly they disavowed the right of others to erase their difference. The struggle for bilingual/bicultural education in Detroit was more than a battle for better schooling, but also one to establish "la raza" as a "distinct people" whose fundamental reality could not be denied.

Throughout the early 1970s two disparate initiatives to improve the public schools in Detroit followed largely separate orbits to their ultimate chaotic intersection. After 1976 desegregation proceeded largely unmodified, but the other initiative, bilingual education, proved to have far less gravity and its trajectory was significantly modified. In seeking improved education for Chicano children, advocates in southwest Detroit had been pursuing bilingual education since 1969.

They largely rejected the idea that the purpose of bilingual education was to ease the assimilation of the community's children into a white, English-speaking American culture, but instead saw bilingual education as a means to cultural cohesion and the reinforcement of a separate, Spanish-speaking, non-white identity. Ironically, the desegregation court also favored bilingual education, but did so because it portrayed Detroit Chicanos as a non-black group that would be adequately served simply by learning English. In this way the implementation of desegregation in Detroit was premised upon the exclusion of Chicano difference from the city's racial order.

The literature on the schooling of Chicanos in the U.S. provides little guidance on interpreting this scenario because, like much of Chicano Studies, it is limited to the Southwest and tends to naturalize that region's environment as *the* Chicano context. The segregation of Chicano students, Americanization through education, creating a pliable labor force, community desegregation efforts, and the institutionalization, however brief, of bilingual education have been primary concerns of scholars focused on such schooling. Gilbert González has argued that schooling functioned as training for low wage labor positions and Americanization to serve a colonial racial order. This view would have been familiar to many of the Chicanos discussed here. Outside the Southwest, some of these concerns, such as the strict segregation of urban Chicano students from whites, were much less salient, while others, particularly a binary black/white racial order that erased Chicanos, were much more so. Few contemporary scholars of Chicano schooling address the interaction of black and Chicano efforts to improve their schools; those who do primarily portray the Black Civil Rights struggle as a significant, but distant milieu instead of a daily circumstance.

Other scholars, most prominently Guadalupe San Miguel and Ruben Donato have found that desegregating black students was a competing narrative for educational improvement, but in most of these cases black students were not the majority as they were in Detroit. Black students outnumbered white students in Detroit from the beginning of 1963. White professional employees were fewer than blacks in the district by 1975, and blacks comprised 63 percent of the city's residents by 1980.[34] Although different, the circumstances faced by Chicano education advocates in Detroit did not have a mediating affect on their critique. As in many other locales, advocates tended to see bilingual education as an avenue to the development of a more distinct ethnic identity. Detroiters concerned with the education of Chicano youth rejected their exclusion from the city's black/white binary. Instead, critics of the education of the community's children asserted that the inadequate education imposed on Chicano students destined them for state spaces of more absolute social control such as the child welfare system, and ultimately, prison. In this narrative, the choice between a theoretical American assimilation and a radical, separate liberation for Chicano, or black, students was laid barren by the omnipresence of Detroit's rapid deindustrialization, globalization, and political marginality.

The process of desegregation was a contested issue within the Chicano community. Although the ultimate decision of Detroit's long-running desegregation case, *Bradley v. Milliken*, included some "educational components" designed to foster student achievement, the primary issue throughout the process was the segregation of black children. The idea that desegregation could be causally linked to increasing the achievement of black children was broadly assumed in proposed desegregation plans, testimony, and public observations of the time.[35] Whether that occurred is not the subject at hand, but rather the conditions faced by Chicano students during this volatile period. At barrio schools such as Western High School, Earhart Middle School, Webster and Preston Elementary Schools, the involvement of parents, community organizations, and allies indicated that the community was far from satisfied with student performance in their schools prior to desegregation.

Although they were students at some of Detroit's whitest schools prior to the desegregation order, Chicano students did not achieve at higher levels than strictly segregated black students. Stanley A. West and June Macklin noted the differential educational attainment of Chicano students in 1970, "in the city of Detroit the median level of educational attainment for those twenty-five or older was 11.0 for males . . . in the barrio . . . median attainments were 6.6 years for males."[36] A 1973 study compared black and Chicano students in southwest Detroit, where the majority of the Chicano population resided, and found that the parents of Chicano students had much less schooling than their black peers.[37] An analysis of elementary school test scores in 1969 found that no school that had a majority of black or Latino student population had scored above the state-designated grade level on recent exams.[38] In 1970 the school district's own study found that sixth grade students in southwest Detroit had a mean score of 4.7, less than the city-wide mean of 5.0 and more than one grade below level overall. Specific scores for Webster Elementary came closest to assessing the achievement of Latino students on their own. The mean score at Webster was 4.8, again slightly below the city mean of 5.0, again demonstrating that barrio schools were far from a privileged haven of high-achieving students prior to the desegregation process.[39]

Nevertheless the result of the desegregation process for the schools in which Chicanos were most numerous was a decrease in their own limited concentrations and an increase in the proportion of black students. Only two schools in Detroit had a majority Latino population, Webster and Preston Elementary Schools. Prior to desegregation both schools had a proportion of white students close to or less than the 26 percent of white students in the Detroit Public Schools overall, with Preston at 19 percent and Webster at 34 percent. Before the ruling in 1975, Webster was 56 percent Latino and 14.1 percent black, while after segregation it was 37 percent black. Preston went from 61 percent Latino, 25 percent black to 54 percent black. Although many elementary schools in Detroit had fewer or no white students, neither school was a local outpost of white exclusivity; of the ten elementary schools in close proximity, four had significantly higher concentrations of white students, ranging from 56 percent to 76 percent white.[40] Due to the placement out of Latino students and the placement in of black students Latinos saw their concentration in, and claim to, each school diminished.

While desegregation valued integration above all else, Detroit Chicanos enacted their desire to build a distinct identity through bilingual education. Neighborhood surveys showed that parents wanted more Spanish-language courses and more material on Mexican culture while community leaders asserted that the purpose of bilingual education was to instill pride in their identity. Margarita Valdez, a local bilingual advocate, portrayed the hope of many that bilingual education would allow Mexican students the chance to use "their language as an *asset* . . . their *culture* as a means of building confidence and pride in their greatness."[41] Adelfa Loera, a paraprofessional working in Webster's Elementary bilingual program, commented similarly, *Creo que una de las cosas importantes que resulta en el programa es que los niños se sienten orgullosos. Orgullosos . . . de su herencia cultural.*" [I believe that one of the important things resulting from the program is that the children feel proud. Proud . . . of their cultural heritage.][42] Valdez and Loera were participants in an ongoing campaign by community advocates to increase the scope of bilingual education and claim it as their own.

Chicano and Latino community advocates pressed for self-determination and control over bilingual/bicultural programs throughout the 1970s. Ignacio González, community leader and teacher at Western High School, wrote in 1972, "It is our unanimous opinion that a program created for the Chicano community should be directed, guided and evaluated by the Chicano community."[43] In the same year Roberto Veliz, editor of a community newspaper, *Nosotros*, objected to the recent lay-off notices received by Latino teachers in Detroit, "*¿Cómo esperamos que un maestro de los suburbios entienda las necesidades y cultura nuestra? Sabemos positivamente que los alumnos latinos que abandonan la escuela secundaria—80% para ser mas exactos—lo hacen debido principalmente a esta razón.*" [How can we expect a teacher from the suburbs to understand our needs and culture? We know positively that the Latino students who leave high school—80% to be exact— do so primarily for this reason.][44] As a result of concerns over governance of bilingual/bicultural programs at Webster Elementary, Teresa Vance, Benita Estrada, Esther Pérez, Juana Alvárez, and Margarita de la Garza formed a separate parents' organization, *El Club de Padres y Educadores de Webster*.[45] In late 1974 a group protested outside the Region II School Board offices to demand that Webster Elementary fill its vacant principal position with a "bilingual bicultural" person as a part of their ongoing campaign against low numbers of Latino staff in the schools.[46] These educators, community activists, and parents believed that improving Chicano children's schooling was inexorably linked to their ability to control programs designed to help them.

Not surprisingly, given their commitment to a "distinct identity," Chicano parents were dissatisfied with desegregation because throughout the formal proceedings of the desegregation case, from 1970 when the School Board issued its first desegregation plan through the court process, until busing began in 1976, they were rarely deemed a group with their own interests in Detroit schools.[47] Over these 6 years the courts considered 11 desegregation plans totaling thousands of pages. Most of these simply excluded students who were neither white nor black.[48] Latino parents first attempted to intervene in the courts after a final plan was developed in 1975. The judge rejected their petition and ruled that as a "language minority" they had "no place" in a racial segregation case.[49]

Community activists identified the lack of recognition of their racial identity as a barrier to their children's achievement. La Sed protested the exclusion of Latinos from the desegregation plan, "We cannot and will not accept any plan which does not consider the Latino as a distinct and separate group."[50] Other parties worked with LULAC (League of United Latin American Citizens) from 1976 until 1980 on legal attempts to intervene in the case. LULAC's efforts to be included in the case were ultimately rejected by Judge DeMascio, who held that, "This case began as and remains a racial desegregation case, and for school assignment purposes Spanish-surnamed students cannot be treated differently than other white students."[51] In this way being defined as "other white students" constrained the ability of Chicanos to preserve and expand their programs.

Conclusion

The resolution of Detroit's desegregation case for Chicanos was that what separated them from their white peers was a basic matter of language learning. Nevertheless, in their efforts to build bilingual education, Chicanos in Detroit rejected the idea that their children were interchangeable with white students. For them supporting bilingual education meant hiring more Mexican American staff, incorporation of Mexican history and culture in the schools, maintenance of Spanish-language ability, and, most commonly, reinforcement of one's difference from both whites and blacks. In their pursuit of bilingual education that reinforced cultural differences, not aided incorporation, Chicanos in Detroit mirrored a phenomenon found in community support of bilingual education throughout the Southwest.

It is through this similarity that Detroit Chicanos' efforts can be seen as a part of the Chicano Movement. Yet the social, economic, and racial geography of Michigan and Detroit presented a different milieu to Chicano school activists than much of the Southwest. Whether they were migrants, immigrants or the children and grandchildren of both, many Michigan Chicanos possessed knowledge and experience of discrimination in the Southwest, especially Texas. However, their experiences being excluded from and discriminated against in Michigan schools reinforced their alienation in unique ways that can inform our understanding of the Chicano Movement and expand the geography of Chicano Studies. In rural Michigan, Chicanos outside the fields were outsiders because they were "migrants," once in schools they felt a greater isolation because they spoke Spanish and the curriculum presented a vision of American that colonized them, and in Michigan's largest school district their attempts to claim a space as Chicanos were, quite literally, judged to have "no place." During the 1960s and 1970s Chicanos in Michigan schools faced erasure and alienation wherever they turned.

From these experiences in Michigan, Chicanos were supposed to learn lessons of assimilation through submission, of allegiance as "whites, Spanish-surnamed." Many learned these lessons and rejected them. Their distance from the lands formerly a part of Mexico, a frequent Chicano Movement talking point, did not blunt their critique. Instead their alienation created a dissonance with the image of the United States as the "land of opportunity" from within America's industrial heartland. In the Southwest, Chicanos were often told that their inequality and poverty were a result of incomplete assimilation and the unfinished incorporation of former Mexican territories. This colonizer's narrative of underdevelopment was more difficult to sustain in the Midwest. Chicanos in the Midwest, like those whose "Pledge to Aztlán" portrayed an America steeped in a history of white supremacy, were better placed to evaluate the ability of the American national project to accommodate them as equals. In the Midwest, Chicanos judged the United States on its own terms and found it wanting.

In 1970s Detroit, Chicanos operated in an environment where whiteness was becoming the racially marked category.[52] The struggle for bilingual education in Detroit could be seen as an attempt, like many others throughout the Southwest U.S., to reinforce cultural nationalism. For some this was the case. Yet Michigan Chicano education advocates went beyond this critique to present schooling as mere training for incarceration. Chicano students, with the support of many parents, walked out of Lansing's Pattengill Junior High on March 9, 1970 for 15 days in direct response to a teacher hitting their peer Eddie Magaña. The short-lived Chicano Movement newspaper, *Sol de Aztlán*, defended the walkout asserting, "The schools do not teach the students, they just police them."[53] Similarly the Detroit booklet, *Ya Es la Hora Latino*, made an even more provocative comparison throughout its text between the fate of young Latinos in the state's child welfare, juvenile justice, or prison systems and those in school. Beginning with its dedication to Juan Herrera, a Chicano from Detroit imprisoned and killed in Marquette Branch Prison, the authors argued that Detroit was using its schools to reproduce a non-employable surplus labor force destined for prison. In this way advocates saw schooling as a form of social control and harnessed regional narratives of Detroit as an increasingly abject "reservation" for those whose aspirations could not be met in a post-industrial America.[54] In this instance regional narratives about the marginalization of black Detroit and Midwest rust-belt politics aided in the development of an anti-colonial discourse among Chicanos.

As the 1970s wore on, the industrial rust-belt, Michigan and Detroit in particular, were often portrayed as the worn-out, washed-up remnants of a bygone era. Yet Detroit's situation was in large part created by the very economic and political processes so closely associated with the late twentieth century: neoliberalism, decline in the structures of social support and solidarity, deindustrialization, outsourcing, and globalization.[55] Just as Detroit, in all its decay and persistence, was in fact an integral part of the United States, migrant workers were indispensable in Michigan, and Chicanos were a part of Detroit's racial order. In arguing for both their difference and presence, Chicanos in Michigan's rural and urban spaces contested the American vision that, as La Sed asserted, had "segregated" them from academic success and discursively excluded them from belonging on their own terms. Instead, they increasingly pursued a national vision of their own.

Notes

1 Ann Laura Stoler, Ed., *Haunted by Empire: Geographies of Intimacy in North American History* (Durham, NC: Duke University Press, 2006), 5.

2 Arturo Rocha Alvarado, *Crónica De Aztlán: A Migrant's Tale* (Berkeley, CA: Quinto Sol Publications, 1977), 151.

3 Sidney Fine, *Expanding the Frontiers of Civil Rights: Michigan, 1948–1968* (Detroit, MI: Wayne State University Press, 2000), 305.

4 Mrs. Robert Newman, "Little Enough Left," *Benton Harbor (MI) News-Palladium*, January 27, 1966.

5 "Says Shelby Migrant School Being Harassed," *Ludington (MI) Daily News*, May 11, 1967; Associated Press, "Furor Erupts Over School for Migrant Children," May 12, 1967.

6 "Protest Settlement of Migrants Here, 'Area Has Enough Problems,'" *Benton Harbor (MI) News-Palladium*, July 31, 1969.

7 The 1967 Saginaw to Lansing march is often labeled the "first march for migrants" in popular memory but it is more properly considered the first statewide march. *Seglares en Acción*, a Mexican-American Catholic group, organized the first march for migrants in Michigan on Easter Sunday, April 10, 1966. Patrick J. Owens, "Mexicans March for Wage Bill," *Detroit Free Press*, April 11, 1966; José Jiménez to Governor George Romney, telegram, April 7, 1966, George Romney Papers, Bentley Historical Library.

8 Tom Chávez to Governor George Romney, June 26, 1967, George Romney Papers, Bentley Historical Library; to Governor George Romney and Ted Blizzard, "Memo Regarding LAUPA Split," 1967, George Romney Papers, Bentley Historical Library; Víctor Hernández to Governor George Romney, April 7, 1967, George Romney Papers, Bentley Historical Library.

9 "Ask Benefits for Michigan Migrant Labor," *Chicago Tribune*, March 27, 1967; "Michigan Campesinos March," *Delano (CA) El Malcriado*, April 12, 1967; Bob Voges, "Farmworkers Demonstrate at Lansing," *Benton Harbor (MI) News-Palladium*, March 27, 1967.

10 Ruben Alfaro and Concerned Citizens for Migrant Workers, "Declaration of Grievances," March 26, 1967, George Romney Papers, Bentley Historical Library.

11 Carlos Falcón and Michigan State Board of Education, *Quality Educational Services to Michigan's Spanish Speaking Community* (Lansing, MI, 1974), 18.

12 These conflicts include a controversy over the United Farm Workers holding grape boycott support committee meetings in the offices of the Michigan Migrant Ministry that were disrupted by growers and later disallowed by the Migrant Ministry. William Bennallack, "Michigan Migrant Ministry Annual Report 1969," January 29, 1970, UFW Michigan Boycott Collection, Walter Reuther Archive; Shirley Charbonneau

to Jim Drake, March 5, 1972, UFW Michigan Boycott Collection, Walter Reuther Archive. Also notable was a campaign by the Women for the Survival of Michigan Agriculture, the Farm Bureau and local growers to have Michigan Migrant Legal Assistance and United Migrants' Opportunity, Inc. investigated and defunded: "Michigan Growers Begin Fighting Back During '75," *Benton Harbor-St. Joseph (MI) Herald-Palladium*, December 31, 1975; Scott Williamson, "Berrien Board Opposes Migrant Aid Unit," *Benton Harbor-St. Joseph (MI) Herald-Palladium*, February 29, 1976; Nick Smith, "Migrants' Aide Says His Office No Threat," *St. Joseph (MI) Herald-Press*, February 26, 1974; Nick Smith, "UMOI Answers Farm Wives'," *Benton Harbor (MI) News-Palladium*, May 17, 1974; Nick Smith, "Probing Migrant's Group: Farm Gals Attack in a Different Way," *Benton Harbor (MI) News-Palladium*, February 12, 1974.

13   Falcón and Michigan State Board of Education, *Quality Educational Services to Michigan's Spanish Speaking Community*, 19.

14   Jesse M Soriano and James McClafferty, "Spanish Speakers of the Midwest: They Are Americans Too," *Foreign Language Annals* 2, no. 3 (March 1969): 322.

15   Hugh Morgan, "Migrant Families Must Work Together in Order to Survive," *Sault Ste. Marie (MI) Evening News*, August 26, 1969.

16   Andres Fierro, interview by Joseph O'Grady, 1990, Oral History Collection, Joint Archives of Holland, Hope College, http://jointarchives.org/Oral%20Interviews/Oral%20Interview%20Topics.htm.

17   Soriano and McClafferty, "Spanish Speakers of the Midwest," 324.

18   *Handbook for Teachers of Migrant Children*. (Lansing: Michigan State Department of Education, 1970), 72.

19   John Peterson, "A Tragic Lesson: Language Barrier Cripples Mexican-American Pupils," *Detroit News*, February 16, 1969.

20   Bob Voges, "City Barber Lobbies for Migrants," *Lansing State Journal*, March 22, 1967.

21   Falcón and Michigan State Board of Education, *Quality Educational Services to Michigan's Spanish Speaking Community*; Minutes of the Second Planning Meeting for the Latino Statewide Conference, January 11, 1975, William G. Milliken Papers, Bentley Historical Library.

22   "Latinos Angry at Educational System," *Lansing (MI) El Renacimiento*, August 29, 1975.

23   Henry F. Graff, *The Free and the Brave: The Story of the American People* (Chicago: Rand McNally, 1968), 382.

24   *A Second Report on The Treatment of Minorities in American History Textbooks* (Lansing: Michigan State Department of Education, 1971), 11, 24.

25   George E. Johnson to Raymond V. Padilla, October 7, 1970, Vice-President for Academic Affairs Staff Files John H. Romani, Bentley Historical Library.

26   Mark Lett, "Migrant Students Get Fall Residency Status," *Mt. Pleasant (MI) Central Michigan Life*, March 16, 1972.

27   Chicanos at Michigan and Linda Guzmán to James O'Neill, May 2, 1972, 1, Provost and Executive Vice-President for Academic Affairs Papers, Bentley Historical Library.

28   Bettie Magee and Others, "A Description of Simulation Technique to Develop Teacher and Counselor Empathy with the Spanish Speaking Student." (1972): 4.

29   Division of Minority Affairs, *A Selected Annotated Bibliography of Material Relating to Racism, Blacks, Chicanos, Native Americans and Multi-Ethnicity*, vol. 4 (East Lansing: Michigan Education Association, 1975).

30   Adelfa Arredondo, *The Miseducation of Chicano Students: Recommendations for Confronting It* (Utah Education Association Minority Affairs Committee, 1976).

31   Ibid., 3.

32   Latin Americans for Social and Economic Development, "Presentation By LA SED and Latino Community To DPS Central School Board on Proposed Desegregation Plan," March 25, 1975, 1, Latin Americans for Social and Economic Development Records, Bentley Historical Library.

33   Peterson, "A Tragic Lesson: Language Barrier Cripples Mexican-American Pupils."

34   Jeffrey Mirel, *The Rise and Fall of an Urban School System: Detroit, 1907–81*, 2nd ed. (Ann Arbor: University of Michigan Press, 1999), Appendix, Table 5 and 6.

35   Eleanor Paperno Wolf, *Trial and Error: The Detroit School Segregation Case* (Detroit, MI: Wayne State University Press, 1981), 13.

36   Stanley A. West and June Macklin, *The Chicano Experience* (Boulder, CO: Westview Press, 1979), 243.

37   James Edward Harris, "The Relationship of the Mobility of Black and Chicano Students to Achievement in Reading and Arithmetic in Selected Detroit Elementary Schools." (PhD diss., University of Michigan, 1973), 47–57.

38   Mirel, *The Rise and Fall of an Urban School System*, 335.

39   Department of Research and Development, *Achievement Test Scores of Pupils in the Detroit Public Schools* (Detroit, MI: Detroit Public Schools, 1970), 13, 29.

40   Mirel, *The Rise and Fall of an Urban School System*, Appendix, Table 5; Office of Desegregation, *Desegregation Plan, 1975–76* (Detroit, MI: Detroit Board of Education, 1975), Appendix C, 8.

41   "Comments on the Title VII ESEA Detroit Bilingual Advisory Council Grant Application," February 22, 1974, Department of Education Papers, State Archives of Michigan.

42   "Nuestro Gente Habla" (Vocero Bilingüe, April 1974), 6, Latino Collections, Michigan State University Special Collections.

43   West and Macklin, *The Chicano Experience*, 243.

44   Roberto Veliz, "Editorial," *Nosotros: La Voz De La Comundad Hispanoamericana De Detroit*, June 1, 1972.

45   "Separate Parent's Club at Webster," *Nosotros: La Voz De La Comunidad Hispano-americana De Detroit*, June 30, 1972.

46   "Pickets Call for Latino Principal," *Detroit Free Press*, October 17, 1974.

47   Mirel, *The Rise and Fall of an Urban School System*, 357.

48   George Cushingberry, *Plaintiff's Desegregation Plan for the Assignment of Pupils, 1975–1976* (Detroit, MI: Detroit Public Schools, 1975), 1A; Michigan State Board of Education, *Six Plans to Achieve Racial Desegregation in Public Schools of the Detroit Metropolitan Area* (Lansing, 1972), 1; Wolf, *Trial and Error*, 313–14, 303.

49   Elwood Hain, "School Desegregation in Detroit: Domestic Tranquility and Judicial Futility," *Wayne Law Review* 23 (1976): 138; Mayo L. Coiner, "Civil Rights," *Detroit College of Law Review* II (1981): 385–86.

50   "Presentation by LA SED and Latino Community to DPS Central School Board on Proposed Desegregation Plan"

51   Judge Robert DeMascio, Ronald Bradley et al., v. William G. Milliken, et al,, 460 F. Supp. 299, 312 (U.S. District Court for the Eastern District of Michigan, Southern Division 1978).

52   For an analysis of racially marked whiteness in Detroit see John Hartigan, *Racial Situations: Class Predicaments of Whiteness in Detroit* (Princeton, NJ: Princeton University Press, 1999).

53   "For Chicano Principal Administrative Treadmill Grinds Slowly," *Lansing (MI) El Renacimiento*, August 15, 1971; "Zapata School," *Lansing (MI) Sol De Aztlán*, March 1970.

54   Thomas J. Sugrue, *The Origins of the Urban Crisis: Race and Inequality in Postwar Detroit* (Princeton, NJ: Princeton University Press, 1996), 4.

55   On neoliberalism, uneven development and social solidarity, David Harvey, *Spaces of Global Capitalism: Toward a Theory of Uneven Geographical Development* (London: Verso, 2006); On the decline of social supports, solidarity through unions and the role of a conservative political vision in Detroit, Heather Thompson, *Whose Detroit?: Politics, Labor and Race in a Modern American City* (Ithaca, NY: Cornell University Press, 2001); On structural economic changes, Sugrue, *The Origins of the Urban Crisis*.

11

SIN FRONTERAS

An Oral History of a Chicana Activist in Oregon during the Chicano Movement

Norma L. Cárdenas

The Chicano Movement is a significant, but often overlooked moment in Oregon history. It is important not only to write the history of the Chicano Movement in the Oregon context, but also to write the "Chicana moment" and Chicanas into that history. Bringing Chicana feminism and oral history methods to bear on the Chicano Movement challenges the dominant historical discourse that has been delimited by the U.S. Southwest paradigm and decenters its masculinist ideologies. This transnational feminist archival project adds to the growing scholarship on Chicana activist historiography by "retrofitting" the historical record with new perspectives on the development of Chicana feminism in the Chicana/o Movement in Oregon. Inspired by Maylei Blackwell's (2011) groundbreaking book, *¡Chicana Power!: Contested Histories of Feminism in the Chicano Movement*, I focus on the rich life history of a Chicana activist in the Chicana/o Movement. My aim is to fill the gaps in the masculine hegemonic narratives with a repertoire of remembrance of Chicana political subjectivity and feminist consciousness in *el movimiento* in the context of Oregon. Heeding calls by Vicki Ruiz and Antonia Castañeda for a regional focus means taking a transnational approach to identity formation across local, regional, national, and transnational borders.

Chicanas are often silenced and excluded in the national historiography, and more so in regional Pacific Northwest history, but are not silent. Scholarship focusing on the Chicana experience in the Pacific Northwest is limited to Yolanda Alaniz and Megan Cornish's (2008) *Viva la Raza*; Elizabeth Salas's (2008) chapter on Chicana *politicas* in Washington state and Latinas in the Pacific Northwest (2006); Lynn Stephen's (2007) work on Mexican immigration and settlement in Oregon; Jerry Garcia's (2003) chapter on Dora Sánchez Treviño and her civic participation in Quincy, Washington; Joanne B. Mulcahy's (2010) book on Eva Castellañoz and *curanderismo* in Nyssa, Oregon; and Isabel Valle's

(1994) *Fields of Toil: A Migrant Family's Journey* about a year in the life of a migrant family in Walla Walla, Washington. Other treatments of the region's Chicano experience, such as Erasmo Gamboa's (1995) *El Movimiento: Oregon's Mexican-American Civil Rights Movement* and Glenn Anthony May's (2011) *Sonny Montes and Mexican American activism*, erase Chicana activism during an especially momentous period.

The larger study from which this chapter is drawn focuses on the life history of María Luisa Alanís Ruiz, whose work in the Chicano/a community has left an indelible legacy on the Pacific Northwest. Her contributions to the Chicano/a community include her activism in the farm worker and student movements during the Chicano Movement, her work at the Colegio César Chávez, and her co-founding of the Chicano/Latino Studies program at Portland State University (PSU) as well as the Portland Guadalajara Sister City Association. The project is truly a collaboration between María and me—a process of shared authority and interest in a narrative in which realities, subjectivities, and identities are co-produced.

As a methodology, I have been collecting oral histories from María since early 2012. She is a repository of historical memory. When prompted with a question, María would narrate her story without stopping, except to ask, "Did I tell you about?" or say, "I have to tell you another story." Comfortably switching between English and Spanish, María would continue offering minute and riveting details. Adding to the archive, I employed ethnographic methods and archival sources such as the Colegio César Chávez and the Valley Migrant League collections as well as newspapers that reveal multiple and contested significations of place, identity, and belonging. A vast majority of archives related to women active during the civil rights era and of those related to the history of Chicana feminism during the Chicano Movement are lost, while some are privately held, such as those in María's home office. This chapter is based on my oral history interview with María and all references are to this source.

Telling and writing María's story in thematic vignettes is the most appropriate narrative form to represent her experiences, perceptions, and changes, including migration, subjectivity, and identity. The vignette form also parallels her stories, which are multilayered and multifaceted, as well as her memory, which shifts from recent to more distant pasts. The themes that emerged from the interviews are interwoven and relate how she negotiated, subverted, and developed her identity and consciousness as a Chicana activist. A feminist visionary, María is able to remember and engage in truth-telling as she self-reflects on her regional identity as well as the spiritual moments in her life.

Childhood—*Traviesa*

Born in 1948 in Linares, Mexico, María was a slender and sick child who was reluctant to walk until she was 3. As a young child, she had typhoid fever that she thinks she may have contracted from a taco cart, and she had to get injections for her delirium. A self-described *traviesa* (troublemaker), María searched for independence, individuality, and adventure. It was a hardship for her father to support the family on his salary in *transportes* (trucking business) while her mother maintained the home. When she was 5 years old, María was sent to live with her paternal grandmother María Luisa "Lichita" in Monterrey for a few years. Despite being a strict disciplinarian, Lichita expressed her love through food, making *fritada*, a soup prepared from *cabrito's* (young goat) blood in *cazos de cobre* (copper pot) and tamales.

A devout Catholic, her grandmother sent María to church and catechism classes. To make her first communion, María had to memorize prayers or she would not be permitted to receive the sacrament. When Lichita found out that María had not learned her prayers, it was already too late because she had planned an elaborate celebration to coincide with the baptism of María's younger sister Cristina. María confessed to her grandmother that the nun was being abusive, chasing her in the patio and hitting her with a leather belt. María ultimately learned to accommodate religion to suit her reality, as she would later become the spiritual leader at Colegio César Chávez, reciting the prayer (in Spanish) at demonstrations.

María and her siblings Eduardo, María del Carmen (Carmela), Mario Salvador, Yolanda, and Cristina Guadalupe (Titina) were all born in Linares, while José Benito and Francisco were born later in Matamoros. As the second-oldest daughter, María navigated the gendered boundaries of her conservative family by refusing the split between public and private spheres and resisting any stronghold of power to control her movement in public. A precocious child, María capitalized on her sociability to win favors from adults, including storeowners and cabdrivers. At age 6, she was sent on an errand for *manteca* (pork fat), after which she boarded a taxi and was driven home five blocks to her grandmother who was *mortificada* (mortified). Another time, she fell asleep from heat exhaustion under her bed on the cool concrete floor and could not be found by her family for hours. Such formative childhood experiences fomented María's disposition for risks so that she could live the kind of life she wanted.

Two pivotal junctures in her life revolve around losing both her parents. In February of 1983, her mother succumbed to brain cancer at age 56. After having surgery to remove the tumor, her mother lived for 18 months with a reduced quality of life. Before dying, her mother asked María for forgiveness, thinking she was too strict, and for "*nunca [me] compró una muñeca [porque] no había dinero*" (not buying her a doll [because] there was no money). Her mother related the story of crossing a body of water to María, which foreshadowed her crossing into the other world. She lived the last days of her life in a nursing home, which exhausted all of her retirement savings. Finding it too painful to live in the home they had shared together, her father moved back to Texas; however, he returned to Oregon in 1991. Having been a smoker for 40 years, he got throat cancer for which he had a tracheotomy. He used an electrolarynx, a hand-held device, but it made his speech incomprehensible to anyone besides his family. In March of 1997, he died at age 80. Aside from being tasked with making both her parents' funeral arrangements, María has balanced her familial responsibilities with freedom, yet her pain is both visceral and palpable, tinged with the anxiety of remembering and forgetting.

Transborder Migration—*Hacer millionario por los chiquillos*

Shortly after her parents married in 1944, her father was recruited as a *bracero*, however he refused to suffer the indignation of disrobing for the physical exam by U.S. immigration and health officials, for which he was sent back to Mexico. Mexican *braceros* were fumigated with the pesticide DDT at the border. He eventually became a U.S. citizen in 1954 with the financial help of a brother-in-law on her mother's side.

After moving from Linares, the family lived in Matamoros, across the border from Brownsville, Texas, from the time María was 11 until she was 18. When María was 12, her sister Cristina fell from a swing and died of an embolism 5 days later; the Texas state police had to contact her father, who was working at a gas station in Harlingen. María recalls the segregated Jim Crow context of learning to speak English in the U.S. Her father paid $8 per month for María to take private lessons in Brownsville. Her mother, in particular, pushed 13-year-old María to learn English, perhaps thinking she could use the English language to defend herself. Despite her parents' encouragement, María had to contend with the school's racist tracking system. She was made to sit at the back of the classroom even though she needed eyeglasses. Fearing punishment from her father, María changed her grades from Fs to As. She was found out later and forced to leave Immaculate Conception Catholic School to support the family with housecleaning chores and caretaking responsibilities. However, her father's low expectations and perception of María's inferior intellect pushed her to academic success later in life. She developed a border identity to fight the disaffection she felt at school and it provided the motivation she needed.

In 1966, when María was 18, her father moved his transborder family to Brownsville, Texas. He refused to cross his family "*sin papeles*" (without documentation) to avoid the dangers and trauma that potentially awaited them had they crossed undocumented. After 12 years, he obtained the two letters of support required. Her father had been working in the United States in Illinois, Wisconsin, and Michigan since 1954, the timing of his return visits to Mexico every 6-12 months coinciding with her mother's pregnancies that resulted in a transborder family.

Tired of working at his current job, and with his eldest daughter (María's sister) suffering from a nervous condition, María's father decided to move the family again. Unfamiliar with social service agencies that might help them, they loaded the station wagon and started the trek north. The car broke down, but by chance they met another family headed to Salem, Oregon at a gas station. The other family invited them to come along with prospects of working in the fields, which illustrates the power of migrant social networks. The man said, "*se va a hacer millonario por los chiquillos*" (he would become a millionaire with the children) by conscripting the children into farmwork. They followed the migration routes from South Texas to Oregon set by earlier migrants in the 1950s.

The family settled in Eola Village in 1968 until 1973 when they moved to Woodburn. Meanwhile, María's older sister Carmela, was interned at the Oregon State Hospital in Salem and would not fully recover. After having spent a few weeks of vacation with her cousins in Monterrey, her sister had returned a different person. Her fiancé called off their engagement. In the early years, she escaped the hospital several times, once boarding a bus and arriving at her aunt's house in Monterrey without any money, form of identification, or her medication. Her care and recovery were limited by the lack of bilingual counseling. She was the first person in Oregon to apply and qualify for a HUD-funded residential facility, where she currently lives and María visits frequently.

Education—"There was Another Me Coming Out"

Both of María's parents stressed the importance of an education, as her father and mother went up to the sixth and third grades, respectively. María understood that education was the means to realize her dreams, albeit reimagined dreams in the new context of the U.S. Soon after moving to Oregon, María met Berna Wingert, an organizer for the Valley Migrant League (VML), who was recruiting students from the fields. "*Déjala*" (let her), said her mother, while her father was less supportive. In March of 1970, Felipe Cañedo and Alfonso Cabrera, graduate students at the University of Oregon (UO), recruited María and other migrant workers like her to the High School Equivalence Program (HEP) at the University of Oregon. In patriarchal fashion, her father thought she was "[*perdiendo*] *el tiempo*" (wasting her time). Another male migrant worker voiced his disapprobation, "*Pa' qué la manda tan lejos, se va regresar embarazada*" (why are you sending her so far, she's going to come back pregnant). Ironically, María would assist the same migrant worker years later with admissions at Colegio, at which point the man remarked, "*cómo se voltean las mesas*" (how the tables got turned). Refusing the gender expectations and sexual limitations imposed on her, she asserted her right to an education. Her father was skeptical of her intentions to advance her education, but he did not try to undermine her desire to improve her life chances. Before María even learned she had passed her General Education Development (GED) test, Felipe had already secured a SESAMEX (Spanish-English Speaking American Mexican) scholarship for her to study at the Language Institute at Oregon State University (OSU).

In María's words, the empowering experience was an embodied transformation: "It felt like there was another me coming out." Motivated by social justice, María was consciously connecting her mind and spirit to action. She epitomized the transition to college for women as she courageously negotiated alienation and family expectations. By September, she was enrolled at the university and living at Callahan Dormitory on the predominantly white campus. For the first time, she was confronted with the notion of her racial and sexual identity in the whiteness of OSU. She experienced extreme culture shock from the new experiences of living with a white female roommate, meeting an African American man in the elevator, and being tutored by a bisexual female Cuban American. Later, she found strength in her circle of friends that included the wives of graduate students. Her racialized, gendered, and class-based experience forced her to find a way to supplement her income. Developing a sense of agency, she bought a typewriter at Goodwill to make extra money by charging $0.25 per page for typewritten papers and reports in spite of her limited English proficiency. She sacrificed her grades because her business was so successful. Her experiences as a working-class college student show that she had to pay for the privilege of an education. It was her working-class consciousness that helped her to develop a Chicana feminist consciousness.

After completing the language program, she enrolled at the UO and graduated in 1974, but because she was missing one course, she did not receive her diploma until 1976. She struggled academically, even though she recorded her class lectures because of her limited English proficiency. As the first to go to college, María represented hope to her family. Her siblings, Eduardo and Yolanda, followed her to UO. Initially, María resented that they chose UO, which she felt restricted her autonomy. Undeterred, she went on to receive a Master of Science in Education Administration and Policy Foundations at PSU in 1998. Paradoxically, in order to transform the university in support of community activist initiatives, María had to ascend the institutional hierarchy to utilize its privileges and resources. She went on to work as an Admissions Counselor and Minority Student Recruiter at PSU, where she helped provide higher education access to formerly excluded ethnic minority students, particularly Chicanas/os. Her struggles to attain full citizenship paved the way for others to follow.

Working in the Fields and Factory—*No sabía de surcos*

Her own female body became the site of a new subjectivity that rejected subjugation. Her first job outside of the home was at age 16 at a Chinese restaurant in Matamoros, Tamaulipas, which involved the policing of her female sexuality. Horrified to find her working at the restaurant's bar, her father ordered her to resign immediately. *Un viejo mañoso* (a dirty old man) was watching her and tried to persuade her dad not to take her. To help her family, María found work as a salesperson at Las Tres Hermanas, at a shoe store La Moda, and at Marco Polo selling fabric, cashmere, and electronics in Brownsville.

Having migrated from an urban city, María recalls, *"no sabía de surcos"* ("I didn't know about rows"). She had no experience in the fields picking, thinning, or hoeing. She described the labor conditions at the Jensen Farms migrant camp near Salem as oppressive and exploitative, with squalid cabins made for chickens, a picnic table, gas stove, refrigerator, and public showers—incomparably horrid "not even in México." Eventually they moved to Eola Village, the largest migrant labor camp with 5,000 people. The piece rate pay was $5 per day or by the crop, which was $0.08 for green beans, $1.50 for strawberries, and $0.20 for hops. After the hop harvest in mid-September, the family worked in other fields. María worked for 2 years as a farm worker, an occupation in which the disciplining of bodies by race, gender, and sexuality controlled workers. In 1968, the family settled in Woodburn, Oregon, where she lived until college.

María later found work at a local factory, Diane's Foods (now called Mission Foods, which is owned by the Gruma Corporation) in McMinnville, manu-facturing hard-shell tacos. She sometimes worked double shifts for $0.90 per hour. For 11 months, she endured working the night shift, the nature of shop-floor work, the heat from the folding presses, and worst of all, the *mal olor* (bad odor). Before long, María became aware that the routinization of labor was exploitative and marginalized workers, particularly female employees. The difficult and dangerous job, with high stress levels, low wages, few benefits, and little job security, gave her the impetus she needed for self-improvement. She was involved in the union struggle for fair wage demands of $1.60 from $1.10 per hour and fair labor practices. With a few of the Mexican women dissenting, the effort was defeated. She recalls one of her dissenting co-workers, Ms. Salinas, who thought María's aspirations of learning English and going to college was possible *"sólo en sueños"* ("only in her dreams").

While María worked hard and was loyal to her employer, she refused to internalize any patriarchal restrictions on her mobility as dictated by her family, co-workers, and society. She credits Berna Wingert, a Chicana from New Mexico working at the VML with providing the affirmation and encouragement she needed to confront the oppression. Her farm worker experience later prompted her activism on behalf of the United Farm Workers (UFW) boycotts. During a weekly picket on Friday in front of a Safeway store, a hostile white male onlooker threw a piece of lettuce that struck María in the face. Agitated, María rolled up her UFW flag and went in pursuit of the man with her picket sign to physically confront him. José Romero, a MEChA (*Movimiento Estudiantil Chicano de Aztlán*) member, beseeched María on the philosophy of nonviolence and diffused the racial incident. Shifting her spiritual understanding, María's capacity for tolerance deepened; however, the racial confrontation allowed María to see her lack of power as a female and to find other forms of resistance. She would continue organizing effective boycotts on the picket lines, first with the grape boycott in 1968, then lettuce, Gallo wine, and Coors in 1970.

Chicanisma and Activism—*"Me salió el activismo"*

Even before entering college, María demonstrated such political consciousness that her parents and siblings teased her that she was "born in the wrong family." Her oppositional consciousness surged, María claims, at age 15, when *"me salió el activismo"* (my activism was born). President J.F. Kennedy's assassination in 1963 was imprinted in María's memory by the attendant emotional turmoil and the closure of the U.S/Mexico International Bridge. Growing up, she defied her parents' curfew, as well as the notions of family, patriarchy, and Catholicism that circumscribed her life. Her fierce self-determination and radicalization primed her for the training and leadership experience that followed next.

Although the Chicano Movement did not reach Oregon until the early 1970s, it was at the University of Oregon at the Chicano Student Union where the ideology of the Chicano Movement took hold. María embraced the Chicana/o label once her racial identity formation had become crystallized. She had developed a sense of racial identity, a cultural awareness, and activist zeal in college, and she benefitted from the collective transformation that challenged white supremacy.

María's activism began in the farm worker struggle and incorporated the urban struggle for education as she navigated college. The historical and social circumstances, such as the farm worker movement and the anti-war movement, elevated her consciousness and provided training for the roles she would later play. With financial aid and recruitment programs, there was also a large concentration of first-generation Chicana/o college students, particularly Chicana students, entering the university under the Three Percent Program, or the Experimental Modification of Admission Requirements (EMAR), which was implemented in the Oregon University System (OUS) in the fall of 1968. In addition, SESAMEX and Project Life, under the auspices of Educational Opportunities Services (EOS), provided opportunities and educational access for Chicana/o students. Graduate students and an activist couple with an affinity for farmworkers, José Romero and Kathy Romero were among a group of Chicanos/as she met that recruited her into MEChA, which they started in 1972. Graduate students such as José Romero, brothers José "Simón" Villa and Roberto Villa, and Cenon Valadez, who had farmworker experience, were instrumental in organizing students around campus and the community for *la causa*. The alienation Chicanos/as felt was assuaged by their numbers even as class tensions between the Chicano Student Union and the Latin American Student Union were growing. A pan-Latino unity between the two student organizations may also have been hindered by different group identities based on their social locations and personal histories.

While at UO, María became the Director of the Migrant Labor Project (MLP), a student-based organization which provided teacher aides, child care, and food for migrant workers. She recalls forcing the state health department to conduct an investigation that led to the closure of the labor camp. For her work with the

MLP, María was honored with the Whitman Award given by Senator Wayne Morse in 1973. They held fundraisers, which included selling *mole* plates and *capirotada*. She also helped organize a symposium that included Rodolfo "Corky" Gonzales and José Ángel Gutiérrez. She participated in a sit-in at the Board of Higher Education and marched in protest of the 1978 Supreme Court's Bakke case, which limited affirmative action in higher education. In 1970, she attended the statewide Poor People's Conference in Salem organized by and for the poor. She attended the Chicana Conference at Lewis and Clark College. María acknowledges that this was the first time the issue of lesbianism emerged for her, even though gender and sexuality issues were raised in the movement in Oregon.

Selected to participate in the *Centro Intercultural de Documentación* (CIDOC), María spent a summer in Cuernavaca, México in 1972 where she was disparaged as a *pocha* (assimilated) and a *traidora* (traitor) to her Mexican culture. As a Chicana student activist, her encounter with Mexican nationals' racialized notions of her identity was confusing; however, she resisted. As a woman, they also deflected her gendered identity and imposed the dominant nationalistic constructions of identity. She was further stereotyped as a tourist, which diluted her ethnic identity. Issues of race, ethnicity, gender, class, and sexuality surfaced during the trip that made María question any transnational political solidarity movement that could have been empowering.

María was also active with the Young Women's Christian Association (YWCA), serving as the Western Region Chicana Caucus Representative for 3 years and attending annual conferences in San Diego, New York, Chicago, and Oklahoma. Resolutions to support the UFW were passed. Even though María did not attend the 1971 *Conferencia de Mujeres por la Raza* at Houston's YWCA that ended with a walkout, the regional factions helped her to explain some of the breakdowns in the conference. Among other complaints was that the YWCA was an Anglo institution that was dominated by white, elite, Christian women at the conference. María negotiated the ideological fissures and formed a gendered solidarity with women across age, race, and class. At one of the conferences, where César Chávez spoke, the YWCA adopted the imperative "[t]o trust our collective power towards the elimination of racism, wherever it exists, by any means necessary." María met Chávez again aboard an airplane when he requested they not serve lettuce. She also met other male leaders of *el movimiento* such as Reies López Tijerina at Mi Tierra Restaurant in San Antonio in 1976 after his release from prison and José Ángel Gutiérrez in Oregon.

After graduating from UO, María worked at Portland's Águila Inc., a bilingual information, referral, and alcoholism counseling group, as the Cultural Coordinator under the Comprehensive Employment and Training Act (CETA), a public service jobs placement program. A grant proposal she wrote in collaboration with Luis Polanco was awarded $300,000 to fund a 2-year outpatient alcohol treatment program. She found the work rewarding and considered earning a Master's degree in social work at PSU.

María credits José and Kathy Romero with fomenting her critical consciousness. Recruited by José, who was then Director of Chicano Studies and later became the Director of Academic Affairs, María started working at Colegio César Chávez in September 1974 as a recruiter. With her independence and a $10,000 salary, María moved to Portland with her sister. Her relationship with the Romeros was also personal; she would babysit their daughter, Shelli. She was gaining independence as she learned to drive, and bought her first car, a 1973 green Chevy Vega, for $99 a month. However, the staff were growing frustrated by the mounting legal and financial problems plaguing Colegio following the resignation of Sonny Montes and eventually José Romero. Interestingly, it was mostly women, including Irma Gonzales, Gloria Sandoval, Hortencia Antillón, and Elizabeth Gorman-Prunty, who remained to stave off closure. For a time, the Colegio staff did not get paid and would divide honoraria among the staff. Despite its 10-year run and national attention, El Colegio never recovered and ceased to exist a short time later.

El Colegio was part of a consortium of Chicano-oriented colleges in the U.S. Unique in its bilingual/bicultural approach, the Colegio administered the College Without Walls program, which granted credit for life experiences and a documented learning portfolio, and was facilitated by a *comité* (committee). El Colegio attracted prominent speakers to campus, such as its namesake César Chávez, the poet Alurista, Teatro Campesino, and Daniel Valdez. At Colegio, María coordinated "*Los Norteñitos*," a youth dance program. She says of the beauty of Colegio, "*Sembramos la semilla . . . Brotó, pero sigue 30 años después*" ("The seed was planted. It grew, and it continues 30 years later"). Despite its closure, the fruit of leadership had transformed the community.

In 1980, she took up her next challenge at PSU where she worked in the Admissions Office. Roberto, her husband, noticed the job announcement in the newspaper and encouraged her to apply. The arduous interview process that started with the committee and concluded with the dean would characterize her experience. María's resilience is evident in the face of institutional and interpersonal violence. In one instance, she was told, "You need to go back where you came from." María submitted her resignation letter when she was offered a better-suited position.

Still a part of the Chicano Movement, there was a push to develop and institutionalize Chicano-Latino Studies at PSU. In 1992, the Hispanic Studies Committee was tasked with developing a proposal for faculty enhancement and curriculum development "in existing courses, development of a team-taught course . . . and development planning for an expanded program on Hispanic and Latin American studies." The committee was composed mostly of white faculty members and a few token Chicana/o faculty and staff. The white members of the committee wanted to enhance their own departments through a faculty seminar with invited faculty speakers and local Hispanic groups. Despite the lofty, long-term goals of interdisciplinary faculty research projects on Hispanic issues in Oregon that would involve undergraduate student research and fieldwork; increased Hispanic enrollment at PSU; enhanced faculty involvement with Hispanic students through mentoring programs, informal advising, orientation programs, or freshman/new student seminars; and support for the hiring of Hispanic faculty in tenure-track positions,

the struggle was hard-fought.

The timing of the committee coincided with the 1992 annual MEChA National Conference at Eastern Washington University (EWU). Politicized MEChA students from PSU attended the conference with a renewed sense of identity and heightened consciousness. Students were formalizing their ethnic and political identities distinct from the Hispanic Student Union and the International Latino Student Union. The students returned to campus, organized, and demanded that PSU adopt EWU's Chicano Studies program model with curricula and services, not the committee's proposed piecemeal program. EWU's Chicano Education Program (CEP) included recruitment, student support services, and the Chicano Studies program. Carlos Maldonado, who was the CEP Director, was also the first Executive Director of the National Association for Chicano Studies (NACS) at Washington. The EWU Chicano Studies program, which was established in 1978, received advice and support from Washington State University (WSU). The University of Washington also had a Chicano Studies program, which was established in 1970. Washington proved to be the state for the germination of Chicano Studies programs across the Pacific Northwest. One of the administrators at PSU, Vice Provost and Dean of Students Juan Mestas, supported the students who mobilized to rally support for the Bachelor's in Chicano-Latino Studies on campus. As the MEChA advisor, María witnessed the students' call to action, mobilizing, and gathering signatures on petitions. Several challenges, from budgetary to bureaucratic, impeded the progress of the program. As an urban public state university, the push came from community organizations off-campus. Faculty from the International Studies and Latin American Studies programs were not supportive.

In 1995, a Chicano-Latino Studies certificate was established at PSU with core courses in the College of Liberal Arts and Sciences. Following a national search, Rubén Sierra was hired as the founding Director of the Chicano/a Studies Program with a joint position in Theatre. Originally from San Antonio, Sierra was an actor, director, and playwright who founded the Seattle Group Theatre. María was recruited by Rubén as founding faculty to develop the Chicano-Latino Studies program. María stepped in as Interim Director at the time of Sierra's untimely death in October of 1998. Later, as Associate Director of Chicano-Latino Studies, she continued to create new curricula (courses such as Southwestern Borderlands, Mexican American Folklore), teach classes (four every term), and serve as advisor to student organizations including MEChA. She established partnerships with off-campus entities such as PSU's Salem Center, Continuing Education, and Portland Community College in Beaverton, and outreach programming such as the Oregon Leadership Institute (OLI), Sí Se Puede Leadership Project, and the Scholarship Gala. She hired adjunct faculty such as Narce Rodríguez, who graduated and worked at Oregon State University. She also invited noteworthy speakers to PSU including: Lalo Alcaraz, Chicano cartoon artist; Victor Villaseñor, Chicano author; and Peter Bratt, film director. For the first 3 years, she also hosted the César Chávez Leadership Conference for high school students across Oregon on the PSU campus. She remains involved by offering workshops.

The year 2004 marked a turning point in her career when she faced a devastating political battle of macho or "chingón politics," ironically after the institutionalization of Chicano/a Studies. In her role as Associate Director, she confronted male supremacy, hierarchical, and individualized leadership. She was called into a meeting by two male faculty members who authoritatively told her she was being "promoted and transferred" to another department. Up until then, there was a racialized and gendered division of labor; however, it was becoming classed. María felt that PSU had institutionalized a male-centered Chicano Studies program. As the only Chicana, María's position alternately had regressed to subjection, alienation, and censure by exclusion and marginalization from the conversation and decision-making process. The divide along gender and class lines mirrors the inherent contradiction between the discourse of liberation and practice of oppression. The two male faculty members used their male privilege to demote María because of her degree (or lack thereof), erase her feminist vision and critical role in the formation of the Chicano-Latino Studies program, and reinscribe the hierarchies of privilege. As one of the administrators of the program, she had solidly helped to build the Chicano-Latino Studies program through Chicana feminist collaboration, participation, inclusion, process, and humility. Her Chicana feminist consciousness and activism were influenced by her own lived experience in the fields, on the picket lines, and in the community, which translated into a daily commitment to awareness of the site of her own privilege in higher education. Nevertheless, the gap between her position and her colleagues' devalued perception of her labor made her dispensable. She described the incident as devastating and demoralizing—"as if she had lost part of her soul." Despite the hidden injuries from the institutional and symbolic violence, María demonstrated tolerance, political clarity, and ethical integrity with her decisiveness. During María's tenure at PSU, she saw professors, such as Elizabeth Flores and Carlos Blanton—two Chicano/a Studies faculty members—leave the program either because they were denied tenure or because of race and gender inequalities. Systematic exclusion and isolation has contributed to the underrepresentation of Chicana/o faculty, resulting in negative implications on the institution, program, faculty, and students.

Feminism—"I was Feminist in a Way"

María claims she was naïve about gender issues when she entered college and yet she challenged the traditional ideologies of womanhood, which is to maintain a home and family, and instead made her own independent trajectory as well as a collective one. For María, feminism was intersected by race, class, gender, and sexuality, and drew from multiple traditions and lived experiences. María acknowledges the agency of her mother, who was unused to rural life, but united the family and wielded authority with her resourcefulness to protect them from poverty. It was in the daily rhythm of migrant life that her mother disrupted patriarchal authority and redefined motherhood. As a stay-at-home mother, she made the labor camp a home for the family, taking care of the everyday routines, particularly the meals from meager resources. For most of the time, her mother raised the children as a single parent. In addition to eating peanut butter and jelly sandwiches, her mother also prepared dishes of *barbacoa*, *lengua*, and *menudo*, delicacies that sustained the family.

One of María's earliest feminist role models was Berna, whom she met at the migrant camp at Eola Village, who invited her to visit the University of Oregon. Education was the site where María subverted male hegemonic constructed identities. Her father had offered her only two options: marry (his *compadre's* son) or go to school. During college, she met Gloria González, a radical Chicana feminist from Tijuana, Baja California. Gloria taught her how to drive a car in a state vehicle while visiting the labor camps. They formed a mostly female *ballet folklórico* group at UO that provided a sense of female solidarity and was a cultural outlet for expression. The Chicana students also formed *Las Mujeres de la Raza*, an organization for Chicana gender and sexuality consciousness; however, it folded because of internal problems caused by *chisme* (gossip) based on patriarchal female competition and alienation. Chicanas struggled to find their own voice while simultaneously balancing the competing demands of the family and the university.

The gender and sexual politics of Chicano nationalism in the Chicano Movement in Oregon were subtle, and the emergence of Chicana feminism occurred from within. Chicana activists questioned the concerns of the Chicano Movement and deconstructed the machismo. The balance between the collective identity of Chicano nationalism and a Chicana's individual consciousness was tensely held. One example of this tension was during a concert at a nightclub where the band members objectified Chicanas with overt sexist and misogynistic jokes saying things such as "making love in the fields." The Chicanos enacted their male privilege in defense of Chicanas' sexuality based on idealized notions of Chicanas in traditional gender roles as wives and mothers. Moreover, Chicanas rejected the Chicanos' nationalist ideologies of race and patriarchy dictating who they could and could not date. María's personal experiences of being sexualized or sexually harassed include an overtly macho Chicano graduate student who felt entitled to ask if she was a virgin. María felt Chicanos were "trying to get in bed" with Chicanas and demanding that "they prove it," using heterosexuality as a weapon to restrict and control their sexual freedom; yet, Chicanos claimed the sexual freedom to date white women. María had a saying for the sexual double standard: "Chicano *de día, gabacho de noche*" ("Chicano by day, white male by night"). Chicanos saving Chicanas from other men was not gender and sexual equality.

As a young woman, María eschewed the feminist label as she did not explicitly identify with white/Anglo feminism. While noting the complications within the feminist tradition, María reveals her ambivalence toward Chicana feminism saying, "I was feminist in a way," which demonstrates the contradictions for both Chicanos and Chicanas. Recognizing feminism as too narrow, she redefined feminism broadly in relation to her gendered life experiences through race, class, and gender. When asked about her feminist consciousness, María critiqued racial politics in the women's movement and the subordination of Chicanas because white feminists "used us." The complexities and contradictions that suffused the women's movement, María felt, were restricted to white/Anglo women's experiences. She felt excluded by the women's movement because she did not share the same feminist identity nor claim the same interests. She explains that her mother and father were egalitarian and that respect toward the family took priority.

Biculturally adept, María learned how to negotiate boundaries that included racist, gendered, and class-based language standards reflecting the white culture of academia. Speaking with an accent that reflects her immigrant/migrant narrative, María has had to invent her own bilingual–bicultural language, challenging notions of citizenship based on national origin. While at PSU, her Mexican-accented English became the target of discrimination by her white female supervisor. Evoking nativist politics, she insisted to María, "People like you need to start at the bottom," indicating a racialized class hierarchy that requires policing to keep people in their place. Denied the relevance of her cultural experience, María was "othered," had her credentials questioned, her accent pathologized, and was told to conform to linguistic norms and acquiesce to psychological behavior modification. Because of her linguistic difference, she was ostracized and subjected to hostile treatment, including intense language repression, negative evaluations, and punitive sanctions such as demanding travel obligations no one else wanted, which ironically required bilingualism. Her supervisor's unearned arrogance allowed her to transfer the burden of sexism to María, who faced a workplace culture that was oppressive and reproduced a racialized and gendered hierarchy. Consequently, María was reassigned to the College of Liberal Arts as the Director of Latino and Community Relations under the direction of Dean Marvin Kaiser. Kaiser, an advocate of multiculturalism, retired in 2011. In her own and her family's best interest, and as an act of resistance, María, herself, decided to retire from PSU after 31 years of service. After all, she had witnessed the impact of the cycle

258 Norma L. Cárdenas

of abuse on her women of color colleagues as their intellectual, emotional, and physical health were compromised at the majority white institution. Rather than be silent, María claimed her agency and consciousness to voice her protest against intolerable working conditions rather than be objectified. By claiming a personal subjectivity, she confronted the harmful effects within the collective.

With greater awareness of issues of gender and sexuality, María was also involved in coalition-style politics. One such organization was *Las Mujeres de Oregon* (Women of Oregon), a statewide grassroots community-building organization, which formed in 1980 and met twice monthly before it disbanded. The ethnic diversity of the group was its strength; however, its internal contradictions such as class heterogeneity and forms of political action were not resolved. María was involved in organizing the "*El Poder de la Mujer Latina*" conference in 2005 at PSU to celebrate and honor the legacy of Chicana activism in Oregon. This event also helped to temper Chicana's individual self-serving agendas.

For María, motherhood was a political choice to practice the "personal is political" dictum. As a Chicana adoptive mother, she used motherhood as a model of engagement for lifting the next generation. Her construction of motherhood included a redefinition of familism, which has allowed her to work outside the home without guilt. She acknowledges that PSU's administration was accommodating to the facts of her life as a mother raising children.

Underscoring her Chicana feminist consciousness, she used her insight and understanding of Chicana/Latina girlhood practices to develop the curriculum for the Sí Se Puede program at PSU, which was integrated with the Chicano-Latino Studies (ChLa) capstone course. She also developed the Adelante Academy, which aims to empower 14–18 year-old Latinas by using embodied knowledge, and a feminist activist pedagogy. The leadership program was developed to inspire and counter the myths of and about Chicana/Latina girls from a health issues approach. Funds from the Legacy Hospital paid for stipends to the 20–60 girls to participate in monthly sessions and hear from invited Latina speakers. The program was short-lived, as María describes it, as "*la avaricia*" (avarice) took over. As she prepared the women leaders of tomorrow, she passed on her ethos of love, which has served to protect María from falling into the trappings of materialism and instead focus on spiritual rewards.

Spiritual Activism—*Una espiritista*

From María's neck hangs a necklace with a pendant of *la Virgen de Guadalupe*, which attests to her embodiment of Chicana resistance and transformative spiritual agency. Bold-spirited, María has reconciled the contradictions of her Catholic identity by recreating her spirituality, which has been a source of female strength and healing. María's survival has depended on her ability to interpret signs and her gift in combatting oppression. As a card reader, María utilizes her *facultad*—which includes faith, humility, and intuition—for healing alienation, illness, and despair, and for offering redemptive remembrance. She constructs her knowledge and identity as *una espiritista* (spiritualist). Her multiple perceptions have allowed others to change who they are and their behavior for personal healing and collective liberation from intergenerational trauma. Her spirituality has facilitated a self-reflexive heightened consciousness and a critical awareness for others.

María's spiritual work is deeply personal and political, bringing together mind, body, and spirit, and providing her a vision for emphatic action. Her stories themselves are spirits that show her love of self and compassion for others and passion for social justice. As a mode of cultural expression, she uses her spiritual activism as a guide toward personal integrity and political empowerment. As a witness to the trappings of materialism and individualism, María's commitment to social justice is undergirded by her humility and way of being.

Community-bridge Work—"You Do It by Heart . . . Do It by Passion"

María's transformative work has been guided by an ethics of love and purpose carried out with feelings, dreams, and passion that transgress boundaries. Determined to eliminate the exclusionary patterns, María's activism has evolved into a transnational focus in which she has improved the social and cultural lives of Chicanos/as in Oregon as well as the transborder lives of Mexicans in Guadalajara. She broadened the civil rights approach to include human rights to make connections with transnational activist groups for social justice. Her involvement with organizations focused on Chicanas/os–Latinas/os has had a gendered focus. *Una "rielera moderna"* (modern trailblazer), María draws on the genealogy of Chicana female activists with transnational and multiracial perspectives to promote economic, social, and cultural rights. A well-respected community leader, María has served on countless committees, councils, and boards.

Having been actively engaged in social struggles for more than 30 years, María remains involved in making and sustaining community. For over 13 years, beginning in 1997, she organized the Scholarship Gala to raise over a hundred $1,000 scholarships for students at PSU, challenging the exclusivity of access to higher education. With the help of Bel Hernández Castillo, she has appealed to philanthropists and celebrities such as Yareli Arizmendi, Ricardo Chavaría, Esai Morales, Edward James Olmos, Lupe Ontiveros, and Tony Plana to serve as keynote speakers.

In addition to the Gala, she has also organized the *Cinco de Mayo* festivities, which is a way to create space, forge memory, and reinforce a transnational ethnic Latina/o identity and culture. For Latinas/os in Oregon, the cultural isolation can be quite unsettling. As founder and President of the Portland-Guadalajara Sister Cities Association (PGSCA), she transcends national borders and builds a sense of collectivity. Started in 1985, the *Cinco de Mayo* celebration at Portland's

Waterfront Park is symbolic of Chicano/a-Latina/o civic and political life, cultural sustenance, and inclusion. When she first made the suggestion, a conflict arose between a Mexican nationalist male leader and María along generational, racial, class, and gender divisions. This is documented in the PGSCA board meeting minutes of February 5, 1985. The first festival included a Cantinflas film series and high school art contest with a $75 budget. The long-established festival attracts more than 300,000 people, proving it to be an important cultural link to the community. Given the geographic isolation of the Pacific Northwest, María recognized that the communal and performative aspects of the Mexican diaspora exist beyond the *fronteras* of the Southwest.

As part of the PGSCA, María receives funding from foundations, but the work is broad-based and reaches organizers and constituents. She established Jardín Portland at El Bosque Las Colomos in Guadalajara, México, which is a replica of Multnomah Falls, Crown Point, and Pioneer Courthouse Square in Portland. Other projects include Villas Mira Valle, which serves as an orphanage; El Colegio Unico, a culinary program; and the *Bombero* (firefighter and exchange) program. In recreating the foods from her youth, María has developed an ethnic transborder identity. Three of her favorite recipes, Aztec pie, *capirotada* pudding, and a *nopalitos* and egg dish, were featured in *The Oregonian* for the third annual *Cinco de Mayo* celebration.

Among her many accolades, she was knighted an Honorary Dame under the Banner of the Rose by the Royal Rosarians in 2005 for her many contributions to Portland. Financially independent, she started her own consulting company in 2011, *Sin Fronteras*, which has partnerships with school districts offering parent education workshops in Portland and at *La Universidad Autónoma de Guadalajara*.

María has been married to Roberto Ruiz since 1985. He has encouraged her to tell and write her story and has been her biggest supporter. True partners in life and work, they share interests and a commitment to the community. They met in 1976 at a *tamalada* hosted by their mutual friend Irma Flores Gonzales, then Board member of Colegio César Chávez. Roberto, originally from Victoria, Texas, lost both his parents when he was a young child. He joined the army and was stationed in Portland, where he has lived since his discharge. With a degree in Accounting from Portland State University, he has worked as a realtor. They have been married for 27 years and have raised two adopted children—Antonio Roberto, who is 20, and Alejandra María, who is 17. Her decision to adopt is part of her motherwork to share her maternal love and transform assumptions about family. The way she speaks about her children—finding them and supporting them—demonstrates her unrelenting commitment to social justice. Adoption doesn't define her family. As a loving and devoted mother, she has helped her children on their journey of self-discovery and self-identity through critical reflection. She is conscious of the hegemonic construction of motherhood, but she holds fast to her feminist convictions of maternity.

Lessons

María's complex life is a panorama of migrant crossings to and within the United States, from the fields to the academy, accented by language that weaves both Mexican and Chicana identities. Empowered by the Chicana/o Movement, she created her own identity in both public and private spheres and consistently challenged boundaries of inclusion and exclusion. Her sustaining power to keep her family together and her survival in racist environments are her rewards individually and collectively for her organizing. Documentation of María's feminist activism during the Chicano Movement in Oregon powerfully exposes the racism, classism, and sexism railed against her in her courageous struggle for access to higher education and for Chicana/o Studies.

Conducting oral history interviews is a rich and powerful site for knowledge production about race, class, gender, sexuality, and belonging. As a privileged witness, I have received from María intellectual lessons, emotional lessons, and most importantly spiritual lessons about courage, survival, and hope. During our first interview at the Woodburn Public Library, I showed deference by referring to María as "*usted*." She insisted on being addressed as "*tú*," and it took several more interviews before I crossed the cultural border where I felt we had established a sense of solidarity and I had become an intimate witness. Through the telling of her individual truths and collective experiences, she has imparted her memories as *testimonio* and has bridged the transcendental divide of thinking and acting.

Feeling overwhelmed at the start soon gave way to exhilaration, as I felt that this project had a longer life and expanded in ways I had not imagined. Pedagogically, I have incorporated students into the oral history project who have directly interviewed María to draw knowledge from her lived experiences and from within Chicana/o communities. By engaging in praxis that applies both theory and method in the service of social change, students will sow the seeds of self-empowerment to reclaim their history and become activists in their own right as María's dreams live on. Another goal of the project is the creation of a Chicana oral history archive that resists the epistemic violence of historical erasure. Finally, the project contributes to a feminist testimonial discourse that pays homage to, and is a testament of, María's social justice activism and voice that inspires solidarity.

Bibliography

Alaniz, Yolanda, and Cornish, Megan. *Viva la Raza: A History of Chicano Identity and Resistance*. Seattle, WA: Red Letter Press, 2008.

Blackwell, Maylei. *¡Chicana power!: Contested Histories of Feminisms in the Chicano Movement*. Austin: University of Texas Press, 2012.

Castañeda, Antonia I. "'Que se pudieran defender (So you could defend yourselves)': Chicanas, regional history, and national discourses." *Frontiers: A Journal of Women Studies*, 2001: 116–142.

Chabram-Dernersesian, Angie. "I throw punches for my race, but I don't want to be a man: Writing us—Chica-nos (Girl, us)/Chicanas—into the movement script." In *The Chicana/o Cultural Studies Reader*, by Angie Chabram-Dernersesian, pp. 165–182. New York: Routledge, 1992.

Gamboa, Erasmo. "El Movimiento: Oregon's Mexican-American Civil Rights Movement." In *Nosotros: The Hispanic People of Oregon*, edited by Erasmo Gamboa and Carolyn M. Buan, pp. 46–60. Portland: Oregon Council for the Humanities, 1995.

García, Jerry. "A Chicana in Northern Aztlán: An oral history of Dora Sánchez Treviño." *Frontiers: A Journal of Women Studies*, 1998: 16–52.

Gonzales-Berry, Erlinda and Mendoza, Marcela. *Mexicanos in Oregon: Their Stories, Their Lives.* Corvallis: Oregon State University Press, 2010.

Hernández, Ellie. *Postnationalism in Chicana/o Literature and Culture.* Austin: University of Texas Press, 2009.

May, Glenn Anthony. *Sonny Montes and Mexican American Activism in Oregon.* Corvallis: Oregon State University, 2011.

Mulcahy, Joanne B. "Oregon voices: 'Know who you are': Regional identity in the teachings of Eva Castellanoz." *Oregon Historical Quarterly*, 2007: 444–457.

Nusz, Nancy and Ricciardi, Gabriella. "Our ways: History and culture of Mexicans in Oregon." *Oregon Historical Quarterly*, 2003: 110–123.

PGSCA. "Board Meeting Minutes." February 5, 1985.

Ruiz, María Alanis. Interview by Norma Cárdenas. (March 3, 2012; April 27, 2012; July 9, 2012; July 17, 2012; July 30, 2012; August 22, 2012; August 29, 2012; September 5, 2012; September 17, 2012).

Ruiz, Vicki. *Memories and Migrations: Mapping Boricua and Chicana Histories.* Champaign: University of Illinois Press, 2008.

Salas, Elizabeth. "Mexican-American Women Politicians in Seattle." In *More Voices, New Stories: King County, Washington's First 150 Years*, edited by Mary C. Wright, pp. 215–231. Seattle, WA: Landmarks & Heritage Commission, 2002.

Salas, Elizabeth. "Latinas in the Pacific Northwest." In *Latinas in the United States: A Historical Encyclopedia Volume 1*, edited by Vicki L. Ruiz and Virginia Sánchez Korrol, pp. 24–28. Bloomington: Indiana University Press, 2006.

Stephen, Lynn. "Latino roots in Lane County, Oregon." 2007. http://cllas.uoregon.edu/wp-content/uploads/2010/06/Latino_Roots_booklet.pdf (accessed July 3, 2013).

The Sunday Oregonian. "Migrant makes big jump from fields to social work." September 10, 1978: 125.

Xing, Jun, Gonzales-Berry, Erlinda, Sakurai, Patti, Thompson, Robert D., and Peters, Kurt. *Seeing Color: Indigenous Peoples and Racialized Ethnic Minorities in Oregon.* New York: University Press of America, 2007.

CONTRIBUTOR BIOGRAPHIES

Rosie C. Bermúdez is a graduate student in the Department of Chicana and Chicano Studies at the University of California, Santa Barbara. Her research focuses on Chicana activism and feminism in Los Angeles during the 1960s and 1970s.

Norma L. Cárdenas is a Professor in the School of Language, Culture, and Society at Oregon State University and her research focus is on the history of Chicanas and Chicanos in the Pacific Northwest.

Mario T. García is Professor of Chicano Studies and History at the University of California, Santa Barbara. He has published a number of books on Chicano history including those on César Chávez, Dolores Huerta, Bert Corona, Richard Cruz, and Sal Castro.

Max Krochmal is Assistant Professor of History at Texas Christian University. His current book project follows a diverse group of ordinary people as they built multiracial political, civil rights, and labor coalitions in mid-twentieth-century Texas.

Gustavo Licón is Assistant Professor of Latino/a Studies in the Center for the Study of Culture, Race and Ethnicity at Ithaca College. His research focuses on the Chicano student movement in California from the late 1960s to the early 1990s.

Jorge Mariscal is Professor of Literature at the University of California, San Diego. His eclectic research has ranged from the literature of Spain including Cervantes to the Chicano Movement.

Lorena V. Márquez received her Ph.D. in History from the University of California, San Diego. She is completing a book manuscript on the Chicano Movement in Sacramento. She is a lecturer in the Department of Chicana/o Studies at the University of California, Davis.

José G. Moreno is completing his Ph.D. in American Studies and Chicano/Latino Studies at Michigan State University. He has taught at Heritage University and Estrella Mountain Community College.

Luis H. Moreno received his Ph.D. in Chicano/Latino Studies at Michigan State University. He is working on a book manuscript on the intersection of labor, migration, and activism in the development of the Mexican community in Oxnard, California between 1930 and 1980. He is Instructor of Latina/o Studies at Bowling Green State University.

Marisol Moreno received her Ph.D. in History at the University of California, Santa Barbara. Her research examines social movement dynamics in the Chicana/o student movement in California universities and colleges from 1967 to 1973. She is a Lecturer in the Department of History at Long Beach State University.

Jimmy Patiño is Assistant Professor of Chicano Studies at the University of Minnesota. He received his Ph.D. in History from the University of California, San Diego. He is completing a book manuscript on the intersection of the Chicano Movement and the immigrant rights movement in San Diego.

Oliver A. Rosales is Associate Professor of History at the Bakersfield College Delano Campus and Visiting Faculty at Bard College Master of Arts in Teaching Program. He received his Ph.D. in History from the University of California, Santa Barbara. He is completing his book manuscript on multiracial civil rights in Bakersfield.

Nora Salas is completing her Ph.D. in History at Michigan State University. Her research focuses on the Chicano Movement in Michigan.

INDEX